AN INTRODUCTION TO SHAMANISM

Shamans are an integral part of communal religious traditions, professionals who make use of personal supernatural experiences, especially trance, as a resource for the wider community's physical and spiritual wellbeing. This Introduction surveys research on the topic of shamanism around the world, detailing the archaeology and earliest development of shamanic traditions as well as their scientific "discovery" in the context of eighteenth- and nineteenth-century colonization in Siberia, the Americas, and Asia. It explores the beliefs and rituals typical of shamanic traditions, as well as the roles of shamans within their communities. It also surveys the variety of techniques used by shamans cross-culturally, including music, entheogens, material culture, and verbal performance. The final chapters examine attempts to suppress or eradicate shamanic traditions, the revitalization of shamanism in postcolonial situations, and the development of new forms of shamanism within new cultural and social contexts.

THOMAS A. DUBOIS is the Birgit Baldwin Professor of Scandinavian Studies at the University of Wisconsin-Madison where he teaches in the fields of Scandinavian studies, folklore studies, and religious studies. He is author and editor of five books including *Nordic Religions in the Viking Age* (1999) and *Sanctity in the North: Saints, Lives and Cults in Medieval Scandinavia* (2008).

AN INTRODUCTION
TO SHAMANISM

THOMAS A. DUBOIS

University of Wisconsin-Madison

CAMBRIDGE
UNIVERSITY PRESS

CAMBRIDGE
UNIVERSITY PRESS

University Printing House, Cambridge CB2 8BS, United Kingdom

Published in the United States of America by Cambridge University Press, New York

Cambridge University Press is part of the University of Cambridge.

It furthers the University's mission by disseminating knowledge in the pursuit of education, learning and research at the highest international levels of excellence.

www.cambridge.org
Information on this title: www.cambridge.org/9780521695367

© Thomas A. DuBois 2009

First published 2009

A catalogue record for this publication is available from the British Library

Library of Congress Cataloguing in Publication data
DuBois, Thomas A. (Thomas Andrew), 1960–
An introduction to shamanism / Thomas A. DuBois.
p. cm.
Includes bibliographical references and index.
ISBN 978-0-521-87353-6 (hardback) –
ISBN 978-0-521-69536-7 (pbk.)
1. Shamanism. I. Title.
BF1611.D83 2009
201'.44–dc22
2008053947

ISBN 978-0-521-87353-6 Hardback
ISBN 978-0-521-87353-6 Paperback

Contents

Contents

Illustrations

Cover. Woman transforming, detail from mural *Freedom*, by Lon Michels (www.lonmichelsart.com), used with the artist's permission. Photo courtesy John Hunter.

Preface

The following study surveys current understandings and research on the topic of shamanism. An initial set of three chapters introduces the "discovery" of shamanism in Western scholarship during a period of intense interaction between indigenous cultures around the world and forces of Western exploration, expansion, and colonization. The set of traditions associated with practitioners designated by the Evenki (Tungus) term *shaman* became generalized in scholarly formulations into an overall norm, one which more recent scholars have also sought to encounter in ancient textual as well as archaeological sources. The antiquity and seeming uniformity of the traditions have been explained through both psychological and historical theories and are a source of enduring interest for scholarly as well as generalist audiences.

A second set of three chapters examines the soteriology and rituals typical of shamanic traditions, as well as the roles of shamans within their communities. The importance of particular understandings of the cosmos and the experience of the shamanic profession as a calling are discussed in detail, with an emphasis on the interaction of personal religious experience and communal needs and expectations. In this context, shamans can be regarded as integral parts of communal religious traditions, professionals who make use of personal supernatural experiences as a resource for the wider community's negotiation of physical and spiritual wellbeing.

Two further chapters survey current research focusing on the ways in which shamanic traditions and techniques can be understood cognitively. Scholars have sought to uncover the mechanisms in the brain through which shamanic trance states are effected, managed, and interpreted. Other scholars working within the area of the ethnography of healing have explored the ways in which shamanic therapeutic acts can prove effective, not only for patients, but also for the broader community as well as for the shaman personally.

A further set of three chapters explores some of the arsenal of performative techniques used by shamans cross-culturally within their professional activities. Music frequently plays a key role in shamanic rituals, as do entheogens – psychoactive substances used for religious purposes. Material culture helps express and effectuate shamanic relations, both for shamans and for their communities. Verbal lore – narratives or incantations performed by shamans, accounts of shamanic experiences, or narratives of primordial or historical shamans – provides a rich pool of knowledge regarding the spirit world and the workings of the shaman within it.

A final set of three chapters examines shamanic traditions today. The same era of Western expansion that led to the scholarly identification of shamanism as a religious phenomenon also led to an intensification of efforts to eradicate or replace it, often in favor of new religious traditions introduced by colonial forces. Communities at times resisted such efforts, retaining at least elements of prior shamanic beliefs even in contexts of profound religious change. Occasionally, communities have revitalized prior shamanic traditions, seeing them as a key for cultural survival and the recovery of lost social cohesiveness. And finally, individuals have attempted to recreate or even adopt shamanic traditions personally on the basis of scholarly information as well as extant evidence regarding the nature or workings of shamanic activities in general. These neoshamanic movements can be regarded in part as a product of a blurring of the conceptual boundaries that once separated Western scholars and their readers from the shamanic communities they sought to understand.

I owe thanks to many for help and encouragement in this project. My colleagues in religious studies at the University of Wisconsin-Madison deserve thanks first of all for having encouraged and supported my teaching in this area. Special thanks in this connection go to Charles L. Cohen and Quitman Phillips, past and present directors of the university's academic program in religious studies. They helped make it possible for me to develop and test a framework for conveying past and current research on shamanism to students with little previous knowledge of the subject. Colleagues in both the university's folklore studies program and Department of Scandinavian Studies were also instrumental in the project, particularly James P. Leary, Ruth Olson, Susan Brantly, and Scott Mellor. My students, too, deserve tremendous thanks, both for their enthusiasm for the topic and for their various insights over the years. Often students became important inform-ants as well as valuable critics of my writing and presentations. In the wider field, I thank especially Thai Vang Yang, Peter Nause, Anna-Leena Siikala, Juha Pentikäinen, Neil Price, Frank Korom, and Timothy F. Tangherlini.

At Cambridge University Press, Senior Commissioning Editor Dr. Kate Brett and Assistant Editor Gillian Dadd were consistently supportive and enthusiastic about the project and helped bring my plans to reality. The three anonymous reviewers who vetted the manuscript at different stages provided valuable advice that greatly improved the final product. Working with the press has been a great pleasure and a rich intellectual experience in itself.

My work was generously supported by the Graduate School of the University of Wisconsin-Madison as well as the Birgit Baldwin Professorship of the university's Department of Scandinavian Studies. This assistance made it possible for me to complete this project within a time frame that sometimes appeared utterly unrealistic and overambitious. Many thanks go to my graduate project assistant Hilary Virtanen, who wrestled with my bibliography and various chapters and provided valuable input throughout that kept the project on track, particularly in its final stages.

As always, I thank my family for their patience and support.

PART I

Introductions

CHAPTER I

Shamanism and the issue of religion

On a blustery winter morning on the campus of a major American research university, I have the opportunity to sit with a unique individual. Thai is an undergraduate anthropology student with a second major in Southeast Asian studies. He is also a *txiv neeb*, what scholars of religion term a *shaman*. Thai is a member of Wisconsin's numerous and thriving Hmong community, a set of people who relocated to the United States from their homeland in Laos starting in the mid-1970s, in the aftermath of the Vietnam War. In Laos, Hmong people lived in mountainous areas, and combined traditional hunting and gathering practices with small-scale agriculture and livestock husbandry. Much has changed in their rebuilding of lives in the United States, but some things remain the same. One of these, at least in Thai's view, is the crucial relation that exists between Hmong people and an unseen but highly influential spirit world. As a *txiv neeb*, Thai is a specialist in these relations, a traveler between the visible world of the everyday and a profoundly different and powerful unseen. Through a set of rituals that hold psychic and physical dangers for the practitioner, Thai travels that spirit world, pursuing, confronting, cajoling, and confounding spirit entities on behalf of his clients and community. Through these journeys, Thai gains information and strategies for curing woes facing his fellow Hmong: sickness, social strains, misfortune. He rescues or recovers fugitive souls that have distanced themselves from their bodies and counters the aggressions of foreign souls that have made incursions on his clients' health or wholeness. He is, in traditional views, a hero. Yet he is also deeply humble, viewing his work as an act of service for the good of others and for the placation of a spirit world at times impetuous and insistent. This study examines Thai's activities within the broader context of shamanism as it has been described and chronicled cross-culturally over the last several centuries. In this broader context, Thai's ritual acts, customs, and worldview can be seen as illustrative of a set of religious practices and understandings that have been important to people in various cultures from time immemorial.

Figure 1. Thai Vang Yang, a practicing Hmong *txiv neeb*, explains elements of Hmong shamanic cosmology in an American university classroom. Photo T. DuBois

By looking at past and present research on these phenomena, this volume seeks to provide a concise overview of a set of traditions of nearly worldwide distribution and deep human interest.

ACADEMIC CONTEXTS

In Thai's community, people speak of two competing religions: Christianity and shamanism. Many contemporary Hmong Americans belong to various Christian denominations. Particularly prominent is the Hmong Missionary Alliance Church, which had already begun to attract followers when the Hmong were still in Laos. In North America, however, the pace of conversion to this and other forms of Christianity has increased exponentially. Christian Hmong retain some of the old customs of their culture, but they do not consult shamans. To do so, in their view, would be to violate a basic tenet of their new religion.

Although this dichotomy is clear and very real in Thai's life, scholars of religion have long debated whether shamanism as we find it in hunter-gatherer or subsistence agricultural communities can actually be called a "religion" per se, or, rather, should be regarded as merely a "component," "dimension," or "role" of certain religions. Within anthropological discourse, the term *religion* has been applied fairly haphazardly, so that its exact scholarly significance is sometimes unclear. In an overview of shamanism, for instance, Piers Vitebsky (2000: 55) writes: "Shamanism is probably the world's oldest form of religion. It is a name generally given to many hundreds, perhaps thousands, of religions around the world." Of course, two different meanings of the term *religion* are invoked in these two sentences, without explicit differentiation: one, a general human phenomenon ("religion") of which specific local varieties can be regarded as variant "forms"; the other, a specific term for local bodies of practices and ideas ("religions"). The former permits us to speak of "shamanism" as a world phenomenon; the latter, to speak of "shamanisms" as locally delimited and specific.

Scholars of religion, for their part, have focused tremendous energy on trying to define the nature and essence of "religion" itself and have found shamanic traditions particularly thorny to categorize. As Roberte Hamayon (2001: 4) summarizes the trend: "shamanism was perceived as a set of elementary components potentially compatible with all religions – if not inherent in the religious attitude as such – and implicitly devoid per se of systemic properties." Because of the decentralized nature of shamanic traditions, in other words, and their seeming lack of the trappings of more familiar Western religions – e.g., an institutional identity, a professional priesthood, a body of explicit dogmas and policies – shamanism did not seem to meet the definitional threshold of "religion." As both Timothy Fitzgerald (2000) and Hans Kippenberg (2002) have shown, such views have in practice more to do with the history and development of the academic study of "religion" than with the phenomena at the center of Thai's supernatural experiences. But in a volume such as this, devoted to providing an introduction, it is important to address such scholarly debates from the outset and define the nature and approach of the analysis to come.

In the chapters that follow, I discuss shamanism as a set of practices and understandings concerning the cosmos, spirits, and human needs. The shaman is a communally recognized professional who cultivates personal relations with helping spirits in order to achieve particular ends for the community: generally, healing, divination, and/or the control of fortune. By entering into trance states through communally recognized rituals, the shaman is able to communicate with spirits, travel the cosmos in search of errant or recalcitrant souls, and minister to the particular needs of clients. Shamanic traditions occur cross-culturally with great frequency in Eurasia and the Americas, particularly in small-scale hunter-gatherer societies as well as those practicing subsistence agriculture. Shamanic practices have also sometimes been incorporated into other religious traditions and, in the current era, have begun to be adapted for use among urbanized Westerners. While the precise relation of these roles and understandings to other aspects of "group-bound religions" (Smart 1973) is left to theorists to debate in other forums, I follow the practice of native scholars like Thai in regarding these shamanic phenomena as essentially religious in nature and often as the conceptual backbone of what a community defines as its religion. As such, it becomes possible to examine the commonalities that obtain between the practices of a Hmong *txiv neeb* like Thai, a Greenlandic *angakok*, a Sámi *noaide*, or a Daur Mongol *yadgan*, while still recognizing the essential distinctiveness of each. A discussion of this stance is presented below.

In his *Discovering Religious History in the Modern Age* (2002), Hans G. Kippenberg traces the development of the field of religious studies as a secular science. As Kippenberg details, the "science" of religion grew largely out of eighteenth-century tracts on the "philosophy" of religion, which was itself an attempt to harmonize a centuries-old tradition of overtly Christian theology with the realities of cross-cultural analysis, state-based religious *Realpolitik*, and historical change. Early studies of the field enshrined Judeo-Christian (or, more specifically, *Protestant*) concepts of God, religious experience, and religious institutions as normative and fundamental, and skewed data or ideas from other religious traditions to fit and justify this largely unquestioned paradigm. Part of this tendency was conscious: scholars viewed Protestant Christianity as superior to other religious traditions, and they were sometimes intent on underscoring that belief in their scholarship. Part of the tendency, however, was unconscious as well: without explicit in-depth familiarity with other religions, it became easy to form definitions which excluded or marginalized important aspects of other belief systems if they did not find close parallels in Judeo-Christian traditions. Antonia Mills and Richard Slobodin (1994) argue in their anthology

Amerindian Rebirth, for instance, that anthropologists working with Native American cultures never fully took stock of the fact that reincarnation is an important feature in many North American Native religions, despite the fact that Native informants were sometimes very clear in emphasizing its importance in their lives. Writes Mills in the introduction to the volume: "Reincarnation belief has been underestimated because it was not part of the Western world-view and hence was not expected; and also because Amerindian and Inuit belief on the subject is varied and complex" (1994: 3). Gananath Obeyesekere (2002: xix) points out, justifiably, that, had the dominant religious background of Western scholars been Buddhist or Hindu rather than Christian, this aspect of Native religiosity would no doubt have been accorded far more attention.

Amid the rampant philosophical shifts of the nineteenth and early twentieth centuries, the field of "religious studies" became dominated by a nostalgic discourse of "tradition" vs. "modernity," dehistoricized into a framework of a purportedly universal sense of the divine at the root of all religious experience. This latter notion found its seminal formulation in Robert Ranulph Marett's (1909) concept of "pre-animistic religion." As Marett wrote: a "basic feeling of awe drives a man, ere he can think or theorize upon it, into personal relations with the supernatural" (1909: 15). This awe experience then becomes refined and interpreted via social, cultural, and historical institutions into the framework of a religious understanding, with attendant rituals and duties associated. As Marett writes:

Thus, from the vague utterance of the Omaha … onwards, through animism, to the dictum of the greatest living idealist philosopher … a single impulse may be discerned as active – the impulse, never satisfied in finite consciousness yet never abandoned, to bring together and grasp as one the *That* and the *What* of God. (1909: 28)

This underlying awe experience, Marett posited, could stand as the definitional basis of all religious expressions the world over.

As Kippenberg chronicles (2002: 125–7), Marett's theory garnered enthusiastic and nearly universal acceptance among scholars of religion in the early part of the twentieth century. It is especially noteworthy, from the perspective of this volume, that Marett made his argument on the basis of what were then termed "primitive" religions – i.e., the religious traditions of small-scale indigenous communities, even if in practice his definition worked to portray as natural and universal a specific Judeo-Christian notion of a single communicative God. Later scholars, such as Rudolf Otto (1950), would take up this purported universal and present it with an even clearer Christian bias. In his seminal work *The Idea of the Holy: An Inquiry into the*

Non-Rational Factor in the Idea of the Divine and Its Relation to the Rational,
Otto asserted that Marett's awe experience (labeled the "holy," or the "non-rational") is brought into relation with various rationalizing features in any given religious tradition. And (expectably), Christianity proved in Otto's view the ideal mix of awe and rational explanations:

> The degree in which both rational and non-rational elements are jointly presented, united in healthy and lovely harmony, affords a criterion to measure the relative rank of religions – and one, too, that is specifically religious. Applying this criterion, we find that Christianity, in this as in other respects, stands out in complete superiority over all its sister religions. The lucid edifice of its clear and pure conceptions, feelings, and experiences is built up on a foundation that goes far deeper than the rational. Yet the non-rational is only the basis, the setting, the woof in the fabric, ever preserving for Christianity its mystical depth, giving religion thereby the deep undertones and heavy shadows of mysticism, without letting it develop into a mere rank growth of mysticality. (1950: 142–3)

While such formulations enshrined Christianity as the pinnacle of all the world's various religious traditions, it presented the "primitive" religions discussed by Marett as inferior: mired in non-rationality, a "mere rank growth of mysticality." From this perspective, the beliefs at the foundation of shamanic interventions into the cosmos became theorized as defective, overly mysticized, or even as altogether outside of the province of religion itself. They were seen as secondary responses to life crises rather than primary expressions of religious insight, since by definition, the "primary" stuff of religion was the purported awe experience. Healing, divination, and the manipulation of luck were regarded as activities somehow below the proper gaze of religion, despite the fact that they are central to many ritual traditions the world over.

A further product of the Western bias evident in these scholarly trends was an insistence on positing the "religions" that respond to this experience of awe as unified systems. Since Western Christian denominations were explicitly demarcated by systematized doctrine, gatekeeping procedures, and provisions for treating internal dissention, scholars viewed these tendencies as fundamental to the very definition of *religion* itself. Thus, Émile Durkheim, in his important study *The Elementary Forms of the Religious Life* (1915), defined religion as "a unified set of beliefs and practices relative to sacred things ... which unite into one single moral community called a Church, all those who adhere to them" (1915: 62). Without this systematized union, beliefs could be defined as "cults" or "groups of religious phenomena" (1915: 57), but not as *religion*. To qualify as a religion, such beliefs – and the people who hold them – had to organize themselves into something resembling a Western "Church." Hamayon (2001: 4) notes the application of such criteria to shamanic traditions: "Scholars ... failed to find in shamanism the institutional features held to characterize a religion as such (doctrine, clergy, sanctuaries etc.)." Such scholarly insistence on institutional features, of course, created a profound definitional hurdle, particularly in the case of small-scale, often largely egalitarian, communities, where the hierarchical and regimented framework posited for "authentic" religions was often foreign, and even distinctly repugnant. In such societies, religious rituals are often carried out within the home, and religious practitioners may be individuals, heads of households, elders, or specialists. Rituals vary in their execution, spiritual relations are private and unique, and small details of the cosmos may differ from practitioner to practitioner. Yet these traditions can easily carry the same significance in individuals' lives as those associated with large-scale, highly institutionalized religious denominations.

By the 1970s, scholars of religion had begun to sense the limitations of a theory of religion restricted to institutionalized awe-centered phenomena, while also usually retaining such assumptions as basic tenets of the field. As Timothy Fitzgerald (2000: 68–9) describes, the influential scholar Ninian Smart (1973) set out to modify the definitional framework of the field to encompass religious traditions where a putative awe experience did not appear central at all. Writing on the basis of E. E. Evans-Pritchard's classic ethnography *The Nuer* (1940), Smart described a set of religions which, rather than focus on awe, locate a sense of fulfillment (i.e., soteriology) on the basis of customary actions. Writes Smart: "Christianity is a religion, and it crosses the bounds of a number of societies; while the religion of the Nuer is essentially group-tied and functions as an abstraction from the total life of the Nuer" (1973: 15; quoted in Fitzgerald 2000: 69). Religion thus becomes, in Smart's analysis, not a doctrinally unified institutionally distinct entity, but rather elements of daily behavior, beliefs, or customs connected with day-to-day life, or responses to personal and/or communal crises, such as feud, disease, death, and misfortune. "Men behave and act religiously, and this is something that the study of religion picks out; just as economics picks out the economic behaviour of the people" (Fitzgerald 2000: 69; Smart 1973: 15).

From an ethnographic point of view, Smart's enlargement of the definitional framework of religion would seem sensible and justified. Yet quintessentially, it proposed a fundamental shift in the methodological assumptions of scholarship on religion. For if "religion" now becomes aspects of life, "behaviors," rather than a unified institution transcending time and society, then the assumed core experience of "awe," depicted by Marett as the foundation of all religious expression, becomes decentered. "Religion" becomes a culture-bound component of daily, seasonal, or occasional praxis, rather than an institutionalization of an ineluctable meditation on a mysterious, transcultural, personal apprehension of God. It becomes the performance of religious behaviors, rather than their institutionalization into a church. Anthropological and sociological approaches thereafter largely adopted this empirical and functional viewpoint, leaving the issues of institutional unity and awe aside, while often retaining the Western notion of unity through terms like "system" or "complex." Illustrative of this shift is the definition which Clifford Geertz presents in his classic article "Religion as a Cultural System" ([1965] 1979). Geertz writes:

Religion is a system of symbols which acts to establish powerful, pervasive and long-lasting moods and motivations in men by formulating conceptions of a general order of existence and clothing these conceptions with such an aura of factuality that the moods and motivations seem uniquely realistic. (1979–80)

The ethnographer's work becomes recognizing the "system" behind religious activities or ideas, which may or may not coincide with institutions designed to achieve centralized control. In a postmodern academic milieu of the late twentieth century, Geertz's confidence in the ability of an analyst to discover such a unified system may itself appear naive.

By the century's end, the field of religious studies appeared primed to interrogate fundamentally the assumptions that had received such unanimous acclaim at the outset of the twentieth century. Timothy Fitzgerald (2000) challenged the awe experience model as covert Christian theology, one which trivialized the religious experiences of individuals in more "group-tied" religions such as Hinduism or Japanese Shinto. Calling for the rejection of the term *religion* altogether, Fitzgerald declares:

Working with the blurred yet ideologically loaded concept of "religion" and "religions" as a starting point can confuse and impoverish analysis, conceal fruitful connections that might otherwise be made, encourage the uncritical imposition of Judeo-Christian assumptions on non-western data, and generally maximize our chances of misunderstanding. (2000: 6)

His viewpoints were echoed by many other scholars in a spirited debate (see, for example, Dirks 1994; Jensen and Rothstein 2000; Gold 2003). Fitzgerald advocates replacing the blanket term *religion* with a trio of other terms: *soteriology* ("the sense of a personal quest for salvation located in a transcendent realm" 2000: 15), *ritual* (symbolic acts undertaken as expressions of religious belief), and *politics* (the interaction of religious activities and social formations). In Fitzgerald's framework, then, the customs and understandings discussed in this volume would fall largely under the rubric of "ritual," while the personal views of shamans themselves regarding the spirits they interact with might well be construed as a variety of soteriology, which may (or may not) be ultimately equivalent to the sense of "awe" posited by Marett. Finally, the social roles of shamans within their communities, or in confrontation with colonial authorities or a changing world, as discussed in the later chapters of this study, would fall under the rubric of politics. By removing the reified and culturally biased term *religion*, Fitzgerald argues, such analysis avoids the potential for becoming enfolded into an underlying scholarly project of justifying – "naturalizing" – Judeo-Christian ideas of God and religion in the manner of ideology. In the coming chapters, then, I follow Fitzgerald's provocative recommendation by using wherever possible specific terms like *cosmology*, *role*, and *ritual*, while continuing to assert – in the manner of Smart – that small hunter-gatherer and subsistence agricultural communities often display a "religion" made up of specific, socially embedded responses to daily events and crises – the practical tasks of the shaman (among others) in general. Whether or not these specific beliefs and behaviors combine into a "unified system" is largely, as I hope the above discussion makes clear, a judgment of interpreters rather than a verifiable empirical fact. From the point of view of shamans like Thai, however, the various concepts and behaviors described in these pages do indeed constitute a unified and highly satisfying system of belief, one which Thai is quite comfortable describing as a religion.

CHAPTER 2

A history of shamanic encounters

The Western scholarly confrontation with shamanic traditions occurred piecemeal over a period of centuries. Crucially, it occurred during – and in part may have helped shape – a process of change in the ways in which intellectuals conceptualized and discussed foreign religions. In the initial encounters, as we shall see, writers approached the phenomena of shamanic rituals from thoroughly Christian perspectives, extending the good/evil dualities of Judeo-Christian thought to encompass in imperfect manner the intricacies of indigenous worldviews and practices. Early on in such encounters, this Christian perspective led writers to view shamanic practitioners as curious and misguided; later, their views turned harsher, as they decried shamanism as irredeemably diabolical. This demonization grew up within Europe itself in confrontation both with shamanic traditions at its periphery and with practices occurring in peasant communities within the continent itself. This stigmatization colored the ways in which writers perceived and portrayed the religious traditions they found elsewhere in the world, particularly in the colonial era. From the Enlightenment onward, these viewpoints took on yet a new tone. Scholars began to interpret shamans as deluded and credulous: simpletons mired in a morass of self-delusion and superstition. These equally negative views only gradually gave way to a scholarly perception based on the ideals of relativism, where religions (at least optimally) were to be considered from the vantage point of their own systems of thought. This chapter surveys these encounters, and the understandings of indigenous religions that the scholarship of the last centuries has produced. It is a chronicle of increasing reification and generalization, as scholars gradually constructed a notion of a single "shamanism" to which ancient and indigenous communities subscribed. This process of characterization is important to recognize and appraise if we are to move beyond its limitations in a survey such as the present study.

EARLY ACCOUNTS

In the textual production of monastic scriptoria and royal courts of the medieval era, amid the various religious tracts and recopyings of Classical thought, there emerge in the twelfth and thirteenth centuries the beginnings of what will eventually become the genre and enterprise of ethnography. In stray and singular texts, writers set down observations regarding the rituals and religious ideas of people with whom they had come into contact through travel, trade, and oral tradition. Harkening back at times to authorities of the ancient world – Herodotus, Tacitus, Prokopeus, etc. – the writers nonetheless anchor their descriptions in the here-and-now, depicting practices observed firsthand or learned about from the reports of credible witnesses. In the Latin text *Historia Norwegiae*, for instance, dated to between 1178 and 1220, we find the earliest account of a Sámi religious ritual, one with what appear to be clear shamanic details. A woman has been struck unconscious by an unseen adversary and two rival shamans attempt to recover her lost soul. Spreading out a cloth to create a ritual space for their interventions, the two men dance, drum, and sing incantations until falling into trance. The inherent danger of their activities is underscored by the fact that one of the two shamans dies while in trance, the victim of an ambush laid by spirit enemies. The other shaman survives, however, and is able to return the woman to health. The shaman tells of having transformed into various animals during his trance, including a whale (DuBois 1999: 129–30).

Even more striking than this account is a later thirteenth-century depiction of divinatory rituals among pagan Icelandic settlers in Greenland. *Eiriks saga* chronicles the Icelandic colonization of Greenland as well as the colonists' forays west to Vinland, apparently mainland North America. In the saga's early chapters, the settlers face a protracted epidemic and a lack of certainty about the coming year. In response, a prominent farmer in the region invites an itinerant seer to his home to perform a divinatory ritual, a custom evidenced in a number of other medieval texts as well as archaeological findings (Jolly, Raudvere, and Peters 2002; Price 2002). The practitioner, a woman named Thorbiörg, is given a special meal made of different animals' hearts and allowed to spend a night and a day at the farm before beginning her acts. Her attire is carefully noted: she wears a cloak and hood made of black lambskin and white catskin, carries an ornamented staff of brass and precious stones, and wears a belt with a pouch "in which she kept those charms of hers which she needed for her magic" (DuBois 1999: 124). At Thorbiörg's bidding, the women of the farm, particularly a newly arrived colonist named Guthrith, gather in a circle around the seer's platform and sing a special incantation. After the performance has ended, the saga writer details: "The seeress gave thanks for the chant, adding that many spirits had been drawn there now who thought it lovely to lend ear, the chant had been so admirably delivered – spirits 'who before wished to keep their distance from us and give us no hearing. And now many things are apparent to me which earlier were hidden from me as from many others'." Thorbiörg is then able to answer the collective and individual questions of her host and his assembled neighbors (DuBois 1999: 125). Where the *Historia Norwegiae* account focuses on a foreign community – i.e., the Sámi who lived alongside Norwegians in the north of Norway – this description depicts divination among the Icelandic/Greenlandic community itself. By the end of the saga, the colony has made considerable progress toward Christianization and, presumably, such rituals have become more rare. But the fact that a thirteenth-century Christian writer could describe such a séance in relative detail indicates that the new faith did not fully supplant pre-Christian modes of divination for at least some time. Such acts belong to the class of rituals that would eventually be stigmatized as witchcraft in later centuries.

At about the same time as the *Eiriks saga* account, an Italian Franciscan detailed his observations of religious traditions in the Mongolian Empire of 1246. Giovanni da Pian del Carpine (d. 1252) was sent by the newly installed Pope Innocent IV to the Great Khan of the Golden Horde with a papal bull directing the khan to convert and make peace. Entering the khan's vast empire at its western periphery in Poland, Giovanni and a fellow friar were swept by horseback over thousands of miles so that they could witness the crowning of Güyük, grandson of Chinggis Khan. The friars' diplomatic and religious mission was an utter failure, yet they survived the experience with their lives and returned to Europe with a wealth of observations regarding the steppe cultures of this mysterious land to the east. Writing of their hosts' religious practices, Giovanni states:

They pay great attention to divinations, auguries, soothsayings, sorceries and incantations, and when they receive an answer from the demons they believe that a god is speaking to them. [Of] this god ... they have a wondrous fear and reverence ... and offer him many oblations and the first portion of their food and drink, and they do everything according to the answers he gives. (Dawson 1955: 12)

Somewhat later but vastly more famous is an account written by the Venetian merchant Marco Polo (1254–1324). Like Giovanni before him, Marco wrote a description of his visit to Kublai Khan, another grandson of Chinggis Khan and the founder of the Yuan dynasty of China. Later scholars have questioned whether Marco Polo himself ever made his famed trip to China, but, in any case, his observations shed interesting light on early shamanic traditions within the ancient empire. Describing procedures for healing, the traveler writes:

[W]hen they are ill they make their physicians, that is magicians come to them, these are the devil-charmers and those who keep the idols (and with these the province is well supplied), and ask them to foresee concerning the sick. And when these magi are come they ask about the manner of the sickness; then the sick persons tell the ills which they have, and the magi, very many of them being gathered together, begin immediately to sound their instruments and they continue this dancing, singing, and playing all together for a long time until some one of these magicians falls all on his back on the ground or on the pavement or on the bed and with great foam at the mouth and seems dead, and then they dance no more. And they say that it is that the devil is entered there inside his body, and he stays thus a great while, in such manner that he seems dead. And when the other magicians his companions, of whom many were there, see that one of them is fallen in such way as you have heard, then they begin to speak to him and they ask him what sickness this sick man has and why he has it. And that one remaining in ecstasy answers. (quoted in Flaherty 1992: 27)

The healer and his assistants are able to determine what sacrifices need to be made to appease offended deities, furnishing the patient and his community with a set of tasks which will restore the sick man's health. Alternatively, if the deities responsible for the illness cannot be appeased, the healers instead predict the patient's time and manner of death. The imagery of spirit possession here resembles strongly that described for Taiwanese shamans some seven centuries later, albeit filtered here through Marco Polo's Christian worldview of devils (Wolf 1990).

These early accounts show a sometimes startling degree of fascination with, or even respect for, the non-Christian practices they depict, especially when compared with the stark condemnations of the era of demonology which would follow some centuries later. Writers – Christian clerics or educated nobles – fully loyal to the mandates of their faith, nonetheless treat their pagan subjects, sometimes begrudgingly, with reverence, and depict pagan rituals at times as efficacious and alluring. The *Eiriks saga* writer closes his account of the divinatory ritual on Greenland with the summation: "Little indeed of what she said failed to come about" (DuBois 1999: 125).

THE ERA OF WITCHCRAFT TRIALS

Within the Christian thought of the time, however, harsher views of magical procedures and practitioners were already emerging. Crucially, the Church hierarchy came to equate purported magic with heresy, and would eventually create an institution, the Inquisition, to hunt down and punish both. Already in his *Warning to the Bishops* of 1140, Gratian explicitly treats *witch* and *heretic* as synonyms, while he describes fantastic nighttime flights of malefactors:

Those are held captive by the Devil who, leaving their creator, seek the aid of the Devil. And so Holy Church must be cleansed of this pest. It is also not to be omitted that some wicked women, perverted by the Devil, seduced by illusions and phantasms of demons, believe and profess themselves, in the hours of night, to ride upon certain beasts with Diana, the goddess of pagans, and an innumerable multitude of women, and in the silence of the dead of night to traverse great spaces of earth and to obey her commands as of their mistress, and to be summoned to her service on certain nights. (quoted in Kors and Peters 1986: 29)

In his classic study of witchcraft and the law, Edward Peters (1978) traces the process by which elements of Classical mythology, and a notion of a high magic practiced by philosophers and magi, became demonized and feminized in medieval European witchlore. It is difficult, if not utterly impossible, to discern whether any of the coerced testimonies extracted from accused witches before their executions in the fifteenth through eighteenth centuries reflect in any way shamanic practices or a shamanic remnant in European folk cultures. Sometimes, indeed, testimonies do seem reminiscent of shamanic ideas, as in the deposition of Anne Marie de Georgel, a fourteenth-century farmwife arrested and burned for witchcraft in Toulouse:

Anne Marie de Georgel declares that one morning when she was washing clothes near Pech-David above the town, she saw a man of huge stature coming towards her across the water. He was dark-skinned and his eyes burned like living coals; he was dressed in the hides of beasts. This monster asked her if she would give herself to him and she said yes. Then he blew into her mouth and from the Saturday following she was borne to the Sabbath, simply because it was his will. There she found a huge he-goat and after greeting him she submitted to his pleasure. The he-goat in return taught her all kinds of secret spells; he explained poisonous plants to her and she learned from him words for incantations and how to cast spells during the night of the vigil of St. John's day, Christmas Eve, and the first Friday in every month. He advised her to make sacrilegious communion if she could, offending God and honouring the Devil. And she carried out these impious suggestions. (quoted in Kors and Peters 1986: 93–5)

This testimony marks the earliest written account of the Witches' Sabbath, a narrative motif that was to recur ceaselessly in the accounts of both Inquisitors and accused witches over the next four centuries.

In his classic study of Italian witchcraft traditions and agrarian cults, Carlo Ginzburg ([1966] 1983) examines Inquisition documents regarding peasant "warriors" who left their bodies to do battle against witches and warlocks. Citing a denunciation against one Toffolo di Buri of the village of Pieris, Ginzburg writes:

This Toffolo asserts that he is a benandante, and that for a period of about twenty-eight years he has been compelled to go on the Ember Days in the company of other benandanti to fight witches and warlocks in spirit (leaving his body behind in bed) but dressed in the same clothing he is accustomed to wear during the day. So Toffolo went to the conventicles in spirit, and for him too the act of going forth was like dying: When he has to go out to fight he falls into a very deep sleep, and lying there on his back when the spirit leaves him three groans are heard, as people who are dying sometimes make. The spirit went forth at midnight, and stays out of the body for three hours between going, fighting and returning home. (Ginzburg 1983: 69)

Such *benandanti* ("good walkers") were also viewed as capable of healing and other acts of beneficial magic. Ginzburg notes that the region of the Friuli, where these traditions flourished, represented an area of convergence between German, Italian, and Slavic cultures, and suggests that their activities may have once been more widespread in Central Europe. Whatever the case, the Inquisition regarded the tradition as heretical witch-craft, and worked assiduously for its eradication.

It is a matter of considerable scholarly debate how much European peasant traditions such as these held in common with the kinds of spirit travel and supernatural dealings of shamans in other parts of the world. It is essential to note in any case, however, that this image of witchcraft came to color European perceptions of shamanism ever after. Equated wholly with demonic contracts and heresy, the shamanisms of indigenous communities were to become prime targets for righteous persecution. They became no longer rituals to be observed and wondered at, but acts of evil to be recognized from the pooled experience of European demonology.

Historians of witchcraft have tried to discover the reasons behind the eruption of violence against all such purported religious heterodoxy during the fifteenth and sixteenth centuries. Scholars have suggested that the numerous trials (and executions) represented a concerted effort by state centers to exercise control over peripheral tracts and communities. In the early Middle Ages, peasants had largely been ignored, left to their own devices, while ecclesiastical authorities focused instead on the middle- and upper-class polities of central cities and royal courts. If such considerations lay behind at least some of the myriad violent persecutions of the era, they almost certainly also affected the indigenous peoples whom Europeans were poised to subjugate in coming centuries. Indigenous practices outside

Europe became equated nearly automatically with the supposed demonism of European peasants, exposing traditional practitioners in far-flung locales to the condemnation of both missionaries and state authorities alike.

ENLIGHTENMENT VIEWS

Cocchiara (1981: 44–60) suggests that the horrors and obvious injustices of the European witchcraft trials eventually aided in the intellectual embrace of an ideal of reason in the human confrontation with the sacred. Seventeenth-century theologians like the German Jesuit Friedrich von Spee or the Anglican Lord Bishop of Rochester Thomas Sprat argued that belief in witches and magic was folly, both for the (alleged) offenders and for the authorities who punished them. God works, such thinkers argued, through natural law, and although it was important for state and church authorities to correct peasant errors regarding divine and supernatural assistance, it was also important to realize that such beliefs were the products of credulous minds rather than direct demonic assistance. Terms like *devilish*, *demonic*, and *diabolical* continued to appear in printed descriptions of shamanic activities, but increasingly in a more metaphorical and patronizing sense. At the same time, however, the suppression of non-Christian rituals and behaviors – "superstition" – and, even more importantly, the suppression of the ritual specialists who claimed authority in such undertakings, remained a key goal of governing polities, particularly as they asserted their control over subject peoples within their expanding empires.

The Recollect lay brother Gabriel Sagard, an early missionary to the Huron of New France, combines deep personal piety with a liberal and tolerant attitude toward the indigenous traditions he observes. His memoirs, *Le grand voyage du pays des Hurons* (1632) proved far more successful than his order's mission, and soon appeared in a second, expanded edition in 1636. Sagard details his hosts' use of healing herbs, sweat baths, and practices of quarantine, the last of which he notes "is a laudable and most excellent custom and ordinance, which indeed ought to be adopted in every country" (Sagard 1939: 198). Of shamanic healing rituals, Sagard describes a joint ritual in which both healer and patient achieve an altered state through hyperactivity:

[T]he patient and the doctor, accompanied by some other person, will make grimaces and utter incantations and throw themselves into contortions to such an extent that they generally become as quite mad, with eyes flashing and frightful to see, sometimes standing up, sometimes sitting, as the fancy takes him. Suddenly a whim will seize him again and he will do as much harm as he possibly can, then he will lie down and sleep some little time, and waking up with a jump he will return to his first fury, upsetting, breaking, throwing everything that comes in his way, with a din and damage and outrageous behavior that have no equal. This madness passes in the sleep that overtakes him again. Afterwards he induces a sweat, with some one of his friends whom he summons, the effect of which is to cure some of these sick persons, and this is what maintains their regard for these diabolical ceremonies. (1939: 201; modified for accuracy in accord with French original, 1639: 372)

Far from regarding these activities as evil, Sagard depicts them as the products of well-meaning delusion:

It is quite within the bounds of belief that these sick persons are not so completely possessed that they do no see the damage they do, but they think they must act like a demoniac in order to cure the imaginations or disturbances of their mind; and by righteous divine permission it generally happens that instead of being cured they jump from the frying-pan into the fire, as the saying is, and what before was only a mental caprice, caused by a hypochondriacal humor or the work of the evil spirit, is converted into a bodily as well as a mental disease. (ibid.)

Sagard is also eager to point out his hosts' desire for a better way and entreaties for knowledge of Christian prayer and healing:

This is why the masters of the ceremony and the members of the council often begged us to pray to God in their behalf and to teach them some efficient remedy for their diseases, candidly admitting that all their ceremonies, dances, songs, feasts, and other tricks were good for nothing whatever. (1939: 202)

No European culture had as great or as varied a host of indigenous peoples within its own continental borders as did the Russian Empire. The vast stretches of taiga and tundra of the immense country were home to myriad communities, each possessing its own language, livelihoods, and religious traditions. Early descriptions of shamanic practices written by travelers and Orthodox clergy note recurrently the laxity of Orthodox faithful in rejecting or suppressing such traditions. The Orthodox priest Avvakum, for instance, exiled to Siberia from 1653 to 1664, describes in his memoirs the deplorable conduct of a Russian officer who consulted an Evenki diviner to determine the outcome of an upcoming battle. Paid by the Russian to procure an answer to his queries, the diviner undertook a sacrifice and trance ritual:

In the evening, the witch brought a living ram close to my hut and began to practice witchcraft over it, by turning it around and around, and finally he had its head off and threw it away. And he started jumping about and dancing and summoning up demons, and, having shouted much, he fell down on the ground, foaming at the mouth. The demons were bearing hard on him and he was asking them: "Will the campaign be successful?" (quoted in Glavatskaya 2001: 238)

Avvakum's text marks the first use of the Evenki (Tungus) root *shaman* as a verbal designation for practices of this sort. A somewhat later Dutch traveler to the region, Nicolas Witsen, would adopt the term *schaman* as a noun in his German text of 1692 (Flaherty 1992: 23).

A similar tendency is evinced in the travelogue of Lionel Wafer, an English surgeon and adventurer whose account of New World travels, *A New Voyage and Description of the Isthmus of America*, appeared in 1699 (1934). Traveling among the Kuna people of what is today Panama, he recounts his party's resorting to a divinatory ritual:

> We presently enquired of these *Indians*, when they expected any Ships? They told us they knew not, but would enquire; and therefore they sent for one of their Conjurers, who immediately went to work to raise the Devil, to enquire of him at what time a Ship would arrive here; for they are very expert and skilful in their sort of Diabolical Conjurations ... We could hear them make most hideous Yellings and Shrieks; imitating the Voices of all their kind of Birds and Beasts. With their own Noise, they join'd that of several Stones struck together, and of Conch-shells, and of a sorry sort of Drums made of hollow Bamboes, which they beat upon; making a jarring Noise also with Strings fasten'd to the larger Bones of Beasts. And every now and then they would make a dreadful Exclamation, and clattering all of a sudden, would as suddenly make a Pause and a profound Silence. (1934: 24–5)

Wafer points out that the diviners' eventual prediction, achieved only after the practitioners had asked the Europeans to leave the building, proved accurate in every respect. It was perhaps as much the willingness of European Christians to resort to such shamanic assistance as concern for the souls of indigenous community members themselves that led to the concerted effort of Enlightenment authorities to continue the work of suppressing and discrediting shamanic activities.

Glavatskaya (2001: 240) views the work of Johannes Schefferus as pivotal in a new missionization effort that would soon aim at eradicating shamanic traditions from the northern peoples of both Scandinavia and Russia. Schefferus, a German professor of rhetoric at the University of Uppsala, was asked by Swedish royal authorities to compile a scientific work on the Sámi. In producing such a treatise, the authorities hoped to demonstrate that the Swedish monarchy did not support or condone witchcraft in the realm. Schefferus's *Lapponia* (1673) drew on the written testimonies of Lutheran ministers among the Sámi to describe Sámi shamanic traditions. Here, in lucid Latin prose, with abundant illustrative woodcuts, we find detailed accounts of shamanic séances, drum divination, and other elements of what would eventually come to be known as classic shamanism. Like most of his contemporaries, Schefferus regards the source of these traditions and powers as demonic, and in the following century, the state churches of both Sweden–Finland and Denmark–Norway would expend considerable energy suppressing them. Internationally, *Lapponia* became an immensely popular work among European intellectuals, appearing in English, French, German, and Dutch within the next decade. It helped shape a Western notion of "primitive religion" in general, and of the set of traditions which came to be known as *shamanism* in particular.

In the aftermath of *Lapponia*, the Russian czar Peter I could no longer turn a blind eye to the evils of witchcraft in his empire. Like his Swedish and Danish counterparts, he came to view it as essential to wipe out the non-Christian practices of Siberian peoples. In 1702, he commanded the *voevoda* of Berezov to procure for him two skilled shamans and to send them to Moscow to be examined. The administrator located two Nenets practitioners, but judging their skills too inferior, failed to send them on to the czar, thereby incurring the ruler's ire (Glavatskaya 2001: 241). By 1711, a decree was put into effect to impose baptism on all peoples of the realm and to destroy their former sacred sites and idols. Glavatskaya writes: "In 1722, the priest Mikail Stepanov burned down seventy-five sacred places in the Ob-river area; in 1723 the Russian administration took away and burned down 1,200 wooden and five iron images of deities belonging to Khanty and Mansi in the Berezov district" (2001: 241). Over the course of a quarter century, some forty thousand individuals were forcibly baptized in an effort to expunge forever the demonism of the natives. Peter's efforts found parallels in the policies and practices of colonial authorities in various parts of the New World.

The view of shamans as enemies of rationalism and truth diffused throughout Europe through the bulk of the eighteenth century. Writing of his travels among the Evenki (Tungus) people between 1733 and 1744, the German scholar Johann Gottlieb Georgi combines ethnographic description of shamanic practices with striking condemnations, describing a practitioner's work as "hocus pocus" and "humbug" and wishing that the shaman could be subjected to hard labor in prison (quoted in Hoppál 1989: 75–6; see Chapter 12 for further discussion). Although the Enlightenment's disapproval of "superstition" certainly led at times to harsh treatment for indigenous cults and practitioners, the attitude could also spawn a good deal of condescension from worldly men of science. Typical is the travelogue of Louis Armand, the baron de La Hontan (1703). Focusing particularly on the Algonkian peoples of the Great Lakes region, the baron explores their religious concepts as well as their healing traditions in detail. In discussing the latter, he writes of "jongleurs," "quacks" who, "being once cur'd of some dangerous Distemper, has the Presumption and Folly to fancy that he is immortal, and possessed of the Power of curing all Diseases, by speaking to the Good and Evil Spirits" (1703: II, 467). La Hontan's disbelief is evident in his description of such practitioners' healing methods:

When the Quack comes to visit the Patient, he examines him very carefully; _If the Evil Spirit be here_, says he, _we shall quickly dislodge him_. This said, he withdraws by himself to a little Tent made on purpose, where he dances and sings houling like an Owl; (which gives the Jesuits Occasion to say, _That the Devil converses with 'em_.) After he has made an end of this Quack Jargon, he comes and rubs the Patient in some part of his Body, and pulling some little Bones out of his Mouth, acquaints the Patient, _That these very Bones came out of his Body; that he ought to pluck up a good heart, in regard that his Distemper is but a Trifle; and in fine, that in order to accelerate the Care, 'twill be convenient to send his own and his Relations Slaves to shoot, Elks, Deer, etc. to the end that they may all eat of that sort of Meat, upon which his Cure does absolutely depend_. (1703: II, 468)

The baron consigns belief here to credulous natives and Jesuits, while he, a worldly man of science, easily sees through the healers' subterfuges. In the same passage, however, La Hontan even extends this image of disbelief to the natives themselves, as he writes of their views of shamanic healers:

Now though every Body railes upon these Fellows when they are absent, and looks upon 'em as Fools that have lost their Senses by some violent Distemper, yet they allow 'em to visit the Sick; whether it be to divert 'em with their Idle Stories, or to have an Opportunity of seeing them rave, skip about, cry, houl, and make Grimaces and Wry Faces, as if they were possess'd. When all the Bustle is over, they demand a Feast of a Stag and some large Trouts for the Company, who are thus regal'd at once with Diversion and Good Cheer. (1703: II, 467)

This same smiling superiority is evident in the writings of Catherine the Great (r. 1762–96). While seeking to continue Peter I's policies of suppression, and fervently hoping to rid her empire of all superstition, she nonetheless chose to depict shamanic practices as laughable. Writing a five-act comedy _The Siberian Shaman_, she portrayed shamans and their clients as deluded simpletons in desperate need of enlightenment (Glavatskaya 2001: 243).

THE DEVELOPMENT OF A "SCIENCE" OF RELIGION

As the era of colonization gave way to permanent subjugation and progressive assimilation of indigenous communities, intellectuals writing about shamanic traditions ceased to view them with the same degree of urgency and fear. Shamans were part of a fading order by the nineteenth century, a window into the curious workings of the primitive mind or a holdover from a different stage in human cultural evolution. Western scholars began to seek out shamans to interview, observe, and analyze, so confident at last in the inexorable triumph of Judeo-Christianity over all trappings of barbarism that they almost regretted the fact. It was in this context that shamanism could at last be viewed with a semblance of scholarly neutrality or even sympathy, the object of study of a new "science" of the history of religion. The combined press of centuries of writing on shamans and their traditions, however, ensured that the tradition would never be looked upon with absolute scholarly objectivity.

The religiously grounded, good/evil worldview of earlier writings on shamanism became replaced at the turn of the twentieth century with ethnographies that aimed at scholarly neutrality and displayed strong comparative dimensions. Particularly important for the study of shamanism was the celebrated Jesup North Pacific Expedition of 1897–1902, organized by Franz Boas for the American Museum of Natural History. The Jesup Expedition brought American and Russian scholars together for the purpose of documenting the peoples of the North Pacific coasts, and resulted in a number of important works, including Waldemar Bogoras's *The Chuckchee* (1904–9), Waldemar Jochelson's *The Koryaks* (1908), and Franz Boas's first studies of Kwagul (Kwakiutl) religion, later revised into his *Religion of the Kwakiutl Indians* (1930). These scholars' meticulous and copious fieldwork set new standards for scholarly detail, as they helped reveal not only the cultural unity of the Bering Sea region but also some of the most widespread features of the region's shamanic traditions. Where earlier observers editorialized freely concerning the moral and intellectual failings of the people they studied, these scholars and those who followed applied analyses based on natural history, evolution, sexuality, and psychology. Further important contributors to this vein of description and analysis include Lev Shternberg, whose 1910 dissertation *The Social Organization of the Gilyak* (1999) presents shamanic callings in psychosexual terms, and R. R. Marett's student Marie Antoinette Czaplicka, whose broad-ranging *Aboriginal Siberia: A Study in Social Anthropology* (1914) became a standard reference work in the field. In it, Czaplicka synthesizes a vast array of prior scholarship to present a detailed view of Siberian cultures in general, with particular attention to shamanic traditions. In addition to offering theories regarding the sexual identity of shamans, she also suggests that shamanism may be a mental response to crises involving persons who are either mentally ill or imbalanced from the abnormal light regimen of the far north, theories that would dominate the field for much of the following century.

Ethnographic approaches to shamanism continued with detailed studies both in the Soviet Union and abroad. Georg Nioradze (1925) and Uno (Holmberg) Harva (1927) provided overviews of the tradition from a Siberian perspective. R. H. Lowie (1934) produced a similar synthetic view for Native American shamanic traditions, pointing to the greater degree of volition and more generalized use of spirit quests in the North American context. Such studies set the foundations for examining shamanism as a widespread religious phenomenon found in many parts of the world.

Czaplicka's psychological theories also attracted later scholars. Sergei M. Shirokogoroff (1935) extended Czaplicka's views and linked them to concepts of the evolution or development of religion. Åke Ohlmarks (1939), George Devereux (1961), and Ernst Arbman (1970) all continued to apply twentieth-century psychological theories to shamanic traditions, focusing on the shaman's personality in particular. I. M. Lewis (1971) viewed shamanism from the framework of social psychology, interpreting the shaman within a broader cultural phenomenon or movement he labeled "ecstatic religion." This psychological tradition can be seen as a backdrop to the cognitive theories of current researchers discussed in Chapter 7.

Undoubtedly, the most influential study of shamanism to emerge in the twentieth century, however, was that of Mircea Eliade. His *Shamanism: Archaic Techniques of Ecstasy* (1964) first appeared in 1951, and was soon translated into English. Eliade built on the detailed ethnographic work of his predecessors as well as the numerous syntheses that had already been formulated, adapting their findings for use in the emerging discipline of the history of religion. The cross-cultural similarities in shamanic phenomena that earlier scholars had regarded as psychological, sexual, climactic, or evolutionary became, in Eliade's eyes, evidence of a historical development which could be carefully reconstructed. Shamanism was conceived of as an archaic technique of ecstasy, a phenomenon that had arisen at a particular moment in the history of religious thought and which had then moved with human populations throughout much of the world. Shamanism thus became part of world heritage, and Eliade could assert that "a knowledge of it is a necessity for every true humanist" (1964: xx). While scholars today often take issue with various of Eliade's generalizations, his work remains a standard in the field, and continues to shape what scholars deem central or peripheral to the concept of shamanism.

In the decades following Eliade, few scholars were able to eclipse his study, despite a sustained international interest in the topic over time. Scholars of the history of religion produced similarly synthetic works, focusing on cross-cultural commonalities and often investigating specific elements of shamanic traditions. Researchers like Åke Hultkrantz (1953, 1979), Anna-Leena Siikala (1978), and Juha Pentikäinen (1989) offered studies that largely adopted Eliade's broader framework, while Hans Findeisen (1957) offered a sweeping challenge by subsuming shamanic ecstasy into a broader category of possession phenomena. On the other hand, among anthropologists, *shaman* became a convenient synonym for earlier ethnographic terms like *medicine man* and *witch doctor*, apparently because it seemed less pejorative than terms born directly of New World and African colonial encounters. Scholars like Hultkrantz (1989, 1998) would preserve Eliade's use, applying the term *shamanism* only to traditions in Eurasia and the Americas and excluding African and Australian traditions from the rubric, thus rejecting the broader anthropological practice. More recently, Alice Kehoe (2000) has argued strongly for returning the term to its earlier Siberian sense alone, critiquing the generalizations which ethnographers have tended to make in applying the term farther afield. In the present overview, *shamanism* is used to describe traditions of spiritual travel characterized by various culturally recognized and defined trance states and undertaken for a range of reasons, including healing, divination, and the management of luck. It is important to realize, however, that the term *shaman* receives different definitions in the works of different researchers, and that questions of characterization are often vehemently debated within the field. Some of these differences will emerge in the various studies cited in the following chapters.

As the above discussion shows, the Western ethnographic "discovery," description, and theoretization of shamanism is deeply mired in the religious and social history of the West. The confrontation of Christianity with other religious traditions spurred at first fascination, then consternation, then eventually condescension. Only in the course of the twentieth century did writers adopt anything like scholarly neutrality toward their subject, sometimes even giving way to a clear sympathy for the worldview or methods of shamanic practitioners. More often, however, shamans were kept at an analytical distance, observed from atemporal psychological perspectives, or from the diachronic vantage point of historical reconstruction, or from the social scientific perspectives of politics and social movements. Thus, the intellectual foundation upon which a study such as the present is founded must be seen as emerging only in the twentieth century, often in distinct dialogue with the earlier, more disdainful, examinations. In the chapters which follow, we focus on the main lines of the twentieth-century study of shamanic traditions, as well as their continuations and modifications in the current century.

CHAPTER 3

Shamanism in archaeological evidence

As we saw in Chapter 2, Western cognizance of shamanic traditions has its roots in the Middle Ages and continues through the Enlightenment era down to today. Medieval authors, however, were not the first persons to describe what appear to be shamanic rituals or specialists. Archaeological data from earlier eras also provide evidence of shamanic activities. In fact, most scholars agree that there exist plentiful grounds for pushing back the historical record of shamanism by many centuries. In some more disputed claims, some scholars would even push the record back tens of thousands of years to encompass evidence derived from some of the earliest known art in human communities. This chapter surveys these sources of evidence and debates surrounding the existence or recognizability of shamanism in the distant past.

TEXTUAL EVIDENCE FROM THE ANCIENT PAST

In the grand totality of human cultures, those which have developed and used forms of writing represent only a tiny minority. Thus, written evidence is unlikely to provide a satisfactory survey of ancient shamanic traditions. Among the existing stores of ancient texts, however, we do find occasional references to what appear to be shamanic traditions, either within a culture which has developed its own system of writing or within an adjacent culture that has taken an interest in describing the religions of its neighbors. Among the ancient Aryans of the Indus Valley and the Zoroastrians of what is today Iran, we find references to the use of an intoxicating plant, which induces a divine ecstasy in those who ingest it. Among the ancient Greeks, we find analogous references to a cult of intoxication connected with the god Dionysus, and occasional references to other visions that entail spirit travel to the world of the dead. Greek sources also provide some evidence concerning Scythian rituals which scholars have interpreted as shamanic. Finally, Chinese sources refer to shamanic rituals among the nomadic

Xiong-nu people, enemies of the Han, whom Western scholars sometimes associate with the Huns. References to ritual procedures in each of these cultures are fraught with ambiguities, but are tantalizing suggestions nonetheless of the antiquity of shamanic traditions.

The *Rig Veda* dates to between 1700 and 1100 BCE and is one of the foundational sacred texts of Hinduism. In it, several deities are identified, including one named *Soma*, the sacred elixir or potion. The Ninth Mandala of the *Rig Veda* is entirely addressed to this deity, and various other poems describe ingestion of the *soma* leading to divine enlightenment. As we shall see in Chapter 9, details of the preparation of the elixir mix in the hymns with characterizations of the wisdom and divine assistance that stem from it, as well as praise for higher gods like Indu and Indra to whom the libation is offered in rites. Typical is the following section of the Ninth Mandala's eleventh *súkta*:

Approach with reverence, mix with the curds, offer the Soma to Indra. Soma, slayer of our enemies, the wise one, the fulfiller of the desires of the gods, do thou shed prosperity on our cattle. Soma, who art cognizant of the mind, lord of the mind, thou art poured forth for Indra to drink for his exhilaration. Pure-dropping Soma, grant us wealth with excellent male offspring – grant it to us, Indu, with Indra as our ally. (Cowell and Webster 1977: 234)

As we shall see in Chapter 9, scholars have debated the botanical identification of this plant. Wasson (1963) suggests that the plant was the psychoactive mushroom *Amanita muscaria*, which would have been brought with the Aryans from the area of modern Afghanistan when they migrated into the Indus Valley. According to Vedic texts, *soma* was known to grow only in the mountains, and Hindu priests gradually lost contact with it, eventually turning to rhubarb as a non-psychoactive alternative. If these references to *soma* depict shamanic reveries brought on by ingestion of the *soma*, they also appear to demonstrate the ways in which shamanic rituals could become incorporated into more complex ritual traditions, such as the propitiary rites presided over by a Hindu priest class.

Soma rituals have a counterpart in ancient Zoroastrianism, where a similar substance, known as *haoma* ("true worshipper"), is likewise personified within the hymns of the *Avesta*, a sacred text that probably dates to around 1000 BCE, although surviving in written form only much later. In Yasna Ha 9 of the *Avesta*, Zarathushtra describes *haoma* as follows:

Thereupon spoke Zarathushtra, "Salutation be to the true worshipper (*haoma*), the true worshipper (*haoma*) is virtuous and well created, the true worshipper (*haoma*) is created truthful, created virtuous, health giver, beautiful of body, good in deed, victorious, golden hued, bending as a branch of tree, the best shining immortal spirit of man, leading it to the spiritual path. O golden wisdom guide me and speak to me, guide me to courage, guide me to victory, guide me to comfort, guide me to health, guide me to prosperity, guide me to growth, guide me to strengthen whole body, guide me to greatness all adorning, guide me to (all) these so that I may go forward as a ruler at will in the world, destroying malice of the evil ones. (verses 16–17; Sethna 1977: 37)

Discussing the botanical substance behind both *haoma* and *soma*, Gavin Flood (1996: 43) suggests the desert plant *ephedra* as an alternative to *Amanita muscaria*. In any case, here again, we find descriptions of psychoactive substance use as a means of effecting shaman-like trances, incorporated into the more elaborate propitiary rites of a complex agrarian religion.

Elements of Greek religion point to similar uses of intoxication, possibly borrowed or adapted from the shamanic traditions of neighboring peoples. The god Dionysus (Dionysos), associated with intoxication, madness, and wine, became known to the Greeks, possibly through contacts with Crete and regions of Thrace (Athanassakis 2001). His cult emerged sometime between 3000 and 1000 BCE, and developed into an elaborate secret society within Greek culture. Seasonal festivals, the "Bacchic revels," as well as its initiatory rituals, appear to have revolved around the myth of the violent murder of Dionysus, in which the deity was torn apart by Titans, devoured, and then reborn (Obeyesekere 2002: 239). Scholars have drawn parallels between this narrative and the call experiences of many shamans, as discussed in Chapter 5. The god's gender ambiguity, close association with wild animals (particularly the panther), animal transformation, and clear connection with intoxication have been seen as clearly shamanic.

By around 500 BCE, the Greeks also knew myths about the hero Orpheus, a man who ventured into the underworld of the dead to try to retrieve the soul of his deceased wife. A Thracian origin is also posited for this myth (Athanassakis 2001: 215). Plato's third-century BCE *Republic* contains a further account of a spiritual journey to the land of the dead. In the final chapter of his work, Plato recounts the vision experience of a warrior named Er, who was killed in battle and then witnessed the sorting of the souls of the just and unjust in the afterlife. Of all the dead, Er selected by the supernatural judges to return to the living as a witness: "When it came to his turn they told him that it was laid upon him to be a messenger to men concerning the things that were there, and they ordered him to listen to and look at everything in the place" (Book 10, 614; Lindsay 1977: 304; see discussion, Obeyesekere 2002: 242). The shamanic nature or origin of these cases of what the Greeks called *katabasis*, descent into the underworld, appear evident (Obeyesekere 2002: 284).

Given the seemingly foreign origins of cults like that of Dionysus, scholars have been eager to posit cultural borrowing as a source of shamanic elements within Indo-European religious traditions. Such elements, it is argued, would have been adopted from neighboring nomadic or indigenous peoples (Eliade 1964: 375ff.; Hultkrantz 1989: 48; Athanassakis 2001). Mircea Eliade (1964: 394) and Åke Hultkrantz (1998: 54) draw on the theories of Karl Meuli (1935) to interpret Herodotus' description of Scythian rituals as evidence of shamanism there. In describing Scythian funerary rites, Herodotus details a final purification ritual for those who have accompanied the corpse in an extended period of feasting and visiting:

After burying their dead, Scythians purify themselves. First they anoint and rinse their hair, then, for their bodies, they lean three poles against one another, cover the poles with felted woolen blankets, making sure that they fit together as tightly as possible, and then put red-hot stones from the fire on to a dish which has been placed in the middle of the pole-and-blanket structure. Now, there is a plant growing in their country called cannabis, which closely resembles flax, except that cannabis is thicker-stemmed and taller ... Anyway, the Scythians take cannabis seeds, crawl in under the felt blankets, and throw the seeds on to the glowing stones. The seeds emit dense smoke and fumes, much more than any vapour-bath in Greece. The Scythians shriek with delight at the fumes. This is their equivalent of a bath, since they never wash their bodies with water. (Book 4, chs. 73–5; Waterfield 1998: 259)

This cannabis-enhanced sweat-lodge custom has been interpreted as a likely instance of the shamanic psychopomp function, in which the intoxicated are presumably leading the soul of the deceased to its proper afterlife destination. Scholars base this interpretation on Siberian shamanic traditions (see Eliade 1964: 395, 209). It should be noted, however, that Herodotus describes the Scythian custom as a form of cleansing rather than as spirit travel, and notes that it is a communal activity rather than the solitary rite of a single shaman. Elsewhere in the *Histories*, Herodotus describes the Massegetae, whom he suggests may be a branch of the Scythians, and who place the fruit of some other psychoactive plant on their communal bonfires to produce a similarly intoxicating smoke:

They have also discovered a kind of plant whose fruit they use when they meet in groups. They light a bonfire, sit around it, throw this fruit on the fire, and sniff the smoke rising from the burning fruit that they have thrown on the fire. The fruit is the equivalent then to wine in Greece: they get intoxicated from the smoke, and then they throw more fruit on the fire and get even more intoxicated, until they eventually stand up and dance, and burst into song. (Book 1, ch. 201–2; Waterfield 1998: 89)

That this communal intoxication may differ from more typically shamanic singular contact with specific gods or helping spirits appears likely from the fact that, as Herodotus reports (Book 4, ch. 79; Waterfield 1998: 261), the Scythians found the Greek cult of Dionysus improper, "on the grounds that it is unreasonable to seek out a god who drives people out of their minds" (Waterfield 1998: 261). Herodotus recounts the stories of two Scythians, one the sage Anacharsis, the other a king, Scyles, who are put to death by their countrymen for participating in these Greek rites. When the Greeks of the Black Sea trading town of Borysthenes host Scyles in a clandestine performance of the Bacchic revels, the townsmen address the Scythians with the following taunt: "You may mock our Bacchic rites, men of Scythia, and the fact that the god takes hold of us, but now the god has taken hold of your own king, and he is in a state of Bacchic frenzy" (Waterfield 1998: 261). Scyles is soon thereafter deposed and beheaded. If the Scythians were shamanic, then, they seem to have practiced a particularly communal variety of the tradition which evinced little interest in the intimate, personalized relations of shaman and spirit helpers or gods described in Chapter 4.

J. Otto Maenchen-Helfen (1973: 267–8) surveys textual and archaeological indications that another nomadic people of Europe's mythologized east, the Huns, may have possessed shamanic traditions. Maenchen-Helfen points specifically to the divinatory activities of fifth-century CE *haruspices*, specialists who foretold the future through examination of the bones or internal organs of sacrificed animals. Rozwadowski (2001: 65) concurs with other scholars who link the Huns to the nomadic Xiong-nu of ancient Chinese history. Scholars suggest that Chinese references to divinatory activities among the Xiong-nu may similarly be regarded as evidence of shamanism in this culture (or cultures) during the first millennium BCE. Auguries of the type associated with *haruspices*, however, are not specifically shamanic, as Barbara Tedlock has shown (2001).

What these various textual accounts of possibly shamanic elements or figures in various cultures of Western and Southern Asia suggest is that shamanic traditions existed to some extent in this region already several millennia BCE. In neither Hindu, Zoroastrian, nor Greek traditions, however, where our evidence is strongest, did they remain the primary religious expressions of the people; rather, as we shall see in Chapter 12, shamanic traditions apparently became incorporated into more complex religious institutions, in which their specifically shamanic character remains recognizable only in the tendency to make use of psychoactive substances and the esteem accorded the resulting altered states, sometimes represented as anthropomorphic deities.

SHAMANISM IN THE ARCHAEOLOGICAL RECORD

Ekaterina Devlet (2001) has outlined a careful methodology for identifying possibly shamanic images in archaeological finds, particularly rock art. For Devlet, a shamanic interpretation of visual motifs is possible when the material culture in question comes from an area, such as Siberia, that is known to have been home to shamanic traditions in the historical era and which has a demonstrated continuity of settlement and culture over time. In such areas, it is often possible to extrapolate to earlier eras of shamanism on the basis of correlations between images in rock art and later attested elements of shamanic tradition. Devlet describes Siberian rock art of Bronze Age Altai, Tuva, and Mongolia which display plausibly shamanic features, including costumes with fringed ornamentation, round or oblong drums, and headdresses that include antlers or rays. The material culture of the region also permits scholars to examine possibly earlier elements of the region's shamanism, such as the use of a bow as a ritual object (Devlet 2007: 49). The decline of shamanism during the historical period can also be traced, evidenced by the appearance and eventual dominance of Christian motifs and depictions within explicitly shamanic art of the post-contact era (2001: 52–4).

Andrzej Rozwadowski (2001) supplies similar interpretations of rock art from the southern Central Asian region, particularly the Tamgaly Valley of southeastern Kazakhstan. Rock art here dates from around 2000 BCE (2001: 66). Rozwadowski finds images that may depict the fringe of shamanic costumes as well as the crozier-shaped staffs associated with shamans of the region in the historical era (2001: 71). Depictions of horses also may be linked to the roles of the horse in this region as a helping spirit and carrier of the dead to the otherworld.

Working with San (Bushmen) materials from South Africa, J. David Lewis-Williams (2001, 2002) explores the relations between rock art and various aspects of the culture's shamanism. Although scholars have doubted the existence of shamanic traditions in Africa, Lewis-Williams's overview of San beliefs and practices (2001: 21) makes a shamanic identification clear: here we find religious specialists who employ prolonged rhythmic dancing, repetitive sounds, and hyperventilation to enter a trance state in which they can heal the ill, summon rain, and attract animals to their communities' hunting ambush places. Writing of San séances, Lewis-Williams states:

At a trance dance in the Kalahari today, women sing and clap the rhythm of medicine songs believed to contain supernatural potency. They sit around a central fire, also believed to contain potency, while the men, half of whom may be shamans, dance around them. As the dance intensifies, the men, usually without the aid of hallucinogens, tremble violently, stagger, and finally enter trance. In a state of controlled trance, they move around laying their trembling hands on all the people present and drawing known and unknown sickness out of them. In a deeper level of trance, the shamans collapse and experience hallucinations such as out-of-body travel. (2002: 120)

Lewis-Williams combines ethnographic data from the nineteenth and twentieth centuries with the extant record of centuries of San rock paintings to delineate the close relation between painting and shamanism in San cultures. Lewis-Williams found that paintings often depicted shamans' visions, and were apparently executed at a ritually important moment, specifically upon the completion of a hunt. Spiritually potent pigment was combined with an equally powerful medium – sometimes a captured eland's fresh blood – to create a vital substance with which to produce the images. Shamans themselves appear often to have been the creators of these paintings, and undertook them not during trance (when their trembling hands would have rendered such work impossible), but in a state of ordinary consciousness. Shamanic art helped "fix" and share potent visions, providing greater continuity and collectivity in the tradition over time. The rock surface itself became a reservoir for spiritual power, which the community members could access by laying their hands on the painted images, and sometimes particular images were carefully overpainted so as to retain and/or augment their power. In this context, then, rock art provides powerful evidence for understanding the details of ritual and worldview within San shamanism.

Neil Price (2002) has demonstrated how textual and archaeological evidence can be fruitfully combined to illuminate otherwise largely forgotten shamanic traditions. In his study of Scandinavian burials from the Viking Age, Price shows how textual accounts of divinatory specialists associated with the Old Norse term *seiðr* can be correlated with grave findings that suggest an operative form of shamanism among Scandinavians during this period. Medieval accounts of *seiðr* practitioners are often strikingly fantastic, and scholars have been obliged to treat such accounts of *seiðr* rituals and ritualists with considerable caution, while nonetheless suggesting possible shamanic linkages (e.g., Strömbäck 1935; DuBois 1999: 121–38). Price's archaeological survey, however, recovers the historical basis behind such accounts. Price finds that probable *seiðr* practitioners were buried with accouterments and apparent reverence that point to a role as a valued religious specialist within the culture. His study demonstrates how archaeological evidence can help scholars sort through the often confusing details of ancient and medieval textual accounts to arrive at a workable hypothesis concerning shamans of the past.

The assumption of uninterrupted continuity, however, can sometimes prove misleading. Examining cast bronze images associated with Khanty and Mansi dwelling sites from the first century BCE to the tenth century CE, Natalia Fedorova (2001) reviews and ultimately rejects scholarly readings of these as shamanic objects. Ob'-Ugrian shamanism was well developed during the historical era, and it might seem natural in this light to regard bronze images of warriors, birds of prey, and bears as shamanic implements, particularly given the cross-cultural significance of both birds of prey and bears as powerful helping spirits in various shamanic traditions. Fedorova, however, presents evidence for viewing both the warrior and bird as reflections of military secret societies that developed among the Khanty and Mansi during the era, a "'heroic epoch' of the Ob'-Ugrians' ancient history, being the period of almost permanent military campaigns" (2001: 63). The bear figures, for their part, correspond, Fedorova contends, with the bear ceremonial, a ritual hunting, killing, and consumption of the bear which was widely practiced in the region during the era. It is important to note, however, that the bear ceremonial did not include an important role for a shamanic specialist: rather it was a familial and/or communal ritual.

SEARCHING FOR SHAMANISM'S EARLIEST MANIFESTATIONS

The above-mentioned textual and material evidence make it possible to posit forms of shamanism in various parts of Eurasia already several thousand years ago. The widespread nature of shamanism today, however – spread over so many continents with such seeming regularity of underlying structure and worldview – has led scholars to suggest a far earlier era for its development, one ranging tens of thousands of years in the past (cf., e.g., Eliade 1964; Hultkrantz 1989). Hultkrantz summarizes these theories to suggest that shamanism has its roots in luck rituals practiced among nomadic hunting peoples in Northern Eurasia some thirty thousand years ago. The Paleolithic hunting culture of Eurasia and the Americas, characterized by highly developed animal ceremonialism, deities known as the masters of animals, and a tiered cosmos would have served as the source and original context for shamanism (1989: 47). The religious practices spread widely along with this hunting culture, reaching the vast bulk of the human populace of the time, apart from areas of Africa and Australia. As various societies adopted agriculture, their religions changed as well, partially obscuring or replacing shamanic traditions, as we see in the discussions of Hindu and Greek religions in this chapter or in greater detail in Chapter 12. From this point of view, shamanism can be seen as a particularly ancient and widespread element of human collective heritage.

Although these theories of origins were originally posited primarily by historians of religion based on the comparison of extant religious traditions from around the world, many archaeologists today have proposed similar theories on the basis of material remains, particularly ancient rock art. Prominent among these was Andreas Lommel (1967), whose *Shamanism: The Beginnings of Art* caused an immense stir in the fields of archaeology and art history at the time of its first publication. Lommel suggests that ancient rock art was made by shamans as visual recordings of trance experiences, often induced by psychoactive substance use. Depictions such as the famous antlered beast-man character in the cave paintings of Les Trois Frères cave, in Southern France, estimated at some 12,000 years old, would in Lommel's reading represent a trance state transformation of a shaman into animal form, possibly to secure hunting success for the community during the current or future hunting season.

J. David Lewis-Williams joined with Jean Clottes (Clottes and Lewis-Williams 2001) to explore some of the possible meanings within rock art from Paleolithic France. Combining the lessons which Lewis-Williams had uncovered in San shamanic painting, Lewis-Williams and Clottes suggest that cave paintings from ancient Europe may sometimes represent shamanic visions. Particular images that had eluded explanation previously could be viewed as possible elements of an emergent shamanic visual discourse: a "fixing" of shamanic visions in the visual plane, where they could be pooled with other community members and possibly resorted to for spiritual help in the future. At least some such representations may correspond, these scholars suggest, to entopic images: visual sensations that are perceived during initial stages of altered states of consciousness, i.e., trance. The ideas of Lewis-Williams and Clottes have been widely applied to rock art in various other parts and periods. Summarizing the focus of this scholarly enterprise to date, Miranda and Stephen Aldhouse-Green (2005: 90) write:

[T]he unifying factor expressed in these "packages" of rock imagery is its production and use within the framework of shamanistic practice and expression. It is against such a backdrop that it is possible to begin to understand some of the apparently unrealistic images that occur on Bronze/Iron Age rock carvings: the half-human, half-animal creatures … the exaggerated antlers on stags, the geometric shapes, such as nets, labyrinths and collections of dots, the beings that disappear into or emerge from cracks in the rock surface, that merge into circles or that appear as dismembered or skeletonized bodies and the images that appear to be stacked one on top of the other.

A number of scholars have taken issue with the theories of Lewis-Williams and Clottes and others approaching ancient rock art along similar lines. Henri-Paul Francfort (2001), for instance, critiques the interpretations of such scholars, noting that their views are often founded on four potentially problematic assumptions: the universality of a cognitive susceptibility to altered states of consciousness, the regularity of certain "entopic" images within such altered states, a universal tendency to express these images in art, and a role for shamans as the artists depicting these images (2001: 31). Francfort challenges each of these assumptions, emphasizing the cultural specificity of perception and the varying functions of visual art in different cultures (2001: 33). Another scholar, Paul Bahn (2001), disputes the universality of entopic images in particular, citing evidence that suggests great cultural specificity in the ways in which altered states of consciousness are experienced and culturally processed. Added to this cultural variability in sensory experience, Bahn notes, are varying cultural norms for the artistic rendering of such experiences in art: what a Western viewer might interpret as a depiction of a trance state may in fact represent something quite different in the iconographic tradition of the culture of the artist.

While archaeologists continue to debate this fascinating set of issues, two salient points remain. First, it is undeniably difficult to argue that images in ancient rock paintings are or are not shamanic, given the fact that we often have little other evidence left to us other than the images themselves. Without the supplemental ethnographic data available for modern shamanic art, in other words, scholars run the risk of circular reasoning, in which features of a painting are regarded as shamanic because the painting itself was produced within a culture that probably had shamanic traditions. The apparent shamanic details then confirm the shamanism, which was assumed in interpreting them in the first place. Lewis-Williams and Clottes offer important qualifications and nuances to their theory to avoid the greatest pitfalls of this considerable methodological challenge. Second, despite such methodological ambiguities, it appears highly likely that at least some rock art, e.g., paintings that contain striking depictions of half-human/half-beast figures, may reflect shamanic traditions which were present in the community at the time that the painting was produced. Whether or not the understandings behind such images correspond precisely to those which a historical shaman might offer is again impossible to determine for certain; scholars have sometimes preferred to use the term "paleo-shamanism" to avoid a too-automatic equation of ancient beliefs with those identifiable among shamanic cultures today (Aldhouse-Green 2005: 29). In any case, these archaeological contributions to the question of early shamanism greatly enrich a discussion which had formerly been the province of historians of religion alone.

With their strikingly widespread distribution and highly recurrent elements, shamanic traditions would easily seem of tremendous antiquity in the history of human religions. Our detailed records of shamanic rituals, however, often go back only a few centuries at most, and seldom permit careful analysis of changes within a given shamanic tradition over time. Scholars have pointed to shamanic elements in ancient Hinduism, Zoroastrianism, and the Dionysian cult of the ancient Greeks, and many scholars have interpreted descriptions of entheogen use or divination in other ancient cultures as evidence of shamanism there as well. Archaeological evidence within shamanic cultures has demonstrated both continuities and processes of change, which add nuance and depth to our understandings of how shamanism has operated within human communities. Common features within shamanic traditions from different parts of the world have led

Figure 2. Inuit *angakok*, bound, with drum by his side, summons his helping spirit.
Drawing included in Knud Rasmussen's *Eskimo Folk-Tales* (1921).

scholars to posit an era of origin for the religious tradition some thirty thousand years ago, yet interpretations of rock art from earlier eras of human history have stirred vigorous debate and call into question our ability to reconstruct religious ideas at such a distance in the past. Nor can we be certain that all shamanisms derive ultimately from a single source: as we shall see in Chapter 7, some scholars regard trance experiences as pan-human mental phenomena, which may independently become cast as that which we call shamanism. Historicist and cognitive theories of shamanism need not be mutually exclusive, of course: many scholars point out that a shamanic tradition that has unfolded in a given locale over the course of centuries may retain features or display a stability in part as a reaction to unchanging cognitive perceptions within shamans' trance experiences. As scholars of various disciplines continue to search for evidence of past shamanic traditions, we may eventually arrive at a fuller understanding of the ways in which this fascinating and important set of ideas developed and became localized within so many cultures around the world.

PART II

Shamanic soteriology and ritual

CHAPTER 4

Cosmology and the work of the shaman

Louise Bäckman and Åke Hultkrantz (1977: 11) point to four prime elements as constitutive of shamanism: a concept of conscious souls or spirits
associated with all elements, a cosmology of multiple (normally unseen)
worlds inhabited by various spirits, a tradition of trance-state spirit travel,
and a specialized role for the shaman as an expert in both spirit travel and
spirit negotiation. Within these broad characteristics, variations abound.

As we shall see in Chapter 6, a single tradition may possess distinct
professionals sharing portions of this supposedly singular shamanic role.
Occasionally (as we noted in the last chapter with reference to Scythian and
Dionysian customs, as we will revisit in our discussion of entheogen use in
Chapter 9), shamans may share their spirit travels with non-shamans, who
may rely on the shaman as an expert guide or authority in cosmic journeys
experienced by all. As we shall see in Chapter 7, too, the term *trance* also
masks a great deal of cultural variation, both in terms of the exact physiological state expected of the shaman and in the times or ritual circumstances
in which trance states are employed. So, too, as this chapter will show, the
cosmological variation evident among various shamanic cultures is extensive, so much so that it becomes questionable whether the blanket characterization of a "cosmology of multiple worlds" is in any way useful as a
scholarly construct.

At the same time, however, a clear logic obtains in Bäckman and
Hultkrantz's formulation: for shamans to journey spiritually, they must
have a notion of a cosmos that contains multiple levels, temporal dimensions, or locales, as well as a notion of spiritual interlocutors with which to
interact. These become important in the shaman's professional duties and
therapeutic strategies (Chapter 8), and many practitioners point to their
knowledge of the cosmos as a prime sign of their efficacy and of the strength
of their relations with spirit helpers. Thus, an examination of ideas of
cosmology common among shamans cross-culturally can tell us a great
deal about shamanism as a set of soteriological ideas and rituals. This

chapter explores cosmologies as they have been documented among sha-manic practitioners from various cultures, past and present.

THE IDEA OF COSMOLOGY

> Think of it this way: the spirits out there are a hundred times more diverse than the things in this world.
>
>   Thai

Cosmology – theories of the nature and workings of the universe – is integral to religious thought. Through the lens of religion, we come to understand our "world" in its material and immaterial senses, and our personal or collective place in its various workings. In its narrowest sense, cosmology is descriptive and historicizing: it explains the world as we find it, and, often, offers a narrative of how it got to be the way it is (its cosmogony). Cosmology is also predictive, however: it creates a model for how things are likely to occur in our lives today, and perhaps how the world that we know will come to an end (i.e., its eschatology). In its broadest sense, cosmology carries a host of implications for how to live our lives: how to think about profound events like birth, maturation, illness, and death; how to respond to instances of great happiness or misfortune; how to interact with other human beings and with the environment in which we find ourselves. In these ways, it becomes, to borrow Peter Berger's (1990) elucidating meta-phor, a "sacred canopy," uniting the details of our daily lives with a broader "cosmic" narrative that offers both meaning and meaningful courses of action. Crucially, as Émile Durkheim noted in his seminal *The Elementary Forms of the Religious Life* (1915), this canopy seeks to account for how things *normally* or *ideally* are, fitting aberrations from the norm into this broader model: "religious conceptions have as their object, before everything else, to express and explain, not that which is exceptional and abnormal in things, but, on the contrary, that which is constant and regular" (1915: 43). Cosmologies also often stipulate parameters for how they are to be illumi-nated or elaborated: depending on the model of the universe proposed, for instance, they may rely upon materialist empirical investigation, superna-tural revelation, insight through contemplative acts.

Roberte Hamayon (1982) notes that the cosmologies of various shamanic traditions tend to rest on a particular theory of the cosmos, an interrelated theory of society, and a mediating and central theory of the individual. For Thai, describing his work as a shaman entails first and foremost describing the cosmos in which we live. As Thai sees it – and as Hmong people have believed for what appears countless centuries – the world is filled with spirits. Animals have spirits, but so, too, do trees, rocks, mountains, bodies of water, and entities like wind and fire. Human beings, for their part, have multiple spirits: a spirit of the shadow, a spirit residing in the body as a whole, and a spirit dwelling in the bones. In addition to these, each human body part has its own spirit: the spirit of eyes, ears, head, arm, and so on. The workings of the world – particularly the interactions of human beings with their physical surroundings – are understood in this view as the interaction of these various unseen but essential spirits.

In Hmong understandings, the world which these spirits inhabit is, like the spirits themselves, more than meets the eye. In addition to that which we can see with ordinary eyes, there exist two further worlds visible to the shaman and spirits alike. Although spirits generally remain close to the physical entities whose essence they share, they may at times become removed to another of these worlds. At death, spirits necessarily migrate to the spirit realm, although some spirits attempt to linger (for various reasons) in the living world, often with problematic results. In sickness and in dreaming, spirits may wander forth from their physical homes, become lost, or become stolen by other spirits. They may travel only a short distance, or they may wander far away. Many ailments facing human beings stem from such a loss of spirit, attributable to any number of causes, from the breaking of tabus, to the ill will of others, to the intentional or unintentional interference of other spirits.

In describing Hmong cosmology, Vincent K. Her (2005: 5) describes three interconnected worlds: the earth (Nplaj Teb), the spirit world of the dead (Dlaab Teb), and an upper realm of the sky (Sau Ntuj). Each realm has ruling figures: Siv Yis, the primordial shaman and ruler of the living earth; Ntxwg (Ntxwj) Nyoog and his assistant Nyuj Vaj Tuam Teem, the fierce rulers of the land of the dead; and Yawm Saub, the benevolent god of renewal. According to accounts which Her cites (2005: 8), Siv Yis was the first shaman and used to live on earth, until his envious younger brother (Ntxwg Nyoog) tricked him into consuming his own son's flesh. Today, he resides on a mountain named for hawks and swallows, located in the remote upper cosmos.

Just as people traverse the earth (Nplaj Teb) in their physical essence, so their spirits can independently wander across the world as well. Such occurs particularly at the time of death. At that moment, one of the individual's spirits remains at the family altar while another accompanies the body to the grave. A third spirit, however, takes leave of the guardian spirits of the home in which the person lived before dying. In traditional Hmong houses, these guardians dwell in particular places: the bedroom, altar, oven, central house pillar, hearth, and main door. Even in the United States, where Hmong often live in houses of markedly different structure, these conceptual places continue to exist in funerary recitations. Once taking leave of these entities, the spirit must retrace its life's steps back to its natal home. Her describes a funeral for a Hmong refugee in Milwaukee, Wisconsin which involved mention of six American cities, a refugee camp in Thailand, and six villages in Laos. Once the natal home is reached, the deceased spirit reunites with the placenta, which was buried in a particular part of the house at birth. Once this occurs, the spirit can enter Dlaab Teb.

Dlaab Teb, the spirit world, has its own topography, transected by a pathway of importance to the deceased's spirit. Mottin (1983: 102) cites accounts that describe this path as crossing twelve mountains, leading finally to the home of Ntxwg Nyoog. According to Her's account, along the way there is a field of sharp grass blades, a three-forked path (where the spirit must choose the middle path), a mountain of perpetual sunshine, a land of giant caterpillars, a cliff with a gnawing jaw, a dragon, a field of crops, and a lake of bitter waters. Thai notes that narrations of this pathway include references to a heavy substance similar to snow and describe a landscape that is cold, where darkness outlasts the light in the day: details which, Thai suggests, may reflect ancient traditions regarding the land from which the Hmong migrated before arriving in tropical Southeast Asia. The spirit follows this path to reach the home of the ancestors, and once it has arrived there, they in turn point out a celestial ladder, which allows the spirit to climb to the realm of Sau Ntuj.

Sau Ntuj is more remote, dominated by its ruler, Yawm Saub. Upon petition, Yawm Saub will grant the deceased's spirit permission to reincarnate, providing the spirit with a "letter of provision" which sets out its destiny in the next life (Her 2005: 22). In other accounts, it is the assistant ruler of the underworld Nyuj Vaj Tuam Teem who provides the written authorization (Tapp 1989: 92). In either case, armed with that letter, the spirit can return to Nplaj Teb (earth) – ideally as a moth – to begin the cycle of life again. In considering these spiritual migrations across the earth to Dlaab Teb to Sau Ntuj and then back again, Her writes:

In this journey ... the deceased does not travel alone. His path mirrors that of the group to which he belongs, as they drift from one village to the next, or one country to another. Their journey covers many places, spanning local, national and international boundaries. This movement shows how the Hmong social experience, similar to those of many other ethnic groups, is characterized by mobility, dispersion and displacement on the one hand, and temporary stasis and belonging (in the form of attachment to places) on the other. This knowledge is crucial to a people's awareness of self and history, making it possible for them to locate, situate and place themselves in time and space, giving them a keen sense of being here and there at once. (2005: 22–3)

Although, in Hmong understandings, every person's spirits thus have the propensity to migrate, Thai, as a *txiv neeb*, has developed an ability to intentionally send his spirit outward into these unseen worlds during his life. Thai uses this skill to pursue or communicate with spirits that have wandered away from living persons, or to contact spirits belonging to other beings. He describes the worlds that he journeys to as realms or levels, each possessing a gate with a guard. There, in the manner of the great original shaman Siv Yis, Thai typically tells his name and asks about the spirit he is seeking. If, as a shaman, he commands sufficient respect – the result of having performed many successful ceremonies in the past – he will receive an answer or directions from the spirit there, and be allowed to travel on to the next station. One pursuit alone would take many hours to conduct and equally many hours to explain. Thai emphasizes that travel of this sort is fruitless, if not completely impossible, without the assistance of a spirit guide who helps the shaman gain admission to the spirit realms. Thai notes that shamans of a different variety (*neeb poj qhe*) are expert in contacting and speaking to the dead. Some shamans know both varieties, but have different guiding spirits for each.

Hmong shamans like Thai have special equipment to help them in their work. They travel to the unseen on a special "horse," a bench that the shaman stands on during the ceremony, and they use special items of clothing and ritual action (discussed in Chapter 10). The ceremony also calls for particular forms of music (see Chapter 9) and oratory (see Chapter 11). On the supernatural plane, Thai uses his horse, equipped with wings, to fly between worlds. He wears a black veil over his eyes during his journeying and is assisted in the seen world by a human helper – his father – who supports his body physically during his various movements, supplying as well the pieces of equipment and other ritual acts necessary for the successful conducting of the ceremony. In the unseen world, Thai is assisted by a special guiding spirit as well as a variety of other spirit helpers (see Chapters 5 and 6).

Although Thai frequently performs such journeying for the purpose of healing, he, like other shamans, also undertakes it for other purposes as well (Chapter 6). His role in doing so is intimately connected with his society and their collective needs. When asked to heal a person (Chapter 8), Thai interviews the patient and his or her family about the details of the illness, then shares that information with spirits that serve as his helpers. They discuss the matter and arrive at theories about what could be wrong. If they suspect a particular spirit to be at fault, they will contact the offending or offended spirit and tell it that they are coming to discuss the matter. Ultimately, the shaman's work of diagnosis requires firsthand investigation, which occurs during a shamanic trance (Chapter 7). States Thai:

I cannot know what the problem is –
I have to go and find the spirit and ask what happened, do research...
Maybe it may have been captured by an evil spirit,
maybe the person was never born with it,
or maybe they did something wrong and the spirit became unhappy so that it left as
    a kind of punishment.
Or maybe an ancestor came back and took it away.
...Think of it this way: the spirits out there are a hundred times more diverse than
    the things in this world.

Once the estranged spirit is found, the shaman and helpers can try to coax it to return home with offerings of rice, egg, and chicken. Sometimes the shaman must address another spirit who has captured the patient's spirit, trick it, or even engage in battle. In general, negotiating with a spirit takes persistence, skill, and goodwill: the shaman often uses his/her reputation and knowledge to convince the spirit to accept an offering of a pig, chicken, or duck which will be made by the patient's family once the illness has abated. If the family neglects to make the agreed upon offering, the result can be very serious for the shaman, as the angered spirits will take revenge on him. But, as Thai notes, "Usually, the Hmong people respect shamans, and whatever the shaman says, if they feel better, they do it." If the ceremony does not result in improved health for the patient, the sick person and family may consult the same or another shaman to try again.

HMONG COSMOLOGY IN A BROADER PERSPECTIVE

Thai's description of the cosmos bears strong resemblance to that characteristic of many other traditions termed shamanic worldwide. The notion of conscious spirits associated with various material entities of the world has been termed by scholars of religion *animism*. Sir Edward Tylor (1871) first identified the concept in his *Primitive Culture*, and asserted that this and other beliefs in *souls* (the term he used) were universal features of all human religion. Early scholars focused on theories of psychological and evolutionary development to account for this widespread premise. From a purely logistic and ethnographic perspective, Louise Bäckman and Åke Hultkrantz (1977: 11) suggest that such an understanding of the cosmos is essential for shamanism in general: it is the interaction of human mediums (shamans) and the spirits of other entities that occupies the central attention of both shamans and their clients, although cultures differ as to how they conceptualize details like the number of human spirits residing within an individual or the kinds of external entities that bear conscious spirits.

Also pervasive in religious traditions designated "shamanic" is a notion of a multileveled cosmos like that Thai describes. The visible world has unseen counterparts or levels, which are often conceptualized as ranging above and below the world which we normally see. Scholars of religion such as Eliade (1964: 259) emphasize that such a cosmology is not necessarily a component of shamanism itself as it exists in a given culture; rather, Eliade suggests, it may represent a conceptual foundation upon which shamans draw to describe and detail their experiences. Setting Eliade's evolutionary theories aside, however, it is clear that the notion of spirit travel requires places to travel to, and these tend to be understood not only in terrestrial terms, but also as spatially differentiated alternative worlds. As Piers Vitebsky (1995: 15) insightfully suggests: "Perhaps 'space' can best be understood as a metaphor for the otherness of the spirit realm."

Some examples of such otherworlds will help clarify the nature of this spatial conceptualization in many shamanic cultures. Merete Demant Jakobsen (1999: 85–9) surveys Danish ethnographic and missionary reports of the realms which Greenlandic Inuit *angakut* were said to visit. Accompanied by his spirit guide, the *angakok* could travel to the bottom of the sea to confront the female deity there whose benevolence is required for hunters to have success. This Mother of the Sea figure (known in other Inuit traditions across North America as Takanakapsaluk, Sedna, or Arnakuagsak) must be wrestled or cajoled, her long hair combed out and her body cleaned before she will release the various sea mammals that traditionally made up the core of the Inuit diet. The route to her home was singularly perilous, featuring treacherous whirlpools, guardian beasts, and a pathway as narrow as a rope's width or a knife's edge, across which the shaman had to pass. *Angakut* could also travel to the moon. The route there led across the sea to a distant land where the sky connects with the earth. From there the path winds past stars until eventually reaching the moon. The journey could only be undertaken at night and might last from nightfall until dawn. Like the journey to the Mother of the Sea, this pathway posed many dangers, including ill-willed spirits and treacherous crevices. The Land of the Dead was a third key destination of the *angakok*'s journeys. The entryway to the preferred otherworld of dead people lay in certain caves or at the bottom of the sea, in close proximity to the abode of the Mother of the Sea. This afterlife destination was described as a realm of perpetual light and plentiful game. Persons of evil disposition, however, were consigned to an afterlife of continual wandering and hunger in the sky. By the late nineteenth century, however – apparently under the influence of Christian cosmology – Greenlanders had begun to describe the land of eternal reward for the dead as located in the sky.

Caroline Humphrey (1996: 119ff.) explores the variety of upper and lower worlds posited by her Daur Mongol informant Urgunge in his descriptions of shamanic travels. On the one hand, these seem to break down into three: an overworld for the spirits of good people after death and an underworld for the spirits of the bad, along with a middle world for living humans. At the same time, however, Urgunge described nine distinct layers of the sky (*tengger*) and multiple underworld realms as well. Of the latter, Humphrey writes:

In Daur stories there is an elaborate nether world, identified with the realm of Irmu Khan, imagined as having many layers (or "compartments" or "prisons"). Irmu Khan had walls and gatehouses, huge guard-dogs, soldiers, palaces, yards, and offices. It was shady … there, lit by a dim, yellowish light. Irmu Khan was imagined as a warrior-king and he bore weapons of every description. (1996: 119)

The spirits of the dead spend time in this ruler's land until being redirected to the sky or to places of retribution beyond the mountains of the seen world. A special class of shamans (*yadgan*) possesses the skills to visit this realm, where they can negotiate with Irmu Khan and potentially rescue imprisoned spirits. Although the realm could be approached through shamanic trance, access could also be gained through certain caves, wells, whirlpools, mountains, or distant travel.

Although Urgunge, as a *yadgan*, did not journey to celestial realms, he knew of their existence to some extent. The *tengger* (sky) is a place in which – or beyond which – various celestial beings dwell, whom specialists of various kinds could contact (1996: 124). As in Thai's discussion of Hmong shamanism, since different shamans may specialize in different varieties of spiritual journeying, such upward, outward, or downward trajectories can often exist as potentially independent entities within the cosmology of the culture, rather than as a necessarily unified vision of the universe. A particular shaman, in other words, may only know about a segment of the many otherworlds identified by other shamanic practitioners in the same culture.

Jean-Pierre Chaumeil (1982) recounts the cosmos described by Alberto, a Yagua shaman of the village of Eden de la frontera on the Marichín River of northeast Peru. For Alberto and his community, the visible world is dominated by the Amazon River, running from its source to its delta. Invisible paths link this seen world to others arrayed in layers above and below. To the east of the Amazon's delta lies a land of the ancestors, people who once lived in a different world at the foot of a great tree. This world is no longer accessible to people, even to the most skilled shamans, who nonetheless seek reunion with it. Below the visible world are three sub-terranean levels: the world of the ground-people, the world of the water-people, and the world of people without anuses. Each of these worlds serves as a source of both illness and potential cures for people in the visible world, and each is visited by shamans in their work of healing. Above the terrestrial world are a variety of other worlds of the sky, visible only faintly from below. At the level of the lowest banks of clouds, there are realms of the vultures, condors, and parakeets, linked to the earth by unseen paths. The spirits of those who have done grave evil (e.g., incest or theft) become transformed into condors and reside in that species' realm. Shamans are able to obtain magic darts from this realm as well, which are useful in their various activities. Above the rainbow and at the level of higher clouds, there exists the "half-world" of the people whose voice is heard in thunder. Higher still is the celestial lake, the reservoir of the rain that falls onto the earth. It is here that sorcerers gain the celestial venom needed for their darts, a substance shared as well by iguanas, spiders, snakes, ants, and scorpions. On the banks of the lake live demons who descend to earth in times of fire to devour the ashes of the dead.

Higher still lives the *rúnda*, the principal spirit of hunting. He descends to earth on great feasts or when the hunting is bad. He gives the human community the animals they hunt in exchange for offerings of beer. Beyond *rúnda*'s level is the world of the moon and its nephew Polaris (the "spirit of the night") as well as a house of fire. A path of fire separates these two beings' worlds from that of the sun and evening star. The spirits of the deceased pass along the Milky Way (the "path of souls") to the "grand heaven," their proper dwelling place after death. In a feature parallel to that discussed for Hmong cosmology, this remote level is also the place of the present home of the primordial shaman. In a reflection of the influence of Christian mis-sionization, Alberto noted that the grand heaven was also the home of the god of the Christians.

Robin Ridington (1988) explores the role of *Naachin* ("dreamers") among Dunne-za (Beaver) people in British Columbia, Canada. Such *Naachin* experience spirit travel and communication chiefly through their dreams. In dream visions, they acquire songs which can aid deceased community members in finding Yagatunne, the trail to heaven. They practice a skill developed originally by Makenunatane, a primordial shaman. Since Makenunatane's time, the dead have listened to the shaman's songs and are able to find their way, despite the confusions that can arise because of the Alaskan Highway and other technological and social intrusions of the twentieth century (1988: 82). Without the *Naachin's* singing, the dead are liable to follow such roads endlessly, becoming frustrated displaced ghosts rather than contented souls at rest in their afterlife world. *Naachin* songs are also seen to maintain the normal passage of the seasons, which might otherwise cease to pass in proper fashion. By "dreaming ahead for every-body" (1988: 78), *Naachin* gain access to knowledge that helps the community prosper in its relations with each other and with the animals essential for subsistence. Writes Ridington, "The Dreamer's journey is a shamanic flight through the appearance of ordinary reality. The dreamer flies to a realm of meaning at the 'center of the universe'" (1988: 79). Such travel is thus incorporated into the ordinary category of dreaming, but with significant differences in meaning and effectiveness. Dreams provide awareness of a cosmos that resembles that of other shamanic cultures.

Although these cosmologies – and many others described for other shamanic traditions of the world – vary considerably in detail, certain commonalities are nonetheless evident. Unseen worlds are multiple, and become known to the human community through shamanic revelation. Shamans rely on spirit guides for assistance in traveling to one or more of these known worlds but often cannot travel to all the worlds known. The cosmologies often pay particular attention to the dead: there are often one or more locales for the spirits of the dead, and the dead must travel there on pathways known to shamans and their spirit guides. In hunting cultures as remote from each other as Inuit and Yagua, there are often deities of the hunt, who require some sort of placation or offering in exchange for hunting success. This, too, often becomes a task for a shaman. In terms of geography, the multiple worlds of the cosmos are often described as vertical in array, but spirits travel horizontally across the worlds as well. The primordial first shaman is often recalled as a key figure in the cosmos, and may live in his own abode, described as remote from the world of the living.

Mircea Eliade (1964) characterizes such multilevel cosmologies as fundamentally tripartite, writing: "The universe in general is conceived as having three levels – sky, earth, underworld – connected by a central axis" (1964: 259). Eliade views variations in the number of upper or lower worlds characteristic of different shamanic traditions as subsequent elaborations, influenced by culture-specific mystical numbers or other historical processes

(1964: 274ff.). Subsequent scholars have criticized such pronouncements as unnecessarily evolutionary, and have suggested as well that they harbor Western – particularly Christian – biases. The "basic" worldview of all religion comes to resemble strongly that of Christianity, while the culturally specific multiple otherworlds, or alternative pathways between them, are marginalized as secondary developments.

Also of concern to many ethnographers has been the precise influence of Christian and/or Islamic missionary activities in promoting a tripartite view among communities practicing shamanism. Most of the ethnographic descriptions of shamanic cosmologies left to us by scholars of the past describe shamanic traditions among peoples already experiencing concerted missionization. The earliest of these accounts were also often written by missionaries themselves, with a clear and expectable tendency to read native cosmologies from the point of view of their own belief systems or to minimize the distinctions between the community's preexisting cosmology and that proffered by the new religion (thereby downplaying differences in cosmological detail). Missionaries thus often made nearly automatic use of concepts from their own religions – e.g., heaven, hell, demons, God – to characterize the beliefs of the people whom they were proselytizing, in the process harmonizing belief systems which in fact may have evinced essential differences in key concepts and understandings. They depicted spiritual travel downward or to the dead as "demonic," and represented travel to upper echelons of the cosmos as akin to concourse with the Christian God. In turn, as the examples above illustrate, shamans in these cultures also incorporated elements of Christian cosmology into their descriptions, making afterlife destinations concur more with Christian notions or inserting the Christian God into their characterizations of the cosmos.

HORIZONTAL TRAVEL AND COSMOLOGICAL ASPECTS OF THE TERRESTRIAL TERRAIN

Although shamans frequently describe their spirit journeys in terms of movement upward or downward through the cosmos, the cosmologies of shamanic traditions often include horizontal, terrestrial, components as well. Thai describes spirit journeys that remain on the level of the seen world and that he may undertake, for instance, to negotiate with the spirit of a physical entity on earth that has become angered at the breaking of a tabu. Scandinavian oral tradition about Sámi shamans tells of powerful individuals who could send their spirits out for clients to find out about conditions far away, or to check on the welfare of family members separated by long distances. Typical is a legend collected in Norway in 1939. A man away fishing asks a Sámi (apparently a *noaide*) to find out how things are going back home. The shaman enters a trance to do so:

He lay down on the floor, and they heard only that he mumbled to himself while he seemed to crawl into his jacket. It took a while before he ... stirred again. His jacket was lying there, but it looked somehow shrunken. Then all at once the jacket began to move, and ... he was there again. Yes, everything was all right at home. Gurina had given birth, and she was sitting and feeding the child. To prove that he had been there, he had brought back a silver spoon. Johan was amazed because he recognized the spoon. (Kvideland and Sehmsdorf 1988: 72)

Cross-cultural evidence indicates that divinatory spirit travel in the seen world – as depicted in this legendary account – could figure importantly in a shaman's professional activities, as we discuss further in Chapter 6. Perhaps because of a predilection for the seemingly more sensational journeying to unseen worlds, however, scholars have tended to marginalize it as an aspect of shamanic duties, as Barbara Tedlock (2001) has noted.

The terrains envisioned in shamanic cosmologies often reflect the environment in which the community lives. As the above examples show, Hmong, Inuit, Daur, and Yagua cosmologies each reflect a community's assumptions regarding landscape, its productive and unproductive regions, and the livelihoods that the community relies upon. Similarly, as Takiguchi Naoko (2003: 132) points out, Miyako shamans of the Okinawa Prefecture of Japan describe not only seven layers of the heavens above, but also seven to nine levels in the sea. The deities dwelling at these different underwater levels can protect people from disease and hardship. On the other hand, if treated improperly, they can take revenge through tornadoes, tidal waves, and typhoons. Shamans on the main island of Miyako knew of eight terrestrial entrance points from which to access the different levels and deities of the sea. According to Martino Nicoletti (2004: 38–9), Kalunge Râi shamans of Nepal associate upward and downward movement in the Himalayan mountains with various spiritual or supernatural goals, from seeking blessing from good spirits living high in the mountains to banishing evils or sickness associated with lowlands. Terrain affords a symbolic canvas upon which to group and differentiate the various positive and negative influences facing the community.

Sometimes the spirit world of the dead in particular is united with places on the earthly terrain. Among Trobriand Islanders of the early twentieth century, the spirits of the dead were known to travel to the nearby island of Tuma. As Gananath Obeyesekere (2002: 29) summarizes Bronislaw Malinowski's ethnography, "On the one hand Tuma is an actual inhabited island ten miles northwest of Trobriand, and on the other it is a place where the invisible spirits live." The dead live in Tuma until reincarnating, and may communicate with their former families through dreams in order to ask for food offerings or convey important messages. Visitors to the island may sense the presence of the spirits and receive information or insights from the experience (2002: 32). In a related vein, Caroline Humphrey notes the ways in which Daur Mongol communities invest the places of death or deposition of past shamans with powerful spiritual significance. Humphrey describes "a landscape linked by a skein of interrelated points of shamanic power. The land itself at such places, though hardly externally marked at all, is a medium for the transmission of shamanic power" (1996: 132). Here the supernatural is overlaid upon the natural terrain, obliterating the disjunction which shamanic cosmologies sometimes entail. If the multiple worlds of the cosmos are distinct, they also possess places of overlap, contact, and interpenetration.

Other aspects of the spirit world also find material expression in the terrain. Among Native American peoples, the landscape sometimes contains key places for sacred contact with unseen forces or beings. Occasionally, these are great mountains or buttes, such as Bear's Lodge/Devils Tower in Wyoming, a site sacred to a variety of Native peoples in the American West (Burton 2002). They may represent the physical sites of great mythic events of the past, and also serve as a privileged place for sacrifices and supernatural communication in the present. In discussing this aspect of Native American religious traditions, Lloyd Burton (2002) writes:

The creation stories, moral lessons, and seasonal rituals of specific indigenous culture groups are cast in specific geographic contexts. A mythic Eden is not the source of human creation for traditionalist members of the Taos Pueblo; it is Blue Lake, an actual body of water in the nearby Sangre de Cristo Mountains that feeds the stream flowing through their village. (2002: 15)

A tendency to sacralize the landscape can be seen as a nearly universal tendency in human cultures. Within shamanic traditions, however, this ascription of supernatural significance helps superimpose a spirit world on the visible terrain of the community's local environment.

As these examples illustrate, vertical cosmologies often contain horizontal, terrestrial localizations. They may also feature earthly portals which connect the seen and unseen worlds. Caves may be pathways to lower worlds, whereas mountains or remote wilderness areas may encompass pathways either up or down. James Brady and Wendy Ashmore (1994) explore the meanings of caves, mountains, and waters among Q'eqchi'

Mayan people of Central America and their archaeological forbears. In this topography of limestone karsts, underground caverns can stretch for considerable distances and are associated with subterranean rivers and lakes. Mayan people of this region regard mountains as essentially hollow, the homes of earth god(s). Caves – both natural and artificial – represent openings to this powerful underworld and access points to sacred waters. Brady and Ashmore demonstrate the close association of cave entrances with both sacred and ordinary dwellings of the Mayan past, and suggest that ancient pyramids in particular may have combined imagery of mountains, caves, and ancestral or royal authority into unified, highly potent architectural symbols.

Although these various visions of a multilayered cosmos posit various interconnections between its diverse layers or realms, some cosmologies envision a single unifying link through a transecting pillar or tree. The eighth-century Frankish emperor Charlemagne is said to have chopped down Irminsul, a great oak which local pagans regarded as the central pillar of the cosmos (Eliade 1964: 263). Thirteenth-century texts from Scandinavia describe a similar sacred tree known as Yggdrasil ("Ygg's [Odin's] horse"). Interconnecting the world of living humans with both underworlds and the sky kingdom of the gods, this tree apparently represented a major thoroughfare for spirit travelers in pre-Christian worldview (*Edda* 1987: 18–19). A strongly reminiscent belief survived among Sámi people into the twentieth century. The Sámi writer Johan Turi noted in his account of Sámi culture in 1910 that the earth is joined to the sky by a pole that leads to the North Star. At the end of time, a celestial ogre, Favtna, will shoot an arrow which will hit this star, causing the heavens to fall and the earth to be crushed and consumed in flames (Turi [1910] 1935: 293).

Although such cosmological details present a rendering of the cosmos as it is believed to exist, shamanic traditions sometimes employ the house as a microcosm or miniature of the cosmos. Eliade (1964: 260–1) points out the frequency of such modeling in Northern Eurasia, where conical house types and tents were traditional. In Sakha (Yakut) views, for instance, the sky was seen as a tent roof, with the stars as holes in the fabric. This same understanding was found among Hmong people, where the sky is seen as the rafters of the world (Cooper 1998: 107). While the home may thus model the cosmos, shamans sometimes represent the cosmos on their drums or other items of paraphernalia, as we shall see in Chapter 10. North Asian (Li 1992: 66), Arctic Siberian (Jankovics 1984), Altaic (Potapov 1999: 27), and Sámi drums (Manker 1950) all include depictions of cosmic features and spirit guides or deities on the drum head, making the drum a cosmic map for the use of the knowing shaman.

Brain researchers have identified particular cells in the hippocampal regions of the temporal lobe that store and recall information about place. These "place cells" allow a percipient to recognize a particular locality regardless of mode of arrival. Together, place cells help create a "cognitive map" that allows the percipient to navigate the known world (O'Keefe and Dostrovsky 1971; O'Keefe and Nadel 1978; Ekstrom *et al.* 2003). Significantly, people can use the same kind of cells and neural processes to navigate in a virtual world created using computer imagery.

Shamanic traditions rely upon cosmologies which are at once complex and yet singularly unified and predictable. The world has visible and invisible dimensions, often conceptualized as separate worlds, which may be vertically arrayed (as Eliade maintained) but may also occupy interconnected or overlapping regions in a horizontal array. Spirits – animate and conscious entities associated with physical beings – exist as invisible components of the visible world and offer the shaman interlocutors with whom to negotiate the issues that face the human community: the onset of disease or ill luck, the need for hunting success, the desire to know with clarity the realities of the present or the future. The shaman navigates the unseen worlds, often with the assistance of other spirits and often with the gratitude of the community whose vision is confined to the visible alone.

In a hunter-gatherer economy, locating resources and finding one's way through the landscape can become defining factors in the relative success of an individual or a community vis-à-vis competitors. The expert hunter knows where and when to find plentiful game, just as the expert gatherer knows where to find sources of food as these become seasonally available. Part of such success lies in knowledge gained by trial and error, and part derives from the fact that the individual keeps such knowledge secret. With resources limited to one degree or another, keeping a prime hunting, fishing, or gathering place secret helps guard it from overexploitation. In a certain way, the shamanic relation to the cosmos is built on this same logic. The effective shaman knows the ins and outs of the unseen cosmos and can bring back for clients or community the kinds of assistance they need. The shaman knows the pathways taken through personal experience, usually with the assistance of one or more spirit guides. Knowing these worlds and bringing back missing information or lost souls makes the shaman heroic, ensuring the individual a noteworthy, sometimes even feared, status within the community at large.

CHAPTER 5

The shamanic calling

I became a shaman not because it was my will
But because it was the will of my shaman spirits
The shaman spirits came to me
To make me a shaman.
                    Paja Thao, in Conquergood and Thao, *I Am a Shaman*

As is the case with many mystical traditions in various religions around the world, the shamanic role is typically regarded as a calling, a supernaturally initiated personal relationship between a living human being and one or more spirit guides. The future shaman may possess certain psychic, emotional, or even physical characteristics that create a shamanic predisposition or potential. The future shaman may also undergo a serious illness or near-death experience that marks entry into a shamanic role. Yet quintessentially, neither illness nor inherent potential is sufficient if the spirits do not elect to invite the shaman into a relationship. This supernatural contact, often experienced as frightening but intensely alluring and ultimately deeply meaningful, forms the focus of this chapter. How do shamans describe their calling, and what steps do they take in becoming aware of their new role and status? Further, given the primacy of spiritual guides in shamanic election, what roles do established shamans play in helping shamans-in-training develop and hone their skills? And how is this process of initiation evaluated and supported by the community which will eventually benefit from the new shaman's activities? These questions form the core of the current chapter and provide as well a foundation for the exploration of shamanic careers discussed in the following chapter.

THE CALL

Shamanism is not like Kung Fu or anything you could practice. Without your spirit you can't do anything.

                                                        Thai

Thai's experience of becoming a shaman occurred at such an early age that he has no clear recollection of it himself, although he knows of it in detail from his parents' accounts. "I don't know how long I've been a shaman – ever since I can remember I have been helping people." In fact, already while still *in utero*, Thai displayed such unusual body movements and constant shaking that his mother – a shaman herself and the mother of nine children before Thai – feared for her very life. Once he was born, Thai kicked and thrashed constantly until he learned to crawl. Then he used his new ability to set up a rudimentary altar, complete with a bowl for sacrificial rice and a stick. He pulled a little chair up in front of his creation and spent hours a day there, showing an unmistakable predilection for shamanic activities. Nonetheless, the little child failed to thrive physically, and at the age of two was far below where he should be in terms of size and weight. He was also stricken with a severe ailment that caused his parents to fear that he would die. They consulted a female shaman in the same refugee camp for help. In a day-long trance the shaman came to understand that, incredible though it seemed to her, Thai had already become a shaman. As Thai reports her testimony: "I heard the drum, his drumming, the sounds of his equipment. I heard all of this for hours and hours, and I couldn't believe it. I checked again and again, but your baby is a shaman, a *true* shaman!" The shaman told the parents to ask Thai if he would like to perform a séance, and, if he should respond affirmatively, to supply him with the equipment and means to do so. They asked him as instructed, and he avidly accepted the invitation. He began to work from then on as a shaman. "The more ceremonies I would do and practice, the healthier I got and I felt better." His health improved as a result. As Thai relates: "Without my helping spirit, I would not be here today; maybe I would be dead."

Thai's account of his becoming a shaman resembles that recorded among other shamans in other cultures around the world. Shamans often point to a period of disease in their personal lives as a pivotal event that led to one or more spirits making themselves available as a resource for healing and survival. The individual may have already displayed certain shamanic predilections – e.g., a sensitivity toward spiritual or emotional topics, a family background in which shamans existed, a series of omens that predicted the individual's future calling. Yet often, it is a specific life crisis that leads the shaman to full and conscious contact with the spirits who will provide guidance ever after.

VOLITION

The question of the future shaman's role in acquiescing to – or even seeking out – relations with spirits has been examined by numerous ethnographers

over time. Waldemar Bogoras (1909) explored in detail narratives of shamanic callings among Chukchi people of eastern Siberia at the turn of the
twentieth century which illustrate some of the ambiguities or variations that
could occur within a single shamanic tradition regarding the question of
callings. Although shamanic spirits (*kélet*) could present themselves spontaneously to a future shaman without any triggering event, narratives of
protracted illness or crisis were commonly cited as turning points in the
development of shamanic callings. One informant, a man named Aiñawát,
recounted meeting with the spirit of reindeer scabies after a severe bout of
illness (1909: 418). Aiñawát found the gaunt, black spirit that appeared to
him particularly attractive and wanted to remain with it permanently.
Bogoras writes:

> The "spirit" hesitated at first, and then refused to stay. He said, however, "I may
> consent, if your desire for my company is strong enough – if you wish me enough to
> take the drum, to handle it for three days and three nights, and to become a shaman."
> Aiñawát, in his turn, refused, and the "spirit" immediately vanished. (1909: 418)

Here, Aiñawát refused the challenges of the call – the difficult and transformative psychic initiation discussed below – and therefore did not progress toward becoming a shaman. The spirit left him, with no negative
consequences. In contrast, another informant, Kátek, responded positively
to the spirit of a walrus head which befriended him in a time of physical
crisis. He had been hunting along the crack in an ice-floe, when he suddenly
became stranded on a small piece of ice surrounded by open water. As the
rough seas rolled over the floe, Kátek battled for survival, while becoming
thoroughly drenched in icy waves. Bogoras writes:

> After several hours of such suffering, Kátek rebelled against his fate, and he was
> about to end the ordeal by stabbing himself with his belt-knife, when a large
> walrus-head suddenly popped out of the water quite close to him, and sang,
> "O Kátek, do not kill yourself! You shall again see the mountains of Uñísak and
> the little Kuwákak, your elder son." Then quite unexpectedly, Kátek saw a large
> iceberg, which drew the block on which he stood towards itself. (1909: 423)

Kátek was able to scramble aboard the iceberg and survive the night, eating
the blubber and wrapping himself in the skin of a seal he caught. Having
survived this harrowing event, he returned to his village, where, Bogoras
relates: "He bade them direct the sacrifice to the walrus-head, and from that
time on he was a shaman. He had some renown among his neighbors, and
his art was in requisition in the village of Uñísak" (1909: 423).

Still another Chukchi shaman, Scratching-Woman, related a calling
experience in which he actively sought out and received the help of the

spirits. Scratching-Woman's father died early in his life, and the boy was forced to work as a laborer for richer families. In this impoverished and undernourished state, Bogoras relates, "he began to beat the drum and to call for the 'spirits,' and one by one he saw all the supernatural beings ... and he made himself a shaman. The ... Motionless Star [Polaris] came to him in a dream and said to him, 'Cease to be such a weakling! Be a shaman and strong, and you will have plenty of food'" (1909: 424).

Such volitional seeking out of a shamanic calling was more common in North America, where, as R. H. Lowie (1934: 312) characterizes it, a more "democratized" shamanism often prevailed. In many North American cultures, adolescents – often particularly males – were enjoined to fast or endure other hardships in order to make contact with one or more spirits. This "vision quest" tradition often displayed many of the characteristics of shamanic initiation, so that, as Bäckman and Hultkrantz (1977: 14) put it, "the boundary-line between the shaman and other visionaries is quantitative rather than qualitative." Illustrative of this tendency are the vision quest accounts which the Ho-Chunk (Winnebago) elder Crashing Thunder included in the autobiography he produced in conjunction with the ethnographer Paul Radin (Radin 1926). At adolescence, Crashing Thunder's father prepared his son for a vision quest by taking him to a sacred place near three lakes and a black-hawk's nest. There Crashing Thunder fasted for a number of days, during which time his father came in the evening to recount for him the vision experiences of other male relatives of the past. One of these, that of Crashing Thunder's grandfather Jobenangiwinxga, may serve to illustrate the genre. Jobenangiwinxga hoped to obtain a vision and blessing of the Night Spirits, supernatural beings who bring about the darkness of night. The young man had a vision of the spirits after four nights, but soon realized that he had simply been duped by masquerading birds. He fasted again for six nights, only to be fooled again by masquerading bluebirds and ducks. Frustrated but determined, Jobenangiwinxga continued to fast for ten nights. Crashing Thunder recounts the events that followed:

Now indeed to its very depths did his heart ache. Ten nights did he fast. Finally the Night Spirits came after him. "Human being, I have come after you." He followed the spirits and they took him to the east; to the site of a Night Spirit village they took him. In the village there was a long lodge standing in the east. There they took him. All the Night Spirits in control of the most powerful blessings were there. When he entered he had to wade through white feathers up to his knees. Many kettles and much food did he see in the lodge. On the outside a buffalo hide was stretched almost across the entire lodge. Then these spirits said to him, "Human being, without giving up, long have you suffered; your heart has indeed been sad. All of the spirits in this lodge have talked about what is to happen to you. I, myself, am the chief of the Night Spirits. This creation lodge, just as you see it, with all that it contains, I give to you. Never shall you be in want of food. Offer up to us as many buckskins as you see here in the lodge. Thus it shall be. The creation lodge of the village of the Night Spirits I give to you. You can go on as many war-parties as you wish and you will obtain everything that you demand of life. All the offerings of tobacco, of food, of buckskins, and of red feathers, that you and your descendants offer to us, they all will come here to our creation lodge and we will accept them." (1926: 25–6)

Later in his narrative, Crashing Thunder also receives a gift of four helping spirits from his brother-in-law, a well-known shaman, who had originally contacted the spirits himself during his own vision quest (1926: 78–9). In Crashing Thunder's account, the brother-in-law states: "I was once blessed by four spirits, brothers, called *Good giant-cannibals*. They said that they had never before blessed any one. They promised me that if I ever got into any difficulties they would help me. They blessed me with long life. Now this blessing I will give you" (1926: 78). Crashing Thunder is asked to fast for four nights in order to make himself worthy of the transfer of the spirits. Here then, the calling of the spirits appears markedly controlled by human interaction, and individuals appear capable of not only selecting the spirits with which they would like to establish relations, but even of transferring these relations to others. It should be noted, however, that, in Crashing Thunder's narratives, the spirits themselves ultimately decide whether or not to reward the young man's nights of fasting with the sought-after blessings: if the spirits are not willing, they cannot be compelled.

Sometimes the line between the spirits' will and the novice's interest in becoming a shaman blurs. Such is the case in the narrative of Nenolo, a Nakwaxda'xw Kwagul (Kwakiutl) shaman whom George Hunt interviewed for Franz Boas in the early twentieth century (Boas 1930: 41–5). In Nenolo's account, his pathway toward a shamanic career began when he stumbled upon an injured wolf. The wolf had tried to ingest a large deer bone, which had become lodged in his throat. Nenolo extracted the bone, while commanding the wolf to repay him in the future with supernatural aid: "I will take out your great trouble and set you right, friend. Now reward me, friend, that I may be able, like you, to get everything easily, all that is taken by you, on account of your fame as a harpooner and of your supernatural power" (1930: 42). The wolf returned to his new friend that same night in a dream. In the form of a man, the spirit Harpooner-Body (Alēxwalal'itax) declared that he would reward the man as commanded:

Take care, friend, I am Harpooner-Body on whom you took pity today, and now I reward you for your kindness to me, friend. There is nothing hereafter that you will not obtain, whatever you wish to get. This also, do not lie down with your wife for four years, to pass through all that you will have to do. (1930: 42)

Soon after, Nenolo found that he now possessed unparalleled hunting luck, particularly in capturing seals. Then, in the summer of 1871, he was traveling with some kinsmen when the party came upon a great quantity of abandoned clothing and food. They gratefully took possession of these things, only to immediately fall ill from smallpox. Nenolo recalled coming to consciousness with his body entirely swollen, red, and oozing pus. All his companions were already dead. Out of nowhere, however, a pack of wolves appeared, led by the wolf that Nenolo had saved. They began to heal him: repeatedly vomiting a foamy substance all over his body and then licking it back up along with the scabs from the smallpox. After several repeated performances of this treatment, Nenolo fell asleep:

Then I dreamed of the wolf who was still sitting there. In my dream he became a man. In my dream he laughed and spoke and said, "Now take care, friend, now this shaman-maker has gone into you. Now you will cure the sick and you will catch the souls of the sick and you will throw sickness into anyone whom you wish to die among your tribe. Now they will be afraid of you," said he to me in my dream. Then I woke up and my body was trembling and my mind was different after this, for all the wolves had left me. Now I was a shaman. (1930: 44)

It is difficult to say in this striking account whether the spirit helper Harpooner-Body came to Nenolo first in the form of a wolf in order to test him, or whether the man's kindness to the wolf and command that he be recompensed with supernatural powers had caused his ultimate transformation into a shaman. In either case, we see that the disease came as a tool of the spirit: a means of transforming the shaman's body and of realigning his social relations. After returning to his village, Nenolo showed no sorrow over the death of so many of his family members, but rather rejoiced in his newfound relation with the spirit helper and the songs which he had learned.

COMPULSION

While volition seems to play a role in some shamanic calling experiences, feelings of compulsion are far more prevalent. Even within the Chukchi society described above, Bogoras noted that terrible consequences could occur if a young person refused a call: "A young man thwarted in his call to inspiration will either sicken and shortly die, or else the 'spirits' will induce him to renounce his home and go far away, where he may follow his vocation without hindrance" (Bogoras 1909: 419).

This element of compulsion is evident in the account of shamanic initiation that Vilmos Diószegi recorded from an elderly Tuvan *kam* shaman in the late 1950s (1968: 279–80). As the old Suzukpen recounted:

It [was] a long time ago. With two of my brothers, the three of us went to hunt squirrels. Late at night we were crossing a mountain … when suddenly I saw a black crow right in the middle of the road. We were advancing in single file, I was the first. I came nearer, but the crow kept crouching in the middle of the road. It stayed right there and waited for me. When I reached it, I threw some snow towards it from a branch. It never moved. Then I hit its beak with my stick. Kok-kok. The knock resounded loudly. What was all this? What was going to happen to me? Because the night before – before seeing the crow – I had already felt miserably. Next day I went back to where I had seen the crow. Not even a trace of it was to be seen, anywhere! Although the others, that is, my brothers, had seen it too. From then on, from the time I hit the beak of that crow, I became very ill. My mind was deranged. I have been suffering for as long as seven years. Finally, I began to shamanize, because everybody kept saying all along: I must shamanize in order to get well again. Nine years after I became ill, I gave in at last and ordered the drum and the drumstick because I had been urged to take up shamanizing.

The *kam*'s account of an encounter with a significant animal resembles that of Nenolo above. At the same time, it is evident here that the crow appears in order to compel the young man into a shamanic life, from which he can have no other escape but insanity.

Jon Crocker (1985) describes the initiatory experiences of Bororo shamans of Brazil. In this culture, the shaman's calling is both entirely compulsory and highly stigmatized:

For the Bororo, a *bari*, a shaman of the *bope* [spirits], is as much cursed as he is blessed. Although the role embodies a variable but definite element of power, it also entails a multitude of liabilities which are collectively thought much to outweigh the benefits. And the premises of Bororo shamanism preclude any element of individual volition, or even of consciousness within the role. The *bope* alone choose their representative, on grounds obscure even to shamans. The individual is free to reject the spirits, but he risks seriously angering them by so refusing their "call." (1985: 198)

According to Bororo tradition, a *bari* always emerges from a particular moiety within the society and must be related consanguineally to a dead shaman. The *bope* first begin to make their presence known to the future *bari* through dreams, particularly of flying, accompanied by the soul of another (1985: 201). Gradually, the prospective *bari* begins to see visions while awake, which are eventually followed by the hearing of questioning voices. He may, for example, see a stone suddenly move, or hear a low grunt or a voice asking where he is going. Crocker writes: "If he says anything about these strange things to other people, the *bope* immediately anger and cease to like him, and may even kill him … A knowledgeable person who understands the significance of these events may deliberately talk about them just so as to avoid being a shaman, but he incurs a certain risk in doing so" (1985: 202). Eventually, the *bope* make their presence known in clearer terms and offer the *bari* the choice of becoming a shaman. If the candidate accepts, he will receive good hunting luck as well as the power to cure diseases. But he and his wife will also become pariah figures within his community – essential professionals whose presence is both feared and polluting.

TRANSFORMATIVE ORDEALS

In many shamanic traditions, once a future shaman accepts the call, a process of spiritual transformation begins. Describing Chukchi shamanism, Bogoras writes:

For men, the preparatory stage of shamanistic inspiration is in most cases very painful, and extends over a long time. The call comes in an abrupt and obscure manner, leaving the young novice in much uncertainty regarding it. He feels "bashful" and frightened; he doubts his own disposition and strength … Half unconsciously and half against his own will, his whole soul undergoes a strange and painful transformation. This period may last months, and sometimes even years. The young novice, the "newly inspired" … loses all interest in the ordinary affairs of life. He ceases to work, eats but little and without relishing the food, ceases to talk to people, and does not even answer their questions. The great part of his time he spends in sleep. (1909: 420)

Bogoras notes that this process is less extreme among "weaker shamans and women" (1909: 421).

Crocker (1985: 203) describes the ordeals which a Bororo *bari* faces while progressing toward full professional status. After the *bope* spirits have been in regular contact with the candidate for some time, they eventually enter him in a violent and frightening experience of possession:

The future shaman returns to the village where he is quickly overcome by sleep. The *bope* enter him for the first time. He suddenly leaps up, babbling and screaming incoherently, and dashes madly around the house and out into the village. Those present grab him and hold him down, while someone goes for the nearest shaman. The *bope* begin speaking through him, although in a very confused way, and he continues to struggle violently. The experienced shaman offers him a cigarette and talks (in a nonpossessed condition himself) with the *bope*. As soon as the novice becomes calm enough to smoke, the *bope* depart with wild whoops, leaving him trembling and sweating. (1985: 203–4)

The initiatory possession experiences continue over the following months, as the novice is faced with various challenges in his dreams. He must resist the advances of the disguised mother of all *bope*, who tries to tempt him into an erection through her alluring behavior. He may be compelled to pass through a great ball of fire, feeling its heat and destructive power. He may be asked to touch a grotesque toad, its body covered with festering sores and warts. Or he may perceive the food he eats during waking life as teeming with maggots and have to ingest it nonetheless. Each time he successfully meets one of these challenges, the new *bari* secures greater future effectiveness for himself as a healer. Crocker notes that these experiences, although secretive and seldom discussed openly by shamans, nonetheless appeared quite standard among all Bororo, and were known in general by shamans and non-shamans alike (1985: 206).

Caroline Humphrey (1996: 33) records an epic account of the initiatory vision of a Daur shaman. The shaman's experience is related as follows:

> At a time when I was seventeen years old,
> Together with all the women,
> *Ikule ekule* having set out to the steppes and the valleys
> *Ikule ekule* having gathered vegetable plants
> *Ikule ekule* [we] were returning home,
> *Ikule ekule* when suddenly with a dazzle arising in my eyes
> *Ikule ekule* [I] stopped understanding anything.
> *Ikule ekule* [I] hardly managed to get home.
> *Ikule ekule* Not knowing why
> *Ikule ekule* [I] myself, weak, knowing nothing,
> *Ikule ekule* fell backwards.
> *Ikule ekule* Since [you] have come to search, I'll tell the
>   communication of the great source.
> *Ikule ekule* [My] physical sensations dimmed,
> *Ikule ekule* and suddenly from the tie-beam
> like the sun in the sky
> a great mirror descended.
> *Ikule ekule* Only just coming to
> *Ikule ekule* [I] took [the mirror], and, it seems,
> *Ikule ekule* in purity and solitude
> [my] whole body turned into powder.
> *Ikule ekule* With a breaking of eighty bones
> *Ikule ekule* ninety bones were twisted.
> *Ikule ekule* And thus [I] myself, becoming radiant,

Ikule ekule in unity with the great spirit,
Ikule ekule [I] myself became glorious, legendary and elevated!

The epic depiction, Humphrey notes, was popular generally during the early twentieth century. The shaman, Nisan, is depicted receiving a mirror, a key device and symbol of the shamanic profession in her region and culture (see Chapter 10).

Mircea Eliade (1964: 50–64) points to a particularly widespread experience of perceived dismemberment and consumption followed by reincarnation in the transformation narratives of shamans from a variety of different cultures. In these accounts – collected from shamans in areas as disparate as Siberia and South America – the novice may experience descent or ascent into an otherworld, where the candidate's body is dismembered and devoured by future spirit helpers. Once this event has occurred, the spirits can reconstruct the new shaman's body from the skeleton upward, recurrently employing magic quartz as a substitute for former bone. Piers Vitebsky (1995: 60–1) records the account of a Sakha (Yakut) shaman regarding this visionary experience, recorded by A. A. Popov in the 1930s:

Then I went through an opening in another rock. A naked man was sitting there fanning the fire with bellows. Above the fire hung an enormous cauldron as big as half the earth. When he saw me the naked man brought out a pair of tongs the size of a tent and took hold of me. He took my head and cut it off, and then sliced my body into little pieces and put them in the cauldron. There he boiled my body for three years. Then he placed me on an anvil and struck my head with a hammer and dipped it into ice-cold water to temper it. He took the big cauldron my body had been boiled in off the fire and poured its contents into another container. Now all my muscles had been separated from the bones. Here I am now, I'm talking to you in an ordinary state of mind and I can't say how many pieces there are in my body. But we shamans have several extra bones and muscles. I turned out to have three such parts, two muscles and one bone. When all my bones had been separated from my flesh, the blacksmith said to me, "Your marrow has turned into a river," and inside the hut I really did see a river with my bones floating on it. "Look, there are your bones floating away!" said the blacksmith, and started to pull them out of the water with his tongs. When all my bones had been pulled out on to the shore the blacksmith put them together, they became covered with flesh and my body took on its previous appearance. The only thing that was still left unattached was my head. It just looked like a bare skull. The blacksmith covered my skull with flesh and joined it on to my torso. I took on my previous human form. Before he let me go the blacksmith pulled out my eyes and put in new ones. He pierced my ears with his iron finger and told me, "You will be able to hear and understand the speech of plants." After this I found myself on a mountain and soon woke up in my own tent. Near me sat my worried father and mother.

Popov collected a comparable account from the Nganasan *nga* shaman Sereptie Djaruoskin (Hutton 2001: 73). In Djaruoskin's vision, his body was reduced to a skeleton by his future attendant spirits, while a smith figure forged him a new destiny as a shaman for his community: "When I entered as a skeleton and they forged, it meant that they forged me. The master of the earth, the spirit of the shamans, has become my origin." Such experiences can prove both vivid and frightening, and may, Eliade suggests, have parallels or imagistic sources in the tortures inflicted upon adepts in the initiatory rituals of many cultures' secret societies (1964: 63). Through it, the new shaman becomes a source of nourishment for the spirits, who in exchange for the shaman's self-sacrifice will then reconstitute the shaman's body in a new, supernaturally strengthened form. It is noteworthy that in the Sakha (Yakut) account above, shamans are said to have specific physical attributes – extra muscles and bones – that destine them to become shamans. Such imagery implies a strong notion of compulsion and fate in the shamanic call.

Although the above descriptions present the spiritual transformation as instigated and implemented by the spirits themselves, human trainers could sometimes be integrally involved in these harrowing physical and psycho-logical experiences. M. A. Czaplicka (1914: 189–90) cites M. A. Castrén's report of a Samoyed shaman's training experience from the middle of the nineteenth century:

[H]e was entrusted to the care of an old shaman for training, when he was fifteen, as he (the candidate) came of an old shamanist family. The means of education was as follows: Two *tadibey* (shamans) blindfolded him with a handkerchief, and then beat him, one on the back of the head and the other on the shoulders, till his eyes were dazzled as with too much light, and he saw demons on his arms and feet.

Such human-instigated pain could apparently have similar effects to that brought about by spirits, underscoring the importance of intense physical sensations in the development of shamanic vocations in many cultures. According to Harvey Whitehouse (2004: 105–12) initiatory pain can result in powerful "flashbulb memories," which can carry particular vividness and attract extensive exegesis within an individual's spiritual life. Narrativization of the events can further reinforce and add depth to these memories, helping create a spiritual resource for the adept in developing an identity and career as a shaman. Pain becomes a pathway to altered states, one parallel to other trance induction techniques discussed in Chapters 7 and 9.

ONSET

As with any important activity managed by strong notions of propriety, shamanic traditions in various cultures tend to display marked norms regarding the onset of a shamanic calling and the ages during which a person may fulfill the role. Exceptions, of course, may occur. It was considered highly unusual in Thai's community that shamanic election should occur at so early an age. Thai relates:

When I started to do a shaman's work and started to help people, people all around the village were all *shocked*. They all came to watch me do it, because they had never seen something like that ... So when I started to do it, my parents wouldn't let me do it in the day, because, even if I did it at twelve midnight people would come to see it ... The people were so many that they broke the wall on our house trying to look in!

The Russian ethnographer G. N. Gracheva found a similar development in a Nganasan community of the 1970s: a four-year-old boy was equipped with a hat and drum and began to enact séances similar to those of his grand-father (cited in Basilov 1997: 8).

Cross-culturally, shamanic election often occurs at puberty, although the candidate may have displayed tendencies that suggested a shamanic aptitude before then. In some traditions, the call could come to adults, particularly, as we have seen, in the aftermath of profound illnesses or life-threatening situations. Vladimir Basilov (1997: 6) points out that Selkup shamans could receive the shamanic illness in adolescence, but also later, while in their twenties. He cites Uzbek female shamans who only received the call after having had one to three children.

Similarly, Karen Smyers (1999: 41) recounts one adult woman's trans-formation into an *odaisan* shaman through her husband's marital infidelity:

She married, had three children, and was leading a fairly typical life until things began to fall apart when she reached forty – triggered, perhaps, by her husband's blatant affairs with other women. Yoshiba-san began to think she was crazy because she could see dead people's shapes, so she went to various shrines and temples looking for help. Finally a shamaness told her that one of Inari's spirit fox helpers was "attached" to her. She needed to enshrine and worship this spirit, she was told, thereby transforming it from a possessing to a protecting one. She performed arduous rituals, including the hundred-day waterfall austerity, learned to control her spiritual abilities, and moved out of her husband's house. Now, like the shamaness who helped her, she makes her living helping other troubled people.

Basilov (1997: 6) also notes that among Uzbek shamans, onset could occur at an even later age. He notes the case of a male shaman who was contacted by the spirits only when he was sixty years of age. Similarly, as Robin Ridington (1988) shows, Dunne-za (Beaver) *Naachin* often began their careers once established as elders. Amma Skookum described her old-age transformation into a *Naachin* as follows:

> That's my own song. About two years ago, I just about died.
> They – one of my husbands in heaven –
> Told me to sing that song. I got better.   (1988: 87)

Among Dunne-za, the songs of the *Naachin* constitute a prime medium of communication between the spirit world (including deceased family members) and the human community. That the gift of singing comes to one late in life makes sense, particularly if the *Naachin* then has a number of close friends or family now in the land of the dead. Summarizing the issue of age, Basilov writes: "Thus, 'shamanic illness' is not necessarily and naturally linked to age-related changes in the body, and it may be presumed that it is caused by factors of a different quality" (1997: 6).

In his overview of Evenki (Tungus) shamanism, S. M. Shirokogoroff found that shamanic illness often occurred after the death of an established shaman (cited in Basilov 1997: 7). As that individual's tutelary spirits began to search restlessly for a new partner, members of the former shaman's clan or community could become ill with symptoms identifiable as shamanic initiatory disease: bouts of confusion, excessive sleep, emotional outbursts, reclusiveness, loss of appetite. Once the spirits determined one individual who would carry on the crucial relationship between the spirits and the community, the other ill persons could regain their health and return to normal status.

While onset of shamanic activities is thus clearly influenced by traditional norms, the cessation of a shamanic career could also be determined by tradition. Writing of Chukchi shamans, Bogoras notes: "On the other hand, it is entirely permissible to abandon shamanistic performances at a more mature age, after several years of practice; and the anger of the 'spirits' is not incurred by it" (1909: 419). While some individuals may remain shamans for their entire lives, other traditions foresee a cessation of shamanic activities or even a practitioner's eventual choice to retire from the profession. Such regulations generally are framed in terms of the spirits' preferences: in some traditions, the spirits prefer young, vigorous shamans to elderly ones, or insist that their protégés have no physical defects. In other traditions, the age and wisdom of an elder are regarded as positive aspects that enhance the shaman's power. Even given these strong cultural norms, however, exceptions can occur, if the spirits choose a shaman of a markedly different age or background.

HUMAN TRAINING

Although relations with spirits lie at the heart of the shamanic calling, many shamanic traditions include an important role for human trainers as well.

Ronald Hutton (2001: 72) notes that while Buryat, Koryak, and Chukchi shamans tended to withdraw from human society in order to receive training from the spirits alone, their counterparts among Sakha, Enets, and Ket peoples relied on a combination of spiritual and human instruction. Without this human education, in these latter cases, it would be difficult for the shaman to establish a career. Human trainers can help the shaman hone skills of use in a séance, or learn esoteric knowledge of value during spirit journeys or healing. Understanding one's shamanic duties often entails a minute knowledge of the culture's cosmology and the mythic history by which the cosmos came to be the way it is. A formal period of training may also help the new shaman become recognized as a professional, conferring the status and notoriety that an advanced degree can provide in Western societies. The place of such formal acts of community recognition will be examined in greater detail in the following chapter.

Diana Riboli (2000: 72–3) notes that Chepang *pande* shamans of Nepal vary as to whether they receive human instruction. Some persons learn their art from other practitioners, while others receive the entire instruction through dreams, or through supernatural abduction in the forest. Riboli reports that Chepang community members view *pande* who have received human instruction as less powerful than those whose training has been exclusively supernatural, suggesting that the former may lack spiritual support or an authentic calling. Similarly, Ruth-Inge Heinze (1988: 56) reports that of the various Chinese, Thai, Malay, and Indian shamans she interviewed, the majority stated that they had received training from the spirits alone. At the same time, in Singapore, several schools existed for training *tang-ki*.

In Korea, training and form of initiation distinguishes two broad classes of shamans. In some regions, *sessŭmu* shamans dominate: these are hereditary shamans who learn elaborate shamanic songs as part of a familial tradition but who generally do not experience spirit possession within the séance. Man-young Hahn (1990: 196) discusses a Cheju Island *shimbang* shaman An Sa-in, who belonged to the *sessŭmu* class and counted himself as the twenty-fourth generation of shamanism in his family. Both of An Sa-in's parents were active shamans, as was his paternal grandmother and great grandmother. When performing a *kut*, he was assisted by his mother, who sang some of the songs required in the ritual (1990: 197–214). In such a familial context, elaborate musical traditions and dances could be effectively passed on from generation to generation. In contrast, in other parts of Korea, inspired, initiated shamans (*kangshinmu*) receive callings from the spirits and acquire formal training only subsequently. Training helps them hone their communications with possessing deities or the spirits of the dead, while also learning songs, dances, and ritual procedures expected of professionals. Within Korean tradition, both types of shaman can be called *mudang*, although outside scholars have argued about whether the hereditary variety qualify as "true" shamans.

In Thai's tradition, most new shamans work with a human master for some time. In the initial training séance, the experienced shaman will journey alongside the student, listening to the student's descriptions and remembering points to go over with the student later on. Later, the trainee will perform alone while the master observes and listens. The séance cannot be interrupted while it is taking place; the master shaman waits until it is over to critique and give advice. To do otherwise would compromise the ceremony, which is not acceptable. The trainee also usually has a helper, often a family member, that undergoes the training as well. They will work together in the shaman's future career. Finding a compatible trainer is not always easy, however: the master shaman's spirit must get along with the novice's; if that is not the case, the novice must search for a new master. A student cannot make a spirit journey without the help of a spirit helper, regardless of personal desire or the assistance of a living shaman. In fact, to attempt such a journey without a spirit would be dangerous.

Among Daur Mongol people, the training of the *yadgan* is similarly formalized, but tied more explicitly to the culture's key calendrical festivals. In this tradition, as Caroline Humphrey (1996: 186) details, the master carefully observes the novice's progress in training. When the novice has reached a suitable level of expertise in controlling interactions with the tutelary spirit, the master instructs the novice's clan members to prepare the ritual garb which the shaman will wear during professional activities thereafter. The novice is then invited to perform a ritual during the triennial festival known as the *ominam*, carefully following the lead of the master but demonstrating in this way the capacity to operate independently as a shaman. Nonetheless, after this performance, the novice will continue to work with the master until the following *ominam*, when at last the new *yadgan* will receive full recognition as a professional in the field.

An interesting record of the human component of shamanic training is contained in narratives written by George Hunt in the 1920s. As Briggs and Bauman (1999: 488) note, Hunt was the son of a high-ranking Tlingit woman and an English father. He was raised at the remarkably diverse trading station operated by the Hudson's Bay Company at Fort Rupert, Vancouver Island, where people of various different tribal backgrounds came into close and daily contact with traders of European descent. Hunt married a high-ranking Kwagul (Kwakiutl) woman, and received the name Māxwalagilis ("Giving Potlatches in the World") at the time of his marriage. Over the years of his collaboration with the anthropologist Franz Boas, Hunt related his shamanic experiences in some four different texts, varying in his portrayal of the experience as entirely real or largely fabricated (Judith Berman, personal communication). In one of these (1930: 13), Hunt relates how he received his shamanic name Qāselid. His account became famous within anthropology through the structuralist reading it received from Claude Lévi-Strauss (1963).

Hunt details the manner in which he was invited and initiated into the ranks of Kwagul shamans. While visiting one of their villages one evening, Hunt witnessed a healing ceremony. At the end of this healing, one of the attending shamans displayed a quartz crystal which he maintained had been extracted from the ill person. He threw it up into the air and a second shaman stated that it had then entered Hunt:

[He] came and stood still in front of the place where I was sitting. He said, "O shamans, important is what has been done by the supernatural quartz for it went into this our friend here, into Giving-Potlatches-in-the-World ... Now this one will be a great shaman," said he. Then all the men turned their faces looking at me where I was sitting. (Boas 1930: 4)

After this public invitation to join the profession, Hunt eventually agreed to become trained as a shaman. The process involved learning not only healing techniques but also tricks of the trade, such as a sleight of hand that allowed the healer to apparently draw a bloody worm out of a patient during healing – actually a small piece of bird down bloodied by biting one's lip during the séance. He also learned how one of the shamans' confederates spied on ill members of various prominent families so that he could relay the information to shamans, who then claimed to have received knowledge of the ailments through their helping spirits. Despite his initial skepticism, Hunt gradually progressed to public healings and enjoyed considerable success in his therapeutic efforts. His account illustrates cogently how human masters could provide elements of shamanic training which would strongly complement the supernatural gifts of the spirits, and which would potentially enable the new shaman to make an effective career within the tradition.

VARIETIES OF HELPING SPIRITS

Scholars of shamanism often divide spirits into the categories of tutelary spirits and helping spirits, and characterize each as either anthropomorphic or theriomorphic. By "tutelary spirit" scholars generally refer to some spirit which enjoys primary status in the shaman's communications and which is regarded as the shaman's essential guide and guardian. "Helping spirits" are lesser figures, who provide assistance to the shaman in particular situations, and who may be summoned by the shaman only when the healing or other task at hand requires specific expertise. "Anthropomorphic" spirits take the form of present or past human beings, either in outward form or in behavior. "Theriomorphic" spirits, for their part, resemble animals. Such categories can be misleading, however, as the same spirit may sometimes play varying roles in a shaman's life or take varying forms. A spirit may be a mix of human and animal forms, or may represent a different sort of entity altogether, e.g., a disease, star, or mountain. The fluidity of form evinced by spirits in some traditions is illustrated by the testimony of a Nanai (Goldi) shaman interviewed by Lev Shternberg in 1925. Although in most cases the *ayami* tutelary spirit took the form of a beautiful Nanai woman, she also adopted other forms at times:

Sometimes she comes under the aspect of an old woman, and sometimes under that of a wolf, so she is terrible to look at. Sometimes she comes as a winged tiger. I mount it and she takes me to show me different countries. I have seen mountains, where only old men and women live, and villages, where you see nothing but young people, men and women: they look like Golds and speak Goldish, sometimes those people are turned into tigers. (1925: 476; quoted in Eliade 1964: 72)

Historical reports indicate that Sámi *noaidit* tended to rely on a combination of anthropomorphic and theriomorphic helping spirits. The *noaide* was called into his vocation by the *noaidegázze*, a set of human-like spirits who lived in a sacred mountain. The *noaide* was able to summon these by means of a spirit bird (*noaideloddi*), and did so when he was in need of their advice or supernatural assistance. Other theriomorphic helping spirits included a reindeer bull that protected the *noaide* during his spirit journeys, and a fish that guided the *noaide* in his travels to the subterranean world of the dead (Bäckman and Hultkrantz 1977: 42–3; Mebius 2003: 170–2). An anthropomorphic female attendant spirit also assisted the *noaide*, particularly when he was under attack from other spirits. Each *noaide* had his own contingent of helping spirits, so that, for instance, one *noaide*'s reindeer bull spirit might well be called upon to battle that of another.

In Daur Mongol shamanism, as Caroline Humphrey (1996: 182–212) details, the collection of tutelary spirits that the Sámi shaman knew as a *noaidegázze* ("*noaide*'s followers"), finds a counterpart in the *yadgan*'s *onggor*. Humphrey recounts the narrative of an *onggor* recorded by Nicholas Poppe in

1930 (1996: 12–13). In it, we see that the particular *onggor* in question represented the fused souls of several different beings. The first of these, Otoshi Ugin, had been a girl born to elderly parents. She was embittered and driven mad by the brutal murder of her parents and set out on acts of revenge that destroyed several villages. A second being, Ganchi Lam, was in life a lama who had tried to defeat Otoshi Ugin but failed, eventually becoming her follower. The third person, Orchin Dog, was a former paralytic whom Otoshi Ugin had cured. These three souls became fused into the *onggor* Guarwan Ayin ("Three Journeys"), destined to remain on earth because of the violence of Otoshi Ugin's acts. Guarwan Ayin became the *onggor* of a succession of important *yadgan* shamans, each of whose souls likewise merged with those of the *onggor* after life. The last soul to be added into an *onggor* was termed the *borchoohor* ("brown-spotted one") and was taken to be a bird spirit of unmatched power (1996: 187). The *onggor* helps the *yadgan* control wild and dangerous spirits (*barkan*), and banish the demonic spirits of unruly dead (*shurkul*). The *yadgan* and *onggor* receive assistance from the *yadgan*'s ancestral clan spirits (*hojoor*). Both *onggor* and *hojoor* spirits are depicted in images and offered propitiary sacrifices.

M. A. Czaplicka (1914: 182–3) summarizes the findings of the ethnographer Sieroszewski concerning Sakha (Yakut) helping spirits. Tutelary spirits (*ämägyat*) were essential to any shaman's work and were publicly acknowledged as helpers. Another set of spirits, however, *yekyua*, were kept hidden from other people in far-away mountain caches. Czaplicka writes: "Once a year, when the snow melts and the earth is black, the *yekyua* arise from their hiding-places and begin to wander. They hold orgies of fights and noises, and the shamans with whom they are associated feel very ill. Especially harmful are the *yekyua* of female shamans" (1914: 182). The effects of an individual shaman's restless *yekyua* depend upon their theriomorphic form: those in dog form may gnaw at the shaman's heart, while more powerful spirits in the form of bulls, stallions, elk, or bears make raucous demands for food. Sakha shamans reported not only being able to see their own *yekyua* through their gift of supernatural vision, but also those of other shamans, and were said to be able to recognize the rise of a new shaman in the vicinity by the arrival of new *yekyua*.

Among Temiar people in the forests of Malaysia, sources of cultural, environmental, and economic destruction also become potential providers of spiritual powers. Marina Roseman (2001) examines the process by which Temiar people may directly experience foreign concepts, objects, or individuals in their waking lives and then meet them in spirit form in dreams:

Foreign peoples and things are socialized in dreams, brought into kinship relations as spirit familiar "child" to the Temiar dreamer as "parent." Strange people, things, and technologies become humanized, even Temiarized, their potentially disruptive foreign presence now tapped for use as a spirit familiar in Temiar ceremonies. (2001: 114)

Such spirit helpers include foreign peoples, trade goods, airplanes, wristwatches, and many other novelties. They appear in dreams in human form and offer a trademark melody, sometimes with additional dance steps and prescribed foods. By performing the song and its adjunct features, the healer brings the spirit helper into the presence of the community, enlisting it as a source of assistance in the present healing. While healers may focus on spirit helpers that they have met in their own dreams, they may also call upon spirits who have contacted other Temiar in the past, sometimes generations earlier. In this sense, the Temiar spirit songs themselves are more communal than personal: like incantations in many shamanic traditions, they represent a collective store of spiritual knowledge and relations, all of which can prove important to the work of a healer or patient.

In Temiar understandings, the supernatural power of the spirit of a tunnel or wristwatch lies in its being a part of the world outside the forest. As outsiders, such beings can soar above the forest canopy, seeking the patient's own wandering or lost spirit, so that the healer may restore it to the body. Made present in the healing ceremony through the performance of a certain song or dance, the spirit may also help the healer root out and banish spirits which have invaded the patient's body. In a sense, as Roseman explains, the Temiar assimilation of foreign beings into its healing system's preexisting world of spirit helpers allows Temiar healers both to acknowledge the sometimes devastating effects of cultural change in their society while also using this change as a source of spiritual power. Such assimilation becomes, she writes, "an act of social suturing, an art of survival, a technology for maintaining personal and social integrity in the face of nearly overwhelming odds" (2001: 110).

In her study of a Korean woman's initiation into the *kangshinmu mudang* (initiated shaman) role, Laurel Kendall (1995) traces the process by which the shaman-in-training Chini came to recognize her spirit helper as a deceased older sister. The family had suffered from a number of misfortunes in the past, including abuse of an alcoholic father and the suicide of the sister when she was nineteen. In a divinatory séance to discover why Chini was not receiving sufficient help from her spirits to allow her to perform expected oracles, her trainer, or "spirit mother," saw the deceased sister in the guise of a destined shaman (1995: 35). This

Figure 3. Inuit drawing of a helping spirit looking in on village activities. Drawing included in Knud Rasmussen's *Eskimo Folk-Tales* (1921).

divinatory act identified the sister not simply as a spirit helper but as Chini's *taesin* – guardian spirit – as well as an embodiment of the smallpox goddess Princess Hogu: "It's Chini's sister who has come here as Princess Hogu, blocking Chini's path. It's clear, she's come here wearing a crown and a court robe, she's come as Princess Hogu to be Chini's guardian spirit" (1995: 35). Once the spirit mother made this observation, details of the sister's death, supplied by the girl's mother, helped confirm its likelihood. In subsequent *kut* séances, Chini was able to speak the words of her sister and performatively demonstrate her identity both as the spirit that had been blocking Chini's progress as a shaman and as the guardian spirit who would subsequently aid her in her calling. In this case, then, although the shamanic relation with a tutelary spirit remains intensely personal and specific (i.e., Chini's unique relation with her dead sister), its actual characteristics emerged in part through collective interpretation.

LIFE-LONG RELATION

Thai and his father suspect that the tutelary spirit in Thai's experiences is a great uncle, who had himself been a great shaman in his life. Such is typical in the form of shamanism which Thai practices, in which the tutelary spirit tends to skip generations. In Thai's clan, such spirits are expected to assist only one shaman of a particular generation, finding a likely adept among the members of his own male line. In other clans, however, the same tutelary spirit may assist several different shamans at the same time. Even in these cases, however, Thai notes, one shaman usually emerges as the spirit's special favorite, sharing the spirit with other family members as needed.

Thai's relationship with his spirit has changed over time. When he was younger – particularly around the ages of seven to ten, he experienced the spirit consciously as an active presence in his mind, talking with him, encouraging him, giving him advice in various cases:

> I had a really close connection to that spirit.
> It guided me through my life.
> It guided me toward what to do.
> It guided me on how to help people.
> It guided me on what's right and what's wrong.
> "This is what you should do and shouldn't do."
> All through my journey, through my life as a shaman.

In those days, Thai could diagnose a client's illness without even asking questions: the spirit simply gave him the information immediately upon seeing the client. As Thai's skills matured, however, the spirit became less prominent, so that at the present time, Thai seldom experiences direct communications from the spirit. He relies on shamanic ceremonies to diagnose clients' illnesses and does not receive premonitions regarding the cause or nature of the ailment ahead of time. Thai does not regard this altered situation as a case of estrangement or abandonment, however. Rather, Thai suspects, the spirit now has confidence in Thai's abilities and is content to watch from a distance instead of actively intervening as before. Alternatively, the spirit may withdraw from communications in order to warn Thai of impending hardships, particularly within his family. Thai still feels the support of his spirit, and is confident of the spirit's engagement in his work as a shaman. Many shamans refer to their relations with tutelary spirits in similar ways. Shamans often find these spiritual friends as important and shaping as any human friends they may possess, and stress the primacy of the spiritual relation within both their professional activities and within their lives as a whole.

While the tutelary spirit is thus a central and sometimes domineering element of the shaman's life, it is often also considered important for the shaman to demonstrate not simply openness to that and other spirits, but a capacity to control them. The shaman's role in the relationship is not entirely passive, in other words. M. A. Czaplicka (1914: 177–8) notes, for instance, that Khanty (Ostyak) shamans were not only able to control their tutelary spirits but even sell them to another shaman. Citing the ethnographer Tretyakov, she writes:

The Ostyak shaman occasionally sells his familiar spirit to another shaman. After receiving payment, he divides his hair into tresses, and fixes the time when the spirit is to pass to his new master. The spirit, having changed owners, makes his new possessor suffer: if the new shaman does not feel these effects, it is a sign that he is not becoming proficient in his office.

SEXUALITY AND GENDER

One of the most powerful means of expressing interpersonal closeness is through sexuality, and in some shamanic traditions, the relationship between a shaman and a tutelary spirit takes on decidedly sexual features. The shaman may experience sexual encounters with a spirit and may come to view the relationship as a kind of marriage. Lev Shternberg (1925) collected one such testimony from a Nanai shaman of northeast China:

Once I was asleep on my sick-bed, when a spirit approached me. It was a very beautiful woman. Her figure was very slight, she was no more than half an arshin (71 cm) tall. Her face and attire were quite as those of one of our Gold women. Her hair fell down to her shoulders in short black tresses. Other shamans say they have had the vision of a woman with one-half of her face black, and the other half red. She said: "I am the 'ayami' [tutelary spirit] of your ancestors, the Shamans. I taught them shamaning. Now I am going to teach you. The old shamans have died off, and there is no one to heal people. You are to become a shaman."

Next she said: "I love you, I have no husband now, you will be my husband and I shall be a wife unto you. I shall give you assistant spirits. You are to heal with their aid, and I shall teach and help you myself. Food will come to us from the people."

I felt dismayed and tried to resist. Then she said: "If you will not obey me, so much the worse for you. I shall kill you."

She has been coming to me ever since, and I sleep with her as with my own wife, but we have no children. She lives quite by herself without any relatives in a hut, on a mountain, but she often changes her abode. (Shternberg 1925: 476; quoted in Eliade 1964: 72)

Similar relations between a shaman and *kele* (spirit) spouse were known among Chukchi shamans (Bogoras 1909: 452). Eliade (1964: 421) points out strong parallels between this relation and that described by both male and female shamans of the Saora (Savara) people of India. Verrier Elwin (1955) included a number of accounts of such marriages in his ethnography of the Saora from the mid-twentieth century. Shamans here could take both tutelary spirit spouses as well as human ones, and produce offspring both in this world and in the underworld of the spirits. Elwin recounts the typical experience of a future female shaman in detail. The spirit suitor appears to his future bride in dreams, adopting the dress and manner of a well-bred Hindu. He uses magic to throw the household into a deep sleep while he attempts to woo the girl into consenting both to marriage and to a professional life as a shaman. Writes Elwin:

In nearly every case, the girl at first refuses, for the profession of shaman is both arduous and beset with dangers. The result is that she begins to be plagued with nightmares: her divine lover carriers her to the Under World or threatens her with a fall from a great height. She generally falls ill; she may even be out of her wits for a time, and wanders pathetically disheveled in the fields and woods. The family then takes a hand. Since in most cases the girl has been having training for some time, everyone knows what she is in for, and even if she herself does not tell her parents what is happening they usually have a shrewd idea. But the proper thing is for the girl herself to confess to her parents that she has been "called," that she has refused, and that she is now in danger. This immediately relieves her own mind of its burden of guilt and sets the parents free to act. They at once arrange the girl's marriage with the tutelary. (1955: 147)

These arrangements include painting an icon of the bridegroom, preparing a sacrifice, and staging an elaborate wedding ceremony more lavish than that usually arranged for human weddings. The couple's subsequent sexual encounters occur either at the family's home or in the jungle, and once a child is born, the spirit father takes it with him to the underworld, returning with it at night so that the mother can nurse it. Despite these concrete, physical aspects of the marriage, Elwin notes: "the relationship is not primarily a sexual one; the important thing is that the tutelary husband should inspire and instruct his young wife in her dreams, and when she goes to perform her sacred duties he sits by her and tells her what to do" (1955: 148). Elwin includes the testimony of several such brides; commenting on her underworld progeny, one such bride states:

So now I was married and five years ago I had a child from my tutelary. I knew it was born for my tutelary used to bring him at night for my milk. People in the village heard him, but my own family slept as if they were dead. Later I married a man in this world, but because I have had a child in the other world I don't think I will ever have one here. (1955: 149)

In fact, however, the shaman eventually gave birth to a son in the human world as well. Dual marriages were not rare among Saora shamans, and often women found it difficult to state which husband they preferred (1955: 146).

Especially in past shamanisms, relations with tutelary spirits might also entail gender transformations, as when, in Bogoras's classic ethnographic account, Chukchi shamans were occasionally compelled by their tutelary spirits to change gender and live out their lives in a reversed gender condition. Bogoras noted that transformation of men into transgendered women was far more common than the transformation of women into transgendered men, but both phenomena were known and accepted among Chukchi at the beginning of the twentieth century (1909: 449–50). Bogoras notes that such transgendered individuals usually underwent their change of gender at the time of first shamanic calling, at the insistence of the *kele* spirits with whom they had formed relations. Although they often entered into a spiritual marriage with this *kele*, it did not preclude them from taking a human spouse as well, and they were much sought after as marriage partners (1909: 451). Bogoras details the dynamics of the three-way marriages that resulted:

Each "soft man" is supposed to have a special protector among the "spirits" who, for the most part, is said to play the part of a supernatural husband, *kéle*-husband ... of the transformed one. This husband is supposed to be the real head of the family and to communicate his orders by means of his transformed wife. The human husband, of course, has to execute these orders faithfully under fear of prompt punishment. Thus in a household like that, the voice of the wife is decidedly preponderant ... The *kéle*-husband is very sensitive to even the slightest mockery of his transformed wife, because he knows that the "soft man" feels exceedingly "bashful," and also because he is doubtless conscious that the position of the latter is ridiculed on account of his obedience to his own orders. (1909: 452)

Although gossip and jest were sometimes directed at transgendered individuals behind their backs, they were also greatly feared for their powers and because of the jealous protection of their spiritual spouses.

As Sandra Hollimon (2001) points out, indigenous peoples throughout North America have occasionally identified explicit roles and statuses for community members which avoid the binary oppositions that had become normative in Western notions of sexuality. Third and fourth gender (Roscoe 1998), "berdache" (Lang 1998), or "two spirit" (Jacobs *et al.* 1997) identities sometimes existed in communities where they were accorded not only acceptance but great respect, perhaps, as Hollimon (2001: 128) suggests, because "among Native North American societies, there is a strong underlying principle that individuals who occupy an intermediate or ambivalent position are spiritually powerful" (2001: 128). The ability to cross or transcend gender boundaries could render such persons particularly effective as shamans, given the shaman's general role of mediating different worlds and

Figure 4. Japanese *itako* shamans open for consultations. Photo courtesy Phil Colley/www.theorientalcaravan.com

social spaces (d'Anglure 1992). Thus, in a number of North American shamanic traditions, shamans who had undergone temporary or permanent gender transformation were known and highly respected. Nonetheless, not all transgendered persons in these societies became shamans, nor did all shamans evince transgender behaviors. The shamanic gender transformation should be understood as a distinct category of spiritual experience, related particularly to the relation of a shaman and a tutelary spirit.

A particularly striking case of modern shamanic gender transformation is discussed by Ana Mariella Bacigalupo (2004) in her study of a Mapuche *machi* (shaman) of southern Chile named Marta. Born and baptized Bernardo, Marta had undergone a gender transformation at the age of twenty-one, when she was called to her shamanic profession by the spirit of her great grandmother as well as the Virgin Mary. Marta's new identity as a woman was not fully accepted by her community, which had over time adopted the majority Chilean heteronormative views and stigmatized gender transformation. Nonetheless, Marta was viewed as a powerful shaman, particularly in the area of fertility rituals in which she specialized. In ritual activities, Mapuche *machi* often alternate gender identities as they embody the four figures – Old Man, Old Woman, Young Man, and Young

Woman – who together constitute the chief deity Ngünechen. In contrast to most *machi*, however, Marta embodied only the feminine beings of the deity and lived outside of her ritual life as a woman. Bacigalupo examines the differences between Marta's views and activities and those of both male and female *machi* of her culture, and explores the interplay of selfhood and gender in a changing Mapuche context. From the broader perspective of shamanism, however, Marta's experience can be seen as a further illustration of the intimate, demanding, and transformative relations that occur between shamans and tutelary spirits, as they negotiate, answer, and live out the shamanic call.

CHAPTER 6

Mediating the spirit world: shamanic roles and careers

The shaman and us, we are like a father of a family and his little immature children.

Khanty informant, reported by Hans Findeisen, *Menschen in der Welt*

The cosmos which shamans describe tends toward both spatial and spiritual differentation. Human beings find themselves in a mysterious web of seen and unseen forces. Frail and limited figures in themselves, they are set in largely unconscious relation to a vast array of powerful sentient beings who hold the keys to success or failure in their lives. Amid this complex and threatening world, the shaman emerges as a crucial mediating figure. Human in current essence, but on speaking terms with the spirit world(s) to which the shaman has occasional and possibly (after death) permanent access, the shaman bridges the gulf between the visible and invisible, the generally known and the largely unknown. Traversing realms unfamiliar to any but other specialists in the trade, the shaman performs tasks for the good of clients or the community at large: negotiating or effecting cures, divining the future, leading the souls of the dead to their proper after-life destinations, securing luck or misfortune for individuals or their enemies. Set apart from other people by these mediating activities per-formed at the edge of the human community and the threshold of the spirit world, the shaman can easily experience a sense of alienation from both human and spirit realms. Yet often, by acting as a bridge between these worlds and interlocutors, the shaman instead becomes central: an esteemed (if not also feared) prime mover in securing the needs of clients and ensuring the wellbeing of the greater community, both human and spiritual.

Although shamans cross-culturally emphasize their relations with spirits as the foundation and driving force within their activities, it is also clear that, as professionals, they enter into particular social and economic relations with their human communities. Cultures in which shamanic traditions thrive often designate specific economic niches in which shamans operate.

They also erect certain normative pathways by which individuals negotiate their status within the community. This chapter focuses on these human institutional factors, elements of shamanic tradition that help create and shape professional shamanic careers.

THE PROFESSIONAL SPECIALIZATIONS OF THE SHAMAN

In their overview of shamanic traditions worldwide, Louise Bäckman and Åke Hultkrantz (1977: 15–17) identify five arenas of activity in which shamans tend to operate cross-culturally: as healer, diviner, psychopomp, luck-bringer/stealer, and sacrificial officiant. First among these is the role of healer, both as a diagnostician and as a provider of therapeutic acts. The mechanisms by which shamanic healing can prove effective are discussed in Chapter 8. Yet, at a very fundamental level, as we will see in this chapter, the role of healer requires both communal recognition and participation. These institutional commitments help establish the shaman as a valued contributor to the health and welfare of the community.

Also important in shamanic careers, however, are divinatory activities: predicting, or even shaping the future through divinatory acts (Bäckman and Hultkrantz 1977: 16). Sometimes divination becomes part of a broader healing ceremony, as when a Hmong shaman employs pieces of horn as a means of determining the nature or color of a sacrifice that will be likely to satisfy or placate an offended spirit. Sometimes, clients consult shamans for specific divinatory assistance: to locate valued lost objects, find out about a coming hunt, or recognize the source or mechanism of some pressing misfortune. Divinatory ceremonies, in fact, can sometimes prove the main activities of a shaman, ones that are greatly valued by the larger community, despite a long-standing scholarly bias against them (see Tedlock 2001; Winkelman and Peek 2004).

Beyond these two widespread roles for the shaman cross-culturally, it is somewhat common for shamans to act as psychopomps, leading the souls of deceased community members to their proper afterlife destinations (Bäckman and Hultkrantz 1977: 17). And finally, shamans sometimes work to secure luck for their clients, to harm or steal luck away from enemies, and to lead sacrifices for the benefit of the community at large (Bäckman and Hultkrantz 1977: 17). These latter activities are by no means as common as that of a healer or diviner, yet they recur in a variety of different shamanic traditions in various parts of the world and can be seen to fit with some of the general characteristics of the cosmos as conceptualized in various shamanic traditions.

Often a single culture will include a variety of parallel or complementary shamanic roles played by the same or completely separate individuals, from specialists in healing, to diviners, to those whose primary responsibilities involve the offering of sacrifices or manipulation of luck. Among Koryak people, for instance, as M. A. Czaplicka (1914: 192) shows, a distinction was drawn between shamans who performed services within a family and those who served non-family members as well. The two spheres of duty implied entirely different professional statuses and roles within the society. Sometimes a practitioner could begin a career within the family context and gradually become drawn into wider service through success in healing and a growing reputation. Often, however, shamans remained firmly entrenched in one or the other mode.

Waldemar Bogoras (1904–9: 430) divided Chukchi shamans into three categories according to their expected duties: those who entered trance as a means of healing, those who divined the future after a short period of drumming and singing, and those who effected cures through incantations. All three varieties of shaman could perform their tasks either to help or to injure other persons. Within shamanic traditions themselves, such divisions often referred not simply to typical actions or fields of expertise but also to likely spiritual partners. M. A. Czaplicka (1914: 195) discusses the distinction in Sakha (Yakut) shamanism between the sky-oriented *aïy-oïuna*, professionals who "take part in spring festivals, marriage ceremonies, fertilization rites, and the curing of diseases" (1914: 195) and *abassy-oïuna*, who make sacrifices to subterranean spirits, "foretell the future, call up spirits, wander into spirit-land, and give accounts of their journeys thither" (1914: 195). While both groups shared the same understanding of the cosmos, they specialized in different varieties of spirit journey, developing relations with different spirits. As Vladimir Grusman, Alexei Konovalov, and Valentina Gorbacheva (2006: 258–9) point out, this same distinction was shared by other Siberian shamanic traditions, including those of Buryat, Tuvan, and Altai peoples. Associated with the symbolic colors white for sky travel and black for subterranean travel, both "white" and "black" shamans were regarded as important supernatural mediators, and both presided over particular communal rituals. Thai notes a similar distinction within Hmong tradition. Although he is termed a *txiv neeb*, a different variety of shamans, *neeb poj qhe*, travel to the world of the dead. They perform their rituals at night, use different equipment and ceremonies, and are consulted when clients wish to communicate with deceased family members. Some practitioners can serve as both kinds of shaman, but do so only with the cooperation of distinct spirit helpers in each case. Grusman, Konovalov, and Gorbacheva (2006: 259) point out a similar possibility among some Tuvan shamans as well, at least during the twentieth century.

In their description of a Buryat shamanic initiation ritual from the Aga region of Siberia, Virlana Tkacz, Sayan Zhambalov, and Wanda Phipps (2002: 10) describe the different roles and verbal resources employed by "black" and "white" shamans within Buryat tradition. In the ritual observed, the two different varieties of shaman performed ceremonies in separate groves but came together for certain elements of the overall ritual. Both their chants and their refrain differed: the refrain of black shamans was no longer comprehensible to modern Buryat shamans, while white shamans employed a refrain that appeared to be drawn from Sanskrit, indicating a possible source in Buddhist practices (2002: 29–30). Differences in material culture and spirits addressed further separated the groups.

Whereas the above distinctions can be regarded as largely organic to the indigenous religious traditions in which they occur, divisions in shamanic role or profile may sometimes derive from differing orientations toward an incoming or competing religious system, a topic we will examine in great detail in Chapter 12. Carmen Blacker (1975: 167) distinguishes between four distinct classes of shamanic practitioner in Japan: Buddhist priests who take on shamanic roles, ascetic *yamabushi* of the syncretic Shugendō order, blind female diviners known as *itako*, and itinerant practitioners who follow traditional pilgrimage routes, dispensing services to clients on request. According to Blacker, the four classes represent different manifestations of an underlying shamanic tradition which came to Japan during its earliest era of settlement and which fused with later religious influences as these took root in Japan's eclectic and decentralized religious culture. Similarly, Neil Whitehead (2002: 5) notes the existence of a separate form of shamanism among Patamuna Indians of Guyana that reflects syncretic fusion with Christianity. The tradition, termed *alleluia*, is regarded by practitioners as wholly distinct from the prior *piya* tradition of shamanic practices. Syncresis of this variety, explored in greater detail in Chapter 12, could lead to marked divisions among practitioners who make use of ostensibly similar techniques and understandings of the cosmos.

In a certain sense, discussing this array of roles and professional identities under the single rubric of *shaman* masks important sources of variation and distinction in shamanic cultures. At the same time, shamanic traditions often speak of an overarching shamanic profession or set of skills, which can be enacted by different individuals with varying specializations, areas of expertise, and techniques. While acknowledging the variety of different subcategories among Chukchi shamans, Bogoras writes:

The shamans, however, combine in varying degrees all these categories of Chukchee shamanism; that is, they converse with spirits, and make them play various tricks before the spectators; then they make the spirits answer the questions and give the necessary directions. If need be, they pronounce incantations, and perform other magical acts. They also perform the magical art in the treatment of various diseases. (1904–9: 432)

FAMILIES AND EMERGENT CALLINGS

The role of the family in helping identify and cultivate a shamanic calling is important, particularly in cultures in which shamanism is passed down intergenerationally within specific family lines. In Thai's clan, a tutelary spirit makes itself available to only one member of the family in a lifetime, so when a shaman dies, the family is anxious to discover a replacement from within their ranks. In other Hmong clans, Thai notes, the same tutelary spirit may elect to develop relations with several different family members, yet generally one shaman assumes primacy in the group. Thai notes that his own family situation was undoubtedly important in his eventual election as a shaman: "I think if I had been born to a different family, it would've been a totally different story." Although Thai's mother is a shaman within her own clan, Thai regards his father as particularly important to creating the context in which Thai became chosen to inherit the clan's shamanic relation. Thai's father had learned a vast amount of shamanic knowledge from his mother, who was also a shaman, and was immediately and consistently supportive of Thai in his calling:

My dad is a very traditional man.
I think that the spirit chose me,
I have a strong belief that the spirit has chosen me because of my dad too.
Because my dad can be a good helper …
Even though he is not a shaman, he knows a lot,
he knows more than a shaman can know,
about the spirit world,
and those spirits' names,
the chanting, and everything.
With my dad's help, and my spirit, then, ceremony after ceremony, as the years
went by I picked it all up. It came naturally …
Without him I cannot do my ceremony.

The notion of shamanic callings passing down through families is widespread. M. A. Czaplicka (1914: 177) notes that among Khanty (Ostyak) people, a shaman generally chose a successor from among the rising generation:

[T]he father himself chooses his successor, not necessarily according to age, but according to capacity; and to the chosen one he gives his own knowledge. If he has no children, he may pass on the office to a friend, or to an adopted child.

Among Chukchi people, as Bogoras relates, families varied with regard to their willingness to allow their children to follow a shamanic calling. Writes Bogoras:

The parents of young persons "doomed to inspiration" ... act differently, according to temperament and family conditions. Sometimes they protest against the call coming to their child, and try to induce it to reject the "spirits" and to keep to the ordinary life. This happens mostly in the case of only children, because of the danger pertaining to the shamanistic call, especially in the beginning ... There are parents who wish their child to answer the call. This happens especially in families rich in children, with large herds, and with several tents of their own. Such a family is not inclined to feel anxious about a possible loss of one of its members. On the contrary, they are desirous of having a shaman of their own – made to order, so to speak – a special soliciter before the "spirits," and a caretaker in all extraordinary casualties of life. (Bogoras 1904–9: 419)

One way in which a family – or broader community – can signal its acceptance of a shaman is through helping outfit the novice. In Thai's community, the equipment of the shaman is procured or preserved by the family: shamanic gear cannot simply be thrown away after a shaman dies. Instead, it is saved for possible use by a later shaman. In the meantime, it serves as protection for the household. Where the family does not possess an item needed to outfit the new shaman, the family members may acquire it through purchase or trade. We will examine the topic of shamanic costume and its production in greater detail in Chapter 10.

ESTABLISHING A SHAMANIC PERSONA

As we saw in the last chapter, shamanic initiation often involves both a spiritual dimension (the development of close relations with one or more powerful spirit helpers) and a human dimension (a period of apprenticeship to some recognized practicing shaman). In both cases, the novice shaman must eventually make some sort of public demonstration of competence in order to attract and secure the community's approval as a new and valued resource. Shamanic traditions often include explicit ceremonies or ritual moments in which the new shaman can display the abilities which lie at the heart of the trade. Doing so with sufficient prowess and confidence are crucial to attracting a willing and receptive clientele.

In modern Korea, professional *mudang* shamans can assemble the paraphernalia they require for their *kut* séances at specialty shops catering to their trade. At the same time, as Laurel Kendall (1995) shows, such purchases tend to be made by family members as a means of supporting the *mudang* in her new vocation, and are usually overseen by the novice's trainer. In addition to looking the part, however, an initiate must also undergo a process of training to learn the dances, techniques, and persona of a successful *mudang*. In analyzing the story of one such shaman-in-training, Chini, Kendall focuses on the performative responsibilities of the novice: "To become a shaman, she must find it in herself to perform as one" (1995: 18). Part of this performance is narrative: the shaman "must create legitimizing autobiographical texts, tales of profound suffering, portentous dreams, and visions, all of which bespeak an inevitable calling" (1995: 25). These stories can develop over time, with the input of more experienced shamans and with the suggestions and interpretations of family and community members as well. An unidentified spirit helper becomes recognized as a particular god or a deceased family member as the result of the vision being discussed as a group. The shaman-in-training assimilates useful feedback into her own narrative, adjusting her future performances.

During the *kut* ceremonies that bring the Korean shaman's formal training to a close, the performative responsibility shifts to speaking the spirits' voices, actively donning costumes that embody particular helping spirits or gods, and inviting them to speak through the shaman's body. On the one hand, as Kendall shows, this act is conceptualized as a type of possession – a seemingly passive opening of the self to another's communicative agenda. At the same time, however, Chini's trainers stressed the shaman's responsibility in letting her emotions loose, actively speaking the oracles, allowing her "gates of speech" to be open. As in other shamanisms that do not conceptualize spirit contact as possession, so here as well, the shaman's role is viewed as active and empowered. And part of the task of the shamanic initiation is to demonstrate the ability and the will to assume the authority demanded of the shaman.

Similar performative thresholds occur in other shamanic traditions, reminding us of the fact that the activities of a shaman – like those of religious specialists in many other religions – always contain a performative dimension. There is such a thing as a "good" or "bad" shamanic performance, and audiences are often canny and active in evaluating performative criteria, as we shall see below.

THE SHAMAN'S ASSISTANT(S)

Thai notes that he cannot undertake any spirit journey without the help of his father. The tutelary spirit that chose and entered into a relation with

Thai is of supreme importance in all of Thai's shamanic endeavors, yet the human assistant also plays an essential role: monitoring the shamanic journey by listening in on the conversations that Thai enunciates while in trance, providing the percussive music that helps launch the shaman on his journey, guarding the shaman's body from harm during the ritual and providing the various pieces of equipment that are needed in given procedures: the horns used for divination, rings used for ensnaring souls, spirit money that must be burned as an offering. Thai's father has served as his son's assistant for the whole of Thai's career, and it is evident to Thai that his help is crucial.

Basilov (1997: 13) notes a similar importance for the assistant of Evenki (Tungus) shamans. The assistant sang along with the shaman in the chants used to induce trance and alternated with the shaman in the beating of the drum during the séance. Although the role of helper could potentially be played by anyone in the community, Evenki shamans tended to have regular helpers with whom they habitually performed.

Basilov (1997: 13) cites A. A. Popov's account of the musical assistance of the shaman's helper in Nganasan tradition:

The Nganasan shaman had a "chanting helper." No shaman will shamanize without one: he is the closest guide of the shaman. The assistant usually began the séance by chanting the "proper" song of a particular spirit. Those in attendance would join in. If the equanimity of the shaman indicated that the spirit was not coming, the assistant changed the melody, singing the song of a different spirit. When the shaman began to beat his drum, the assistant summoned the spirits with a recitative. During the ritual, he repeated the shamanic hymns, in this way sustaining both the shaman and his spirits. If the séance was being performed for an especially severe emergency illness, a relative or the shaman's wife could be the assistant.

COMMUNITY ACCEPTANCE, COMMUNITY PARTICIPATION

Despite an initiatory phase in which the shaman may exhibit marked reclusiveness and emotional outbursts, the shaman eventually comes to function in an intensely social manner. Healings and other ritual duties are performed in public, often with public participation a mandatory feature and a key to the event's therapeutic value. This social aspect of the shaman's career means in practice that the shaman is exposed to far more social screening and evaluation than the discourse of singular relations to dominant helping spirits might imply. The community must accept a shaman as valid, consult and heed the shaman's advice in times of need, and perform those tasks expected of the community in the shamanic economy. In a variety of ways, then, the community is not simply the recipient of shamanic services, but the shaper of a shaman's career.

This communal role is underscored strongly in the ceremony known as *shanar* in Buryat tradition (Tkacz, Zhambalov, and Phipps 2002). A *shanar* is undertaken at a shaman's request to strengthen relations with helping spirits. The ritual is accompanied by persons filling the roles of father, mother, children, and other assistants. In explaining the ritual to modern participants, the shaman Bayir Rinchinov declares:

> A shaman has no road to the Thirteen Northern Spirits. Even if he were to go right near the Baikal [a place of origin in Buryat shamanic tradition] they will not consider his offering. They will only accept his offering through the Father, Mother, the Children of Heaven, the Guardians and the Cupbearers ... If we don't do this part of the ritual, the Thirteen Northern Spirits will never accept our offering. (Tkacz, Zhambalov, and Phipps 2002: 67–8)

In return for their participation, the grateful shaman will regularly pray for these assistants, making an annual offering on their behalf during the following three years (2002: 174). While participating, community members may appraise the validity of the ritual, ascertaining that the shaman is a reliable source of assistance in future times of need.

Margery Wolf (1990) explores the events which led a rural community in twentieth-century Taiwan to reject a woman who appeared at first to have received a shamanic calling. Wolf lived in the village of Peihotien when a local woman suffered a hysteric episode that involved her throwing herself into a rice paddy. Her husband sent her to a mental hospital for a short time, but she soon returned, with the aid of her mother. She reported having been contacted by a god and asked to worship the deity Shang Ti Kung. A *tang-ki* (shaman) of Shang Ti Kung was consulted and examined the woman but stated his opinion that she had been visited by a ghost rather than a god. The woman, Mrs. Chen, subsequently asked to worship a different god, Wang Yeh, and then still another, and began to function as a new *tang-ki*, holding consultations for people who came to see and hear her and appraise her health. Mrs. Chen's mother acted as her interpreter in this new role.

The community was initially strongly interested in the woman's situation but soon decided that the original shaman's diagnosis had been correct: Mrs. Chen had been attacked by a ghost rather than invited by a god. Wolf notes that the village had no *tang-ki* of its own at the time and that, foreseeably, they would have welcomed Mrs. Chen's new status. Several factors combined, however, to cool local interest in her candidacy. Primary among these was the fact that Mrs. Chen was an outsider in the village, having moved there in the recent past and not belonging to the dominant clan of the locale. Her outsider status was coupled with the villagers' distrust of her husband, who seemed to want to profit from his wife's newfound calling, and whose drinking habits may have lain behind some of the anxieties which Mrs. Chen had complained of before the episode. Mrs. Chen's situation seemed to deviate too much, Wolf suggests, from the community's shamanic norm, which features a predominantly male, unpresuming *tang-ki* typically associated with local gods and ancestors. Had Mrs. Chen belonged to the village's majority clan, and possessed male relations of suitable stature and credibility, her pathway to a shamanic career might have been assured. Wolf speculates on Mrs. Chen's motivations in the context of personal maintenance of self-hood within Taiwanese village society:

I continue to wonder whether or not Mrs. Chen, on that fateful day when she threw herself into the rice paddy, was not, as some claimed, trying to get to the river. Suicide (often by drowning) is a solution for many (younger) Chinese women who have trouble creating a new self in a strange place. Perhaps when she was pulled out of the muck of the paddy, she made one final attempt to join the social world of the village by way of a god who had more reality for her than the people among whom she lived. Unfortunately, her self was so poorly established that she could not carry it off. The self that spoke with the gods could not be used to construct a self that could survive in a social world constructed by strangers. (1990: 429)

S. M. Shirokogoroff recorded a similar pivotal role for community members in the selection of a shaman in a Manchurian village (summarized in Basilov 1997: 9). After the death of a local shaman, two clan members emerged as possibly experiencing a shamanic call. One of these, the deceased shaman's former mistress, began to disappear into the forest at night and reemerge only later, exhausted, confused, and bruised. The other candidate, the deceased man's son, had significant dreams and occasionally awoke at night to spontaneously perform shamanic acts. Uncertain which individual had been called, the community assembled to evaluate both candidates. In the resulting trial, the older woman failed to enter a trance state, while the young man managed to perform a strongly convincing séance by the fourth night of the event. He was thus embraced as the new shaman of the community. Writes Basilov:

Why such an outcome? ... One of the reasons for the failure of the woman was, beyond doubt, the unwillingness of the majority to have her as shaman. She was handed a damp, bad-sounding drum, laughed at, and the like, which doubtlessly prevented her from concentrating ... It was decided that she was not controlling the spirits, but the spirits her, and therefore could not become a shamaness. (1997: 9)

Given such extremely critical and potentially hostile audience evaluation, it is not surprising that many Inuit shamans, for instance, repeatedly down-played their activities before and after performance as inadequate, foolery, or even deceptions (Hunt 2002: 32). Assuming the performative mantle of the shaman could hold significant perils if the community refused to accept the individual's status.

Edward Schieffelin (1995) helps explain the reasoning behind this central attentiveness to community wishes at the outset of a shaman's career through examining the ways in which the community functions within the performances of established shamans. As we will see in greater detail in Chapter 8, the community is often a crucial component of shamanic healing, one that works with the shaman to discover the causes of a patient's problems and to suggest or enact possible therapeutic strategies. Without the community's engagement and support, the shaman can often accom-plish little. Thus, securing and maintaining that community support is essential for the shaman's career.

In Schieffelin's study, two Kaluli shamans of New Guinea cooperated in a séance held to discover the cause of a local child's ailment. The older and more established shaman, Aiba, possessed deep learning but was not known as a particularly good performer of the musical pieces that make up the spirits' communications with the human community. Nor was he well acquainted with the circumstances concerning the ill child or family in question. His counterpart, Walia, was younger and less established, but was regarded as an extremely gifted singer. He also possessed more local knowledge about the social dynamics of the village and the dealings of the patient's families with neighbors, as well as an attentiveness to the social needs and interests of his audience. In the séance itself, as Schieffelin demonstrates, the audience rejected as inconclusive or irrelevant the utterances of Aiba's spirits, while becoming rapt with attention by the story of resentment, witchcraft, and danger that Walia's spirits presented. Schieffelin notes: "A Kaluli séance is a much more loosely structured, dialogic and improvisatory kind of event than rituals are usually characterized as being in anthropological literature" (1995: 63–4). In this context, the shaman must build audience approval for any therapeutic course of action not only through performative expertise, but also through building strong audience rapport. Walia's attentiveness to the audi-ence's situation and engagement of the audience in helping puzzle out the causes of the disease helped secure his performance as efficacious.

Inuit séances accorded a similar importance to audience participation, again underscoring the crucial importance of the audience as a component of an *angakok* shaman's activities as well as career. As Hunt (2002) notes:

The *angakok*'s communication with the spirits takes place within the *qasgiq*, with a large mixed audience in attendance. The audience is essential, both to witness and encourage the *angakok* and to admit to any transgression which may have offended the spirits. It is said that the *angakok* is able to detect a dark cloud that is invisible to ordinary people which gathers around a transgressor. (2002: 30)

Knud Rasmussen (1921) recounts the means by which an *angakok* could enlist the community in discovering the cause of an illness or other problem:

If the helping spirit has communicated to them the name of a person who is threatened with illness or other danger, they never, during a public incantation, mention the actual name; they content themselves with allusions that can put their hearers on the right track; and when the latter guess the name of the person implied, the magician breaks out into moans, shouting – "Yes, it is he. You spoke the name. Oh! I could not help it – I had to say what I knew!" (1921: 152)

Such performances allow the community to acknowledge their possible prior awareness of the problem underlying the supernatural disturbance, while also sharing the culpability and possible hostility that could arise through direct accusation of another community member's wrongdoing or impropriety. Sometimes, the purported culprit's offending acts could be small, e.g., slight breaches of tabu; yet, if these were acknowledged by community members as possible sources of the problem at hand, the séance could come to a close with a feeling of finality and clarity of action. Writes Rasmussen:

Sometimes a very eager *angakok* will adduce the most extraordinary causes for an illness. Once, I remember, Piuaitsoq's little child fell ill, and Alattaq was summoned to hold an incantation, to which the whole village was invited. He called upon his spirits and conjured them until far into the night, and discovered that the reason of the child's illness was that once, for fun, the little one's fox-skin breeches had been put on a puppy! (1921: 153)

Indiscretions in the area of clothing were regarded as serious misdeeds, Rasmussen notes, perhaps since they threatened to lead astray the spirits who inhabit the world.

The *angakok* functions, Hunt points out, as a social device for uncovering and resolving community tensions. Hidden conflicts are brought into the open when the *angakok* returns from a spirit journey with indications that tabus had been broken, or that an aura of misdeed surrounds one or another member of the community. Writes Hunt:

At one level, of course, the *angakok* fulfills the people's real need of reassurance, as well as providing a safe outlet for confessions of indiscretions that would otherwise rapidly give rise to severe tensions within such close-knit communities. Eskimo survival depends on close cooperation and sharing, and festering tensions would undermine the viability of the group. Without a mechanism for resolving differences, Eskimo communities would become fragmented and vulnerable. (2002: 41–2)

Given this powerful role of the community in bringing about any shamanic healing, it is evident that gaining and maintaining the community's support must lie at the heart of a shaman's professional activities. Without a community's acceptance, a shaman can seldom build a professional career.

A different side to the issue of community "acceptance" is the possible normative experience of a pariah status for persons recognized as shamans within the community. Even in societies in which the shaman is regarded as a crucial member of society, it is not uncommon for shamans to feel alienated, feared, or even ostracized by their ambient communities. Among Bororo people of Brazil, for instance, the *bari* shaman and his wife are both recognized for their essential role in the community's life and yet completely shunned by their neighbors and families (Crocker 1985: 211). Writes Crocker: "The shaman and his wife are to be avoided, except when their services are needed. The only aspects of their existences which draw them back into community life and furnish some status are those deriving from the ritual positions they may occupy within their respective clans and through the complex set of relationships involved in the representation of the dead" (1985: 211). Acceptance of a shaman's efficacy is thus not always synonymous with social popularity, nor can we assume that a shaman is always viewed heroically. In fact, as our discussion of spiritual aggression below makes clear, views of shamans may vary from strongly positive to strongly condemnatory.

SPIRITUAL AGGRESSION

Magicians are sometimes soul-stealers; the people affected then fall ill and die. Some little time before our arrival at Cape York a man named Kajorapaluk had been murdered "because he stole souls."

Knud Rasmussen, *Eskimo Folk-Tales*

The same confidence in supernatural abilities that made the shaman a valued member of a family, village, or locale could also lead to nagging distrust of the shaman – or other community members – as potential spiritual aggressors. In a world in which the overall quantity of luck was regarded as severely limited, and in which disease and misfortune were regarded as the products of unseen aggression, other people could easily become suspected of performing evil – be it to enemies, to family and neighbors, or to seeming allies. In some traditions, shamans actively attempted to do harm for the sake of gain; in others, shamans with negative intent were categorized as separate from those striving to help others.

The same shamanic relationships between humans and their spirit helpers that held such capacity to help and cure could also prove dangerous if marred by acts of disrespect. Among Dunne-za (Beaver) people, as Robin Ridington (1988: 52–3) notes, a person could be endangered whenever another person, intentionally or unintentionally, offered food or items that were closely associated with the spirit helpers at the center of the person's adolescent dream quest. In Dunne-za tradition, dream quest visions were kept secret, but nonetheless could be guessed at by the precautions the person took in daily life after returning to the community. If a person avoided a certain kind of meat, for instance, it could indicate that that person had experienced a dream vision involving that animal. The act of consuming food made of the body of a spirit helper constituted a kind of spiritual cannibalism, which could result in the person becoming a cannibal in general life as well. As Ridington notes: "The person who became 'too strong' is called *Wechuge* ... a cannibal monster who hunts and eats members of his own community ... a superhuman cannibal monster, capable of hunting people in the way that people hunt animals" (1988: 53). In order to prevent a person from becoming "too strong," family members strive to encircle the person in human relationships, reincorporating the would-be cannibal into a fabric of human relations before the dreaded antisocial tendencies emerge. What is crucial to note is that the same spiritual relationships that help the person act effectively for self and community can equally become a source of danger, particularly through the meddling or ill will of other community members.

The folklorist Just Qvigstad collected a story of a particular variety of Sámi *noaide* from Johan Johanson Aikio in 1890 (1927: III, no. 151: p. 434). According to Aikio: "There is a certain kind of *noaide* who is called an 'eater *noaide*' [*boranoaide*]. This type can do nothing but evil through taking the lives of others." Here the *noaide* is regarded as a potential aggressor, often striking out at family members or close associates. These attitudes could lead to a great deal of fear when dealing with a *noaide*, and the potential for attributing any loss of health or good fortune to the likely machinations of the shaman. As discussed in Chapter 11, tales of the past irascible *noaide* Káren-Ovllá, and others of his era, were still widely known to Sámi raconteurs nearly a hundred years after his death. Káren-Ovllá had purportedly been responsible for the death of his son, the blinding of his wife, and the death of a nephew as well (Qvigstad 1927: III, no. 149, 1: pp. 420–7). At the same time, his acts often seemed to occur without his conscious will: his helping spirits read his thoughts and acted in response, punishing those who questioned or hindered the *noaide*. Occasionally, too, the spirits retaliated against Káren-Ovllá for acts that they regarded as insulting or belittling. The element of fear in the relationship between a shaman and helping spirits can be powerful: the shaman must be careful to maintain the upper hand with the spirits, lest they come to dominate the relationship to the detriment of all. Perhaps the *boranoaide* was one whose relations with spirit helpers had developed an imbalance, leading to the dominance of the spirits and resulting in unbridled aggression toward other community members. In this sense, as discussed in earlier chapters, the shamanic spirit relationship with the shaman firmly in control differs from the classic definition of passive spirit possession. The spirits are capable of doing either good or ill, and it is part of the task of the shaman to harness their powers for the advantage of the community.

Knud Rasmussen (1921) reports negative tales told of the Polar Inuit *angakok* Qilerneq, who lived in the same village as a once mighty hunter named Tâterâq. Rasmussen notes that special terms existed for an *angakok* who could call down misfortune on others, and that such shamans often accomplished their evil through creating a *tupilak*, an automaton beast made of the body parts of other animals that was capable of murdering or physically injuring a victim. Rasmussen recounts the tale of Tâterâq's misfortune:

Tâterâq had caught a tupilak; one autumn day, as they were making their way home from the chase, towing a walrus, a seal came to the surface just in front of the kayaks. Tâterâq was at once beside himself with hunting ardour, and shouted and comported himself generally like a madman. He rowed forward and harpooned the animal, and it was only after he had killed it that he grew calm again. When they got home and cut it up, they discovered that the animal had been made by an *angakok*. The chest was like a human being's, and the rest of the bones had been taken from different animals. A short time afterwards, Tâterâq fell ill, and gradually his body died. He, who used to be one of the best seal-catchers, has now lain for several years paralysed and helpless on a sledge among the houses. It was thought that it was old Qilerneq who had made this tupilak. (1921: 155–6)

Qilerneq's chief wrongdoing here appears to have been that he had been hostile to Tâterâq in the past. Once Tâterâq took ill, suspicions turned to the *angakok*. Such suspicions contributed to the occasional pariah status of shamans discussed above. They hinged upon Qilerneq's reputation for effectiveness in shamanic activities, but coupled with a suspicion of possible mean-spiritedness as well.

In her overview of traditional Tlingit shamanism, Barbara Iliff (1997: 37–8) describes the kinds of supernatural aggression which a practitioner called *nakws'aati* ("master of sickness") was said to perform. The *nakws'aati* was not a shaman (*ixt*) per se, but a spiritual competitor who made use of similar supernatural resources:

> The [perpetrator] used a kind of "sympathetic bewitchment," that involved the magical manipulation of body leavings, like nail parings, hair, spittle, and excrement. These substitutes for the intended victim were fashioned into a bundle which would be placed in a human corpse, the body of a dead dog, or among cremated ashes and allowed to rot, thus making the victim fall sick. When the patient's illness could not be cured with herbal remedies or through the extraction of spirit intrusions, the shaman would be compelled to leave his body in order to allow a series of spirits to speak through him, identified by their distinctive accouterments. (1997: 38)

If the spirits identified a *nakws'aati* among the assembly, that person was bound, starved, beaten, or nearly drowned until admitting the aggression. Once the transgressor admitted the activity, there was hope that the victim would heal. Such evil was suspected to occur within families, and to be motivated by both greed and envy. It undermined the trust and security of the extended family group, the base of Tlingit society and identity, and was thus viewed as doubly deleterious. Belief in such supernatural aggression continued long after the end of active shamanism, and survived the language shift from Tlingit to English (1997: 37). In English-speaking Tlingit communities, the *nakws'aati* became known as a "witch." In examining the experience of accused *nakws'aati*, Iliff (1994: 60) writes:

> There were undoubtedly cases where people were unfairly accused because of their social oddities and low social esteem. Orphans, slaves, and persons exhibiting unusual behaviors were often accused and punished severely and, conversely, high-status people were known to be treated leniently. The shaman had virtual power in these cases and could draw upon cultural mechanisms to preserve the status quo, even if justice wasn't ultimately served.

In this tradition, then, the *nakws'aati* is not viewed as a subclass of the *ixt* (shaman), but rather as an entirely separate class of practitioners. Iliff details the contrast between them:

> [T]he shaman's practice was in accord with culturally agreed upon principles of inheritance and ritual action, with the shaman as the exemplary individual through which spirit power was deliberately manifested. While the "calling" may come involuntarily to the novice (usually a nephew of the former shaman), the first

public acknowledgement of spirit possession occurred during the funerary feast for the deceased shaman. Within this socially sanctioned environment, the songs of the previous shaman would be sung by those present to honor the predecessor and his spirits that were being passed down, to inspire the novice, and to form a bridge between the living and the dead ... The [*nakws'aati*], on the other hand, lived outside the sanction of his group because of the unconscious and reckless manner in which he manipulated spirit powers. From Tlingit accounts it is known that a person hoping to become a [*nakws'aati*] intentionally sought out malevolent spirits, usually alone, often in the graveyard at dusk, and motivated by an overwhelming desire to harm. The particulars about how the [*nakws'aati*] acquired the use of supernatural power are not clear, because Tlingit people have been reluctant to discuss the subject. Copulation with dead spirits and handling the bones of the dead were cited as means of becoming possessed with malevolent spirit power. It is not known if [they] acquired songs, incantations, formulas, or visions as a result of their spirit contacts. In fact, it appears that because they lacked a ritual structure, they became unconscious agents of the power they contracted with, and were never fully in control of the outcome of their deeds. (1994: 61–3)

Thus, whereas the *ixt* stood as a recognized and valued spiritual intercessor, who maintained control over the spirits with whom he dealt, the *nakws'aati* purportedly operated on a clandestine level, with spirits that he was ultimately unable to control. The two classes of practitioners are clearly distinct, but rely upon the same shamanic understanding of the cosmos and theories of sickness and misfortune.

This view of the shaman as a potential aggressor helps explain the pariah status of Bororo shamans as reported by Crocker (1985: 211). Given the *bari* shaman's great powers and roles, avoiding close contact with him would seem advisable. Similarly, as Michael Harner (1972) has shown, Shuar (Jívaro) people also regarded their shamans as threats. Writes Harner:

Shamans (uwis'in), more numerous than outstanding killers, often wield considerable power in the neighborhood. The bewitching shamans (wawek, or yahauc'i: bad shaman) derive their social influence primarily from the fear in which they are held by their neighbors. Their mildly expressed wishes are often interpreted as near commands by laymen. The curing type of shaman (peŋer iwis'in: good shaman) exercises a less ominous type of social power, deriving primarily from the fact that his neighbors tend to view him as an important asset to their welfare. They warmly court his favor in order to assure themselves of his future willingness to cure them or members of their family. (1972: 116–17)

Shuar tradition thus identified different varieties of shaman, depending on their propensity to cause harm. All shamans, however, were regarded as possibly dangerous.

One of the most chilling accounts of aggression within cultures that practice shamanism is the *kanaimà* described by Neil Whitehead (2002).

Among Patamuna people of Guyana, a secret cult has revolved around the ritual murder and consumption of human victims since at least the sixteenth century. Whitehead describes this secret society as "distinct but related" from two other shamanic complexes: *piya*, a constellation of indigenous customs similar to that described in this study, and *alleluia*, a syncretic religious tradition drawing on both shamanic and Christian concepts (2002: 5). The relation of these forms of shamanic tradition and the ritual assault at the core of *kanaimà* is the focus of Whitehead's study. In Patamuna mythology, as Whitehead shows, *piya* is the gift of the deity Piai'ima, who created the first shamans and gave humans the magical plants used in rituals and cures (2002: 98–9). Piai'ima has a brother, Makunaima, who is a malicious figure responsible for many human scourges, including venomous snakes, scorpions, and stingrays. The *kanaimà* assault tradition is also viewed as the creation of Makunaima, and explicitly contrasted in the culture with the *piya* of Piai'ima. As with many shamanic traditions, this multiplicity of shamanic roles includes both helpful and hurtful forms, and adds ambiguity and complexity to any conceptualization of shamanism as a whole. Along with Robin Wright, Whitehead has also co-authored an anthology of articles focusing on similar traditions of sorcery and aggression in other Amazonian traditions (Whitehead and Wright 2004). Their work provides a valuable overview of aggressive sorcery as practiced in Amazonia and as described by ethnographers over the last century.

REPUTATIONS

As the quotation which opens this chapter illustrates, shamans can sometimes become figures of great respect and prestige within their communities, even in traditions in which they may also be feared. Hans Findeisen (1934: 41) found that Khanty communities looked up to their shamans as sources of wisdom and guidance in this world as well as sources of supernatural aid from beyond the visible realm. Thai, too, finds himself regularly consulted by members of his community – sometimes persons much older than he – concerning a whole host of personal decisions. "The Hmong people have a lot of respect for their shamans, and I feel that responsibility very strongly," he states.

Writing of Siberian shamans in general, M. A. Czaplicka (1914: 176) states:

The wizard who decides to carry on this struggle has not only the material gain in view, but also the alleviation of the griefs of his fellow men; the wizard who has the vocation, the faith, and the conviction, who undertakes his duty with ecstasy and negligence of personal danger, inspired by the high ideal of sacrifice, such a wizard always exerts an enormous influence upon his audience.

The reputation of a shaman – born of performative competence, a proven track record of success, and an air of concern for the community and its needs – is a powerful aid and aspect of the professional shaman. On the other hand, Czaplicka points out reputations could be negative as well. Referring to the highly convincing and authoritative shamans noted above, she quotes the ethnographer Sieroszewski as stating: "After having once or twice seen such a real shaman, I understood the distinction that the natives draw between the 'Great', 'Middling', and 'Mocking' or deceitful shamans" (1914: 176).

As with any professional, the shaman's recourse to potential clients is affected integrally by questions of reputation and professional success. A shaman who has effected remarkable cures or rightly predicted momentous events will receive more requests for consultations than one whose success rate has been low. Without clients, of course, the shaman cannot perform any of the duties which the tutelary spirits may wish to share with the human community, and may find it difficult to further a career as a source of supernatural assistance within a given locale.

Shamans may become shapers of their own reputations through both their performances and their narrative recounting of spiritual experiences, a topic to which we will return in Chapter 11. The shaman's audience may often obtain only a vague inkling of the shaman's adventures through witnessing a séance or broader ritual event, and thus it falls to the shaman to supply missing details concerning spirit journeys, encounters with supernatural beings, negotiations with souls, etc. Well-performed and convincing narrations naturally attract greater notoriety than inexpertly delivered accounts. At the same time, shamans are also often expected to display humility or modesty when discussing their powers, lest they anger the spirits who have helped them accomplish their deeds. This humility may preclude open boastfulness about one's impressive powers or overt mention of one's proven success rate.

The shaman may also figure, however, as a memorable character in the narratives of others. Shamans may be recalled for their heroic deeds or suspected of underhanded or mean-spirited dealings. The Ho-Chunk (Winnebago) elder Crashing Thunder reported having heard accounts of his ancestors' spirit quests from his father at the time of his own period of fasting (Radin 1926: 25–6). Community members learned and retold the supernatural experience narratives of prominent community members, thereby helping secure these persons' reputations as spiritually blessed or gifted within their communities. The narratives also helped establish or maintain a community's shared notions of what spiritual journeys consist of, and how they may unfold as events or as performances.

Knud Rasmussen (1921) collected both positive and negative stories about *angakut* during his expeditions among Inuit people. In a positive example, he heard a former client tell about a shaman named Nivigkana, who had entered into trance in order to heal another community member's sled dog. In her trance, Nivigkana saw that a spirit had stolen the soul of the dog in question. According to her own account, Nivigkana had boldly demanded the spirit to return the dog's soul and predicted that the dog would get better as a result. Rasmussen's grateful informant noted: "It [the dog] did recover, and Nivigkana's fame spread through the village" (1921: 155). Nivigkana's role in the healing was first conveyed by her own narrative of her spirit journey. But the spread of her fame in the village can be attributed to persons like Rasmussen's informant, who recounted the healing to others and praised her success.

Carmen Blacker (1975: 242–4) notes the case of a Japanese shamanic practitioner Mrs. Hiroshima Ryūun, whose healing exploits were carefully recorded by a pupil in a manuscript book. Spanning the shaman's long career, the manuscript recounted details of the healer's exciting, sometimes harrowing, experiences, carefully set down for posterity. Blacker gained access to the book through the healer's daughter, who still conserved the text some decades after its completion.

Thai notes that when a Hmong shaman is unsuccessful in aiding a patient, the patient is simply encouraged to try a different shaman. The tutelary spirits of shamans vary in their powers and interests, and the fact that one shaman's treatment was unsuccessful does not preclude the possibility that another's might yield positive results. In many traditions, however, shamans may become locked in fierce competition for clients, or may find themselves pitted against each other by rival villages or clans. George Hunt, a man of Tlingit and English ancestry served as Franz Boas's linguistic informant for Kwagul language. Hunt recounted his own experience of shamanic competition after he healed a very ill woman of the Gwetela Kwagul (Kwakiutl). A more experienced shaman of the vicinity, a Walas Kwagul man named Aíx:ag:idālag:îlis, had boasted that he was the only real shaman around, yet he had repeatedly failed in his attempts to heal the woman. Hunt, known by his shaman name Qāselid, performed an impressive healing ritual which involved seemingly sucking the disease out of the patient and displaying it to the community as a bloody worm. Immediately after this treatment the woman recovered (Boas 1930: 29). The patient's father expressed his gratitude to Hunt and his wife but warned them of the envy of the other local shamans, particularly Aíx:ag:idālag:îlis:

"Now take care, look out, you and your wife, for all the men see in the minds of the shamans that they are ashamed for what you did last night. I mean this, that you should be careful of them," said he. (1930: 30)

In Hunt's account, Aíx:ag:idālag:îlis eventually sends for Hunt and asks for his help:

It won't be bad what we say to each other, friend, but only I wish you to try and save my life for me, so that I may not die of shame, for I am a plaything of our people on account of what you did last night. I pray you to have mercy and tell me … Was it the true sickness [you took] or was it only made up? For I beg you to have mercy and tell me about the way you did it so that I can imitate you. (1930: 31)

Hunt extracted from his colleague details of all his sleights of hand and other tricks, but did not divulge his own technique for simulating the extraction of a worm from a patient. Soon after, the older shaman left the vicinity, shamed by his loss of reputation among his community:

[H]e went away for shame on account of the talking of all the men, for they said he should be ashamed because he did not let all the men see the sickness of the sick person that he referred to as the thing sucked out of him; for always many blankets were paid to him, and a large canoe was paid to him, when the sick one was a respected person. (Boas 1930: 33)

Hunt was warned to avoid Aíx:ag:idālag:îlis if he should come upon him, since the latter might well retaliate for his loss of status by murdering his rival.

Scholars have often attributed such conflicts to economics, positing that shamans vie with each other in order to monopolize the healing practices of a given locale and thereby generate greater profits for themselves. Yet ethnographic reports often reveal that shamans make little sustained profit from their activities, or that their income fluctuates wildly according to the wherewithal of their clients. Karen Smyers records the up-and-down income of *odaisan* shamans associated with Japanese Inari shrines:

Their income is highly erratic: most on principle will not charge a set fee but trust the client to give what she can. Yoshiba-san had no money at all one day; the next day, a satisfied client arrived with a gift of 1 million yen ($8,000 at that time). The money was soon gone, however, for she made generous donations to the offering boxes of the *kami* [spirits] at the shrine in thanks for this boon. She trusted that her *kami* would take care of her and that when she was again reduced to nothing, someone else would come through – and this did seem to happen. (1999: 41)

Rather than looking to monetary gain as the main source of shamanic motivation, more recent ethnographers have focused on other forms of compensation: e.g., the establishment of the shaman in a personally meaningful profession, the shaman's integration into a grateful and supportive community. Often, the shaman's sense of self-worth, both within the community and within the spirit world, is based on continued and effective rendering of shamanic services, so that the curtailment of these activities could lead to an identity crisis.

Given such high stakes in terms of career, self-respect, and reputation, shamanic traditions often possess particular performative venues which allow shamans to compete openly without loss of life. Verbal duels or other activities permit rival shamans to display their skills and determine whose spirits or personal gifts are of greatest significance, while endangering neither's life nor potential as a source of future healing. Success in these shamanic contests could also enhance a shaman's reputation and bolster successes in healing or other services. We will explore such verbal genres in greater detail in Chapter 11.

OUTSIDERS

Although shamans frequently arise and live out their performative careers within their own families, clans, or villages, outsiders may sometimes function as shamanic professionals as well. Barbara Tedlock (2001) notes that, cross-culturally, shamanic diviners are often cultural outsiders, persons whose cultural or personal alterity contribute to the aura of supernatural acuity key to a successful career. George Hunt, too, was a foreigner in some respects to the communities in which he functioned as a shaman. His wife's Kwagul culture was quite distinct from either his mother's Tlingit society or the culture of his English father. Perhaps it was in part his alterity that led to his success in the healings he described to Boas. Bogoras notes several Chukchi shamans who were popular among the Russian population as healers, one in particular who had become known by the epithet *shamanchik* ("little shaman") (Bogoras 1904–9: 424). Thai, too, notes that soon after his arrival in the United States, he was consulted by an Anglo-American who asked Thai to cure him. The man had read about Thai in a local newspaper and sought him out for help. Thai noted that he had been able to heal the man and that he had been paid rather handsomely. In Thai's view, any person who needs help is a suitable patient for him and his spirit helpers.

At the same time, shamans often pointed to outsiders – particularly skeptical ethnographers – as factors that diminished the effectiveness of their séances. Particularly when the outsiders were openly dubious or dismissive, these attitudes could greatly undermine the efficacy of the ritual for both the shaman and the community. Peter Freuchen described for Knud Rasmussen an elaborate séance he attended among Inuit people (Hunt 2002: 30–6). After several hours of chanting and other ritual activities, in which the *angakok* Sorqaq seemingly disappeared into the spirit world and only slowly returned, the aged shaman supplied the community with the following explanation of their recent misfortunes:

The Great Spirits are embarrassed by the presence of white men among us and will not reveal the reason for the accidents. Three deaths are still to come. So as to avoid more tragedies, our women must refrain from eating of the female walrus until the winter darkness returns. (2002: 36)

DEATH

From the beginning of the shaman's career, death is always a close and likely event. The psychic transformation experienced during the shaman's first calling, the shaman's repeated spiritual journeys into unseen worlds, the negotiations with the souls of others – all of these experiences either threaten the shaman's life or provide a foretaste of the condition of the soul after death. In the perspective of many shamans, every ritual experience may prove fatal, as the shaman relies on wit and the goodwill of spirit helpers to tackle opponents of otherwise unsurpassable power. Death is eventually inevitable, for the shaman as for all human beings.

Caroline Humphrey (1996) notes the importance of Daur shamans after their deaths. The spiritual transformation that brought them into a shamanic career has changed their natures so profoundly that they are never the same as other human beings again, even after death. The *yadgan*'s body was thus disposed of in a special manner: placed above the ground and equipped with the shaman's mirror and other tools, which were hung from a nearby bier. From here, the *yadgan* would be able to merge with the tutelary *onggor*, ready to reach out to a new adept in the coming generation. In the meantime, the *yadgan*'s grave was recalled as a place of power and danger, where a lack of proper reverence could result in serious illness or madness.

In the 1950s, Vilmos Diószegi (1968) was able to visit the grave of a Tuva shaman that had remained undisturbed since the shaman's death many years earlier. In this case, too, the body had been placed above ground, surrounded by the shaman's paraphernalia as well as offerings of food and drink. Diószegi writes:

It is a quiet birch grove, undisturbed by human steps … The corpse of the shamaness is already lying on the ground, a few thick, decaying branches are spread around it. The reindeer jacket is torn, wild beasts and dogs might have destroyed it. The wooden dishes are empty, the teacup contains but rainwater, or melted snow. But, the shaman's staff, put up against the birch-tree, still stands there triumphantly! Careful hands tied it to the trunk, it cannot fall, the falling leaves could not yet hide it. The snow, the rain and the sun had faded the colours of the ribbons, but they are still fluttering in the breeze, even now. (1968: 255)

Neither Diószegi nor his Tuvan companions dared disturb the grave, but rather left it to continue its slow dissolution into the elements of nature.

Shamanic traditions often share particular ideas regarding the death of a shaman. The shaman's spirit may be welcomed into a separate afterlife location, as was noted in Chapter 4, or may return to the human community as the tutelary spirit of the next generation's shaman, as Thai notes in his own clan. Before dying, the shaman may select an heir to the powers or spiritual relations at the core of the shamanic calling or simply allow the spirits to make their own selection in the future. Although Bogoras (1904–9: 225) reported meeting Chukchi elders who had retired from a shamanic calling and now apparently lived perfectly ordinary lives, the idea of a life-long transformation into an interlocutor with the spirits is very widespread cross-culturally and reflects the tremendous notoriety of the shaman's profession in its traditional contexts (see Chapter 5). Whether destined from birth to become a shaman or transformed into one through processes of election or ordeal, the shaman's eventual spiritual distinctiveness finds expression in a funerary tradition often entirely distinct from that surrounding other deaths in the community.

Singular in spiritual experience and yet highly social in professional function and career, the shaman depends upon the ambient family, clan, or community as strongly as the community depends on the shaman. Recourse to supernatural assistance is a resource of tremendous value to a community, particularly one with a small number of members, great dependency on the vagaries of hunting, fishing, and gathering, and limited means of addressing serious threats like disease or misfortune. In this context, the shaman often plays a central role and is accorded prestige, or perhaps fear, in recognition of this fact. Although shamans may describe their callings first and foremost through reference to spiritual interlocutors, it is often their human communities which spell the success or frustration of a shamanic career. For the shaman cannot mediate between the supernatural and human if the human community does not deign to participate in the act. The loss of shamanic careers through cultural and religious change is a topic we will examine in more detail in Chapter 12. It is poignant to recognize the fragility of a shamanic calling that, on the one hand, seems to offer nearly unlimited recourse to supernatural aid but which, on the other hand, may be foiled by the skepticism, hostility, or dismissal of a decidedly human community. The shaman of traditional shamanism is an intensely social being, one serving a community whose interests ultimately animate both the shaman and the spirit world.

PART III

Examining ritual effectiveness

CHAPTER 7

Séance, trance, and the shamanic mind

"A first definition of this complex phenomenon, and perhaps the least hazard-ous will be: shamanism = technique of ecstasy" (Eliade 1964: 5). So states Mircea Eliade, in a work which would come to define the study of shamanism for much of the second half of the twentieth century. For Eliade, *ecstasy* here entailed at least three distinct features: a particular psychological and physio-logical state (i.e., "trance"), a set of techniques used to induce it, and a culturally (or more precisely, mythologically) shaped set of understandings of the cosmic events occurring during the state itself. Writes Eliade: "the shaman specializes in a trance during which his soul is believed to leave his body and ascend to the sky or descend to the underworld" (1964: 5). This view represented more-or-less the consensus of the earlier ethnographies Eliade used as his sources, and it certainly exercised influence on ethnographers who came after him as well. Few subsequent scholars have rejected the centrality or defining role of trance in the study of shamanism, although some more recent scholars (e.g., Hamayon 1993) have certainly begun to question this scholarly tradition. So essential indeed did the trance appear to scholars at the beginning of the twentieth century, that Waldemar Bogoras (1904–9) depicts Chukchi shamanism in devolutionary terms chiefly because it seemed to lack frequent and powerful trance states:

In other cases the shaman actually "sinks"; that is, after some most violent singing, and beating of the drum, he falls into a kind of trance, during which his body lies on the ground unconscious, while his soul visits "spirits" in their own world, and asks them for advice. Chukchee folk-lore is full of episodes referring to such shamanistic trances; but in real life they happen very rarely, especially in modern times, when shamans are so much less skilful, than of old. (1904–9: 441)

According to Bogoras, Chukchi shamans of his day seldom, if ever, achieved trance state, even if they simulated it at times: "In important cases, even at the present day, the shamans, when treating a well-to-do patient, will at least pretend to have sunk into the required unconsciousness" (1904–9: 441). This chapter focuses on this "required unconsciousness" as an implement and an ideal of shamanic practice. How do shamans achieve this state – if it is customary for them to do so – and what happens physiologically during unconsciousness? What alternatives to unconscious trance exist within shamanic traditions and how are these alternatives managed within the shaman's performative economy?

Where Chapters 4 and 5 focused on the cosmology of shamanic traditions, and the frequent destinations of shamanic spirit flight as reported within practitioners' narratives, this chapter summarizes the vast amount of scholarship that has been generated to describe and explain the shamanic trance from an outside, "objective" perspective. The studies examined in this chapter can at times appear ironic, in that they often both seek to see the trance as if through the shaman's own eyes – i.e., arriving at a precise understanding of the perceptions and emotions associated with the state of shamanic ecstasy – and yet may reject or set aside the shaman's own explanations regarding the supernatural nature of the visions and sensations experienced. Scholars have tended to gloss the shamanic trance as a psychological or even pathological event rather than as a spiritual experience. In the most recent cognitive studies of trance states, however, scholarly agendas have begun to shift, as we shall see: researchers today often strive to reconcile biological and cognitive findings with shamans' own descriptions or experiences of altered states, recognizing the shamanic trance as a powerful and adaptive element of human religiosity. It is this burgeoning area of shamanic research today which we explore in the following pages.

THE PHENOMENOLOGY OF TRANCE

F. A. Anisimov observed an Evenki (Tungus) séance during fieldwork in Siberia in 1931. His description helps illustrate what scholars of shamanism have come to think of as the "classic" trance experience. The séance took place at night inside a tent. The shaman, aided by an assistant and dressed in special ritual garb, took his place on a small platform. He was surrounded by representations of his spirit helpers. As the fire was damped, the shaman began drumming, swaying, and singing. The assembled community joined in on the chorus of the invocation songs that he began with, until after some time, the shaman began to improvise lines of his own, calling to his spirit helpers for assistance. By listening to the shaman's song (as we discuss further in Chapter 9), the audience could discover what the various spirit helpers looked like and whether they came willingly or unwillingly to help in the present task: the healing of a patient's illness. As the spirits began to arrive, the community could hear the sounds of their cries, snorts, and flapping, punctuated at times by cessation or resumption of the shaman's loud and sometimes rapid drumming. They could also hear the shaman's instructions to the spirits, ordering them to guard the tent or to set out toward one or another spirit realm to learn the cause of the patient's illness. Chief among the attending spirits was the *khargi*, an animal double of the shaman. The shaman's performance became more and more frenzied, as he sang, drummed, and danced loudly, acting out the heroic journey of the *khargi* in pursuit of the sought-after knowledge. Anisimov continues:

The shaman leaped into the air, whirled with the help of the tent thongs, imitating the running and flight of his spirits, reached the highest pitch of ecstasy, and fell foaming at the mouth on the rug which had been spread out in the meanwhile. The assistant fanned the fire and bent over the shaman's stiffened, lifeless body. The latter, representing at this moment his *khargi* in the land of the *khergu* (the world of the dead), was outside of this seeming corpse. The assistant, fearing that the shaman might not return to the land of *dulu* (the middle world), persuaded him to return as quickly as possible from the lower world, orienting himself by the light of the fire which he (the assistant) had kindled in the tent. The shaman began to show signs of life. A weak, half-understandable babble was heard – the barely audible voices of the spirits. They signified that the *khargi* and the spirits accompanying him were returning to the middle world. The shaman's assistant put his ear to the shaman's lips and in a whisper repeated to those present everything that the shaman said was happening at the time to the *khargi* and his spirits. The shaman's weak, barely audible whisper changed into a loud mutter, unconnected snatches of sentences and wild cries. The helper took the drum, warmed it over the fire, and started to beat it, entreating the shaman (that is, his *khargi*) not to get lost on the road, to look more fixedly at the light of the tent fire, and to listen more closely for the sound of the drum. The drum sounded faster and louder in the hands of the assistant; the shaman's outcries became ever clearer and more distinct. The drum sounded still louder, calling the shaman, and finally became again the accompaniment of ecstasy. The shaman leapt up and began to dance the shamanistic pantomime dance symbolizing the return of the *khargi* and his attendant spirits to the middle world (*dulu*). The shaman's dance became more and more peaceful, its movements slow. Finally, its tempo slowed, the dance broke off. The shaman hung on the thongs, swaying from side to side in time with the drum. (quoted in Siikala 1978: 233–4)

From here, the shaman was able to relate the advice he had received from ancestors regarding the illness and its expulsion. The remainder of the séance involved continued drumming, dancing, and oratory, during which the shaman offered the spirit of the disease a sacrifice (a reindeer), and cajoled, threatened, and finally forced it to depart from the patient. Capturing the spirit, the shaman's helping spirits were depicted in song and oratory harrying it mercilessly, before the shaman, dancing and singing wildly, carried it to the lower world to be abandoned there. The shaman then identified the rival clan and shaman who had sent the disease, and directed his *khargi* to seek out and punish these aggressors. Finally, the shaman danced an ascent into the sky, where he was able to entrust the soul of the patient to the protection of celestial deities, including the Christian God (Siikala 1978: 235–7).

Two centuries earlier, the Norwegian missionary Jens Kildal described a similar trance ritual among Sámi people. His account of the séance runs as follows:

When a Sámi has become seriously ill people believe that his soul has left his body for Jápme-aimo [the land of the dead] and the *noaide* and all neighboring Sámi and relatives are fetched, and a *noaide* meeting is held. The assembled pray for the sick person in a *joik* song, asking Jápme-áhkká [the goddess of the dead] to release the patient's soul so that it may return to its body. Meanwhile, the *noaide* makes magic to this end, drinks aquavite, and is affected; he walks violently around on his knees, takes glowing fire in his hands, cuts his hands with a knife, and takes hold of the magic drum in order to beat it. After having behaved this way with great eagerness for a long while he falls down dead to the ground and remains lying there breathless for three quarters of an hour. During this time he undertakes a journey down into Jápme-aimo in the guise of his *basseváreguolle* [fish spirit helper] in order to negotiate with Jápme-áhkká about sacrifices to her in return for the patient's soul, so that he may bring the latter with him up from Jápme-aimo and back to the sick person. While [the rescue] in Jápme-aimo depends on the promise of the *noaide* about such and such a big sacrifice for the release of the soul from there, it sometimes depends on the speed of the *noaide* that, with the aid of his *basseváreguolle*, he may catch the soul from the dead without their noticing it.

All the time the *noaide* lies there breathless a woman continuously sings *joik* eagerly, partly to remind him of his task in Jápme-aimo, partly to revive him; and for this highly necessary singing she will be paid by the *noaide*.

When *basseváreguolle* has brought the *noaide* unharmed up from Jápme-aimo and back into his own body he begins to draw breath and to move. Then he relates how his journey was and how big a sacrifice he had to promise Jápme-áhkká before he, with the help of his *basseváreguolle*, received from her the sick person's soul that he carried with him back again. (quoted in Bäckman and Hultkrantz 1977: 45; spellings modernized)

Kildal's account appears more a characterization of typical shamanic séances rather than an explicit recounting of a single occasion. Nonetheless, with a Sámi wife and considerable expertise in Sámi language, his description is probably fairly accurate.

Both Anisimov's and Kildal's descriptions contain a number of features typical of North Eurasian trance induction, including rapid drumming and singing, intense, painful activity and hyperventilation, and an eventual collapse into rigid and inert trance. The return to consciousness is followed by a narrative account of what the heroic shaman has witnessed, as well as (in the case of Anisimov's Evenki séance) a resumption of the musical performance. As we shall see below, the "debriefing" stage may also involve extended communal investigation concerning what the shaman's visions might mean. The ritual's aftermath is marked by the shaman's sense of euphoria and exhaustion (Siikala 1978: 44).

THE PHYSIOLOGY OF TRANCE

Michael Winkelman (1986, 1992, 2000) has explored the physiological nature of shamanic trance, locating its sources and mechanisms within the brain. Particularly important in this respect is the hypothalamus, which controls both the sympathetic nervous system (operative during waking states) and the parasympathetic nervous system (operative during relaxation and sleep). By sending nearly instantaneous chemical messages to the adrenal medulla, the hypothalamus can relax muscles and slow heart rate and breathing, conserving the body's energy during sleep. According to Winkelman, the kinds of physical collapse described in Anisimov's account can be regarded as instances of sudden complete parasympathetic dominance, from which the person only slowly recovers as the hypothalamus gradually returns dominance to the sympathetic nervous system.

In evolutionary terms the hypothalamus belongs to the oldest part of the brain and exercises broad control over muscular responses to states such as anger, hostility, and pleasure. It in turn is modulated by a part of the "younger brain," the cerebrum, specifically the temporal lobes. These bilaterally symmetrical regions of the cerebrum are responsible for hearing, memory, and the limbic system (i.e., emotions). Two small centers within each temporal lobe, the hippocampi, play a central role in the limbic system, memory, and spatial navigation. It has been discovered experimentally that certain stimuli can "drive" the septal nuclei of the hippocampi to relay a message to the hypothalamus, causing it in turn to induce parasympathetic dominance. These driving agents include many of the stimuli typically found in shamanic séances, such as rhythmic music, fasting, extensive motor behavior, stereotypy of movement, pain, meditation, and various hallucinogens. Crucially, once this parasympathetic collapse has occurred for the first time, the brain's resistance to it lessens in the future, a phenomenon known as "kindling." It becomes progressively easier, in other words, to fall into trance. In a process known as "tuning," the shaman can further train the brain to enter the trance state as an easy, nearly automatic, response to certain ritual behaviors, such as singing, dancing, or drumming. Ideally, Winkelman theorizes, this kindling and tuning are key parts of the shamanic initiation process, by which the shaman comes to have control over the onset and cessation of trance states.

Scholars can recognize the altered state of consciousness described above not only by the physical disposition of the body, but also by observations of brain waves produced by various regions of the brain during trance. These waves are measurable by electroencephalography (EEG). In normal waking life, the brain displays desynchronized, relatively fast-wave activity dominated by the frontal cortex of the cerebrum (Winkelman 2000: 76). As the various parts of the brain attend to the myriad stimuli and processing typical of waking activities, they each produce their own electric waves, generally falling into the category of "beta waves," with a frequency of 13–40 cycles per second. Once the hippocampal septal areas of the temporal lobes are driven to induce trance, however, they begin producing alpha waves, typical of sleep and imaginative states. These waves are slower, 8–13 cycles per second, and are characteristic of the optic lobe in particular. This slow-wave activity then spreads to the frontal lobes, causing the entire brain to begin to produce alpha as well as theta waves (4–7 cycles per second), which become deeply synchronized. These features constitute the distinctive brain-wave profile of an altered state, which can be recognized cross-culturally in persons undergoing trance and which correlates with percipients' experience of visions of various kinds. Winkelman suggests that the physiological characteristics of these altered states serve as the experiential basis of shamanic traditions worldwide. He writes:

Shamanistic traditions have arisen throughout the world because of the interaction of innate structures of the human brain-mind with the ecological and social conditions of hunter-gatherer societies. This is possible because this altered state of consciousness basic to selection, training, and professional activities occurs spontaneously under a wide variety of circumstances. These altered state of consciousness experiences can be induced naturally as a consequence of injury, extreme fatigue, near starvation, ingestion of hallucinogens, perceptions of natural phenomena, bioelectric discharges, or as a consequence of a wide variety of deliberate procedures that induce these conditions ... Consequently, shamanism was reinvented or rediscovered in diverse cultures as a result of those experiences and because the experiences provide important adaptive capabilities. (2000: 77)

Research along these lines contributes to a movement within ethnography known as the "anthropology of consciousness" as well as the psychological movement known as "neurotheology" or the "cognitive science of religion." These interrelated scholarly enterprises seek to locate the causes or features of human religious behaviors in the structures and functioning of the human mind (see Persinger 1987; McKinney 1994, Ramachandran and Blakeslee 1998; Newberg, D'Aquili, and Rause 2001; Whitehouse 2004; Austin 2006; Tremlin 2006). Scholars posit that supernatural experiences as such are either natural perceptions of complex brain functions or evolutionarily adaptive responses to stimuli such as pain, illness, and threat. Significantly, Winkelman's theory of shamanic trance offers an ahistorical means of explaining the widespread distribution and continuity of shamanic traditions around the world: rather than regarding shamanic traditions as a set of practices which arose in one place and gradually spread, in other words, Winkelman suggests that shamanic trance may have been repeatedly discovered due to recurrent tendencies in the human brain.

TRANCE AND EPILEPSY

Early ethnographers noted an occasionally significant correlation between epilepsy and shamanism. As a result, scholars posited that shamanism functions to provide both an explanation and a purpose for epileptic seizures. Temporal lobe epilepsy is a medical condition in which portions of one or both of the temporal lobes frequently experience seizures. These neurological disturbances can involve varying parts of the temporal lobes, but the neocortex, hippocampi, and amygdalae often figure as key regions. Given the role of the hippocampi (and possibly also the amygdalae) in the trance states described above, it is easy to note the possible connections between epileptic tendencies and trance-state facility.

Researchers on epilepsy have differentiated seizures on the basis of relative gravity (Commission on Classification and Terminology of the International League Against Epilepsy 1981). At the slightest level, the person experiencing a seizure may notice differences in sensation: a feeling of strange familiarity (*déjà vu*), unfamiliarity (*jamais vu*), or even amnesia. The person may also experience powerful emotions such as happiness, anger, or fear, or perceive sounds, smells, or tastes which are not readily apparent to others in the vicinity. More significant in magnitude and duration are seizures that involve larger portions of the temporal lobes and that result in noticeably altered states of consciousness. In these, the epileptic may stare, remain motionless, display altered or unusual speech, or move parts of the body involuntarily. At the most severe level, such seizures may spread beyond the temporal lobe to the rest of the brain, leading to marked physical effects, including muscle spasms, foaming at the mouth, stiffened torso or limbs, involuntary urination, loss of muscle tone, and shallow or even stifled breathing. A victim of this sort of seizure may be thrown to the ground by muscle failure, writhe in seeming pain or confusion, and cry out in apparent anguish as the body becomes rigid and inert. Such features frequently resemble elements of trance states described in ethnographic literature, leading scholars to posit that observed trances were in fact seizures affecting temporal lobe epileptics.

In studies of temporal lobe epileptics, further, Vilayamour Ramachandran (Ramachandran and Blakeslee 1998) found that such individuals often displayed enhanced responses to religiously charged words, images, and symbols. Noting that epileptic patients sometimes have religious experiences during seizures, Ramachandran writes:

God has vouchsafed for us "normal" people only occasional glimpses of a deeper truth ... but these patients enjoy the unique privilege of gazing directly into God's eyes every time they have a seizure. Who is to say whether such experiences are "genuine" (whatever that might mean) or "pathological"? Would you, the physician, really want to medicate such a patient and deny visitation rights to the Almighty? (1998: 179)

Whereas Ramachandran and Blakeslee discuss such experience from a Judeo-Christian perspective, the implication of such evidence is that such seizures in a shamanic religious tradition might well be interpreted as instances of trance. Thus, in such cases, temporal lobe epilepsy could come to be regarded as a physical predilection for shamanic experience and lead the epileptic to be socialized into a shamanic role. In areas where the shamanic calling is said to run in families in particular, a genetic propensity toward epilepsy could become a significant feature in the selection and encouragement of new shamans.

It is important to note, however, that, after a careful review of past research on auditory driving and epileptic seizures, Peggy A. Wright (1991) found no conclusive evidence that the intense rhythms of the typical drumming ceremony may induce seizures in participants with certain varieties of epilepsy. The temporal lobes may show a greater readiness to experience seizure, in other words, but this tendency is not triggered by the procedures typically used to induce trance within the séance. And even if temporal lobe epilepsy may enhance trance induction in certain instances, epilepsy as such is not a *sine qua non* of shamanic function. People in cultures that practice shamanism can function as shamans without epileptic tendencies, and epileptics can go through life without assuming a shamanic role. Further, the frequently involuntary nature of epileptic seizures could prove detrimental to a shaman's status and career, as it would signal to trainers or community an inability to control the spirit world. Ideally, the shaman must be able to call upon both trance states and the spirits when needed, and resist their communications at other times. Entering such states involuntarily might be acceptable for a shaman in training, but would likely prove a liability for the established practitioner.

Merete Jakobsen (1999: 50) cites Birket-Smith's early twentieth-century description of the mental condition of the Greenlandic *angakok*: "Behind all the mad behaviour of the *angakok*, which outsiders often denounce as simple fraud, there lies a disposition of a sick mental life. It is first and foremost highly strung individuals, hysterics and epileptics that perform as *angakut*." Along with epilepsy, hysteria has been posited as a contributing factor to trance susceptibility in many shamanic traditions. The notion that shamanic trance induction arises from a tendency toward hysterical behavior, particularly among peoples living in Arctic regions, arose as a theoretical construct at the turn of the twentieth century. Both Bogoras (1910) and Czaplicka (1914) make claims along these lines, and still in the 1960s, George Devereux (1961) characterized shamans as "neurotics." Bogoras cites numerous examples of Chukchi shamans with strong hysterical and at times suicidal tendencies. Typical is his description of a man named Akímlakê, who often sought weapons during times of ceremonials as a means of killing himself:

Once, at a thanksgiving ceremonial at which I was present, he began his usual search, and came to me, among others, explaining with signs his desire for a knife, in order to be able to destroy himself … I really had a knife on my belt; and a Russian Cossack who sat next me proposed laughingly that I give it to Akímlakê. Hearing this, the women of the house raised a frightened cry. Akímlakê, however, who doubtless was stung by the taunt implied in the words of the Cossack, suddenly picked up from the ground a long, sharp-pointed chip of wood, and, baring his abdomen, put one end of the stick on his body, and the other against my breast. Then he made a thrust forward with the whole weight of his heavy body. The chip, of course, was snapped in two. One end flew up and hit me on the brow very near to the left eye, leaving an ugly gash. The other end cut a deep scratch entirely across the abdomen of Akímlakê. I wonder that it had not been driven in. All this was done so quick that nobody had time to interfere. Akímlakê with much coolness picked up a handful of snow, and, wiping off the blood from his abdomen, quietly went to another tent. In half an hour, when he was no longer thirsting for blood, I asked him about his actions; but he disclaimed all knowledge, and expressed the utmost wonder when showed the bloody scratch on his own abdomen. (1904–9: 442–3)

The psychopathology theory was taken up by other scholars as well. Åke Ohlmarks (1939: 100) saw the Arctic's brutal environment and distinctive light regimen as the very cradle of shamanism, and suggested that shamans further south were obliged to find other ways of inducing trance once the tradition migrated out of the Arctic region. Hallucinogens, as well as "feigned" trance, became in Ohlmarks's view signs of a devolution from the pristine hysterical conditions of the tradition's place of origin (see Chapter 9). Although such theories lost ground in the post-war era, they found partial echo in the writings of later figures, such as Ernst Arbman (1970).

The psychopathology theory rested in part on the notion of "culture-bound syndromes" – the idea that particular cultures or societies are plagued with distinctive, sometimes unique, forms of mental illness. In the Arctic regions, various culturally identified ailments – including the Sakha (Yakut) *menerik*, the Nenets and Khanty *omeriachenie* (a Russian term), and the Inuit *pibloktoq* became viewed as evidence of a pan-Arctic tendency toward severe hysterical episodes, which in turn could serve as the experiential basis of shamanic trance. Art Leete (1999) details the manner in which Russian scholars made frequent use of such somatic models in characterizing the behaviors of indigenous Siberians whom they observed. Recent research on the topic of culture-bound syndromes, or folk illnesses, has pointed out, however, that adoption of folk categories as empirical facts holds many pitfalls, particularly since the terms used within ordinary culture for perceived illnesses are extremely variable and imprecise (Simons and Hughes 1985; Prince and Tcheng-Laroche 1987). Both Thomas Miller (1999) and Lyle Dick (1995) have pointed out, further, that folk constructs of illness became inextricable parts of a colonial enterprise when they entered Western medical and anthropological discourse, serving to further exoticize, infantilize, and disempower Native populations.

Lyle Dick (1995) presents a cogent argument to this effect in a careful review of scholarship regarding Inuit *pibloktoq*. Dick shows, for instance, that the term *pibloktoq* originates in 1894 in the travel journal of Josephine Diebitsch-Peary, who transcribed it as she heard it pronounced by an Inuit guide. Diebitsch-Peary was accompanying her husband, the polar explorer Robert Peary, to Northumberland Island at the time. There, she witnessed an Inuit woman's powerful emotional outburst at seeing Peary and his company in her village. Robert Peary would later refer to such outbursts as a culture-specific hysteria in his popular polar accounts of 1907 and 1910, writing: "the adults are subject to a peculiar nervous affection which they call *piblokto* – a form of hysteria" (quoted in Dick 1995: 3). Peary's assessment in turn led the New York psychiatrist A. A. Brill, a prominent Freudian of the time, to write a scholarly paper on the condition, establishing *pibloktoq* as a scholarly verity (Dick 1995: 3). Yet, as Dick (1995: 10) shows, no such Native term actually existed in Eastern Canadian or Western Greenlandic dialects of Inuktitut. Dick suggests that the actual term Diebitsch-Peary may have heard could be *pilugpoq* ("he/she is in a bad way"), *perdlerorpoq* ("he/she is mad"), *perdlerpoq* ("he/she is starving"), or *pirdlerortoq* ("a drum dance fit"), terms that indicate a wide array of different phenomena. Further, such bouts of putative hysteria seemed to arise particularly in response to the stresses of Inuit contact with Euro-Americans, and with Peary in particular, whose mania for reaching the North Pole led him to make considerable, and often unreasonable, demands of his Native crews. Bouts of putative hysteria often freed men from dangerous tasks they were being ordered to do, and may have rescued Inuit women from the sexual advances of white men whom they were expected to serve in various ways. Writes Dick:

"Pibloktoq" did not constitute a specific disorder but rather encompassed a multiplicity of behaviors associated with Inuhuit psychological distress. These apparently included reactions of acute anxiety, symptoms of physical (and perhaps feigned) illness, expressions of resistance to patriarchy and possible sexual coercion, and shamanistic practice. What these diverse phenomena shared in common was that they were largely confined to the early twentieth century, and often precipitated by the stresses of early contact with Euro-Americans. (1995: 23)

By the 1930s, reports of "pibloktoq" had virtually disappeared, although the medical and anthropological literature remained convinced of its existence. Medical researchers, for their part, have suggested that the symptoms reported could stem possibly from calcium deficiencies (Dick 1995: 3) or overconsumption of vitamin A (Landy 1985), or from mental disturbances arising from the distinctive light cycle of the Arctic region. The reported outbursts' association with shamanic rituals in a number of the accounts may reflect Euro-American misunderstandings of the ritual acts individuals undertook in response to the crisis situations they faced.

Eliade (1964) noted the prevalence of psychopathology among shamans, but rejected either the notion of an Arctic predominance in its manifestation or its centrality for defining the nature or role of shamans in general. He writes:

The alleged Arctic origin of shamanism does not necessarily arise from the nervous instability of peoples living too near the Pole and from epidemics peculiar to the north above a certain latitude ... [S]imilar psychopathic phenomena are found almost throughout the world. That such maladies nearly always appear in relation to the vocation of medicine men is not at all surprising. Like the sick man, the religious man is projected onto a vital plane that shows him the fundamental data of human existence, that is, solitude, danger, hostility of the surrounding world. But the primitive magician, the medicine man, or the shaman is not only a sick man; he is, above all, a sick man who has been cured, who has succeeded in curing himself. (1964: 27)

For Eliade, it is this fact of being cured – of having gained control over one's psychic trials – that allows the shaman to function effectively within the community. Personal and spiritual pain becomes a foundation for helping others. Writes Eliade: "shamans, for all their apparent likeness to epileptics and hysterics, show proof of a more than normal nervous constitution; they achieve a degree of concentration beyond the capacity of the profane; they sustain exhausting efforts; they control their ecstatic movements, and so on" (1964: 29). Siikala (1978: 47), echoing Eliade's view, adds further that shamans must use their trance state to meet very high expectations from their patients and communities. Rather than simply giving way to personal emotions and views (as in hysteria), the shaman must marshal the visions and perceptions received for specific instrumental ends aimed at helping other people, doing so with an authority and a confidence that convince both community and patient of divine assistance. In this sense, the shaman behaves in a manner nothing like the hysteric (Walsh 1997).

TRANCE AND SCHIZOPHRENIA

Richard Noll (1983) confronts another long-standing assumption among Western ethnographers, i.e., that shamans are in fact schizophrenics. Noll cogently demonstrates the invalidity of this assumption on the basis of clinical definitions of schizophrenia itself. According to Noll, schizophrenics and shamans differ in at least five key areas. First, where the schizophrenic experiences altered states of consciousness as involuntary events which impair normal life and impede goal-oriented activities, the shaman learns to move voluntarily between normal and altered states of consciousness, employing the latter for specific goal-directed ends, such as healing, divination, or communication with the spirit world. Second, the schizophrenic's hallucinations tend to be derogatory and auditory in nature, while the shaman experiences primarily positive and visual communications. Although the shaman may also report some auditory sensations, Noll maintains that the visual component is far more central to the shaman's experience. Third, the schizophrenic becomes delusional through an inability to distinguish normal from altered states of consciousness. The schizophrenic's world thus becomes jumbled and disordered, and the schizophrenic may easily become paranoid and confused as a result. In contrast, Noll argues, the shaman's world is divided into highly ordered and clearly differentiated worlds: the normal realm of the everyday, and the highly charged supernatural realm of the spirit world. This latter world can only be accessed through specific rituals undertaken by individuals with special gifts. As a valued medium, the shaman acquires a positive and confident view of self. Fourth, the schizophrenic's experiences are patently maladaptive, impairing normal function and relations, while the shaman's experiences are explicitly adaptive: highly valued skills that the community gratefully acknowledges and makes use of. Finally, perhaps in response to the above differences, the schizophrenic frequently displays a flattened emotional affect, becoming detached and often depressive, while, in contrast, the shaman not only displays a heightened personal affect but becomes highly attuned to the needs and feelings of other people, particularly patients and their supporting community members. From Noll's perspective, then, past ethnographers' frequent and indiscriminate application of psychological terms like *neurosis* and *schizophrenia* greatly distort scholarly appraisals of shamanic states, careers, and social status. Such pronouncements, Noll argues, are essentially amateur misdiagnoses and ignore the salient points of the diagnostic criteria developed within clinical psychology itself.

TRANCE AS VISION

Although the shamanic trance may prove an intense psychological state in itself, Noll (1985) argues in a later article that shamanic traditions cultivate trance not for its mental characteristics but for its usefulness in obtaining and sharing visions. For Noll, "mental imagery cultivation" is a prime aim of shamanic training, and possibly the primary goal of trance experiences. Noll identifies a series of steps by which shamanic trainees learn to experience and recount their visions. At the initial stage of training, a novice shaman reports trance experiences to elders or more experienced shamans. These individuals then help the neophyte fit the visions into the tradition's *"mundus imaginalis"* – the communally shaped understandings of the supernatural world and its communicative predilections. In successive narration of such visions, the trainer helps the neophyte hone and develop areas of the vision that hold the greatest resonance for the community (e.g., visual descriptions and particular details or impressions) while downplaying aspects which depart significantly from the established tradition. Key to trainers' evaluative statements is an interest in concrete detail that can serve to increase the verisimilitude of the report for an audience. The trainers also instruct the neophyte on how to recall the vision, so that the shaman can summon forth a past vision at will for cogitation or recounting. These powerful visions then become part of the shaman's own arsenal for describing the spiritual world and conveying its needs to the community. By listening to the shaman's accounts, the community in turn sees its view of the supernatural confirmed and is encouraged to "remember" the sacral world by reenacting it in specific rituals.

In their interviews with the contemporary Buryat shaman Bayir Rinchinov, Virlana Tkacz, Sayan Zhambalov, and Wanda Phipps (2002) record reminiscences that indicate a cultivation of shamanic vision much like that described by Noll. Bayir Rinchinov describes his interactions with his father as follows:

> I started seeing when I was four ... My father had the gift of sight, but my mother did not. My father understood I also had this special gift and he would ask me very specific questions. If I saw someone on a horse, he would ask me: "What kind of rider do you see? What is he wearing? What color is his horse?" They were very concrete questions because he wanted to understand how clear my visions were, how specific. (2002: 4)

Noll's theories regarding visionary training are supported by recent research in the area of religious memory summarized by Harvey Whitehouse (2004: 105–12). According to Whitehouse, perceptions which occur during intense ritual experiences – such as those associated with shamanic initiations – can result in "flashbulb memories," vivid recollections that may remain virtually unchanged in a person's mind for years, and which are recalled in a precise, sequential ("episodic") form. The events captured in this unique manner within the brain are not mundane: they are usually marked by intensity and a high degree of personal consequence from the point of view of the perceiver (2004: 107). Such memories are apparently generated in part through the strong involvement of the limbic system, particularly the amygdala and/or the hippocampus – i.e., the same brain centers implicated in the onset of shamanic trance. As Whitehouse writes: "There is significant evidence for a distinctive profile of neurological processing associated with the encoding of emotionally arousing memories" (2004: 106).

From this evidence, it is possible to suggest that shamanic visions can exist as flashbulb memories in the shaman's mind. Researchers have further noted that repeated narrativization of such memories – characteristic of the shaman's training as well as professional activities – can reinforce them, adding new layers of significance, "exegesis," perhaps, as noted above, with the input or guidance of the shaman's trainers or community members. The memories become the basis for profound personal reflections, shaped by the cultural knowledge of trainers or community. While victims of post-traumatic stress disorder find themselves unable to control or avoid such flashbulb memories, the shaman learns to call them up purposefully as part of subsequent trance induction or other ritual activities (2004: 110). Finally, Whitehouse notes ethnographic evidence that the act of witnessing others undergoing similar experiences – e.g., the initiation or trance induction of another shaman – can reinforce one's own memories, leading to a supplemental "schematic" memory as well, rich in explanatory detail and specificity useful for future repetition of the ritual itself (2004: 112). In this sense, systems of shamanic training may help maintain understandings of shamanic cosmology and techniques not only for neophytes but for their trainers as well. The novice's visions become part of the collective *mundus imaginalis*, potentially modifying or augmenting that which the community maintained before.

We can glimpse part of this exegesis of vision in Laurel Kendall's (1995) chronicle of the training experiences of a novice *mudang* in contemporary South Korea. Kendall recounts the ways in which more experienced shamans, the novice's trainers, helped interpret and even shape the new initiate's visions. When the shaman-in-training, Chini, saw a vision of the god known as the Heavenly King but failed to say so during the *kut* séance, her trainers Kwan Myŏngnyŏ and Kim Pongsun upbraided her for not sharing the information:

KWAN MYŎNGNYŎ: You get the vision and then you speak. Understand? How can we understand the words of the spirits?

KIM PONGSUN: … If the spirits come up right before your eyes and you don't announce them, then what's the point?

CHINI: Uhm, this time, the Heavenly King appeared; I saw him. I thought it was him; I thought I saw the Heavenly King.

KIM PONGSUN: *Ahyu!* If he appeared, then why didn't you gesture with your hands, "I need a crown like such and such?" [*She demonstrates the appropriate gesture.*] You've got to come out with it. (1995: 46)

Here the young shaman is taught to share details of visions with her trainers, who can then help interpret the memories and recognize details or issues for further elaboration. Such exegesis, as noted above, helps both fix the memories in the shaman's mind and helps shape them, at least in terms of their interpretation. In her professional activities, the *mudang* must learn to act out or recount her visions immediately for the benefit of her audience, whose input will similarly tie the visions to an interpretive framework based on the clients' needs and experiences. Without her cogent performance of the visions, the audience would have no access to the supernatural communications occurring within the shaman's world, and, thus, would not be able to benefit from them.

Just as Western scholars have sought explanations of the trance state or memory recall in the workings of the brain, so the capacity to see visions themselves has been explained as a product of brain function. Ramachandran and Blakeslee (1998: 85–112) suggest that some percipients who report particularly vivid or unusual hallucinatory experiences may have a condition known as Charles Bonnet syndrome. They write: "Charles Bonnet syndrome is extremely common worldwide and affects millions of people whose vision has become compromised by glaucoma, cataracts, macular degeneration or diabetic retinopathy." Percipients see wildly unusual imagery – animals, people, or other objects appearing where they do not seemingly exist, or vivid colors or movements of objects that appear bland and immobile to others. The images appear absolutely realistic within the percipient's mind, while the percipient may also be able to clearly recognize them as figments of the imagination. Citing a British study of elderly people with visual handicaps, they write: "Out of five hundred visually handicapped people, sixty admitted that they hallucinated, sometimes only once or twice a year, but others experienced visual fantasies at least twice a day" (1998: 105). At the same time, they note, "people who have these symptoms are reluctant to mention them to anyone for fear of being labeled crazy" (1998: 87). Hallucinations – complex and creative impositions of the imagination onto the mind's conscious perceptions of the visual field – become sources of embarrassment or unease, attributed to age or a declining intellect. In contrast, the shaman, whether in training or as a mature professional, may receive strong encouragement to share such visions, leading to an appreciation and even cultivation of this particular difference in neural function. Brain researchers are only beginning to understand the complex relations between visual perception and the imagination, relations more evident in the hallucinations of persons whose visual data is limited by impairment, but characteristic of human sight in general.

ALTERNATIVES TO UNCONSCIOUS TRANCE

Although scholars have pointed to unconscious trance states as the core of shamanic spirituality and function, many descriptions of past or present shamanic séances depict trance as a fairly minor part of the overall séance.

In Anisimov's description of the Evenki séance described above, the trance is followed by a wide variety of other ritual behaviors which prove essential for the healing ceremony's effectiveness. Kai Donner's description of a Selkup séance observed between 1911 and 1913 shows a similar tendency:

When the performance begins the fire is allowed to go out in the tent, the witch prepares himself a suitable place at the back of the yurt, opposite the door, and seats himself on a special reindeer skin, and the listeners group themselves around him. Amid utter, tense silence he grasps the drum, standing in front of the fire, sits down again, presses the drum to him, and with noisy yawns begins to show that he is falling asleep and leaving this world. At the same time he puts his cap on his head and having yawned sufficiently sleeps for a moment. On waking he is completely changed, his movements appear unconscious, he is as though in a stupor, he pays no attention to his surroundings, and his voice is altogether different. To begin with he beats the drum very softly and hums wordless tunes or fits in a language unknown to his listeners to his song. He whispers so that the drum booms, he whistles, yawns and moans. It sounds as though various animals are running round the sides of the drum and their sounds echo on every side. In this way he summons all his assistants, the spirits and animals of the air and the underworld. Gradually the drumming grows faster, becoming rhythmical, and the shaman begins to sing his song. (quoted in Siikala 1978: 212–13)

From here, the shaman goes on to narrate his spirit journeys, discovers the spirit needing placation, and dramatically negotiates the size and nature of the sacrifice to be made, all in the hearing of the assembled community. Once this information has been conveyed to the community, the séance ends with the shaman's return to an unconscious state:

He drinks a few cupfuls of water, prays for the last time that he may be set free, and falls to the ground. The performance is over, the spirit has returned to his body and the witch falls into a sleep which may last for many hours. (1978: 214)

In this account, it is clear that the shaman has concourse with the spirit world and that states of unconsciousness are experienced or depicted, yet the bulk of the séance occurs through a conscious form of altered state.

In discussing trance experiences, Thai reported a similar situation. During the ceremonies that involve spirit travel, Thai retains the ability to hear the people around his physical body, although their voices grow fainter as his concentration focuses on the spirits and the spirit travel at the center of the ritual. For Thai, the trance state is one of attending to two simultaneous realities, a visible world seen by his clients and assistants, and a spiritual world experienced uniquely by him. His verbalizations of what he is seeing and hearing allow his audience to comprehend the ritual's mechanisms, constituting a blow-by-blow account which, Thai notes, has great importance for the effectiveness of the séance. Complete unconscious trance, in other words, would not only be unusual for this Hmong practitioner but also detrimental from the point of view of the audience's needs and expectations.

Louise Bäckman and Åke Hultkrantz (1977: 20) point out the dangers of limiting the definition of trance or the validity of séance to only those moments in which the shaman loses consciousness: "[T]here is another form of shamanic experience that Eliade's definition does not account for, *viz.*, the enlightenment of the shaman through the arrival of auxiliary spirits. So many séances of divination and curing take place in a state of ecstasy … without the shaman's soul leaving him." Bäckman and Hultkrantz suggest that altered state forms may vary, and, indeed, many ethnographic accounts such as that of Thai above demonstrate that a shamanic consultation that consisted only of parasympathetic collapse would not necessarily be regarded as successful. Perhaps the scholarly focus on the unconscious trance itself betrays certain romantic or aesthetic notions about effective supernatural experiences on the part of ethnographers of the past: a desire for truly exotic ritual acts that would appear integrally different from the prayer or other spiritual experiences more familiar to practitioners of Western religious traditions. Yet from the performative perspective, it is often the shaman's stirring narration of the spirit journey, and the hearing of the voices of spirit helpers or spirit enemies speaking through the body and movements of the shaman that create the most powerful impressions of the séance itself. With its oratory, song, dance, occasional ventriloquism, and startling feats of physical and manual dexterity and stamina, the séance can be a stirring sensory event, one which depends upon a shaman who is conscious and active for at least a large portion of its duration. Thus, altered states which permit the shaman to retain some active control of body and voice are important to the success of the shamanic role.

TRANCE AND THE ACCUSATION OF FEIGNING

Franz Boas's collector of Kwagul (Kwakiutl) narratives, George Hunt, related the story of his own initiation into the shamanic profession in the 1920s (Boas 1930). When established shamans within the community designated Hunt as a possible initiate, the latter balked, having had little interest in shamanic practices before. After some hesitation, however, Hunt acquiesced, and his trainers began to instruct him in the various ritual acts of importance to the shamanic trade. The first of these was trance. Hunt recalls the demonstration he observed. The leader of the assembled shamans first ordered one of the shamans to demonstrate the trance:

"Take care, friends, and let us begin to teach him the beginning of the ways of the one who wishes to be a shaman, the one who faints and who trembles with his body when the quartz crystal is thrown into his stomach. Now go on, friend Life-Owner, and try to pretend to faint that it may be seen by Giving-Potlatches-in-the-World here from you," said he. Then Life-Owner sat down on the right hand side of the house. For a long time lasted his breathing. Then he was turning on his back and he stretched out. Then he trembled with his body. Then four shamans went and took hold of him as he went around in the house and he cried, "Haai', haai', haai'" trembling with his body. As soon as he reached near the door of the house he stopped. (1930: 7)

The account goes on to detail Life-Owner's lack of breath and the various means by which the other shamans revive him. Although the account states that Life-Owner was asked to "pretend" to fall into trance, upon recovering, he showed no awareness of what had taken place, and the other shamans told him he had temporarily died (1930: 8). It is difficult to tell from Hunt's narrative whether the writer regarded the performance as a masterful piece of feigning or the product of a highly developed ability to induce trance. Given that Hunt produced his account for Boas, a "man of science" upon whom Hunt was financially reliant, at least part of his apparent skepticism may derive from his assumptions regarding what he thought Boas might think about shamanic rituals and techniques. Hunt's report underscores the classic difficulties of obtaining truly open communication on sensitive topics within an ethnographic encounter shaped by marked differences in status and culture.

Even if a traditional community were to suspect a shaman of somehow feigning, making such a judgment could be very difficult as well as potentially deleterious on both social and supernatural planes. Traditional audiences have not had access to complex diagnostic machinery such as electroencephalography; instead, they have had to judge the onset and course of trance states through only the simplest and least invasive forms of observation. The frequent occurrence of the séance in darkness and the demands of proper decorum during the event itself further limited audience scrutiny. And thus, it has often been assumed – particularly by skeptical ethnographers – that the shaman at times merely feigns the trance state. It is easy to find scholarly opinions in the published literature on shamanism to the effect that shamans intentionally dissemble in order to attract attention or mislead clients. Kendall (1995: 19) suggests that such scholarly tendencies may stem from an unwillingness in Western society to allow for the co-occurrence of both authentic religious experience and performative showmanship: the presence of one has tended to be viewed as the negation of the other. Thus, a séance that includes overtly performative aspects – e.g., sleight of hand, ventriloquism – is viewed as "fraudulent," and the validity of its other elements summarily dismissed. This scholarly skepticism has been furthered by a prevalent opinion among many shamanic communities themselves that the art of shamanism is on the decline and that truly great shamans lived only in the past (see Chapter 11). This Native view, combined with the realities of cultural change that accompanied most of the ethnographic records left to us, have led scholars to view "true" trance as a glimmer of a bygone era.

It is important to note, however, that the assumption that trance has declined in frequency or authenticity is not verifiable in any real fashion. It is true that trance figures strongly in oral narrative within shamanisms, and that shamanic traditions tend to speak of earlier shamans as having been far stronger than the shamans of the present day. Yet such is typical of heroic discourse in general, especially when linked to mythic progenitors. Further, feigning mental states to one degree or another is a long-standing and very human tendency, and it is very possible that past shamans were as expert in counterfeiting trance as were/are their descendents. Much of the ethnographic materials left to us come from periods of intense intercultural contact and substantial destruction of indigenous livelihoods and world-views, so it is natural to assume that such ethnography reflects degradation of the indigenous religious practices as well. But to deny the possibility that "pre-contact" shamanisms may have also engaged in subterfuge, or to assume that such acts were less then than they are now, is ultimately to imagine an era when all prayer was heartfelt and every act sincere, an assumption which our ethnographic data in no way support. Ultimately, even with the most elaborate of modern machinery, we cannot definitively judge what is occurring in another person's mind, and modern ethnographers are far more hesitant to describe shamans as "charlatans" than were their predecessors of a century ago.

ECSTATIC TRANCE VS. POSSESSION

Because shamans often act out and give voice to spirit helpers during the séance, scholars have sometimes regarded trance behaviors as a form of possession. Other scholars see a distinction between the empowered, authoritative air of the shaman during trance, and the more passive, involuntary air of the "victim" of supernatural possession. The shaman, it is said, sends the soul outward, while the possessed person suffers the intrusion of a soul from outside, either voluntarily (to gain some assistance from the intruder) or involuntarily (especially in cases of illness or self-destructive behavior). Shamanic traditions often describe concourse with spirit helpers in positive terms, while possession traditions may describe similar concourse as harrowing, unpleasant, and abusive.

Theorists have debated extensively the relations of ecstatic trance and possession. Some have wished to see shamanic ecstasy and possession states as part of a single complex (e.g., Findeisen 1957; Lewis 1971), while others (e.g., Eliade 1964; Paulson 1964) have wished to maintain a clear distinction between them. Gilbert Rouget (1980: 30–1) asserts that shamanic ecstasy is marked by characteristics that easily distinguish it from possession. For instance, the shaman induces the trance personally, contacting spirits and inviting communication, and remaining in control at all times. These behaviors contrast with that of the possessed individual, who takes a more passive role in the onset of the trance, being spiritually ambushed by a communicating spirit. Further, the shaman's intentional trance induction usually involves the performance of music, in which the shaman figures as a key performer and participant, while the possessed individual is often the passive recipient of musical performance or other trance-inducing proce-dures. Even given such clearly drawn distinctions, however, Rouget readily admits that a single individual can sometimes undergo either or both experiences, or that a given experience can prove a composite of the two (1980: 36). He suggests in fact that the two states are poles in a single continuum (1980: 36), a view seconded by Louise Bäckman and Åke Hultkrantz (1977: 20). Ruth-Inge Heinze (1988: 87–94) suggests that this continuum can be differentiated along two axes: on the one hand, the degree of control retained by the percipient; on the other, the degree of mental self-awareness maintained. Where the "classic" shamanic state of ecstasy entails both heightened control and heightened self-awareness, the classic possession state entails extreme loss of control and a mental state of marked dissociation. A shamanic possession trance, as described below, lies somewhere between the poles, exhibiting a continued sense of control but a dissociative mental state.

One way to measure the degree of control and mental self-awareness which the shaman maintains during a séance is to examine the shaman's statements about the experience post factum. Bäckman and Hultkrantz (1977: 20) note that Eliade's focus on ecstatic trance ignores the frequent ritual procedures in which shamans allow spirits to enter their bodies as a means of communicating with the human community. Rouget (1980: 34) cites ethnographic accounts of Hmong shamans who reported no memory of what had transpired during sessions in which spirits spoke through their bodies (i.e., possession states). Similarly, Heinze (1988: 145–7) presents a case study of a Chinese shaman in Singapore who reported no memory of any of the communications she received while possessed by the Goddess of Mercy. It was her husband who was obliged to note her verbalizations and help interpret them after the fact. In a detailed ethnography of a contemporary Buryat shamanic ceremony, Virlana Tkacz, Sayan Zhambalov, and Wanda Phipps (2002) record similar moments in which the shaman Bayir Rinchinov indicated no knowledge of the communications that had occurred through his body during trance. The participants in the ceremony relied on the shaman's possession states to help divine the attitudes and concerns of the spirits with whom they were attempting to communicate. At one point, the spirit speaking through Bayir's body asked the assembly to ask Bayir if he had been offended by any of the events that had occurred thus far in the séance. When the spirit eventually left Bayir, the other assembled shamans inquired about his feelings and he replied that he was in no way offended (2002: 142–4). This complete dissociation between the shaman's own consciousness and that of the possessing spirit could strike the assembly as funny at times, as when a newly recovered Bayir asked his counterparts if the visiting spirit had bothered to give him a blessing during the trance (2002: 112). Such accounts parallel those reported of Chinggis Khan's divinatory rituals during the seventeenth century, as described in Chapter 12. A lack of memory of the trance implies a state of dissociation, the hallmark of a voluntary state of possession. Where such possession can occur as part of a shaman's professional life, initial contacts with the spirits early on in the shaman's career may be described as wholly involuntary possession states, marked by all the fear, confusion, and emotional turmoil usually associated with possession in other contexts.

ECSTATIC VS. "ENSTATIC" TRANCE

A further area of comparison lies between what Gananath Obeyesekere (2002: 164–8), following Eliade (1964: 417), terms the "ecstatic" vs. "enstatic" trance. If ecstasy involves sending the spirit outward, Obeyesekere states, enstasy entails turning one's thoughts inward. Since Buddhism does not posit the existence of a soul, such an entity cannot be imagined to leave the body (2002: 165). Instead, the meditator gains access to insights intuitively during extended meditation, or through communications from gods to the meditator during the trance state. At the same time, Obeyesekere suggests, such acquisition of knowledge, although in Buddhist understandings a result of inwardly oriented meditation, may in fact come to resemble outward spirit travel in everything but name. Writes Obeyesekere:

On one level the Buddhist meditator lets his mind penetrate *inwardly* as he recollects his own past lives (through enstasis). But if he is to get at the past lives of others or witness the dissolution and coming into being of past and present universes, either he must seek the help of a god ... or he must let his mind penetrate *outwardly* into other cosmic realms (through something like ecstasies). But this surely means being able to reach out of the body, and, as with other Indic virtuosos, on occasion being able to project a mind-image of the physical Buddha. If my line of speculation is correct, what seems to have happened here is that ecstasy has been absorbed into enstasy; the samana has incorporated into his very being some of the attributes of the shaman. (2002: 167)

Obeyesekere's view parallels Hultkrantz's (1989: 48) suggestion that South Asian enstatic meditative regimens such as yoga may have developed out of earlier shamanic ecstatic techniques, such as those glimpsed in the *Rig Veda*'s (Cowell and Webster 1977: 136) description of *munis*: "silent ones who wear the wind as their girdle, and who, drunk with their own silence, rise in the wind, and fly in the paths of the demigods and birds (Obeyesekere 2002: 167). As the Buddha learns to achieve the same enlightenment through inward meditation, so Buddhism replaces the concept of ecstasy with enstasy, while retaining the same central role for trance and the trance percipient. Larry G. Peters (2004: 15) comes to a similar conclusion in his comparison of yoga and shamanic trance in Nepal and Tibet. As he puts it: "yoga has incorporated and interiorized (embodied) the symbolism and rites of shamanism" (2004: 15). Similarly, Andrzej Rozwadowski (2001: 72) suggests that the dervish tradition within Islamic Sufism owes its trance induction techniques to local shamanic traditions. Such absorption of shamanic methodologies into succeeding religions will be discussed in greater length in Chapter 12.

Shamanic trance, the assumed heart of shamanic traditions, thus presents a wide range of different characteristics and interpretations. As Winkelman (2000) suggests, it may be possible to identify a specific variety of altered state that correlates (at least ideally) with designated trance phenomena in various cultures, perhaps in conjunction with moments of parasympathetic dominance. These states, as Whitehouse (2004: 105–12) suggests, may involve powerful visions, etched into the mind as flashbulb memories, and subsequently interpreted and used by the shaman and community in mutually agreed upon and effective ways. Yet such trance states exist in any case only in conjunction with other performative events of the séance, ones which may supplement or even supplant the trance itself in the eyes of the community at large. Scholars, in attempting to account for trance induction, have tended to turn to pathological models – e.g., epileptic seizures, hysteria, culture-bound syndromes, schizophrenia – marginalizing in so doing the cosmological explanations supplied within shamanic traditions themselves or the adaptive, communal means by which novice shamans are trained to narrate and interpret their trance experiences. A tendency to somaticize in order to demystify shamanism dominated scholarship for much of the first half of the twentieth century, leading to a portrayal of the shamanic trance as an involuntary, passive, mental state rather than as a carefully cultivated bodily technique. Current research that seeks to integrate physical, particularly cognitive, elements of trance experience with their uses and interpretations within a shamanic tradition can, in contrast, deepen our respect for ancient traditions that make use of altered states as a favored vehicle for religious experience, within shamanism as well as in other religious traditions of the world.

CHAPTER 8

Shamans, clients, and healing

It is not fitting to write down all the Sámi methods of healing in this book, because this book will be read all over the world, and it is not proper for many learned gentlemen to hear all these methods. For they would not believe in them and would only ridicule the Sámi for their foolishness. But if they could only see what the Sámi can do, then they would be astonished by their power and wonder where it came from.

(Johan Turi, *Turi's Book of Lappland*)

More so than virtually any other aspect of shamanism, the issue of healing challenges Western presuppositions regarding veracity and interpretive objectivity. For even if we are able to adopt a neutral attitude to informants' narratives of supernatural interlocutors or spirit travel and accept as positive the mystical experiences and trance states described so far – key elements in typical shamanic traditions – the claim or fact of therapeutic efficacy makes fundamental demands on our very understanding of fact. On a certain empirical level, we all would seem to be able to agree that a patient became well or did not, prospered or declined, survived or died. In the event of a positive turn, we should be able to say that the therapy worked; in the event of the negative, that the therapy failed. Yet nothing so clear-cut obtains in the ethnographic data. In the realities of the healing process – be it Western medical or shamanic tradition – seemingly sound therapies sometimes fail, while seemingly unsound ones sometimes prove effective. Healing acts that would seem to hold little prospect of truly helping a patient are sometimes met with startling success, creating a quandary that Western researchers have recognized, sometimes begrudgingly, as the "placebo effect." On a deeper level, ethnographic data sometimes reveal communities whose very definition of health differs substantively from that assumed and enshrined in somatically circumscribed Western medicine. A course of therapy may treat elements of a stolen soul or injured supernatural relations that find no counterpart in Western medicine, apart from the broad framework of psychopathology. And sometimes, the therapy may be considered a success even when the patient dies, generally a sign of utter failure in Western medicine apart from the relatively new discipline of palliative care. No wonder early ethnographers, faced with such perplexing phenomena, often preferred simply to declare all shamans charlatans and their methods humbug or quackery. To give up on the surety of healing or acknowledge the multiple pathways toward its achievement threatened the very essence of ethnographers' understanding of reality.

Perhaps the various lessons of twentieth-century relativism or its later postmodernist sequelae have created for us today a less solid ground from which to criticize and dismiss shamanic healing. Or perhaps it is the combined wisdom of modern research in medical anthropology, community medicine, and alternative health movements that has broadened researchers' understandings of what constitutes health and healing. Whatever the case, scholars of shamanism today are far less prone to deny the efficacy of shamanic therapies for patients and communities that value them. In this chapter, we examine the ways in which contemporary ethnographers, psychologists, and medical researchers have come to conceptualize the effective potential of shamanic healing. How do shamans "heal"? What do their patients gain from the therapies they administer? And how do the mechanisms of these healing methods compare with those defined as normative in Western medical practice?

In order to answer these questions, we focus below on three issues decisive for understanding shamanic healing on its own grounds as well as in comparative perspective. First, following the lead of ethnographers of medicine, we shift the focus of inquiry in the healing situation away from a close-up on the patient and healer alone toward a more complex, negotiated relation between patient, healer, and community. This shift in viewpoint allows us to take into consideration some ethnographic data that might seem extraneous otherwise but which, in fact, prove decisive to the workings of shamanic healing in certain cultures. Second, we acknowledge the fact that therapeutic strategies usually grow out of a healing tradition's theories of disease etiology. When we understand how a culture conceptualizes health and illness, it becomes easier to understand the methods the culture possesses to effect healing, and possibly, by extension, the methods by which these therapeutic strategies prove efficacious. Finally, stepping back from these culturally specific considerations, we ask whether certain cross-cultural phenomena may be characteristic of shamanic therapies in general. The notions of catharsis, placebo effect, and symbolic healing rise as possible explanatory models, particularly when coupled with intense social bonding. The chapter as a whole reveals, I hope, not only the plethora of ways in which shamanic healing can prove effective, but also how shamanic cultures exploit the power of explanation, ritual, and human relations to optimize the body's mysterious but undeniable capacity to heal.

Before launching into this examination, however, let me note that this chapter will not examine the host of effective medicines that shamanic traditions around the world have developed through the ages. When a Western doctor today prescribes morphine, that professional makes use of a substance first used as an entheogen in shamanic contexts, as we shall see in Chapter 9. Many other important medicines in use today likewise derive from the therapeutic arsenals of shamanic and other traditional healers from various parts of the world, adopted into Western medicine, stripped of their ritual uses, and transformed into seemingly neutral pharmaceuticals. This act of borrowing can be seen as an acknowledgement of the medical achievements of shamanic practitioners over time. The ethnobotany of shamanism is a rich and varied topic which cannot be fully covered in a survey of this length. Some attention will be paid to entheogens in Chapter 9. Yet it should be acknowledged here, as the great Sámi healer and writer Johan Turi noted in his text of 1910 (quoted at the outset of this chapter), shamans often possess formidable pharmacological expertise, which, combined with ritual acts and intense human interactions, may achieve remarkable cures.

THE THERAPEUTIC TRIANGLE

In her examination of healing rituals among Wana people in Sulawesi, Indonesia, Jane Atkinson (1987, 1989) presents observations that appear confusing at first from the perspective of Western medicine. Where Western healing focuses on the patient as the prime site of both pathology and therapy, Wana healing rituals are aimed much more concertedly at the community as a whole. Great attention is paid to the preparations of family and community as a planned séance approaches: various items must be procured and made ready for the healing ceremony, and the entire community is encouraged to contribute to the event in a show of solidarity (*kasintuwu*). During the ensuing séance itself, the focus shifts to the shamanic healers – *tau kawalia* ("people with spirits") – who persistently call for the attention of all assembled and occasionally fall unconscious during their concourse with the spirits. On such occasions, the unconscious healer may need to be revived by another healer present, and/or offered foods which will appease the hungry spirit. The spirit signals its food or drink preferences by means of riddles which the shaman recites, while the community together labors to decode and then act upon them. Meanwhile, the ill person – the central "patient" of Western medical practice – may not even be present at the event. If, in fact, the patient is not in attendance, *tau kawalia* may substitute a house post or bottle as an effective surrogate.

It is difficult to understand such medical procedures from an analytical framework that focuses myopically on the patient alone, or even on the patient–healer dyad. Instead, as Atkinson notes, ethnographers of healing need to make use of a descriptive model which takes into account the negotiation of patient, healer, and community in complex, culturally regulated ways. Writes Atkinson: "If one envisions a triangle composed of shaman, patient, and audience, it follows that the relationship of any two elements is dependent on the relationship of each element to the third" (1987: 342). In the Wana case, the relations between shaman and community are particularly elaborated, leading to a decrease in the centrality of the patient, the figure considered most central in most Western therapeutic traditions. Atkinson's Wana case underscores dramatically the cultural variability of healing traditions, while establishing the premise that a "successful" therapy is one that satisfies the potentially varied expectations of patient, healer(s), and community alike.

Although the Wana tradition may at first seem extreme in its focus on community and healer over the patient, the dynamics of its healing ceremonies find parallels to varying degrees in many other shamanic traditions as well. It may be that only one individual is suffering from a particular somatic or psychological condition, but nonetheless, the illness itself is often experienced communally, as the individual's family, friends, neighbors, and trading partners perceive and react to the suffering they see and the changed behaviors that the illness has occasioned. When illness occurs, systems of interdependence and mutual support are disrupted; prospects for present or future welfare are imperiled, economic and emotional relations are distorted or destroyed. As a result, disease can often spawn a collective malaise, which may be marked by anxiety, guilt, and frustration, and which requires a healing process of its own. It is often precisely this collective therapy which a shamanic séance can supply, one which stands to benefit both the community and the individual patient. Some further examples help illustrate this tendency.

Laurel Kendall (1995, 2001) has explored the healing traditions of Korean shamans in a number of articles. Describing the familial tendencies typical of the *kut* séances she observed, she writes:

Generalizing from many *kut* ... I would describe an "ideology of affliction" wherein all manner of problems – medical, financial, and social – are *symptomatic* of a household's troubled relations with its ancestors and gods ... In all of these *kut*, the entire household and the full sum of the problems and aspirations of all its inhabitants become the subject of healing. The idiom of healing is a series of reconciliations between the living members of the household and their gods and ancestors who appear in sequence in the person of costumed shamans. (Kendall 2001: 27)

In this system, the ultimate cause of a patient's illness lies in the misbehaviors of the collective, particularly in relation to its ancestor deities. Affliction results as punishment for misdeeds, and specific illnesses or problems result as manifestations of the affliction. Thus, a woman in a family that had skimped on its offerings to ancestors was accidentally shot in the chest by a stray bullet when out working in the fields. Her ailment required Western medical treatment, which the family procured, and which proved effective in saving her life. But from the family's point of view, the underlying etiology of the shooting lay in their collective misdeeds, reparable only through placation of the spirits' injured feelings through offerings prescribed and realized in a *kut*.

Kendall (1995) also presents a concrete example of such communal therapy in her examination of one Korean woman's road toward professional status as a shaman. A young woman, Chini, although recognizing a calling to become a *mudang* (shaman), nonetheless found it difficult to allow the spirits to speak fully through her in *kut*. Her experience of spiritual blockage was eventually attributed to the presence of a frustrated deceased sister, who had been destined to shamanhood, but who had committed suicide at age nineteen. In a *kut* performed for the family by Chini's shamanic trainers, the family experienced communications from both the deceased sister and the alcoholic father, who had abandoned the family. As Kendall writes: "As in any *kut*, the appearance of the ancestors gives voice to a larger family story of pain, recrimination, and reconciliation" (1995: 39). As with many other forms of healing, effective therapists are often former patients themselves, and in this case, initiatory *kut* help provide a model for how bringing forward family trauma can lead to a sensation of relief.

Amanda Harris (2001) explores the role of collective space and action in Iban healing. Iban people of Borneo have resided traditionally in longhouses. These structures have a balance of private apartments (*bilik*) and communal hallways (*ruai*), both of which become important in shamanic healing. While a male healer (*manang*) traditionally undertakes séance activities in the public hallway, family members and friends may crowd around the patient in the contiguous private space of the *bilik*, adding their own touch and presence to the healing event. Interrelating the two healing components, Harris writes:

The application of medicine (*ubat*) became a collective pursuit in which healing power did not derive from *ubat* alone, but a combination of *ubat* and people. Meanwhile on the longhouse *ruai* Manang Ipoi continued to summon his assisting spirits (*yang*) and other celestial *manang* to his aid, and through the words of the *pelian* chant the search for the errant *semengat* [invisible aspect] began. But in a sense this became a background to the bustle of healing work in the *bilik*, where ministrations continued in intimate association with visible and affective dimensions of the patient. (2001: 137)

Harris maintains that scholarly focus on the *manang* alone has tended to overlook or marginalize the role of the community in orchestrating therapeutic acts. In the Iban longhouse it is evidently the interplay of familial and communal, the demonstrations of concern and care from both, that creates the most powerful therapeutic context for the healing. The *manang*'s long song performances – crucial in their own way for healing – occur in tandem with the community's therapeutic contribution of sympathetic "presence." As we shall discuss below, the sociality of such an event itself can prove decisive for its efficacy, as patients respond to the social bonding inherent in such temporary and intentional reconfigurations of their contexts.

The shaman's therapeutic acts may address communal issues indirectly, while focusing ostensibly on the patient's healing as a separate task. Marina Roseman (2001) explains how shamanic practitioners among forest-dwelling Temiar people in Malaysia touch on communal experience of deforestation and environmental degradation within the spirit songs intended to cure patients of specific maladies. In distinction from the Wana or Korean cases discussed above, where the therapeutic acts are specifically aimed at a collective malaise, in the Temiar case, shamans address communal ills as an ancillary issue, one which we might well overlook but for the analytical framework that compels us to examine the patient–healer–community triad as a whole. By singing songs and employing spirits derived from the encroaching world outside the rainforest (e.g., the spirits of airplanes or canned sardines or Chinese laborers), Temiar people assimilate these potential or real threats into their own supernatural worlds, asserting control over them. The act reestablishes the Temiar community as the center of the Temiar world and conveys the community's ongoing control over its own destiny.

DISEASE, ILLNESS, AND SOMATICIZATION

In his study of phenomena which he labels "religious healing" among Greek Orthodox fire walkers (*astenaria*) Loring Danforth (1989: 52) cites

Kleinman's distinction between "disease" and "illness." For Kleinman, a disease can be defined as a verifiable physiological pathology, with or without noticeable symptoms. *Illness*, on the other hand, is defined as the "psychosocial experience and meaning of perceived disease." Typically, of course, disease and illness are united: disease, the physical disorder, is perceived and interpreted by means of the socially constructed notion of illness. Yet, as Western medicine has demonstrated, one may suffer from a life-threatening disease such as cancer with little or no inkling of its existence, while, on the other hand, one may complain for years of physical symptoms or problems of an illness for which a Western physician can discover no cause. The former can be described as a hidden disease, the latter as an evident illness with no identified underlying disease. In traditional societies, Kleinman suggests, disease is recognized only by symptoms, and illness in general is typically viewed as meaningful: a protracted or sudden challenge in one's life that carries with it temporary or profound implications for one's experience and survival.

Obscuring Kleinman's distinction between disease and illness is the concept of *somaticization*, a process by which, Danforth states, social or emotional problems become expressed through bodily ailments. A prolonged backache or fatigue may arise as a response to stressful situations in one's life, yet the illness as such will also be a disease, provided it correlates with somatically verifiable physiological manifestations. According to Danforth (1989: 53), "somaticization is particularly common in societies where mental illness is heavily stigmatized." In contexts such as rural Greece, Danforth suggests, issues of social or emotional adjustment can be expressed and discussed through reference to ailments – loss of sleep, stomach pains, fatigue – and potentially addressed through healing activities that seek to restore bodily health through processes of social reintegration and validation. The bodily ailment becomes in this framework the conscious target of healing intervention, while the underlying social or emotional disorder which may have led to it receives covert treatment.

ETIOLOGY AS CURE

The way in which disease is conceptualized within a culture carries with it a set of assumptions for what constitutes a workable or efficacious therapy. As an example, in a medical tradition which attributes disease to unseen microbial invasion (as in Western medicine) it will seem logical to look for agents – poisons or potent substances of other sorts – which will kill the microbes in the patient's body. If, on the other hand, disease is viewed as a loss of something – e.g., a loss of soul or power – the likely therapy will be one which seeks to restore what is missing. Thus, understanding notions of disease etiology within shamanic traditions can help us understand how and why particular treatments are regarded as effective.

In their discussion of Sámi shamanism, Louise Bäckman and Åke Hultkrantz (1977: 44–5) note that shamanic traditions often conceptualized disease as either an instance of soul loss or of soul invasion. In the former case, the errant spirit or soul must be tracked down and restored – often literally blown – back into the patient's body. In the latter case (where disease is seen as a form of possession), the intruding spirit must be banished, often through harsh invocations or clever pleading, but sometimes through a dramatic sucking of the offending entity out of the patient's veins or skin. These ancient and very widespread notions of disease become localized and refined within particular cultural traditions.

Thomas D. DuBois (2005: 71ff.) describes the diagnostic rituals of *xiangtou* healers in a small village of northern China. In the 1930s, female mediums made diagnoses at night, with all the lights out. Sitting on a large brick platform (*kang*), surrounded by sacrifices of boiled eggs and wine, the *xiangtou* questioned the spirits about the patient's illness and then allowed the spirits to speak through her body. One contemporary healer described her acts as taking the pulse (*haomai*) of the patient: sitting on a *kang* and pinching the cloth of her pants, the healer addresses the spirit of the fox and other beings. If the ailment is a *xu* sickness, i.e., brought about by evil deeds, unsettled human ghosts or animal spirits, the *xiangtou* will potentially be able to identify its cause and effect a cure. Ordinary physical illnesses (*shi*) may also be caused by an underlying *xu* disorder. Typical treatments involve placating the offended spirit(s) through admitting the error and offering sacrifices (2003: 74). Sometimes, however, spirits attack a victim out of simple spite or mischief: such is particularly the case with fox spirits. At the same time, fox spirits prove powerful spirit helpers for the *xiangtou* and may be cajoled into curing patients' illnesses as well (2005: 76). Health is thus regarded as the maintenance of harmonious relations with the spirit world and an attentiveness to proper bodily and social decorum in all aspects of life.

Jane Atkinson (1987) details concepts of soul-loss in Wana understandings of health. Normal life is marked by the presence and integration of a given individual's various soul-parts, all of which are constantly subject to withdrawal, loss, or theft. When soul-parts dissociate from the self, illness results. Shamanic healers – *tau kawalia* ("people with spirits") – allow parts of their own beings to wander out in quest of the patient's missing soul-parts, thus risking their own self-integration and health for the good of another. Soul-parts can withdraw in response to hurtful actions or improper behaviors, or they may wander off or be stolen. Part of the *tau kawalia*'s work is to discover what soul-parts have gone where and to take appropriate therapeutic steps on the basis of this diagnosis to retrieve them. Crucially, here, etiology predicts treatment: wandering souls must be sought by wandering souls.

Carol Laderman (1995) describes the array of different disease etiologies identified by Malay *bomoh* healers:

The Malays believe that most illnesses result from a humoral imbalance, and treat them with herbal remedies, dietary adjustments, thermal treatments, blood letting, and massage. Should ordinary health problems not respond, or an illness appear to be unusual in kind or in course, a suspicion may arise that the sufferer's problems are due, at least in part, to attacks of spirits (*hantu*), either sent by ill-wishers or acting on their own initiative; or to an imbalance of the component parts of the patient's Self. (1995: 115)

The latter two situations are ones which may require a shamanic séance (*Main Peteri*) performed by a shaman (*tok 'teri*). *Hantu* spirits – examples of "intruding souls" – sent by others of ill will or arriving of their own accord, gain access to the body when the individual's store of inherent spirit (*semangat*) is reduced. *Semangat*, present to some extent in all beings, can leach away from a person as a result of such forces as misfortune, emotional trauma, or social conflict. As *semangat* escapes, the strength of the body's defense against *hantu* ebbs, and the body becomes more vulnerable to disease. The *tok 'teri* may then need to call back and reinstate missing *semangat* through the *Main Peteri* in order to cure the ailment. Sometimes the *tok 'teri*, in conjunction with an assistant (*minduk*) must also address or negotiate with the spirit guards that act as gatekeepers around the body. These guards – essential to the integrity of the body as a whole – must be exhorted to do a better job retaining *semangat* or staving off *hantu* incursions. The healer relies on divination during the *Main Peteri* to determine what sort of *hantu* have attacked and which guards need to be addressed.

While *semangat* figure as important factors in such supernaturally controlled disease, imbalances caused by inner winds (*angin*) also pose potential threats. In Malay understanding, as Laderman details, a person's body must be able to let inner winds flow outward without obstruction. If a social situation or personal choices fail to allow the expression of these inner winds, they may build up inside the person, again causing illness. Typical symptoms include: "backaches, headaches, digestive problems, dizziness, asthma, depression, anxiety, in short, a wide range of psychosomatic and affective disorders" (1995: 120). The *tok 'teri* and *minduk* cure *sakit berangin* ("wind sickness") by giving name to the source of pent up wind and performing a narrative song that describes its history, as we shall discuss below. If the patient is short-tempered, for instance, the trapped inner winds may belong to *Angin Hala* ("The Wind of the Weretiger"). Performing the story of the Weretiger helps free and manage the trapped winds of the patient and ensure a return to health, a verbal cure akin to others we will explore in Chapter 11. The diagnosis of disease in the Malay system thus allows for a variety of different etiologies, each of which implies a different set of therapeutic responses. The failure of one therapy will lead the healer to suggest different disease etiologies, which in turn will lead to different therapeutic strategies.

Healing by narrative

In his classic article "The Effectiveness of Symbols" within his *Structural Anthropology* (1963), Claude Lévi-Strauss suggests that shamanic healers, like Western psychotherapists, assist their patients in constructing a reading (interpretation) of their illness. This primarily narrative and symbolic understanding of what is happening within the patient's body or life then serves to alleviate or even resolve the patient's problems. Western patients within psychotherapeutic or medical settings can experience a sense of healing as they accept the narrative of their ailment's etiology. Even when this identification consists of little more than a diagnostic label (e.g., "chronic fatigue syndrome," "neurosis"), patients may report a sense of relief or wellbeing as a result of this naming process. In psychotherapy, however, as in varieties of shamanic healing, this initial naming of the problem may be followed by a series of more detailed therapeutic acts aimed at exorcising the offending spirits, addressing the causes of the trauma, or bringing closure to the detrimental situation. Working through the agreed upon problem allows the patient to take control of the situation, transact feelings, and discover means for restoring health.

In detailing the therapeutic methods of Japanese *itako* healers, blind women who use song and divination to address patients' needs, Takefusa Sasamori (1997) writes:

People who consult an *itako* are more interested in asking "why" they have been afflicted with a particular illness than "what" that illness might actually be. The patient might ask why the disease attacks him of all people, and, in this context, want to know the cause of his miserable fate. The *itako* will give him an answer so that his suffering can be put into a meaningful context. Through this kind of understanding, he will gain the strength to endure his pains. (1997: 93)

As the patient discovers the narrative cause of the disease, the *itako* also provides a set of actions which will undo the stated conflict: e.g., an angered deity must be placated by certain offerings, or a cosmically offensive misbehavior must be curtailed. Such instructions give the patient an opportunity to feel in control of the situation again, and to take positive steps toward regaining health.

Whereas the *itako* provides narrative explanations based on personal insight and communications from spirits, Malaysian healers involve their clients directly in recognizing the exact agents responsible for their illnesses. Carol Laderman (1995) describes the therapeutic response to Malay patients who display a build-up of inner winds (*angin*) within their bodies:

The Inner Winds of a patient who has been diagnosed as suffering from *sakit berangin* ["wind disease"] must be allowed to express themselves, released from the confines of their corporeal prison, enabling the sufferer's mind and body to return to a healthy balance. In healing ceremonies, the band strikes up appropriate music as the shaman recites and sings excerpts from the story of the *angin*'s archetype. When the correct musical or literary cue is reached, the patient achieves trance, aided, as well, by the percussive sounds of music and the rhythmic beating of the shaman's hands on the floor near the patient's body. (1995: 120)

In this therapeutic framework, narrative and music fulfill a key role, while the healing team (the *tok 'teri* and *minduk*) cooperate with the patient to propose and eventually identify the explanation that best fits the patient's personality. A person of great inherent charm or creativity may suffer from built-up winds related to *Dewa Muda* (a demigod), while a patient plagued by dissatisfaction may suffer from winds related to *Dewa Penchil* (a legendary king). Identification of the culprit winds occurs as the healers, aided by musical accompaniment, seek the assent of the patient. The patient's falling into trance signals the aptness of the proposed diagnosis and allows the salutatory freeing of the winds to occur. As a result, the patient will be expected to feel better, unless other disease-causing agents (e.g., loss of inherent spirit *semangat* or attack by foreign spirit entities, *hantu*) further complicate the situation.

Seeking to interrelate the narrative tendencies of shamanic therapies and symbolic healing within Western tradition, James Dow (1986) has proposed a broader framework for understanding how a patient and healer negotiate treatment. Dow identifies four steps which he describes as the "universal aspects of symbolic healing":

1. The experiences of healers and healed are generalized with culture-specific symbols in cultural myth.
2. A suffering patient comes to a healer who persuades the patient that the problem can be defined in terms of the myth.
3. The healer attaches the patient's emotions to transactional symbols particularized from the general myth.
4. The healer manipulates the transactional symbols to help the patient transact his or her own emotions. (1986: 56)

In Dow's formulation, both steps one and two essentially involve narrative: the accounting for the etiology of a disease through some story about how the world or the cosmos works. In the first step, the patient, shaman, and community share an understanding of the world and how disease came to be a part of it, or how it comes about today. It may be a narrative that involves, for instance, easily angered spirits, or angry dead, or ill-willed living neighbors, or humors that need to be balanced for health to continue. The second step then involves applying this general understanding to the patient's own case, pointing out the irregularities that have resulted in the patient's ailment. In the third step, the shaman then convinces the patient (and the community) of the shamanic ability to correct this situation, leading the patient to set confidence in the séance or other treatment that will follow. Finally, in the fourth step, the shaman performs the promised procedure, transacting the patient's emotions and leading to a feeling of empowerment, action, and (hopefully) wellbeing.

One of the recurring criticisms of explanatory models like the ones described above, however, is that not all shamanic traditions seem to rely so clearly on narration as a therapeutic agent. In some traditions, ethnographers have noted, the words performed by a shaman in a séance are barely audible to the patient, or are so encased in oblique metaphor or poetic language that they become barely intelligible except to an expert. In other cases, the patient may be far separated from the healer, lying in a different room, or potentially even in a different house at the time of the ceremony. Clearly, in cases such as these, narrative cannot play the same role that it seems to play in situations like those described above. To understand healing mechanisms in such other instances, other models are necessary.

CATHARSIS

Another model for explaining the positive effects of shamanic healers is through the notion of catharsis. By vicariously experiencing the pain or intense emotions of another, the theory holds, a patient – or broader community – can release and lessen their own pain, leading to a sense of wellbeing.

Jane Atkinson (1987), drawing on the earlier work of Thomas Scheff (1979) suggests that the mechanism at work in the Wana séance is catharsis. As the Wana *tau kawalia* undergo the trials of their seance, Atkinson argues, they ideally attract the gratitude and attention of the entire community. The attending audience is led to see the healers' willingness to allow their souls to wander as a temporary but highly risk-fraught disintegration of self for the needs of another. By witnessing the séance, including frightening moments when one of the *tau kawalia* may lose consciousness and demand ritual intervention to ensure successful return and reintegration, community members may experience a sense of catharsis. Writes Atkinson: "If a shaman's request is not attended to, not understood, or not granted, the danger is that the shaman's soul will go off hurt in the company of his spirit familiars, leaving his body unconscious and unresponsive to treatment" (1987: 348). By attending to the healers' requests and supplying their needs, the community becomes involved in actively preventing a catastrophe. Their participation also enhances a sense of solidarity and communal identification potentially lacking in a culture of relatively mobile shifting agriculturalists. And, posits Atkinson, the community's ability to respond appropriately to the shaman's life-threatening situation in turn may act as catharsis for the community in its contemplation of the situation they cannot otherwise directly ameliorate: the plight of the patient.

ACTIVATION AND SOCIAL BONDING

Robert Desjarlais (1995), in examining the therapeutic methods used by Yolmo shamans in Nepal, suggests that they may rely on a process which he terms "activation":

My understanding is that the rites do, at times, have a positive effect, tending to work through indirect, tacit means – the less obvious aspects of ritual – to negate a sensibility bound by loss, fatigue, and listlessness and create a new one of vitality, presence, and attentiveness. Simply put ... [the shaman] changes how a body feels by altering what it feels. His cacophony of music, taste, sight, touch, and kinesthesia activates the senses. The activation has a potential to "wake up" a person, alter the sensory grounds of a spiritless body, and so change how a person feels. (1995: 143)

This same reliance on a combination of meaningful acts is reflected in Harris's (2001) discussion of Iban healing, mentioned above. The sensation of communal concern and care, evidenced tangibly in presence, touch, and interaction, can have powerfully therapeutic effects of its own.

Ede Frecska and Zsuzsanna Kulcsar (1989) have attempted to discover the physiological means by which social bonding can prove salubrious in human healing. Examining the production and uptake of endogenous opioid peptides in the brain, Frecska and Kulcsar note that these opioids help the brain experience and convey a sense of wellbeing. Experience of social affiliation – bonding, feelings of unity or communal identity – results in increased production of these peptides, which in turn leads to an enhanced feeling of happiness and trust. Endogenous opioids also produce sensations of euphoria and analgesia, making them valuable in combating pain or trauma. And further, they can increase the body's ability to combat disease (immunocompetence). Acting particularly on the orbital front cortex of the brain, as well as the temporal lobe and amygdalae, these peptides constitute the brain's chemical means of telling itself that all is well. In contrast, sickness and forms of social withdrawal or depression (the kinds of ailments often described in shamanic traditions as spirit loss or spirit illness) involve precisely the opposite phenomenon. The individual withdraws from social interaction, and, consequently, experiences decreased levels of endogenous opioids. Healing rituals, with the shaman's intense focus on helping the patient, and the likely warm presence and encouragement of community members, can furnish a dramatic surge in endogenous opioid exposure, produced by the patient in response to the social behaviors of others, or possibly transferred to the patient via olfactory or tactile contact with healers or others. The patient, charged with this powerful feeling of affiliation, enjoys all the benefits of an endogenous opioid peak, which may be accompanied by a ritual procedure that seeks to link the sensation to future altered behaviors. In discussing shamanic therapy among Native American communities, Frecska and Kulcsar note that depressive states "often refractory to Western therapeutic approaches [are] ... responsive to healing ceremonies through personality depatterning and reorientation in altered states of consciousness" (1989: 81). The séance itself can thus create both the mechanism of affiliation (endogenous opioids) and the tangible demonstration of affiliation (social intercourse), leading to a mutually reinforcing change in viewpoint that can be experienced as a profound sensation of belonging, trust, peace, and wellbeing. In this model, shamanic therapy succeeds not so much through the intellectual efficacy of a convincing narrative as through the more primal, nearly infantile sensation of the tender embrace. Tellingly, Frecska and Kulcsar point out, the brain's formative experiences of fluctuations in levels of endogenous opioids occur in response to the presence or absence of the mother.

HEALING THROUGH PLACEBO

Shamanic healing apparently makes use of varying channels in the human nervous system to effect a positive change in attitude as well as overall health. A final, further avenue within this complex gamut of influences is that which medical researchers have labeled the placebo effect. The power of belief in the efficacy of a particular therapy – regardless of its normally measurable physiological effects or potential – is a factor of profound significance in all healing traditions. Although Western medical research tends to test therapeutic effectiveness against placebos to measure the "actual" efficacy of a given substance or procedure, the reality of the placebo itself as a healing mechanism is often construed as somehow illegitimate or misguided. It is standard to talk of potentially useful drugs, but "mere placebos." Indicative of this tendency is Philip Singer's (1990) statement in his study of a Filipino faith healer's use of sleight of hand in curing patients:

The question of healing was specifically not addressed, since almost every type of disease may respond to placebo treatment, including the common cold, hypertension, or multiple sclerosis. (1990: 444)

The fact that placebos are so effective is not presented in Singer's study as a sign that they are a "wonder drug" but that they are discountable. Because their mechanism lies within the functioning of the brain rather than within the physiological combating of intruding microorganisms or other disease-causing factors identified in Western medicine, they are regarded as somehow beside the point. In shamanic healing, in contrast, the placebo effect is evidently exploited to the greatest degree possible, for the benefit of patient, community, and healer alike. Shamanic healing cross-culturally often makes use of sleight-of-hand illusions, ventriloquism, and other tricks of the trade as means of convincing a patient of the shaman's power in controlling the spirits and disease.

In his classic study of Chukchi shamanism, W. Bogoras (1904–9) writes:

There can be no doubt, of course, that shamans, during their performances, employ deceit in various forms, and that they themselves are fully cognizant of the fact. "There are many liars in our calling ... One will lift up the skins of the sleeping-room with his right toe, and thus assure you that it was done by 'spirits'; another will talk into the bosom of his shirt or through his sleeve, making the voice issue from a quite unusual place." (1904–9: 429)

"Tricks" of this sort helped convince patients and communities of a shaman's efficacy, leading to confidence in the treatment and its likely effects. Significantly, Bogoras observed that many Chukchi people of his day could see through their shamans' tricks, but nonetheless allowed them to proceed. Bogoras attributed their jadedness in this respect to contact with cultural outsiders.

During the same era, however, Franz Boas documented a more complex situation in his publication of George Hunt's initiation as a Kwagul shaman (Boas 1930: 1–41; Lévi-Strauss 1963: 175). Hunt did not at first believe that the shamans who offered to teach him their trade were reputable, but he nonetheless consented to receive shamanic training. Among other things, he learned how to simulate sucking a worm from the body of a patient. During a séance, he learned how to hold a small amount of down in his cheek. Biting down on his gum or tongue during the ceremony, he was able to make the down bloody. He could then spit the down out and claim that he had sucked it out of the patient's body. This "worm" was said to represent the disease that had afflicted the patient. As discussed in Chapter 6, Hunt recounted the success of this therapeutic ploy in his dealings with an ill Koskimo patient. A more experienced shaman of the patient's own community, a man named Aíx:ag:idãlag:îlis, had already tried to heal the woman unsuccessfully. Hunt, known by his shaman name Qãselid, performed a very impressive healing ritual:

I tucked up both sleeves of my shirt and I asked that four times for a long time the song leaders should beat fast time as is done ... for their shamans. Immediately they beat fast time. The first time I felt what was referred to by her as her sickness [a swelling]. Now I saw Aíx:ag:idãlag:îlis lying down on his back near the place where I was sitting. Now, evidently he tried to find out about me, for he was watching me. When the song leaders had beaten fast time four times, I pretended that my body trembled. I applied my mouth and immediately I sucked. I had not been sucking long when I raised my head and at the same time the song leaders stopped beating fast time. Then my mouth was full of blood mixed with the down [that had been concealed there], the alleged worm. Then I spat the blood into my hand and I tilted my hand so that all the men and women could see the blood as it ran into the water in the wash basin. As soon as all the blood was out they all saw the alleged worm, the down that stuck on the palm of my right hand. Now I stood up after this and went around the fire in the middle of the house. Now I was singing my sacred song and also a sacred song against the shamans, made for me by Fool [Nenolo], the shaman of the Nakwaxda'xw Kwagul. As soon as I arrived at the post, the place to which Aíx:ag:idãlag:îlis had stuck his red cedar bark, I took off the alleged worm, the sickness and I stuck it on to the post. Then I left it and went and felt of the woman ... Then she spoke and said, "For what was felt by you, great supernatural one? I felt it when you took out the sickness that now sticks on the post," said she. Then I arose and went to the post. I took off the alleged sickness, the worm. I asked someone to get a small piece of soft cedar bark for me ... I wrapped it around the worm, the alleged sickness, and I buried it in the hot ashes of the fire in the middle of the house. Now this was finished after this. (1930: 29)

It is certain that at least part of Hunt's own success in this case lay in the power of the placebo effect.

Such is not to imply, however, that the community simply engages in a willing suspension of disbelief in each and every instance. In fact, communities can be extremely discerning and critical of would-be healers. Edward Schieffelin (1995) describes the various ways in which Kaluli audiences appraise and authenticate séances they attend:

The authenticity of a medium could be judged on several points. Important in the long run was a reputation for successful cures. But in the immediate event it was a medium's quality in séance that was scrutinized. As a basic minimum the songs had to be well composed, poetically well constructed (with proper framing of place-names within a range of poetic devices) ... well sung, and capable of occasionally moving audience members to tears. Further, the voices of the various spirits had to be recognizably different from the medium's natural voice and from each other. Various vocal pyrotechnics, such as bird calls (representing spirits who arrived in the form of birds) and other kinds of vocalizations thought to be only producible by spirits, lent further verisimilitude to a séance. Finally if the spirits spoke about matters that the audience believed the medium couldn't possibly know, this was a very strong indication of séance authenticity. Kaluli were usually very annoyed if they suspected a medium was attempting to deceive them with a false séance. (1995: 67)

Schieffelin notes that disbelief did not always lead skeptics to declare their views publicly. Reticence was sometimes the preferred course of action, since the family and supporters of the patient could grow very angry if the shaman's work was summarily discounted. Further, the shaman could grow to resent the critic and possibly curse him in the future. For this reason, when community members suspected falsity in a séance, they looked for indirect means of bringing it to a swift close. Circumspection of this sort could help a community retain a view of shamanic acts as generally powerful and efficacious, even when, privately, individuals might suspect the veracity of one or another healer.

For the placebo effect to work, confidence in the cure must be as complete as possible: halfhearted performance on any side – be it in the shaman or shamanic ritual or in their perception by patient or community – could undermine the effectiveness of the entire act. And thus, our examination of shamanic healing comes back to where we began the chapter: with the complex interrelations of patient, healer, and community. Researchers are only beginning to understand the myriad ways by which human beings heal themselves. The more we know, however, the more evident it becomes that a model of health that looks at the body in isolation from the mind or the individual's social context is notably incomplete. In shamanic traditions, where somatic interventions could be far more limited than in contemporary Western medicine, or where certain diseases defied easy treatment, the efficacious influence of narrative, symbol, catharsis, social bonding, and placebos was not to be dismissed, particularly when combined with existing medicinal remedies. Over centuries of therapeutic trial and error, shamans developed powerful means of achieving and improving health in their communities. And often, in the decline of shamanic traditions due to processes of religious change or colonialism, communities lost a tremendous resource for social and physical health, one only imperfectly replaced by the Western medicine that had supplanted it.

PART IV

The shamanic arsenal

CHAPTER 9

Music and entheogens: pathways to ecstasy

As the previous chapters have shown, participants of shamanic traditions tend to regard altered states of consciousness – shamanic trance or similar mental states – as pivotal elements in human interactions with the super-natural. Through the trance, the shaman comes into direct contact with a powerful and highly interested spirit world, one capable of maintaining or restoring individuals' health, welfare, and luck. Within the framework of the séance, community members can witness the shaman's entry into spirit realms, although much remains invisible to any but the shaman and those assisting in the ritual.

In this chapter, we examine two of the key tools employed in shamanism to achieve trance states: music (along with dance) and psychotropic substances administered for religious purposes (termed by scholars *entheogens*). These are frequent elements of shamanic traditions worldwide and have faced occasional, sometimes virulent, suppression under succeeding religious systems. They display a powerful capacity to seize control of a shaman's consciousness and propel the willing spirit traveler into unseen dimensions of the surrounding cosmos. In addition, they help shamans share their experiences of the spirit world with others, shape bodily sensations of ritual participants or audiences, and compel clients or communities toward health and relief.

Both ritual music and movement and the administration of entheogens tend to play key roles in conveying the nature and efficacy of shamanic rituals. They may help identify a situation as a shamanic ritual, calling attention to the shaman's powerful acts and alerting the audience to the fact that a supernatural performance has begun. Further, they also serve as media through which shamans may achieve trance states or as the very idiom through which spirits choose to communicate with the human community. Spirits may speak or act through song and dance, or the spirits of particular psychotropic substances may address shamans directly as animate beings during the séance. In the case of music and dance in particular, performances may serve not only as a medium for human communication with spirits, but also as an acoustic and visual record of the resulting supernatural encounters, detailing events which otherwise would remain unknown to the observing audience. Dance in particular allows the shaman to act out the speakers or messages received in dramatic, but often cryptic form. Sometimes music can serve as a record of communications after the fact as well, as when a shaman returns with a particular set of healing words or knowledge of a particular spirit encapsulated in a song. We will examine each of these functions below, while querying as well the possible physiological mechanisms by which music and entheogens achieve their effects.

MUSIC

> Music has Charms to sooth a savage Breast,
> To soften Rocks, or bend a knotted Oak.
> I've read, that things inanimate have mov'd,
> And, as with living Souls, have been inform'd,
> By Magick Numbers and persuasive Sound.
>
> William Congreve, *The Mourning Bride*, 1697

In the scholarly discovery of shamanism during the eighteenth century, Western travelers were often struck by the intense, rhythmically insistent musical performances which accompanied shamanic séances. Practitioners or their assistants beat drums at a rapid and unflagging pace, clanged cymbals or bells, and/or chanted songs of power and complexity. They responded to the music bodily: through dance, hyperactivity, and dramatic shifts from action to torpor. Scholars, intent on remaining distant from the proceedings they witnessed, sometimes found themselves inexorably drawn to the emotional experiences at the center of shamanic rituals by the music they heard, describing it in retrospect with a sense of awe or even terror.

The use of music as a device for framing and identifying a shamanic ritual is evident in many ethnographic records of shamanic traditions. Basilov (1997: 12) notes that in Nenets' shamanic performances, music constituted the single medium that bound together shaman, audience, and spirit world: "the Nenets accompanied each striking of the drum with shouts of 'goi! goi! goi!' As the cries of the participants intensified and blended with the general noise, the shaman would begin to summon the spirits." Similar communal participation in the music of shamanic rituals occurred, Basilov notes, among Khakass and Ket peoples as well.

Norman Bancroft Hunt (2002: 30–6) recounts the experiences of the ethnographer Peter Freuchen, who observed an Inuit séance performed by the *angakok* Sorqaq and an assistant in the early twentieth century:

Krilerneq, Sorqaq's assistant, tied up the old *angakok*, who had completely undressed, and extinguished all seal-oil lamps except for one tiny flame. He placed the shaman's drum and drumstick next to Sorqaq, who ... was completely immobilized: his arms were secured behind his back with a stout rope above the elbows, his thumbs were lashed together with strips of rawhide, and a rope extending from these wrapped around his ankles so that his feet were drawn up beneath him.

Sorqaq began to sing in his ancient cracked voice while the spectators shouted encouragement and praised him for his great abilities. For a long time Sorqaq chanted, breaking his song every so often with a despairing cry that this *tunghat* had forsaken him and he would be unable to travel through rock and plead with the spirits, or that his power would leave him at the mercy of their tricks and make it impossible for him to return to the people.

Each time he uttered his words of despair the crowd yelled that he could make it, until the *qasgiq* [ritual hall] was filled with shouts and cries urging him on. Slowly his chant increased in strength and tempo, while the drum which the Eskimo say "plays itself," began to beat faster. The *qasgiq* trembled with the sound of the drumbeats. Seal-skins crackled through the air, or could be heard passing through the ground beneath the audience's feet. Krilerneq's voice boomed in accompaniment to Sorqaq's song, which was becoming wilder and wilder, while the audience sang and shouted. Freuchen lost track of how long this "infernal din" lasted, but recalls that he held on to Krilerneq's arm to make certain that he was not party to any trickery on Sorqaq's part. Finally the *angakok*'s voice became fainter and then stopped. Krilerneq relit the lamps. Sorqaq had disappeared. (2002: 34)

In this account, it is evident that music played a key role not only in framing the ritual event but also in helping effectuate the shaman's trance and spirit travel. Singing allowed the practitioner to communicate with his helping spirits and to seek the encouragement and emotional support of the human audience, which participated actively through their own singing and shouts. The curtailment of the shaman's singing marked the end of the first phase of the ritual and would resume only when the *angakok*'s voice was heard returning to the earth.

Boudewijn Walraven (1994) notes the cooperation between the Korean *mudang* shaman and her musical accompanists, who help her execute the *muga* (song) involved in a given *kut* séance:

Usually a *muga* is sung by one *mudang* alone, but the musicians often assist her with cries of encouragement and occasionally they join in the singing. On the East Coast, in some *muga*, the drummer sings a phrase, after which the *mudang* sings a line. The drummer repeats the phrase, while the *mudang* sings a new line and so they continue. The drummer constantly repeats the same words, the lines of the *mudang* change all the time. In such songs the task of the drummer is to give support, he is not an independent singer. In parts of the *kut* with a theatrical element, such as one often finds at the end of a ceremony, the contributions of the drummer are of great importance, when he takes part in humorous dialogues. When more than one *mudang* participates in the singing, there is usually one who sings the song itself, while the others sing refrains or encouragements. (1994: 28)

Man-young Hahn (1990: 196–217) presents a musical transcription of a Cheju Island shamanic *kut* featuring such elaborate interplay of multiple shamans and musicians. Shifts in tempo and instrumentation helped accentuate moments in the *kut* so that the audience could better follow the supernatural events described in the songs. Here we see the cooperation of shaman and assistants in the creation of the ritual's music, although in this case, the audience appears more passive, watching the performers' combined song and dance. The importance of encouragement appears key: the shaman must be assured of the desire of the assembly to see the supernatural communication occur in order to receive the proper inspiration and courage needed to leave the security of ordinary consciousness. That music and dance constitute the context in which such encouragement occurs appears both logical and characteristic within shamanic traditions.

While performing their songs, the Korean *mudang* may also make use of elaborate dance steps and props. Lee Yong-Shik (2004: 64ff.) details some of the typical implements used in such dances. Fans are seen as cosmic seats that permit the spirits to enter the shaman's body during the *kut*, while flags of different colors symbolize the client's good and ill luck as well as the shaman's tutelary spirits. Swords and daggers are used in divinatory acts, and some varieties of shaman will stand upon sharp blades during the performance. As Lee describes: "The shaman dances with the freshly sharpened *jakdu* [fodder blades] to soothe the deities who will protect her … She licks the blades and hits her cheeks, hands and legs with the *jakdu* in order to check whether deities will allow her to perform *jakdu tagi* [the blade dance]." If the deities indicate their readiness, she mounts the sharpened blades and dances on top of them. Writes Lee: "The performance of *jakdu tagi* demonstrates the mysterious power of the deities which Hwanghae shamans embody and makes the ritual an awesome spectacle" (2004: 69). The close association of music and material culture here is evident, helping create a richly multisensory experience that moves both audience and performer alike.

Takefusa Sasamori (1997) surveys the role of music performance in the shamanic rituals of *itako* shamans from Japan. As a rule, *itako* are blind and female, and draw on a repertoire of songs that includes Buddhist sutras. Given their blindness, aural channels take particular prominence in the *itako* ritual acts, which generally feature massage, patting, and song. Sutras are performed to heal illnesses, exorcise invasive spirits, accomplish divination, locate missing objects, and sacralize particular public ceremonies. For musical accompaniment, the *itako* uses prayer beads, bows, hand-bells, a characteristic fan-shaped drum, and small bells attached to figures of the deity Oshira (1997: 91). These instruments mark rhythm, but also accomplish supernatural tasks as well: prayer beads can be rubbed on affected areas as a cure, and bows made of catalpa, mulberry, or maple, and strung with human hair, can lure spirits into attendance (see also Blacker 1975: 160–1). The *itako*'s bodily movements may be kept to a minimum, but can sometimes include dramatic dance routines involving two accompanying staffs.

In many shamanic traditions, music also constitutes part of the symbolic code by which particular spirits, shamans, or community members are identified within a ritual. Lisha Li (1992) describes the ways in which audience members can eavesdrop on Manchu shamans' spirit travel through observing shifts in instrument use or rhythm. Changes in the characteristics of the shaman's performance indicate changes in locale or interlocutor during the shaman's spirit journey, although all such elements are invisible to the attending audience. The shaman uses drumming to summon and communicate with deities, while the sound of shaking waist-bells in the shaman's ongoing dance is intended to evoke images of thunder and thereby frighten or mislead demons (1992: 54, 59). Particular rhythms, all based on odd numbers, are used to denote the shaman's movement through the cosmos and spiritual addressees. Writes Li:

> According to some old shamans, the "Old Three-accented Patterns" are for worshipping the gods who live in the sky region, the "Five-accented Patterns" are for passing the intention of the gods to the people, the "Seven-accented Patterns" are for driving away the demons and the "Nine-accented Patterns" are for dealing with all living beings in different regions of the cosmos, i.e., humans, gods, and demons, etc. ... Many people understand the meanings of these rhythmic patterns, especially the "Old Three-accented Patterns" which are the most widespread ... Experienced people even know, through the particular rhythm used together with other elements of the performance, which level of the cosmos the shaman has reached and whom the shaman is contacting. (1992: 58–9)

Li further notes that accentless drumming with single beats is used to mark transitions between cosmic regions, further delineating for the audience the path and progress of the journeying shaman. Such symbolism creates another means by which the shaman can draw an audience into the ritual, engaging the assembly as an integral, if seemingly passive, part of the event.

Not only can music identify place and type of being involved in a séance, it can also sometimes identify specific individuals. By singing a shaman's personal song, for instance, a knowing community member can invoke that individual or communicate vital messages through music (DuBois 2006: 66–72). Caroline Humphrey (1996: 185) recounts a telling example of this use of song in her account of the Daur Mongol *yadgan* Mendüsürüng:

> Mendüsürüng, who had grown up in the Hailar district, remembered [the shamans] Pingguo Saman, Huangge Saman, Lam Saman, and Jaban Saman. As he talked Mendüsürüng constantly broke into song. He was overcome by the melodies, one like a lullaby, another like a romantic entreaty, and a third confident and happy. These were the signature-tunes of individual shamans. They were the musical refrains (*iroo*) from longer chants (*gisaar*). It seems that many of them had been melodies from popular folk-songs, and that a shaman would gather tunes from the people and transform them into his or her own song by replacing the words and inserting the tune into a longer chant ... I realized that each shaman left aural traces, which were the most spontaneous memories of them. Mendüsürüng once wrote, "The sound of the shaman's voice can take away your heart". (1996: 185)

Robin Ridington (1988) examines the role of shamanic singers among Dunne-za (Beaver) people in British Columbia. In Dunne-za culture, elders may acquire the skill of becoming *Naachin* ("Dreamers"). The songs they learn through their dream visions serve as communications between deceased community members and the living, confirming the former's arrival in the land of the dead. By performing songs gained through visions, *Naachin* can confirm such arrivals or even help effect them, as the spirits of the dead wander along *Yagatunne*, the trail that leads upward from this world to the next. By singing and dancing along with the *Naachin*, the community members can ease the passage of others – or themselves – to the next world (1988: 87). As the *Naachin* Charlie Yahey put it in an oratory which Ridington recorded in 1965:

> This song is supposed to be really kicking.
> It sounds like white man's music on the record player.
> White men's music isn't going to do anything for you.
> It won't help you get to heaven.
> This kind of music – when you hear it, it's hard to make it.
> Somebody really prays to God – it's not going to be hard.
> Somebody gets stuck getting up, sing, sing.   (1988: 82)

Yahey's words signal both the cosmic importance of his songs and his personal frustration with a culture that was losing touch with the

Naachin tradition and the vital communications such music contains (see Chapter 12).

In a series of studies on the Temiar people of the forests of Malaysia, Marina Roseman (1991, 1995, 2001) has similarly described the place and function of music as a symbolic code in Temiar shamanic activities. Among Temiar people, as among Dunne-za, spirit helpers make their presence known to the community through dreams, during which they may convey a melody as well as possible dance steps and words. This signature song then becomes a means by which healers can call the spirit helper into presence and enlist it in curing the maladies of an ill community member. Temiar healers have experienced a wide range of spirit helpers from the outside, including spirits of other nationalities (e.g., Chinese loggers, Japanese occupation forces during the Second World War), and technologies (e.g., trade goods, airplanes, wristwatches, canned sardines). Each of these provides a musical signature that fits into the preexisting framework of Temiar spirit helpers.

Within this shamanic tradition, practitioners expect that communications from the spirit world will take musical form. Particular genres exist that describe and dictate the shape and sound of such songs, and these are shared widely in Temiar culture, although with some distinctive regional and local variations. When performing a spirit's song, a core remains stable, while the performer is also accorded license to expand and adapt it to the circumstances of the healing ceremony (2001: 118). This performative authority may stem in part from the fact that in Temiar tradition the shaman becomes the surrogate parent of the spirit helper: the shaman asserts control over the relationship through choosing when and how to perform the spirit's song. Roseman (2001: 111) points out that music in particular holds power in Temiar understandings because it is detachable: it crosses social, generational, and even cosmological boundaries, creating linkages that allow the shaman to move between otherwise disconnected areas or statuses. In a very real sense, the musical repertoire of the community becomes a chronicle of the spirit contacts it has experienced over a span of generations.

Scholars of musical perception have investigated the ways in which music can achieve the emotional and psychological effects which are evident in these accounts of shamanic performance. Robert Jourdain (1997: 303) discusses the ways in which music can relieve the effects of even severe Parkinson's disease and notes: "It is remarkable that something so powerful as music is so unnecessary" (1997: 304). Describing the heightened effects of music on frontal lobe as well as limbic system activity, he writes:

As our brains are thrown into overdrive, we feel our very existence expand and realize that we can be more than we normally are, and that the world is more than it seems. This is cause enough for ecstasy. (1997: 331)

The mechanics of music sensation are complex. Melodies are processed in a region of the temporal lobe known as the primary auditory cortex. Specific neurons within the cortex respond to specific pitches, although all cells fire to some extent when confronted with auditory sensations of any kind (Jourdain 1997: 52). The primary auditory cortex then conveys input to surrounding cells, the secondary auditory cortex, where they are further analyzed. Here right-brain and left-brain functions differ: the right-brain secondary auditory cortex cells help sort and analyze simultaneous sounds, discerning hierarchies of sounds and harmonies. Left-brain auditory cortex cells analyze the succession of sounds and hierarchies of sequencing, such as rhythm and dance steps. Given that the left brain is responsible for processing language, this focus on sequencing is to be expected (1997: 57).

As Daniel Levitin (2006) points out, the jumble of phenomena which we conceptualize as thought works largely through processes of neural interconnectivity between different brain centers, and in the case of musical understanding, these connections include primary and secondary auditory cortex cells, frontal regions responsible for processing musical expectations and structure, the cerebellum and the basal ganglia, the latter two probably further involved in processing rhythm and meter. Crucially, the limbic system is also activated in musical reception, as musical stimuli cause neural firings in the nucleus accumbens, connected with both the amygdala and the hippocampus via the mesolimbic pathway. Writes Levitin: "The rewarding and reinforcing aspects of listening to music seem ... to be mediated by increasing dopamine levels in the nucleus accumbens, and by the cerebellum's contribution to regulating emotion through its connections to the frontal lobe and the limbic system" (2006: 191). When we listen to music, our brain's various cells and centers come to synchronize with the impulses derived from the pitches, harmonies, rhythm, and tempo of the music, responding to their own ability to do so through the release of endogenous opioids. The brain in a sense enjoys becoming entrained to this outside stimulus and, given the right conditions, as discussed in Chapter 7, can eventually undergo the complete parasympathetic dominance characteristic of trance states.

Although Judith Becker notes the value of physiological models of musical perception, she also emphasizes the role of culture in shaping personal as well as communal responses to music. She writes:

The scripts of music and emotion, the habitus of listening, can be helpfully understood as a process which is supraindividual ... in which the relationship between music and emotion needs to be understood as extending beyond the minds and bodies of single musicians and listeners, that is as a contextually situated social practice. Emotions relating to music are culturally embedded and socially constructed and can usefully be viewed as being about an individual within a community, rather than being exclusively about internal states. (2001: 151)

For Becker, music achieves its effects within a framework of culture, which may harness the physiological mechanisms of the brain's perceptive system to the end of religious and social communication. Her view is echoed by that of Gilbert Rouget (1980) and Laurent Aubert (2006). Aubert states that the efficacy of music "does not rely solely on the nature of the sounds, their acoustic properties, but also upon the social function attributed to the music and the aural codes it admits in a particular situation, codes immediately perceived and applied by adepts in a position to be affected by the music" (2006: 17; my translation). Jourdain (1997: 303) notes significantly that the music that works to relieve the Parkinson's symptoms of one person may not do so for another: cultural concepts and communal tastes help shape the sequences of sound and rhythm that an individual identifies as pleasurable, connected, or efficacious, and only those that exhibit a certain degree of "flowingness" from the individual's cultural perspective will stave off the jerking loss of motor control that torments the advanced Parkinson's syndrome patient. Jourdain suggests that the key to all such musical experience is the perception of stimuli which either meet or defy our culturally grounded patterns of expectation: truly "moving" music treads a fine line between meeting the expectations dictated by genre and typical style, on the one hand, and startling the listener with unconventional, unexpected, stimuli, on the other. Emotional engagement with the music comes through cognizance of this complex negotiation of expected and unexpected turns (1997: 312).

ENTHEOGENS

As with examinations of shamanic gender (Chapter 5) or supernatural aggression (Chapter 6), scholars' views of entheogen production and use have often been shaped by ideas derived not from the shamanic traditions themselves but from outsiders' social mores. Western scholars have on occasion felt it important to take moral positions on the use of mind-altering substances. With some notable exceptions, for the bulk of the history of the field, researchers have not only documented but also deplored the use of entheogens, regarding them as a sign of the delusional or decadent nature of the shamanic calling. In the late 1960s and early 1970s, young American researchers such as Michael Harner (1972, 1973) and Carlos Castaneda (1968, 1972) embraced psychotropic substance use as paths of human enlightenment, only to distance themselves later from these same positions, and have come to present substance use as a misguided or unnecessary element of shamanic practice, as we shall see in Chapter 14. Scholars have frequently rejected a truly neutral attitude toward this aspect of shamanic practice, despite the fact that it is widespread throughout the world and often considered crucial for the shaman's commerce with the spirits. In the following discussion, we examine entheogen use as a culturally identified pathway to shamanic trance states, parallel to that afforded by other trance induction techniques described above and in Chapter 7.

As with music, entheogens often help frame and identify shamanic rituals for their communities. The collection, preparation, and administration of psychotropic substances are events which allow the community to observe the onset of the ritual procedure and possibly to play a role in its performance. Where such preparatory acts are part of the shaman's occult lore, part of the apprenticeship of novice shamans may include learning the techniques involved in collecting and creating the necessary substances. Often, shamanic traditions possess subtle rules for the preparation of entheogens, and elaborate narratives may exist regarding the community's discovery of and initial use of the substances in question. As we shall see below, a survey of several entheogens from different shamanic traditions around the world can illustrate the variety as well as the similarity of such concepts cross-culturally.

A number of scholars have sought to amass and document the diverse findings regarding use of psychoactive substances worldwide (Ott 1993; Schultes, Hofmann, and Rätsch 2001; Rätsch 2005). In addition, a comprehensive website is operated by the Erowid organization, devoted to "documenting the complex relationship between humans and psychoactives" (Erowid 2007). These sources provide information on a wide range of plants traditionally used as entheogens, along with occasional details regarding the myths or rituals associated with their use. A selection of some of the substances best known within documented shamanic traditions are presented below. This survey is by no means exhaustive, but is intended to convey some of the varieties of knowledge and practice associated with shamanic entheogens cross-culturally.

One of the best-known and most widespread entheogens of the Eurasian cultural area is the fly agaric mushroom (*Amanita muscaria*). This species of fungus is red, yellow, or occasionally white, flecked with raised white spots (Schultes, Hofmann, and Rätsch 2001: 34). It grows in symbiosis with pine, fir, and birch in thin forests, and contains several compounds of psychoactive nature: muscimol, ibotenic acid, and muscazone (O'Neil 2006, monographs no. 6,312, 4,877, and 6,311). Together these chemicals make the mushroom a powerful psychedelic deliriant which can also serve as a potent analgesic. Already in the mid-seventeenth century, Western travelers noted the use of this substance as a psychotropic in Siberia (Pearson 2002: 98). At the turn of the twentieth century, Waldemar Jochelson confirmed its use as an entheogen among Siberian shamans, such as those of the Koryak people of eastern Siberia (Pearson 2002: 98). He describes the hallucinatory experiences of Koryak shamans as follows:

Fly Agaric produces intoxication, hallucinations, and delirium. Light forms of intoxication are accompanied by a certain degree of animation and some spontaneity of movements. Many shamans, previous to their séances, eat Fly Agaric to get into ecstatic states ... Under strong intoxication, the senses become deranged, surrounding objects appear either very large or very small, hallucinations set in, spontaneous movements and convulsions. So far as I could observe, attacks of great animation alternate with moments of deep depression. (quoted in Schultes, Hofmann, and Rätsch 2001: 83)

As discussed in Chapter 3, R. Gordon Wasson (1963) posited that the esteemed *soma* of the *Rig Veda* may have referred to *A. muscaria*, although the substance would have become replaced by other plants as the Aryans migrated into the very different biotope of the Indus Valley (see Flattery and Schwartz 1989). Wasson notes the secondary ingestion of the substance through consuming the urine of people who had eaten the fungus, and suggests that Vedic references to this custom correlate with eighteenth-century accounts of similar practices among Russian villagers living in Siberia (1963: 235). Schultes, Hofmann, and Rätsch (2001: 82) include a Koryak myth about the creation of the mushroom from the spittle of the god Vahiyinin:

The culture hero, Big Raven, caught a whale but was unable to put such a heavy animal back into the sea. The god Vahiyinin (Existence) told him to eat *wapaq* spirits to get the strength that he needed. Vahiyinin spat upon the earth, and little white plants – the *wapaq* spirits – appeared: they had red hats and flecks. When he had eaten *wapaq*, Big Raven became exceedingly strong, and he pleaded: "O *wapaq*, grow forever on earth." Whereupon he commanded his people to learn what *wapaq* could teach them. (2001: 82)

Big Raven here fills the role of a mythic primordial shaman, the first of his culture to access the powers offered by the spirit world through psychoactive plants such as *A. muscaria*. Jonathan Ott (1993: 333) discusses a twentieth-century account of the fungus among Anishinabe people of the Great Lakes region as well, although it is difficult to determine the age of the tradition in this area.

Gary Lincoff (2005) recounts fieldwork he undertook in 1994 and 1995 among Evenki and Koryak shamans of eastern Siberia. Both communities made use of *A. muscaria* as well as other medicinal plant substances in their healing and ritual traditions. Particular importance was attached to mushrooms found growing in close association with birch trees (*Betula ermanii*), which are regarded as a cosmic pathway between the visible world and various otherworlds (see Chapter 4). Lincoff's Koryak informants in particular harvested and used only those *A. muscaria* mushrooms found near a single birch tree held sacred by the community. Lincoff also includes details from an interview he conducted with the Evenki healer Tatiana Urkachan. Urkachan described herself as a seventh-generation shaman, and noted using *A. muscaria* as a medium for spirit travel as well as an ingredient in poultices she prepares for patients suffering from inflammations and arthritis. Her spirit travel was undertaken to heal community members of somatic, mental, and spiritual ailments.

Plants of the genus *Datura* within the family Solanaceae have been widely used as entheogens in both Europe and North America. Large, spindly shrubs of *Datura certocaula*, *D. inoxia*, *D. metel*, and *D. stramonium* contain a variety of delirium-producing compounds, including atropine, scopolamine, and hyoscyamine (O'Neil 2006, monographs 875, 8,406, and 4,858). Among the Native American peoples of the southwestern USA and Mexico, *D. inoxia* ("Stinkweed," "Toloache," "Toloatzin," "*hierba del diablo*") was often employed for a variety of spiritual activities, including spirit travel and divination. It was occasionally used as an entheogen during male puberty rites of passage. Dried roots were steeped in hot water to make a potent tea.

Amy Arnett (1995) notes that *D. stramonium* ("Jimson Weed") is so known because of its unintentional ingestion by British troops at Jamestown, Virginia in 1676. The resultant delirium was described by colonial writers and marks the first written account of the substance in North America. The plant is also known as Locoweed (a term also used for *Cannabis*), Angel's Trumpet, Thorn Apple, Devil's Trumpet, Mad Apple, Stink Weed, Sacred Datura, and Green Dragon, terms that reflect the plant's frequent association with supernatural activities, as well as its trumpet-shaped flowers.

Another member of the Solanaceae family, *Atropa belladonna* ("Deadly Nightshade") was widely used as a deliriant in Europe. Its botanical name is derived from the name of the Greek Fate Atropos and the Italian *bella donna* ("beautiful woman"), referring to its frequent use as an eye dilator among wealthy Western women in the eighteenth and nineteenth centuries. Its various common names include Sorcerer's Cherry and Witch's Berry, referring to its strong association with sorcery in European folk tradition (Schultes, Hofmann, and Rätsch 2001: 88). Schultes, Hofmann, and Rätsch (2001: 90) record sixteenth-century reports of solanaceous hallucinations in which people imagined themselves turning into fish or geese and behaved accordingly, complete with flopping on the ground, honking, or flapping arms like wings. Related Solanaceae trees of the genus *Brugmansia* figure in some South American recipes for *ayahuasca* (see below).

Pearson (2002) notes that ingestion of Solanaceae has been linked to perceptions of animal transformation (as illustrated above) as well as out-of-body flight (2002: 105–7). Preparations of the plant are also smoked or made into poultices to apply to various parts of the body. Pearson writes:

Topical activity is typical of the *Solanaceae* family. Zuni rain priests, for example, applied powdered roots of *Datura meteloides* to their eyes in order to commune with the Feathered Kingdom ... Yaqui sorcerers of northern Mexico were known to rub crushed *Datura* leaves on their genitals, legs, and feet to experience the sensations of flight. (2002: 106–7)

In North America, peyote stands as a prime entheogen. Native to the desert scrub biotopes of Northern Mexico and Southern Texas, the low-growing, round cactus species *Lophophora williamsii* or *L. diffusa* contains the hallucinogen mescaline (O'Neil 2006, monograph 5,905), a psychomimetic alkaloid that acts as a powerful hallucinogen. Archaeological evidence attests to its use as an entheogen in the areas in which it grows natively already two to seven thousand years ago (Schaefer 1996: 141). Today, it is used ritually by Native communities across a wide range of the continent. In ethnographic literature, it is generally referred to as *peyote*, a term deriving from the Nahuatl word *peyutl*.

Stacy B. Schaefer (1996) discusses the ritual uses of peyote among Huichol Indians in Northern Mexico. Huichol people consider *hikuri* (peyote) a central element of their spiritual lives. Through sharing the cactus with community members in carefully prescribed rituals, the shaman (*mara'akáme*) shares access to spiritual worlds beyond that normally visible and guides them in their journeys. The entheogen allows for the kind of "democratizing" of shamanic experience characteristic of many North American shamanic traditions, as discussed in earlier chapters.

Schaefer's description of Huichol peyote rituals illustrates the ways in which entheogen use can become deeply embedded in communal norms

and customs within shamanic traditions. The normal procedures for ingestion occur within an annual pilgrimage to the area where it grows, Wirikúta
(San Luis Petosí, Mexico). Schaefer characterizes the rituals:

> The preparation and consumption of peyote is always done within a strictly
> ceremonial context. Eating peyote ... is a highly ritualized activity likened to the
> partaking of sacramental food. The optimal manner of ingesting peyote is in
> Wirikúta, when it is freshly harvested. Peyote cannot be eaten until all of the ritual
> obligations are performed by the pilgrims. The peyotéros [peyote collectors] must
> first stalk it like deer in Wirikúta. Afterwards, the pilgrims collect peyote in the
> surrounding area in their woven baskets, known as *kiliwei*. No peyote is eaten until
> the shaman indicates that the time is right to do so. (1996: 148)

Family representatives as well as individual *mara'akáme* shamans look to a
single leading shaman for guidance in the ritual, the Nauxa, or Keeper of the
Peyote, who leads a ritual both on a sacred mountain and in the pilgrims'
camp. The Nauxa blesses all the participants, as well as the peyote, and takes
responsibility for doling out the cacti to community members throughout
the event. During the night following the gathering of the cacti, the event
unfolds as follows:

> Everyone eats his or her peyote and the *mara'akáme* begins the chanting that will
> continue through the entire night. While the *mara'akáme* carries the souls of the
> pilgrims along the journey of his song, Nauxa makes certain that the pilgrims are in
> the physical and mental states that facilitate their out-of-body travel along this path.
> Five times during the night, when the pilgrims must circle the fire after a cycle is
> completed in the *mara'akáme*'s song, Nauxa places the same amount of peyote as
> originally consumed in front of each pilgrim ... although the individual parti-
> cipants decide ahead of time on the dosage they plan to take, it is Nauxa who
> distributes the peyote and who, in doing so, keeps the road open for all the pilgrims
> to travel. (1996: 152)

Following this night-long ritual, the pilgrims return to their family groupings to repeat the ritual there with family members who did not participate
before. Again, Nauxa plays a role distributing the peyote to each family who
then perform their rites around the shrine of their ancestors, a *xiriki*.

Although all community members (including children) are thus invited
into the shamanic experience of spirit travel, in practice, it is the *mara'akáme*
who understands the travel better and sees the spirit world with greater
acuity. Schaefer quotes a Huichol shaman:

> [W]hen *mara'akámes* who have reached a very high level look into the fire they will see
> Tatewarí – Grandfather Fire – as a person, an old, old man with grey hair and a wrinkled
> face. He speaks to the *mara'akámes* and they listen to him ... The *mara'akámes* use their
> mirrors and their *muviéris* (feathered wands) to understand him better. The other

people, the ones who aren't as far along on their "path," don't see this old man in the fire. They will only see rattlesnakes, speckled lizards ... and mountain lions, who are the special messengers of this god – his representatives. (1996: 160).

The shamans thus acts in two key capacities in Huichol peyote ingestion: they effect and maintain the ritual in which peyote is to be consumed (thereby limiting its consumption and guarding against its misuse by communal members) and they help interpret and guide participants in relating their hallucinatory visions to the culture's various deities and supernatural entities. In this way, they function much like spirit guides do for shamans in general, sharing their knowledge of the supernatural world with others who have less experience of its complexities.

The kinds of culture-specific uses of peyote described above also occur alongside a more generalized use of peyote by members of the Native American Church, a syncretic religious organization which dates to the mid- or late nineteenth century. Formally incorporated as a religion in 1918, the Native American church spread quickly throughout Native American reservations and today finds adherents in more than fifty different tribes, with a combined membership of some 250,000. Adherents of the religion share peyote in communal services, which also include prayer and contemplation, songs, and rituals. Sweat lodges are a frequent component of Native American Church ritual activities as well. The development of "Peyotism" as a religious movement is discussed in Chapters 12 and 14.

One of the most widespread entheogens in Amazonian shamanic practices goes by the generic name *ayahuasca*. In practice, thick, brewed liquids known by this name may contain a wide variety of different plants, depending on local conditions and tradition. Most typically, these include the bark of *Banisteriopsis caapi* or the closely related *B. inebrians*, woody vines native to the rain forest biotope, as well as the leaves of *Psychotria viridia* or *Diploterys cabrerana*. Sometimes a single local tradition may identify multiple brews for different hallucinogenic effects. Among Tukano people of the Vaupés River Valley in Colombia, for instance, six distinct varieties of *ayahuasca* ("*kahí*") are identified, differing in both strength and visionary nature. The strongest of these, *Kahi-riáma*, is described as useful in divination, while the second-strongest, *Mé-né-kahí-má*, is said to cause visions of green snakes (Schultes, Hofmann, and Rätsch 2001: 124).

Schultes, Hofmann, and Rätsch recount a Tukano myth that attributes *B. caapi* to divine sources. The Sun-father impregnated the first woman, causing her to give birth to the plant. As the plant aged, he in turn gave men their semen (2001: 131). The authors also note the strong prevalence of powerful snakes and felines in *ayahuasca* visions:

The repetitiveness with which snakes and jaguars occur in Ayahuasca visions has intrigued psychologists. It is understandable that these animals play such a role, since they are the only beings respected and feared by the Indians of the tropical forest; because of their power and stealth, they have assumed a place of primacy in aboriginal religious beliefs. In many tribes, the shaman becomes a feline during the intoxication, exercising his powers as a wild cat. Yekwana medicine men mimic the roars of jaguars. Tukano Ayahuasca-takers may experience nightmares of jaguar jaws swallowing them or huge snakes approaching and coiling about their bodies. Snakes in bright colors climb up and down the house posts. Shamans of the Conibo-Shipobo tribe acquire great snakes as personal possessions to defend themselves in supernatural battles against other powerful shamans. (2001: 126)

Kenneth Kensinger (1973: 11) surveys uses and views of *nixi pae* (*ayahuasca*) among Cashinahua people of Peru, noting its frightening aspects in this culture and the resultant tendency of users to partake of it only in community:

Although each man operates on his own, the group is very important, as it provides him a contact with the real world, without which the terrors of the spirit world through which he is traveling could be overwhelming. Frequently a group of men will line up on a log, each one wrapping his arms and legs around the man ahead of him. Only the men who are "strong," i.e., those who have had many years of experience with *ayahuasca*, will not maintain physical contact with at least one other person. *Ayahuasca* is never taken by a person alone. (1973: 11)

As Michael Harner (1972: 153; 1973: 5) points out, however, among other Amazonian peoples with greater degrees of individualism, such as the Shuar (Jívaro), *ayahuasca* intake is normally practiced alone. Both Benny Shanon (2002) and Ralph Metzner (1999) explore the accounts of numerous Westerners who have ingested *ayahuasca* for spiritual purposes. Grob (1999: 242) points out the strong belief among urban *ayahuasca* users in Brazil that communal use of the substance (as administered in certain religious communities) is the only means of ensuring that it will lead to what interviewees term "the path of simplicity and humility." Without the communal context, they fear, the same substance can easily lead to inflated and destructive feelings of self.

The principal hallucinogenic ingredient in *ayahuasca* is N, N-dimethyltryptamine (DMT; O'Neil 2006, monograph 3,262), a powerful hallucinogen which is derived principally from *Psychotria viridia* or *Diploterys cabrerana*. As Schultes, Hofmann, and Rätsch point out (2001: 127), however, this compound normally cannot cross the blood–brain barrier maintained within the body to protect the brain from harmful chemicals. The chemicals harmine and harmaline (O'Neil 2006, monographs 4,613 and 4,616), derived from *Banisteriopsis caapi*, however, inhibit the production and distribution of monoamine oxidase (MAO), the enzyme responsible for breaking down DMT in the bloodstream, allowing the entheogen to enter and affect the brain. Harmine and harmaline are also central nervous system stimulants on their own.

Charles Grob has studied the effects of long-term *ayahuasca* use among Brazilian members of the movement União do Vegetal (Grob 1999: 237–42). He found that it helps in treatment of addiction, depression, and anxiety, and that it causes an increase in the number of serotonin receptors on nerve cells. Serotonin is an important monoamine neuro-transmitter which operates in various parts of the body. In the brain, the raphe nuclei release serotonin in order to stimulate such strong emotional expressions as anger, aggression, and sexual attraction.

Although the variety of active compounds found in shamanic entheogens around the world defy generalization, certain regularities do emerge from comparative analysis of their physiological effects. Many hallucinogens mimic the effects of the neurotransmitter serotonin, increasing and disrupt-ing the flow of messages between brain cells (Pearson 2002: 103). Others (euphorics) mimic the effects of endogenous opioid peptides such as dop-amine: neurotransmitters in the brain that stimulate cognition as well as relaxation and can produce analgesia and euphoria (Frecska and Kulcsar 1989). As noted in the discussion of *ayahuasca*, still other substances inhibit the action of monoamine oxidase, the chemical responsible for deactivating opioids once they have delivered their chemical message. As a result of all of these effects, the brain's processing of "reality" may become distorted, as new stimuli flood the mind and propel the percipient into powerful sensations outside normal perception. Pearson writes of hallucinogens:

[T]he chemical effects of hallucinogens cause the brain to undergo a massive and global change – a major ecological shift for which the brain appears to be inex-plicably ready. These substances seem to have a unique ability to fundamentally transform the functions that we consider to be uniquely human – the way we think, feel, and act. They alter and shift cognitive and symbolic capacities, aesthetic sensibilities, and our linguistic and imaginative capacities – the very kinds of brain functions that constitute the fabric of what we experience as "mind." (2002: 103)

Perhaps these effects do not arise so much from the brain's "inexplicable readiness" so much as from the fortuitous recurrence of certain chemicals crucial to the central nervous system's internal communication system in various plant substances that a person may chance to ingest. In the hunting and gathering lifestyle that engaged the human species for tens of thousands of years, individuals came to sample a vast array of potential food sources over time. Some of these were recognized immediately as deleterious and abandoned, perhaps after cases of toxic poisoning within the community. Others became staples of daily or seasonal diets. Still others may have become recognized as causing profound changes in mood or outlook, perhaps providing glimpses of an unseen spirit world or a deeply meaningful cosmos. When combined with the worldview and practices that lie at the heart of shamanic traditions, these became part of the human stock of entheogens, culturally recognized tools for spiritual enlightenment.

FROM ENTHEOGEN TO PUBLIC SCOURGE

While psychotropic substances have thus played a pivotal role in human religiosity over millennia, they have also occasionally wreaked great harm on individuals and human relations. Many such substances are strongly addictive. The regular intake of addictive chemicals can cause the body to produce less of its own neurotransmitters, causing a permanent chemical dependency which the body is unable to reverse. The individual comes to need the substance to maintain even a normal level of awareness or well-being. When the use of such substances is regulated and explained within a set of religious practices, this addictive propensity can often be held in check, or at least its effects mitigated. Intake is limited to moments of ritual need, or is confined to periods of specific ritual activity. The sacrality of the substance further inhibits users from engaging in casual ingestion. When, however, the same substances become viewed as purely recreational, the potential arises that they may become the objects of compulsive intake, creating substantial physical or economic liabilities for the user. Individuals as well as communities can be deeply damaged by unmanaged drug use. We survey the issues surrounding such crossover substances through an examination of alcohol, tobacco, and opium.

That alcohol served as an entheogen in many forms of shamanism is a certainty. The Sámi writer Johan Turi (1918–19) writes about the *noaide*'s use of alcohol in turn-of-the-twentieth-century Sweden:

And the *noaidit* look in brandy too, and they see all the things and the one who has stolen them. And if someone has become beset by ghosts, and he goes to a *noaide* for help, then the latter asks: "Have you got any brandy?" And if he has, then he helps him. And then he sees how the misfortune has been sent. (1918–19: 17)

The association of alcohol with divination here reflects deep-seated attitudes about the supernatural aspects of alcohol, and its capacity to reveal elements of the unseen world. Throughout history, it has frequently been used within festivities and celebrations as a means of heightening emotion and eliciting altered states of consciousness. It is perhaps not surprising that the class of alcoholic beverages in general is termed "spirits."

Alexander von Gernet (2000) reviews the use of different species of tobacco among Native American communities. Both *Nicotiana rustica* and *N. tobacum* were used in spiritual traditions, although the former was more common due to its greater hallucinatory effects. Indigenous rituals throughout the Americas still rely on tobacco to some extent as a means of blessing or purifying ritual elements and as a possible accompaniment to other forms of entheogens (Weiss 1973: 43; Schaefer 1996: 155). Bradley Bennett (1992: 486) notes the use of both alcohol and tobacco as adjuncts to *ayahuasca* in Shuar (Jívaro) shamanic practice. Although Europeans were initially recipients of tobacco as a novelty, by the late sixteenth century they had become major marketers of it to other Native groups, extending its cultivation and use to the Great Lakes area and eventually west across the entire continent. Some sixty other substances were also smoked by various North American peoples, a number of which had psychotropic effects (von Gernet 2000: 74). Von Gernet notes (2000: 78) that tobacco use permitted shamans to share supernatural sensations. As with peyote use described above, smoking helped create a "democratized shamanism ... in which all members of an egalitarian society had the potential to 'dream' and acquire spiritual power for themselves and their community."

The opium poppy (*Papavera somnifera*) was also traditionally used as an entheogen among many Middle Eastern and Asian traditions (Booth 1998). The thick latex derived from poppy buds contains a variety of active substances, including morphine, codeine, thebaine, and papaverine (O'Neil 2006, monographs 6,276, 2,463, 9,276, and 7,019). Substances derived from it are classified as euphorics, muscle relaxants, and analgesics. Martin Booth (1998: 11) has chronicled the spread and variations in use of this important substance. While peoples of Central and South Asia developed traditions of direct ingestion, either in solid form or in solutions, peoples of East and Southeast Asia developed methods of concentrating and smoking opium instead. Opium was used as an entheogen in various shamanic traditions throughout this region, although it gradually became transformed into a recreational drug, especially in urban environments. In cultures in which it had a shamanic use, however, addiction rates are lower. Joseph Westmeyer (2004: 124) cites epidemiological data from Laos which indicate that Hmong seek help for opium addiction at an earlier point in their addiction than their Lao counterparts. This difference seems to reflect a perception among Hmong people that addiction is a serious aberration requiring treatment rather than an expectable by-product of opium use.

After two centuries of largely unregulated trade in psychotropic substances, states in the early twentieth century began to place limits on their sale and production. American regulations were initially focused on indigenous populations alone: restrictions on alcohol sale and peyote use targeted Native communities well before any comparable limitations were proposed for the broader population. The Bureau of Indian Affairs outlawed the sale of alcohol to Native Americans in 1907, and soon tried to expand the ban to include peyote as well (Slotkin 1956: 51–6). The Bureau worked hard during the following decade to find legal justifications for a ban, despite frequent Congressional hesitation. Weston La Barre (1989: xii) cites Senate hearings on banning peyote in 1937, in a bill sponsored by D. Chavez of New Mexico (see also Slotkin 1956: 54). At that time, anthropologists staved off the impending ban by testifying about the positive effects of the substance within the framework of Native American spirituality. Despite such legislative defeats on the federal level, lawmakers were successful in criminalizing peyote use on the state level, through a variety of different laws enacted from 1917 to 1929 (Slotkin 1956: 56). While some of these were eventually repealed, pressure remained in other quarters for their reinstatement or extension. When in 1990, the US Supreme Court ruled that states had the right to prohibit peyote use, despite its importance in the activities of the Native American Church, the US Congress responded with the Religious Freedom Restoration Act of 1993, which reasserts the right of Native communities to adhere to traditional practices including entheogen use, despite prohibition of the substances in other contexts. Today, peyote use is a guaranteed right of members of the Native American Church, who may purchase supplies only from certain licensed vendors. As we shall see below, this legal exemption for indigenous use became a model for international legislature as well.

The selective ban on alcohol accomplished by the Bureau of Indian Affairs regulation of 1907 led to broader measures intended to affect the entire American society. By 1919, Prohibitionists had convinced legislators to outlaw alcohol altogether, amending the constitution to do so. The 18th Amendment was not repealed until 1933. Parts of the United States and other Western states remain "dry" today, a characteristic they share with observant Islamic states.

On the international level, trafficking in psychotropic substances met with legal restrictions through treaty agreements. The International Opium Convention of 1912 was signed by some thirteen nations in The Hague,

Netherlands and represents the first such agreement of its kind. Today, the UN Convention on Psychotropic Substances regulates the sale and production of prohibited chemicals internationally, with various Western states providing national legislation to implement the convention's directives. These include the US Psychotropic Substances Act, the UK's Misuse of Drugs Act, and the Canadian Controlled Drugs and Substances Act. Responsibility for identifying a substance as harmful rests with the World Health Organization. The UN convention's Article 32, however, allows exemptions for "plants growing wild which contain psychotropic substances … and which are traditionally used by certain small, clearly determined groups in magical or religious rites." This exemption is meant to permit entheogen use among shamanic practitioners, as in US toleration of peyote use. According to the convention, however, exemptions may only be made at the time that a given nation signs or ratifies the treaty, meaning that the legislation does not provide for the discovery of previously unknown entheogens or the spread of entheogen use from one nation or group to another.

The latter case occurred in Brazil, where *ayahuasca* use eventually spread to the general population through the various syncretic religious movements discussed in greater detail in Chapters 12 and 14. While some of these – such as the Church of Santo Daime – remained largely rural and peasant-oriented, the movement known as Centro Espirita Beneficente União do Vegetal (UDV) spread to urban areas and attracted members from the educated middle class. Largely through the activism of UDV members, the Brazilian government legalized use of *ayahuasca* for spiritual purposes throughout Brazil in 1987 (Grob 1999: 225). As Charles Grob relates, Brazil thus became "the first nation worldwide in almost 1600 years to allow the use of plant hallucinogens for spiritual uses by its non-indigenous inhabitants."

This precedent affected American law as well, when in the late twentieth century, a community of Brazilian emigrants sought to continue their traditional use of *hoasca* (*ayahuasca*) in their new home of New Mexico. The community, members of the UDV movement, attempted to import *ayahuasca*, only to find their shipment confiscated by state authorities. Claiming protection under the US Religious Freedom Restoration Act, the group sued for the right to continue their traditional use of the substance as an entheogen. In 2006, the US Supreme Court ruled that the community did indeed possess the right to use *hoasca*, just as members of the Native American Church are guaranteed the right to use peyote.

Recounting a vision that combines both music and entheogen use, Stacy Schaefer records the testimony of a Huichol peyote user:

Figure 5. Altai shaman's costume, collected by A. V. Anokhin in 1911. Note extensive use of tassels and inclusion of manufactured bells obtained through trade. Peter the Great Museum of Anthropology and Ethnography, Kunstkamera, Russian Federation. Photo courtesy Juha Pentikäinen.

One woman told me that when she was deep within the peyote a man came to visit her. It was the god of the wind Eka Tewari (Wind Person). He spoke to her and told her she had to remember his song. He began to sing for her and repeated the song until she knew it well. In the morning she related this to the mara'akáme [shaman], who told her she must sing the song for the whole temple group. Once she sang it out loud for everyone she knew she had it memorized. She says that it is now a part of her forever. (Schaefer 1996: 159)

The link between music and entheogens is powerful and, from the point of view of many, natural. Both pathways allow shamans to access complex spirit worlds so as to bring wisdom and insight back to the human community. Both pathways also permit shamans to share at least part of their experiences with other community members, who may partake of the music, dance, or entheogens alongside their religious specialists, particularly in cultures practicing forms of "democratized shamanism." In these cases, the shaman becomes not only a medium but also a guide to the surrounding spirit world.

Sometimes such sharing eventually creates a recreational custom which no longer carries with it the deep spiritual associations of previous intake traditions. Alcohol, opium, and tobacco use today may be regarded as pleasurable, but in most cases are no longer essentially associated with shamanic traditions. Other communally shared entheogens, however, such as peyote and *ayahuasca*, continue to maintain a close association with notions of spirit journey and shamanic sacrality, even when these have become adopted into ritual traditions or movements that hinge on collective imbibing and experience, or when they have become transferred to communities that lack or reject a long-standing relation to a shamanic tradition. It is undoubtedly the ritual traditions that help preserve this role, underscoring from one generation to the next the functional role of entheogens, like music and dance, in offering users access to a meaningful and efficacious spirit world.

CHAPTER 10

The material culture of shamanism

In many ways, shamanic rituals privilege sound over sight. During the séance, the shaman's words and singing, often sustained by vigorous drumming, cries of excitement and/or mimicry of animal sounds combine to create a rich collage of acoustic stimuli which evoke for the audience an intricate world of unseen spirits and events (Chapter 9). Frequently, visual channels are intentionally blocked in shamanic rituals: séances may occur in the dark, with the light of the fire extinguished, and key spiritual events may take place while the shaman's body lies motionless on its stage, offering little outward indication of the dramatic events unfolding in the spirit world.

Yet the visual is frequently also of importance in shamanic traditions, and finds powerful expression in various elements of material culture: the shaman's costume and implements, the potent objects within a shaman's kit, the masks or sculptures that embody key deities, the altars or stages that serve as a focus for the shaman's activities (Pentikäinen *et al.* 1998). In this chapter, we examine the material culture of shamanic traditions with attention to the form and function of objects. More enduring than song or speech, albeit seemingly less important, these elements of shamanic expression concretize the relations between shamans and the spirit world, as well as those between shamans and their communities. Shamanic material culture cues on a visual plane the unseen world of relations and beings that make shamanic practices possible.

COSTUME

Purev and Purvee (2004: 165–70) survey details and symbolism of Mongolian shamanic garb. Shamanic costumes collected from the 1960s or recovered from earlier archaeological sites vary by locale and type of shaman. They often were made of roe deer skin but have differing appliquéd fabric bands and fringe. Colors carried symbolic meanings that shamans could identify precisely. A Hotgoid shaman's gown includes owl feathers on its shoulders, and the vestments of Hurlar and Darhad shamans feature a similar use of eagle feathers. Groupings of owl and eagle feathers also grace extant headdresses, with feathers arranged in numbers that held cosmic significance (e.g., three, nine, seven, twenty-one), or that were seen to symbolize the number of past shamans in the practitioner's family (2004: 172). The Hotgoid costume also contains fabric flaps that resemble wings. These features clearly signaled to the shaman's community linkage with powerful raptors which the shaman could mimic in spirit flight or to whom the shaman appealed for spiritual guidance. Both the eagle and owl were ancient totems of the Mongols (2004: 172). Embroidered images of human faces or skeletons on the costume or headdress also expressed particular deities or ancestors and the physical situation of the shaman.

While the deer, raptor, and human body were thus important elements of Mongolian shamanic imagery, the snake also figures prominently in shamanic costumes (2004: 177–8). As an important messenger between various deities and the shaman, the snake found logical representation on the costume. Strands of cotton or wool were twisted to make imitation snakes, which were then covered with fabric and stitched to different parts of the costume. In some regions, these "snakes" remained highly abstract and were often accompanied by a long tassel. In other regions, the simulations were furnished with head, eyes, nose, and tail. A costume created in 1925 includes some 118 different snake tassels, arrayed over the shaman's heart, arms, legs, armpits, shoulders, collarbone, and chest (2004: 178). Eliade (1964: 152) cites customs among Altai shamans that stipulate inclusion of 1,070 snake images on a single costume. Although such details create a powerful visual impression, they also achieve an acoustic effect: often shamanic costumes in various cultures accentuate the practitioner's movement through clanging metal or bone pendants, bells or tassels (Iliff 1997: 47). Lisha Li (1992: 54) notes that Manchu shamans used percussives attached to the waist as a prime means of signaling elements of the spirit journey and the interlocutors with whom the shaman was interacting (see Chapter 9).

While some of the materials used in Mongolian costumes were of local manufacture, others were often Chinese in origin. Costumes that might appear at first to be unified wholes turn out to be creative amalgamations of different elements referring to various spirit helpers, deities, and social relations. In summarizing such costumes, Purev and Purvee write:

According to this research, and explanations of some shamans, it is evident that shaman clothing is not only a spirit image of a person or a roe deer. On the contrary, it is a whole system or assembly of the spirits of many animals such as antelope, snake and human. (2004: 165)

In a tangible sense, costume replicated what the shaman's words described: a remarkable merging of spiritual essences which created the basis for supernatural acts capable of transcending and transforming the concrete realities of the world.

While some of the visual elements of the costume thus made outward statements of a shaman's relations with the spirit world, others served as personal reminders for the shaman's own notice. As an example, Purev and Purvee note the *samalga*, a pendant made of antelope skin or multicolored fabric that was arrayed so as to hang down from the headdress before the shaman's eyes. The pendant was regarded as a means of attracting the spirits, but it also served as a protection for the shaman during ritual activities. It symbolized good and bad deeds, cosmic realms, and various virtues (2004: 174). The variety of meanings of the pendant probably reflects the individualized nature of shamanic understandings, and the fact that one shaman might interpret a costume element differently from another. In any case, the pendant's placement made it impossible for the shaman to see without confronting this tangible reminder of key elements

Figure 6. Nganasan shaman Turbyaku Kosterkin and his wife Valentine Kosterkina during séance. Note drum and tassels of headdress, obscuring the shaman's outward vision. Taimyr krai, Russian Federation. Photo courtesy Juha Pentikäinen.

of worldview and relations. As we shall see further below, obstructions to the shaman's ordinary vision are frequent in costumes cross-culturally: veils (such as Thai uses in his form of Hmong shamanism) are characteristic of some costume traditions, and in those traditions in which masking is common, the masks may have only small or even entirely absent eye holes.

Kendall (1995: 31) explores the performative dimensions of shamanic costumes in the region in which she conducts fieldwork:

> The costumes that the shamans wear are more than theatrical artifice; they are vehicles for the spirits' presence. Each trove has been dedicated to a particular spirit, either a member of the shaman's own pantheon or a particularly potent spirit of a client household. In particularly dramatic manifestations, spirits with unusually pressing business may appear out of turn when a shaman reaches spontaneously for their costume, clothes herself, and then gives them voice … the garment [the shaman] chooses will reveal the claims of a particularly potent spirit.

Here the shaman possesses multiple costumes, each attached to a particular deity. At the same time, the basic form of the costume remains the same, as do the accompanying implements used in the *kut* ceremonies. Halla Pai Huhm (1980: 32) describes the typical vestments used: blouses of white, blue, yellow, and light green (many with cuffs or draw-strings of other colors), *ch'ima* skirts of white, blue, and red, and various implements like hats, fans, swords, belts, and jackets that allow the performer to embody and express the various beings invoked in the ritual.

Similarly, Barbara Iliff (1994: 103) notes that Tlingit shamans made use of multiple costumes:

> The garments, like other types of shaman's objects, were particular to a certain helping spirit or spirits and when worn in conjunction with other accouterments during the séance, aided in the impersonation of these spirits by the shaman … The final product was a visual and aural expression of the individual doctor's powers related directly to his visions.

During the same séance, the shaman could change garments several times in order to convey different spirit interlocutors.

In hunter-gatherer cultures in which individuals may possess few articles of clothing other than a basic set of garments, the receipt and use of garb reserved solely for supernatural activities could carry great symbolic significance. Caroline Humphrey (1996) discusses the ways in which procuring a costume helped mark the stages of a shaman's training in Daur Mongol tradition:

> When the teacher judged that the young shaman was learning well, he requested the clanspeople to prepare the magical gown, a long and expensive undertaking.

Then the young *yadgan* would be inducted at the great triennial ritual called *ominam*, at which the pupil followed his teacher in every step of the performance. The young shaman was then an authorized *yadgan*, but not yet qualified to wear a shaman's crown; she or he wore a red cloth covering the head. More training took place over the next three years, until the next *ominam* was held. After this the shaman could wear a crown and was considered fully qualified. (1996: 186)

Providing the costume and its additional accouterments allows the community to acknowledge the new role which the adept is acquiring, and helps the novice shaman establish a career (Chapters 5 and 6). This role in outfitting the shaman finds parallels in many shamanic traditions around the world. Barbara Iliff (1994: 103) notes that in Tlingit culture, for instance, a training *ixt*'s sisters and female cousins assumed the responsibility of creating his ritual garb, both tanning the hides to be used, and then sewing them into the costumes themselves.

In the contemporary world, procuring a costume may involve painstaking preparation and assembly of components or, in the case of Korean shamanism, may simply involve buying a ready-made costume at one of the shamanic supply businesses that now thrive in modern Korea. Among contemporary Buryat shamans, a similar shift has occurred, but shamans regard it as a loss: where earlier shamanic capes (*nemerge*) were made to the accompaniment of important magical words, the tailors of today no longer know such formulas (Tkacz, Zhambalov, and Phipps 2002: 46) In Thai's Hmong community, the costume and other implements of the shaman's gear may entail the added complication of importation: Hmong people living outside of Laos must find ways of preserving or obtaining items that suit shamanic purposes in an alien cultural environment. Thai notes that in his community, shamanic gear cannot simply be thrown away after a shaman dies. Instead, it must be saved for the possible use by a later shaman. In the meantime, it serves as a protection for the household.

Regardless of the source of shamanic items like costumes or other implements, their usefulness is often negligible until they have been "activated" by a shaman. Barbara Iliff (1994: 117) notes such a view among Tlingit people, and Lisha Li (1992: 73) describes a similar concept among Manchu shamans. Smearing the object with blood was the Manchu way to enliven and sacralize shamanic drums. Jon Crocker (1985) details much the same notion in Bororo shamanic tradition (see below). Among Altaic shamans, as Potapov (1999: 27) details, the ritual "revival" of a drum consisted first of a ceremonial feast attended by the shaman's kin as well as other shamans of the district (1999: 27). The shaman then sought the soul of the animal whose skin formed the drum head. Once found and captured, the soul was

Figure 7. Yupik shaman in costume with patient, Nushagak, Alaska, 1890s. Note mask and exaggerated false hands. Photo by Frank G. Carpenter. Courtesy University of Washington Libraries.

forced into the drum, enlivening it ever after. The shaman then embarked on a spirit journey in order to present the drum to deities for approval. If the drum did not pass muster, it had to be corrected or the shaman could suffer illness as punishment (1999: 28).

MASKS

Crucial to shamanic costumes in many cultures are masks. As extensions of the costume over the very face of the practitioner, they create a lens through which the shaman views the outside world, while shaping in turn the ways in which outsiders perceive the shaman. Through dance and impersonation, the shaman may become one with deities or spirit helpers, manifesting them for the broader audience to see.

The Navy officer George Emmons procured more than a hundred Tlingit shaman's masks during his time in Sitka from 1882 to 1899 (Iliff 1994: 91). Some passed into his hands through sale by their owners; others he apparently removed from shamans' graves without familial permission. Barbara Iliff discusses the ethical implications of this fact in light of the US Native American Graves Protection and Repatriation Act. Although the masks were dispersed to a variety of museums across North America, Emmons saw the value of keeping shamanic kits together as unified assemblages, and so the masks are often preserved in conjunction with headdresses, staffs, rattles, and other artifacts associated with the original owner's shamanic practices.

Iliff (1997: 37) describes the ways in which the Tlingit *ixt* used masking in healing ceremonies. Once the shaman had achieved trance state, he often spoke in secret languages known only to the spirits. He also made use of a selection of masks, shifting between these during the ritual just as he shifted between costumes. One shaman named Setan transferred his masks to the collector George T. Emmons around 1860. He owned some nine masks (one more than the ritually perfect number of eight – Iliff 1994: 110), including ones depicting spirit helpers (a Tlingit man, a raven, and a sculpin), a friendly spirit of the air, the spirit of a drowned man who had transformed into a land otter, and various depictions of the shaman in the midst of key activities: singing, wearing a bone nose ornament, displaying a face painted with the dorsal fin of a blackfish (1997: 40). During healing ceremonies, the *ixt* might don particular masks at the spirits' bidding and act out their communications, allowing the spirits to use his body as a mouthpiece (1997: 38), much like the Korean *mudang* during *kut* rituals. Like Mongolian costumes, Tlingit masks often display a fusion of animal and human forms, evocative of the otherwise unseen supernatural transformations that occur within the shaman's spirit travels.

Significantly, in contrast with Tlingit masks used in other ceremonies (such as potlatches), shamanic masks did not have bored eye holes. Called "eyes solid," such masks obliged the shaman to rely upon his *yek* spirit guides for assistance in moving and dancing. Writes Iliff: "[these] were not dance masks in the true sense but the palpable means by which a shaman became transformed into his spirit beings and the vehicle by which he temporarily manifested the active presence of the spirit" (1994: 108).

Because of the close association between masks and the beings they represent, many shamanic traditions possessed rules for how the masks were to be stored or treated when not in ceremonial use. Norman Bancroft Hunt (2002: 63) describes the ceremonial masks of Iroquois collective shamanism. Iroquois culture rested traditionally on two potentially opposed subsistence activities: hunting and slash-and-burn agriculture. The former was presided over by the deity Tawiskaron ("Flint

Figure 8. Kwagul Mask of Tsunukwalahl, photographed by Edward S. Curtis c. 1914.
Library of Congress LC-USZ62–52217.

Giant"), while his twin brother, Tharonhiawagon ("Sapling"), presided over agriculture. Two societies of shamans existed in further reflection of this dichotomy: the False Face Society of the hunting livelihood, and the Husk Face Society of agriculture. Members of the societies created and made ritual use of masks that depicted the floating head spirits that bring both disease and healing. The False Face masks were carved from living wood and featured "grotesque distorted features that represent the symptoms of the illness" (2002: 64). Husk Face masks had similar functions but were made of corn husks. These masks were said to actually become the spirits they depicted, so that society members had to exercise great care when handling the masks, lest they offend the spirits. When not in use, the masks were carefully wrapped in white cloth and stored face down, so that the spirits could rest.

Galina Gračeva (1989) discusses shamanic masks among Nganasan and Enets shamans. Sometimes of metal, sometimes of wood, such objects were not apparently worn but rather treated as sculptures of deities (1989: 152). Two wooden masks collected in 1971 present highly abstract images of faces, differentiated as male or female through both details and wood type. Appliquéd metal eyes, bear teeth, and inscribed grooves or markings helped characterize them as images and sacred tools. They were conserved by a woman guardian on a ceremonial sled until they were accessioned as museum artifacts during the Soviet era. The line between masks and sculptures was fine, with the question of whether the objects were ever worn often unclear. Such a situation is paralleled in Tlingit tradition, where masks intended to be worn co-occurred with those meant as idols (Iliff 1994: 40).

DRUMS, MIRRORS, AND STAFFS

Few elements of shamanic paraphernàlia are as characteristic and as redolent of meaning as the drum. Although not all shamanic traditions feature the drum, it is nonetheless very common cross-culturally, and has been found among shamanic practitioners from North Eurasia to northern North America, with occasional recurrence in such far-flung locales as southern Chile (Hultkrantz 1991: 19–20). Both a musical instrument and an imposing material object, the drum offers practitioners a wide variety of ways of contacting the spirit world and of demonstrating those contacts to a human community.

Lisha Li (1992) presents a typology of North Asian shamanic drum construction, noting the occurrence of both single and double-headed drums, with different forms of frame reinforcement. As Li notes, the single-sided drum held particular significance as a means of calling spirits, and the rhythmic patterns played by the shaman during performance informed the knowing audience member of the shaman's progress through the various worlds beyond the visible (see Chapter 9).

Leonid Potapov (1999) surveys the shamanic drum among Altaic Turkic-speaking peoples of Central Asia. The drum was an essential tool of the shaman's arsenal, and was never shared with others. When not in use, the shaman carefully concealed it in the forest, never bringing it inside the home (1999: 29). Potapov writes: "Possessing one's own drum gave to each shaman the possibility of autonomous existence within the theological community of Altaic shamanism and its cult" (1999: 25). Construction of the drum, although simple, was governed by strict rules:

The shaman did not have the right to make his own drum, but rather this was the obligation of people living in his neighborhood. It was made simultaneously by several people, exclusively male, under the direction of the future shaman, who, in turn, was guided by the commands of his own ancestral spirits, former shamans. (1999: 27)

The Altaic drum was a hoop structure, reinforced behind by a cross-piece made of wood and metal. It was regarded as a tool for inducing trance, a vehicle for spirit travel, and a place for sequestering recovered souls.

Vilmos Diószegi (1968) collected widely in Soviet Siberia in the late 1950s. He was able to document a broad range of shamanic traditions conserved by people of that time as memory lore. Among his findings were elaborate accounts for how Tuvan (Soyot) craftsmen approached the task of constructing a shamanic drum. One such account tells of a group of men preparing the drum to the shaman's own specifications:

I made the drum for the shaman called Takka. He went into a trance one evening, in order to find out where we should go to find a tree. He said, we must go to the snow-capped "Silky" mountain because a certain kind of cedar-pine grew only there. The shaman came with us and he pointed out the right tree. There were three of us there, besides him. We left in the morning and came back the same night. We ... felled the tree. The shaman himself told us how to cut it out. But after pointing out the tree, he went home. We cut the plank from the tree, there on the spot, and bent it too. Two of us curved it around the trunk of the felled tree. One was smoothing one end, the other was shaping the other end upon the trunk. The ends were fastened with two double wooden pegs at the point where they touched. But this was not enough, the plank was not yet evenly bent, so we traced a circle upon the ground and stuck some wooden spikes around it into the earth, in the middle of the circle we made a fire, and we shaped the final form of the rim around the spikes. Furthermore, we cut off enough of the trunk for the handle to the other parts of the drum. But the rest of the work we had already carried out back home. The drum was ready within three or four days. (1968: 251)

While members of this clan thus cut down the tree to be used for the drum, they acknowledged that other clans were careful to leave the tree standing, cutting only the part of it necessary for constructing the drum.

Maria P. Williams (1995) details the construction of Tlingit shamanic drums. Her discussion illustrates the care that went into constructing drums and further illustrates the kinds of regulations that could obtain regarding those employed in their construction:

I contacted Mr. Watson Smarch, a Tlingit drum maker who lives in Teslin, British Columbia. Teslin is an inland Tlingit village. Mr. Smarch is one of the few individuals that still makes drums using traditional methods. It is time consuming and can take an entire winter to make a drum. The frame is the most difficult part of the process. Mr. Smarch said that the wood must be worked in water, heated and resoaked in a long process called kerfling in which the wood is bent into a round shape. The head of the drum is from the foreleg of a deer; often this part of the animal is damaged when the game is skinned or dressed. Instruments are always made by the members of opposite clans ... This is an aspect of reciprocity which existed between the moieties. (1995: 87)

Ernst Manker (1938) as well as Anna Westman and John E. Utsi (1999) provide a formal typology for the seventy surviving Sámi shamanic drums. In the South Sámi areas, an oval-shaped frame drum made from pine or spruce was common, reinforced behind with cross staves. The North Sámi variant was fashioned from hollowing out the burl of a pine or spruce tree, and thus had a smaller, rounder shape and a different back. Both the frame drum (*gievrie*) and the bowl drum (*goabde*) were completed with a drum head made of leather from a non-reproductive reindeer cow or a calf. Juha Pentikäinen (1995: 170) notes that the great Copenhagen fire of 1795 destroyed a vast wealth of drum evidence that had been collected and archived there from the Dano-Norwegian missions. Many drums were also summarily burned or otherwise destroyed during the era of intense missionization in both Denmark–Norway and Sweden–Finland.

Lisha Li (1992: 65) summarizes the various meanings of the drum in North Asian shamanic traditions. The drum itself can represent the sun amid the shamanic cosmos, a lake, a horse, or a reindeer. Its wooden construction links it inevitably to the World Tree, and elements of its structure are often associated with passages between cosmic realms (see Chapter 4), or with typical means of travel such as boats or horses. The drum head in turn not only links the drum to spirit helpers, but also offers the shaman a canvas upon which to depict spirit guides, cosmic features, or other important information. Li (1992: 66) notes the prevalence of images of snakes, frogs, tortoises, and bears on North Asian drums. Maria P. Williams (1995) discusses the symbolism of a particular Tlingit drum head. Although the drum had been owned by a man who belonged to the Raven moiety, the drum head featured a fused man-bear image more typical of the moiety of the Eagle. Writes Williams:

I had other knowledgeable Tlingits look at it. Austin Howard, a Tlingit elder, said it was more than likely that the mysterious Man/Bear figure related to the previous owner's personal vision or some type of supernatural experience such as a guardian spirit. (1995: 86)

The drum head thus becomes a place for promulgating in visual form the spiritual relations upon which its owner relies. In Tlingit culture, where personal vision quests were common among non-shamans as well, these relations could occur without the communally recognized designation of *ixt*. Sometimes, however, shamanic drum heads contain no pictures: Hultkrantz (1991: 14) notes, for instance, that Tuva shamans erased their images after each performance, redrawing them when the drum was to be used again.

The drum head could also serve as a map of some kind. As M. Jankovics (1984) notes, Arctic Siberian shamans tended to feature the night sky on their drum heads, with the North Star at its center. Further south, among Altaic peoples, more attention was paid to constellations. Potapov (1999: 27) reports that Altaic shamans in the 1920s told of using such depictions on their drums to help navigate the heavens during spirit journeys. On Sámi shamanic drum heads, the details of cosmic mapping varied: on the oblong drums of the south, a stratified cosmos was often depicted, with various deities and ritual items shown as vertically stacked layers. On the rounder drum heads of the northern region, on the other hand, the drum head was dominated by a central rhomboid image of the sun, with deities and objects arrayed on rays emanating from the center or around it, a distribution that has led Bo Sommarström (1991) to suggest that they represent a star map. Other symbols on the drums, however, referred to earthly locales, such as *sieidi* altars (see below) or graves. Sámi used their drums also for divination: by placing a metal ring on the drum head and beating the drum, the shaman or family head could observe the images crossed by the ring as the membrane vibrated, thereby arriving at a prediction regarding an issue at hand. The same custom recurs in eastern North America, among Naskapi and Montagnais peoples in Labrador, where it was used to predict the whereabouts and number of game before a hunt (Hultkrantz 1991: 19).

Where the drum head could provide a place for the public presentation of shamanic knowledge and relations, the back or interior of the drum could sometimes offer the practitioner a place for more private declarations. On Sámi frame drums, amulets, bone fragments, and teeth could be hung from the cross-pieces, while tin nails were driven into the frame to mark each bear killed in a ceremony officiated by the *noaide* (Westman and Utsi 1999: 10). Bowl-shaped drums could feature carved images of suns or other powerful entities on their back sides as well. The wooden cross-piece of Altaic drums became not only a handle, but also a depiction of the shaman's helping spirit(s). Always carved of fresh wood, the handle generally took the form of a human figure with one or two heads (Potapov 1999: 26). Occasionally, it could be dressed in strips of cloth representing clothes (1999: 30). In the meantime, the perpendicular metal cross-piece on the inner side of the drum represented not only the spirit helper's arms but also a bowstring which the shaman could use to fire arrows at attacking spirits (1999: 26).

Given its intensely meaningful nature, it is not surprising that shamanic drums were at times disposed of along with the deceased when the shaman died. Sometimes, however, the same drum could be passed down within a family, just as shamanic spirits could pass from generation to generation. Lisha Li (1992: 74) recounts the story of an Inner Mongolian shaman, Ma Qinshou, who instructed his family to recover a drum that had been buried with a deceased shaman from their clan. Writes Li:

When Ma was first "caught" by the soul of this dead shaman, he went into a trance, told people where this shaman's drums and set of waist-bells were buried, and asked people to dig them up. Then a new "life-cycle" of his "revived" drum started with its new user. Such a drum is considered more mystical and alive. (1992: 74)

Whereas many shamanic traditions thus view the drum as an intensely personal supernatural device, transferable only through careful actions of acquisition and revivification, some shamanic traditions allow for communally owned drums. An example can be found among Chepang *pande* shamans in Nepal. As Diana Riboli (2000: 96) details, *pande* drums, made of *sandan* wood and goat hide, were prohibitively difficult items to procure, as state restrictions severely limited the felling of trees and goat skin was very scarce in the region. In this situation, *pande* shared drums as a means of practicing their art.

Kira Van Deusen (2004: 18–20) notes the importance of mirrors as a further shamanic device in many North and Central Asian traditions. Using the mirror, the shaman can see the unseen or the yet to come. Alternatively, as Virlana Tkacz, Sayan Zhambalov, and Wanda Phipps suggest (2002: 32), the mirror (Buryat *toli*) can be viewed as a protective item, deflecting evil that may be directed at the shaman by other individuals or spirits. Van Deusen recounts narratives from modern shamans regarding their acquisition of their mirrors, today generally manufactured items but formerly locally made:

A Buriat shaman I met was given her mirror in a museum in Mongolia by a worker who said "I felt that the mirror should belong to you." Khakass shaman Tatiana Kobezhikova tells about going to visit a friend in another city on her own birthday. The friend said to her, "I have something for you. When I was up north, an old man came to me and gave me this mirror. He said I must give it to a person who will come to me on her birthday – and he described you!" (2004: 20–1)

Such tales can be regarded as counterparts of Bayir Rinchinov's elaborate account of acquiring *toli* included in Chapter 11.

Mircea Eliade (1964: 153) notes that mirrors in the past were often of polished copper and were interpreted differently from culture to culture, e.g., "the mirror is said to help the shaman to 'see the world' (that is, to concentrate), or to 'place the spirits,' or to reflect the needs of mankind" (1964: 154). Like the drum, it was sometimes described as a steed or vehicle.

Although Diószegi (1968: 238) found abundant accounts of shamanic drums among Tuva (Soyot) people, he also recorded details about shamanic staffs. Staffs were often an accompaniment or counterpart to the drum throughout the Siberian culture area, and, among Tuva, the staff often marked the novice shaman in particular:

The new shaman had first only been equipped with the shaman staff and he got the drum only after he had already become a good shaman. The staff was the tool of the shaman. It had always been made of birchwood and was usually painted red, with red clay, found in the mountains. If the shaman had been equipped with only a staff, he had to get around "on foot." After two or three years the new shaman could request his drum ... The shamans also kept their staff after having obtained their drum. There were shamans who kept their staff all their lives. For instance, the shaman called Khoban, shamanized all his life with a staff. It is up to the spirit to decide this: he "informs" the shaman whether he wants a drum or not. However, the shaman equipped only with a staff might be just as powerful as the one who has a drum. (1968: 238)

Nanai and Dolgan shamanic staffs often displayed ornamentation that depicted the multilevel cosmos and/or the World Tree motif (Pentikäinen *et al.* 1998: 116, 177). In examining evidence for shamanism in Viking Age Scandinavia, Neil Price (2002: 175–87) notes the particular prominence of the staff in medieval accounts of magical practitioners, as well as grave-finds of persons who seem to parallel the textual descriptions. In the latter case, the staff would represent a case of complete displacement of the drum considered so vital in other shamanic traditions, including that of Nordic Sámi.

KITS AND COVERT PARAPHERNALIA

Where costumes and masks can be regarded as highly public embodiments of a shaman's profession, elements of kits are often quite the opposite. Objects of powerful supernatural nature – fragments of the skin, claws or teeth of spirit helper animals, talismans, devices for accomplishing healing or divination – were often stored in a private assemblage, often a pouch or bag. Shamans guarded the contents of such kits assiduously, and generally limited access to them to trusted associates or apprentices.

Among Bororo people of Brazil, as Crocker points out (1985: 208–9), the material goods of the *bari* become viewed as contaminated, and must be treated with great care. The *bari*'s personal possessions must be kept secure from others, and if any are stolen or destroyed, the *bope* spirits are likely to visit their anger upon the offender as well as the *bari*. The *bari*'s worn-out clothing must be disposed of by burning, and his knife is tabu for anyone to touch aside from the *bari* himself and his wife. Concerns regarding *bari* possessions extend to items made for the *bari* as gift offerings, as Crocker notes:

Sometimes persons give the *bope* [spirits] through their shaman, a pot, or skewer (*joto*), or special kind of fan, in gratitude for a cure. All such items are among the equipment used by the *bari* in the preparation of *bope* food: the pot for cooking and storage, the *joto* to stir and pick out pieces of boiling meat when cooked, the fan to renew the fire and cool the possessed *bari*. If any of these things break, the *bope* inflict an illness on the original maker, and often on the shaman as well. So they are constantly remade by the giver or one of his affines. The utilitarian character of these cooking instruments is much superceded by their symbolic importance, at least for the skewer and fan. The shaman uses them in his mystical battles with the host of evil *bope* who attack the village at night, and their form is determined by this function rather than the more mundane one. (1985: 209)

Paul Radin (1926: 17–18 fn. 10) details the meanings of the war-bundle tradition among Ho-Chunk (Winnebago) people:

The war-bundle was the most sacred object among the Winnebago. It consisted of dried animal skins, other parts of animals, reed flutes, etc. all of which had some symbolical meaning. The various animal remains, for instance, were supposed to give the owner the powers of these animals, the sound of the reed flutes was supposed to paralyze his enemy and make it impossible for him to walk. Each clan possessed at least one such bundle and whenever the tribe went on the warpath, this bundle was carried on the back of some individual esteemed for his bravery. The power of this war-bundle was such that it would kill anything or anybody who approached it, the only exception being a menstruating woman. For this reason the war-bundle was always carefully guarded and protected and women were not allowed to see it or come anywhere near it.

In the Ho-Chunk tradition of collective shamanism, these war-bundles paralleled the private assemblages found in other shamanic traditions.

Barbara Iliff (1994: 90–1) has described the typical elements of Tlingit private assemblages:

One of the most potent of the curing items (called *skutch* by Emmons) was not art in the strict sense but an amulet made from a bundle of plant and animal parts, human hair and sometimes including carved charms … So powerful was it that it was not brought inside a house unless the shaman was practicing.

The skutch often contained animal tongues, seen as the site of supernatural power. Pelts were also regarded as repositories of supernatural power. Writes Iliff: "An unidentified Sitka shaman carried a stuffed mink skin whose strong spirit ate up sickness" (1994: 90–1). Iliff notes that Tlingit kits could also include foreign objects: coins, wooden canes, Inuit ivories, etc., signaling the notion that foreigners could connote spiritual power (1994: 118).

In Nganasan tradition, as Galina Gračeva (1989) shows, the shaman's potent implements were arrayed on a special sled, oriented toward the east. Sacred objects such as shamanic masks were placed face up on the sled, with other items arrayed around them on the sled itself or on the ground. The assemblage was carefully tended and guarded by female family members. Gračeva recounts an occasion during which such a site was disrupted:

Once it happened that a middle-aged Nganasan male, a good story-teller, who imagined himself to become a shaman, deliberately overturned the whole sledge with the shaman's outfit on it. So strong were the ties of the sledge with the woman's life that she got sick and almost died; her daughters had a difficult time nursing her back to health. (1989: 149)

After the aged guardian's death, her daughters, fearing pillaging of the items, sequestered the kit in a sack, and eventually turned it over to a museum in the early 1980s. In this way, they sought to avoid the supernatural repercussions that might result from an improper caretaking of the materials.

In several publications, Barbara Iliff (1994, 1997) has examined the ethical questions surrounding the study and possible public display of such items: should the privacy and supernatural potency of such elements of shamanic activities be respected as arcanum, or is it permissible for museum personnel from a different culture or later period to mount the items for others to see? Barre Toelken (2003: 55–6) recounts his experiences with a Pomo elder and basket-maker Mabel McKay. Mrs. McKay was reticent about allowing outsiders to view a basket decorated with red woodpecker scalps, quail topknots, other feathers, and beads. The power of the basket, she explained, could harm people who came upon it unawares. When allowing one such basket to be photographed for a museum catalogue, Mrs. McKay turned the basket upside down, apparently to protect viewers. Toelken writes of later seeing a similar Pomo basket on display at another museum, apparently presented without any inkling of its significance. He writes:

> I wondered what Mabel McKay would think if she could see that icon of her tribe's most serious ideas about health, healing, and power hanging in an antiseptic glass case, far from home. Should it even be there on display? … Was the basket given willingly by an Indian who had "decommissioned" it? Or was it given to the museum by a generous donor who got it "somewhere," not knowing that he was meddling with someone's cultural patrimony? Questions like these are difficult to answer, but they remain important nonetheless. (2003: 56)

Indigenous communities have increasingly taken an interest in recovering sacred items from museum collections, seeking to restore decorum after more than a century of appropriation and examination in the interest of Western science. A good example of such processes of repatriation is described in the case of the Omaha sacred pole and white buffalo skin, described in Chapter 13 (Ridington 1997; Ridington and Hastings 1997). The legal framework for such acts of restoration in the United States lies in the Native American Graves Protection and Repatriation Act of 1990, a landmark piece of legislation which seeks to reverse the effects of scientific pillaging of indigenous artifacts and traditions over the last several centuries.

SCULPTURES, HORSES, AND ALTARS

While costume, drums, masks, and kits represent key implements of shamanic practice, shamanic traditions often also include sculptures and offering places as the recipients or sites of ritual acts. Sculptures can represent or even embody spiritual interlocutors with whom the shaman may converse and toward whom acts of respect or appeasement are performed. In many shamanic traditions, practitioners maintain sacred spaces that act as repositories for ritual implements or the focus of specific ceremonies. Such sacralized places may be localized in a home, arrayed on

Figure 9. Neng Nor Lee's Hmong shamanic altar, Eau Claire, Wisconsin. Photo courtesy James P. Leary.

a moveable conveyance like a sled, or rooted in the natural landscape. Occasionally, it is the grave of an earlier shaman that acquires this sacral charge, acting as both a resource and a source of potential danger for the community.

The sculptures used in shamanic rituals are often strongly abstract, with features that emphasize the spirits' hungry or insistent natures. I. P. Soikkonen collected a Sakha (Yakut) sculpture in 1928 that was used in rituals to ensure human and livestock fertility. Stored in a secluded place normally, the sculpture was placed by the fire during the ceremony. The

Figure 10. Sakha (Yakut) effigy figure, collected in 1928 by I. P. Soikkonen. Peter the Great Museum of Anthropology and Ethnography, Kunstkamera, Russian Federation: Photo courtesy Juha Pentikäinen.

sculpture represented a spirit that wished to devour the souls of children and calves; by treating it kindly in the ritual, the shaman sought to convince it to leave the community in peace. In other traditions, sculptures may be dressed, coddled, and fed as a means of propitiating the assistance of associated spirits.

Carmen Blacker (1975: 149) discusses the *oshirasama* figures used by Japanese *itako* in their rituals. The *oshirasama* are essentially staffs, with a carved figure of a horse or woman's head on one end. Each *itako* possesses two, which she wields in her communications with the spirits. The carven heads are carefully covered in fabric, with a new layer added each year. Blacker notes preserved exemplars with upward of a hundred such layers, indicating continued use of the objects over several generations. An accompanying narrative recited by *itako* relates the birth of silkworms from an amorous relation between a girl and a horse (1975: 150).

A special category of sculptures related to the *itako* tradition and common cross-culturally are depictions of horses. In some traditions, such as that of Buryat shamans, the sculpture could take the form of a hobby-horse which the shaman might figuratively ride during shamanic journeys (Pentikäinen *et al.* 1998: 108; Diószegi 1968: 42). Vilmos Diószegi (1968: 239) notes that Tuvan shamans often portrayed their staffs as horses. He recounts a ceremony parallel to the enlivening rituals discussed above in which a shaman's staff was made ready for supernatural use. The shaman made an offering of a reindeer, placing a portion of its heart and brisket, along with tea and milk, in front of the new staff. The shaman's oratory included direct address to the staff: "White birch-staff: be my horse, be my friend!" (1968: 240). The shaman holding such a staff could be said to be riding or walking with a horse. The same tradition also sacrificed horses as a gift to the deities of the sky (Grusman *et al.* 2006: 258). In Thai's Hmong practice, the "horse" is actually a bench which the shaman mounts during ceremonies. Thai notes that the bench transforms into a bird in the spirit world, and was essential for his practice. He notes: "Without the horse, I could go nowhere." That horses take on such prominence probably reflects both their status as a prestige means of conveyance in the visible world and their considerable spiritual associations in various mythological traditions. Bird, cervid, and fish sculptures also figure prominently in many shamanic art traditions and similarly represent spiritual conveyances to otherworlds.

Altars within the home are important sites of prayer and ritual in many shamanic traditions, particularly those influenced by religions that normally include household altars, such as in many Asian traditions. Thai notes that Hmong shamanic altars vary in size and complexity with the growing experience of the shaman. The greater the status and success of the shaman, the larger and more elaborate the altar. In general, such facilities include a shelf for making food offerings to the spirits – generally eggs, rice, and water – as well as a place for burning incense. A bridge of string and sticks leads from the altar to the door and allows spirits to locate the altar when approaching the home. A Hmong altar documented by James P. Leary (Figure 9) demonstrates in its multiple levels the attending shaman's considerable skill. A gong used in séances hung on the side of the altar, while finger bells were stored on a lower shelf. An animal jaw bone was displayed in the center of the upper shelf. Paper decorations (*ntawv neeb*) were prominently displayed, and the shaman, Neng Nor Lee, noted that these must be replaced once a year to keep the spirits content. The altar was also the site at which the shaman made an annual accounting of rituals and deeds undertaken.

Caroline Humphrey (1996: 210) describes the altar and accouterments collected from the son of a deceased Daur shaman in the late 1930s. The goods were kept in a black tent in which the family lived as well, and included a drum, a black chest in which the shaman's costume was stored, two horse-headed iron sticks, and two masks. Offerings of meat were placed in the masks' open mouths, and both meat and alcohol were offered at the altar to obtain the help and favor of the spirits. In the particular household which Humphrey describes, the black shamanic altar stood alongside a competing red Buddhist altar, leading to considerable personal and supernatural turmoil for the family. Eventually, the shamanic altar and its goods were transferred to a museum, leading to an improvement in the family's fortunes.

Among nomadic or semi-nomadic peoples like the Nganasan (Enets) of Siberia, shamanic goods could be stored on special sledges, placed in the open on the tundra and oriented in a particular direction (Gračeva 1989: 145). Masks were placed face-up on such sledges, and costumes were kept in cloth bags. Offerings could be made on or around the sledge, rendering it both a place of storage and a more formal altar. Gračeva notes the dilemma faced by one Nganasan family when the mother of the household, an accomplished shaman, passed away:

The changing situation in and around the settlement, the presence of numerous newcomers – builders, electrical crews, etc. – did not allow the outfit to be left in the tundra on a sledge as had been done before, for fear of profanation and pillaging ... So one of the daughters put the outfit in a sack and kept it in a cold place in her apartment ... The fact that the whole outfit remained in the house undoubtedly troubled the young woman. When, in the spring of 1982, the settlement was visited by a group of collectors from the Tajmyr District Museum ... she was happy to pass it to the museum's workers. (1989: 149)

The young woman's reticence about keeping her mother's costume and other equipment in her home derived from a fear of angering the spirits through improper tending:

According to the traditional belief of the Nganasans, the idols that are abandoned and are not taken proper care of, i.e. are not fed, are not given new clothes and pendants, can become evil and can give trouble to people who stay near them. (1989: 149)

By transferring the goods to the district museum, the woman sought to avoid the anger of spirits offended by the curtailment of the tradition of the sledge altar custom.

Sámi shamanic sites were not located in the home, but rather were distributed across the landscape in relation to prime resources the community

Figure 11. Khanty idol, dressed in strips of cloth. Collected by U. T. Sirelius, 1898.
Photo courtesy Suomalais-ugrilainen Seura.

wished to exploit and preserve. As Hans Mebius (2003: 144–6) shows, the *sieidi* (altar) was often a piece of wood or a free-standing stone, frequently reminiscent of a person in shape. Trees were sometimes pared down to stumps, or were uprooted so that their roots became branches. Sámi practitioners – both *noaide* shamans and others wishing to obtain help or good fortune – brought offerings to the site where the *sieidi* lay, generally in a secluded place kept secret from persons not belonging to the community, and often off-limits to women as well. Offerings could be buried around the *sieidi*, and blood from the slaughtered animals was used to coat the altar.

Figure 12. Sámi *sieidi* stone, "Orrit," Rávttasjávri, Sweden.
Photo courtesy Mikael Svonni.

Such offerings were aimed at optimizing the community's luck in hunting
and were addressed either to specific deities or to an unnamed spirit of the
sieidi itself. *Sieidi* stones intended to increase fishing luck were generally
located in proximity to a lake or stream and were slathered with fish fat
rather than blood.

Natural sites also became places of sacrality in Japanese shamanic tradition, as Carmen Blacker (1975) details. Often, mountains in particular could
become "opened" – i.e., sacralized – by contact with a shamanic ascetic.
Mt. Fuji, Mt. Fushimi, Mt. Haguro, Mt. Kōja, Mt. Nantai, Mt. Ontake, all

possessed significance as sites of supernatural power, first made available to later visitors by knowing shamans. Writes Blacker:

"Opening" a mountain or a temple site ... means releasing its latent holiness. All the time it has been a "thin" place, through which the other world and its perilous power could show through. But until the ascetic arrives it has gone unrecognized and uncelebrated. By dwelling there and by practicing meditations and austerities on the spot, the ascetic acknowledges its power, concentrates it into a centre from which which worship can be conducted. (1975: 245–6)

As Karen Smyers (1999: 47) notes, modern Japanese continue to perform highly individualized rituals on these sites today, often without feeling the need for intermediary priests. Rock altars, springs, waterfalls, and statuary within the site focus pilgrims' attention and act as catalysts to prayer and worship (1999: 176). In the Japanese case, landscape and human beings together appear essential in establishing a site as sacred.

Sacralization of the landscape is also evident in many Native American shamanic traditions, where particular mountains, lakes, or other elements of the terrain have functioned as favored sites of ceremonies, vision quests, and other shamanic functions since time immemorial (Burton 2002). Cultural outsiders might easily fail to recognize such sites as sacred, but within the shamanic communities themselves, the sites often received the same marks of respect and fidelity that one might expect to see accorded an altar of human manufacture and ornamentation. Petroglyphs, burials of sacrificed animals, and other evidence can sometimes attest to long-standing ritual activities at such sites, sometimes demonstrating ritual activities that stretch back many centuries.

The shaman's grave could also become a kind of altar for the surviving community. Because of their unique relation with the spirit world, shamans are often considered to merit a different kind of grave than their more ordinary counterparts. In many cultures, the body is elevated and exposed to the elements as a fitting means of transferring the shaman's soul to its post-life existence. In other cultures, great care is taken to bury the shaman with all pertinent supernatural devices as a sign of respect. As Caroline Humphrey (1996: 193–202) has shown, the places of rest of deceased Daur shamans were regarded as filled with power, and persons who unwittingly came in contact with such sites could suffer serious illness if they offended the spirit(s) residing there. Her account of the fate of a family who failed to properly honor the goods of a deceased shaman serves as an apt final image for this chapter. In the account, a woman, now elderly, recalls the decision of her grandfather to refrain from passing on his shamanic spirits and role to anyone in the younger generation. The old man's decision became integrally tied to stipulations regarding the final disposition of his corpse as well as his costume:

In my clan there was an old man and he had sons and a grandson. When he was dying, the old man said "I do not want to pass on my powers to younger generations ... Now that my life is ending I will fold my *jawa* [shaman's costume] and with leather thongs it will be tied up." So he did what he said, folded and bound up the *jawa*, with seven ties. This way seven knots and that way four knots, backwards seven and forwards four, and he said a spell (*tarni*) and put it in a box. This *jawa* is sacred and must be put in a high place like the edge of a cliff or on a mountain. (1996: 211)

The family followed the old man's directive for storing the costume at first, mounting the box in which it had been placed on the top of a granary. Fearing that the box would be looted during the Cultural Revolution, however, the family eventually disregarded the shaman's injunction and buried the goods. Thereafter, they suffered numerous and unexpected misfortunes, including suicides among the young generation and a freak drowning accident. Rather than attributing these to the kinds of cultural breakdown and anguish which often characterize indigenous communities subjected to concerted colonization (as detailed in Chapter 12), the woman concluded her narrative with a clear attribution of the cause of the family's miseries to its treatment of the shaman's gravegoods: "The people said this was caused by the violation of the old man's will, burying the *jawa*" (1996: 212). The sacred items that had accompanied the family's shamanic practices for generations now became concentrated sources of retribution, delivering punishment to the family for its collective abandonment of prior relations with the spirit world and for its improper handling of ritual imperatives.

The material culture of shamanism tends to convey two overlapping messages, seemingly opposed but nonetheless integrally connected. First, it emphasizes the performative role of the shaman. By acquiring, donning, and employing particular items – costumes, masks, drums, paraphernalia, kits, and altars to name just a few – the shaman can assume a particular role that is recognized by the community and regulated by strong norms of expectation and esteem. "Looking the part" is an essential element in the shamanic economy, a key means by which both the human and the spirit world comes to recognize a person as a functioning shaman. Equipping a shaman becomes both an act of investment by the community and an act of investiture: a formal recognition of a new status that will prove essential for the welfare of the collective.

Second, these items all come to hold a sacrality in and of themselves that may defy the assumptions of superficiality that Westerners tend to associate with terms like "costume" or "prop." Through special enlivening rituals or repeated supernatural use, the items acquire a sacral weight of great consequence, both for the shaman and for the wider community. Shamanic items are heavy with meaning and power, and ethnographers have repeatedly noted that when communities abandoned their shamanic traditions, they often were at a loss to know how to dispose safely of the material goods that had sustained that tradition in their midst. Gračeva notes the decision of a Nganasan family to donate the goods to a museum, thereby removing them from the realm of the family's direct responsibility and liability; Humphrey tells the story of a museum receiving a Daur costume and kit so that its associated spirits would stop their warring with the family's newfound Buddhist spirituality. In any case, as we will see in Chapter 13, communities have sometimes sought to reverse these decisions generations later, repatriating sacred objects into a community whose ancestors once saw the objects as key bridges between the visible world and the spirits beyond. Sometimes exquisitely fashioned, sometimes unassuming, sometimes barely distinguishable from random assemblages of natural elements, the material culture of shamanism evinces a weightiness of significance that can prove both startling and profoundly revealing of shamanic ways of viewing the world.

CHAPTER II

Shamanic verbal art

It is a point of irony that the very elements that many shamans regard as their greatest tools as well as their greatest demonstrations of artistry and effectiveness nonetheless prove difficult, if not impossible, to translate. These elements are items of verbal art: specialized vocabulary, narrative, poetry, incantations, and other elaborate, often characteristic genres. Shamans not only prove expert artisans of such oral genres, they also often become the subjects of others' narratives. The mythic origins of the shamanic calling are related in detailed accounts of a primordial shaman, an era of cosmic unity destroyed by human folly, or a struggle between forces in support of or against the human community. In the current era, neighbors, clients, and enemies alike may tell or retell stories about a shaman's healing deeds, spiritual journeys, personality, career, or foibles. In some cases, such narratives may long outlast the active practice of shamanism in a locale, creating a lingering cultural memory of a once intact religious system. On the other hand, in cultures where shamanism remains vibrant as a tradition, such tales can serve as narrative models of both idealized and stigmatized shamanic behaviors: part of the communal code of conduct for shamans and their clients within the community.

WORDS OF POWER

For shamans in many traditions across the world, language not only records or expresses a practitioner's power, it also creates it. Shamanic training often entails a long process of memorization of words and narration. A special vocabulary separates the shaman's efficacious speech from that of ordinary communication. Long poems or narratives help the shaman negotiate with spirits and convince clients or audiences of the authenticity and likely effectiveness of the shaman's performance. As Laura Kendall (1995: 31) shows in her study of *mudang* initiation in modern Korea, such scripts may take many weeks to memorize but must be recited forcefully and with complete conviction, as if occurring to the shaman firsthand:

[C]harged with divine inspiration, she must proclaim the long lists of spirits associated with each segment of the *kut* as the visions appear before her eyes, and transmit the spirits' oracles. Her performance implies a spontaneous flow of visions, but in fact the lists of spirits are learned and difficult to master.

In describing Nepali shamanism, Gregory Maskarinec (1995) makes a similar observation:

The long public recitals and the short private *mantars* (standard Nepali: *mantra*) of Himalayan shamans are polished, well-constructed, orally preserved texts, meticulously memorized through years of training. These texts constitute the core of every shaman's knowledge. By their accurate recitation, shamans intervene to manipulate and change the world. In learning them, shamans acquire the knowledge necessary for their profession and obtain a complete, detailed view of the world and its participants. What you learn to say is what you learn to do. Shaman texts create shamans. (1995: 6)

Shamanic oral traditions vary as to whether such verbalizations are to be memorized verbatim or left open to improvisation. In recording the views of contemporary Buryat shamans, Virlana Tkacz, Sayan Zhambalov, and Wanda Phipps (2002: 14) note that some shamans memorized chants word for word, to be performed verbatim each time a ritual was undertaken. Others, however, employed stock phrases and imagery in an improvisational manner, seldom repeating the same prayer twice in the same manner. At least at present, this variation is considered an accepted part of the shamanic profession and a sign of the different relations shamans maintain with their spirit helpers. At the same time, an uninspired performance, showing a paucity of verbal preparation, inspired spontaneity, or performative authority was unmistakably marked as a failure and could lead to a refusal of the spirits to cooperate with the shaman's requests (2002: 98).

Knud Rasmussen (1921: 153–4) describes the specialized vocabulary of Greenlandic Inuit *angakut*. The objects of the hunt could not be mentioned by name, but were rather referred to by circumlocutions, known by anthropologists as *noa* terms. The arctic fox, for instance, was known as *teriangniaq* in ordinary speech, but in shamanic incantations was referred to as *pisugkaitsiaq* ("the wanderer"). Metaphorical terms were used for people as well: the ordinary term for a person was *inuk*, but in shamanic vocabulary, the term *tau* ("shadow") was used, suggestive of the shamanic concept of spirit travel and of shadows as a metaphor for the spirit. Other items were also described poetically: the term *puak* ("lungs") was replaced by *anerneqarfit* ("that which draws breath"); the term *qamutit* ("sledge") was replaced by *sisoraut* ("that which one slides forward").

Such vocabulary rendered the *angakok*'s speeches richly poetic but also difficult to understand. The alternative lexicon may have allowed the practitioner to hide his statements from the beings referred to, or, alternatively, to gain greater control over the beings through demonstrating knowledge of their hidden or more powerful names.

Polynesian cultures distinguish between highly charged sacred names or objects – termed in Maori language *tapu* – and those which hold no special power and can therefore be used in ordinary situations (*noa*). By employing a *noa* circumlocution, a speaker can avoid summoning the being referred to, something that would occur immediately were the *tapu* term enunciated. Avoiding use of the *tapu* further helps preserve and maintain its sacrosanct nature over time. The term *tapu* passed into English in the eighteenth century as *tabu/taboo*. Such linguistic behaviors reflect an ancient and widespread confidence in the efficacy of words not only to describe but also to attract and shape individual destinies.

While traditional circumlocutions could render a song cryptic to a novice audience member, the texts of shamanic oratories and songs could sometimes prove challenging to experts as well. Vilmos Diószegi (1968) notes:

The experience I had with the shamans of the Buryats, Sagays, Karagasays and reindeer-keeping Soyots proved that the real difficulty was not in searching for the shaman song, or recording it, but in transcribing it. Because, not even the shaman himself understands his own sentences ... He has no definite text, and those sentences he drones out while entranced, are just as strange and unknown to him as to the listeners. (1968: 238)

Of course, it is difficult to state definitively whether the lack of comprehension that Diószegi encountered among elderly Siberian shamans in the late 1950s was the product of years of inactivity under the harsh dictates of Soviet religious suppression or a sign of a freeing of the shaman's poetic sensibilities through the experience of dramatic performance. In any case, since the shaman's words may reflect communications from a wide array of spirits, it would be expectable for at least some of their oratory to escape the complete comprehension of even highly learned fellow shamans. And in some cases, as Edward Schieffelin (1995: 69) observes among Kaluli shamans, it is not unusual for shamans in some traditions to give voice to communications in languages foreign to both the shaman and the community at hand.

Because verbally referring to disease or other difficult situations could be regarded as an act of aggression, Rasmussen (1921) reports that the Greenlandic *angakut* were careful about how they named other people in their verbal performances. During a séance, the *angakok*'s words were repeated by an elder, who shouted encouragement and urged the *angakok* to be forthcoming with all pertinent information (1921: 53). This act helped clarify the shaman's utterances for the audience, but also shared the responsibility and potential blame for any information conveyed. The revelation of a person's name could become the object of a long process of hinting. The *angakok*'s frequent protestations regarding the explicit naming of malefactors could shield the practitioner from blame or suspicions of intentionally calling down disease or misfortune upon another, something which could expose the shaman to suspicions of treachery or aggression (Chapter 6).

In a similar way, Thai, as a contemporary Hmong *txiv neeb*, never intimates that a patient is going to die, even if his helping spirits have revealed the fact to him: "You never say someone's going to die. You never say that to them. You just tell them to 'Try again, find another shaman. Then you will be all right.'" Thai recalled the case of a Hmong patient whose Western physician told him he had only a few months left to live. Thai reported that the son of the patient punched the doctor in the mouth and broke off all further consultations. The patient's family turned to Thai to provide shamanic therapy and the man lived long past his expected end date.

FROM WORDS TO POEMS

Boudewijn Walraven (1994) explores the poetry within Korean *muga* songs. A typical *kut* séance consists of some twelve (or more) parts, each devoted to one or more deities. The dramatic as well as the supernatural dimensions of the *kut* are sustained by shifts in costume, dance, ritual acts, and songs. These may be narrative or lyrical in nature, or represent incantations or prayers (1994: 15). Walraven includes a *muga* intended to convince the Grandchild of Samsin (a deity associated with childbirth) to allow a patient's engorged breastmilk to flow:

> Deity who takes care of breastfeeding,
> Grandchild of Samsin!
> Please help us, make the milk flow
> As gushing out of the well of the Dragon King of the East Sea,
> Gushing out of the well of the Dragon King of the South Sea,
> Gushing out of the well of the Dragon King of the West Sea,
> Gushing out of the well of the Dragon King of the North Sea,
> Like [the water] of the Dragon Pool of the Sasil Dragon King in
>   the Centre

So that [milk] will be left after feeding,
So that [milk] will be left after it has been squeezed out.   (1994: 16–17)

Muga can also represent the voices of deities or unseen spirits who wish to communicate with the living through the *mudang*, as in the following message from a dead person to an audience of mourning family members:

Ay, sad, sad it is!
The body that was alive yesterday
Has become a ghost, become a spirit
Why is it, that I belong to the shades?
Today I go to Paradise, to the Ten Kings [of the Underworld]
My kind and dutiful daughters-in-law and descendants!
Because you all have made a great effort,
I will help you, I will support you.
I will help you to pass the three years of mourning for me nicely,
To pass the three months after my death comfortably.
I will see that you, my descendants precious as gold,
Will rise high, will be honoured.
I will give you gain and I will give you growth.
Don't worry, thanks to all my descendants
I go to Paradise,
And become a cherished child of the Lord Buddha
I will go to Paradise, flying up steadily,
I will go to the Ten Kings.   (1994: 17)

In both these texts, the *muga* represents a direct address facilitated or performed by the *mudang*. Other *muga*, however, may include narratives, e.g., myths of the birth and careers of particular deities or shamans, or the origins of prominent dynasties (1994: 94–5). Some such texts reflect the influence of Buddhist thought and narrative genres, imported into Korean culture from China (1994: 98–105). *Muga* are transmitted from one generation to the next within shamanic families or as part of the training which a novice *mudang* receives during her apprenticeship (1994: 24). New songs could also appear to practitioners through dreams, although these often contain highly traditional images and phrasings that tie the new work to already established *muga* within the tradition (1994: 26–7).

In recording the events associated with a Buryat *shanar* dedication ceremony in contemporary Siberia, Virlana Tkacz, Sayan Zhambalov, and Wanda Phipps (2002: 25) provide a translation of the chant which one shaman made at the outset of the ritual:

From far away, from the Northwest
From a distant beautiful place

The sound of my drum
Covers the land like a mist.
The beautiful instrument that I hold
Was crafted, made by
The heavenly white smith.
I call to you, oh seventy-seven smiths.
I bring you strong wine.
I beg you, taste it.
Listen to me, hear me well.
Drink the strong wine
Brought to you by this humble son.
Look kindly upon it.
Look after me and protect me.
Listen to me, hear me well.

The purpose of the chant was to empower the shaman's implements, as detailed in Chapter 10. As in the Korean examples, symbolic directions and stock phrases and epithets help render the oration both recognizable and efficacious to human and supernatural audience alike. Delivered in the proper manner, such orations helped the ritual progress from one stage to the next, demonstrating at the same time both the authority and the verbal dexterity of the shaman.

That part of the shaman's work traditionally was to discover, learn, and use verbal formulas – prayers, petitions, incantations, charms – is readily apparent from many ethnographic accounts as well as occasional epic or narrative renderings. In the thirteenth-century Old Norse Eddaic poem *Hávamál*, a narrator – apparently a shamanic practitioner or possibly the god Óðinn – provides a catalogue of charms he possesses. His listing finds parallels in other Eddaic poems as well, including *Sigrdrífomál* (The Lay of Sigrdrífa), in which a valkyrie spirit teaches such spells to her warrior partner Sigurð. In *Hávamál*, the narrator claims words capable of helping and healing, blunting weapons, breaking bonds, stopping flying spears, having success or invincibility in battle, reversing ill will, quenching fire, soothing tempers, calming waves, driving away witches, compelling the dead to speak, attracting women and ensuring a woman's faithfulness (Terry 1990: 32–4). Typical are strophes 148 and 149, which relate the speaker's knowledge of spells useful in battle:

I know a third [spell]: if I should need
To fetter any foe;
It blunts the edge of my enemy's sword,
Neither wiles nor weapons work.

I know a fourth [spell]: if I should find myself
Fettered hand and foot,

> I say the spell that sets me free,
> Bonds break from my feet,
> Nothing holds my hands. (Terry 1990: 32)

The poem attests to the narrator's knowledge of the spells, but coyly leaves the actual words unrecorded, perhaps preserving their efficacy for future use. Such spells suggest the needs and life experiences of a warrior and reflect, perhaps, the uses to which magic was put in pre-Christian Scandinavia. It is significant that both *Hávamál* and *Sigrdrífomál* were written down some two centuries after widespread Icelandic conversion to Christianity: clearly, on some level, the magical wisdom of the past was still remembered and valued by the descendents of pagan Icelanders. Somewhat more homespun charms were written down in complete form by Anglo-Saxon monks at about the same time: charms for healing diseases, expelling stillborn infants, and curing lunacy were diligently copied and apparently performed by Christian monks (DuBois 1999: 104–12).

Such examples reflect a strong and enduring embrace of verbal art as a key component of supernatural intervention, and underscore the performative nature of such acts. Edward Schieffelin (1995) describes a Kaluli séance in which the community carefully assessed both the content and style of the orations of two vying shamans: the audience's attentiveness to the performers' discourse concerning disease etiology and therapy reflects a community highly accustomed to critical appraisal of shamanic verbal performances. In the end, the audience favored the shaman who offered both the best verbal performance and most compelling diagnosis of the problem at hand.

While such accounts point to audience attentiveness to every syllable of a practitioner's oratory, the unique lexicon and poetic flights of the shaman might well prove a barrier to audience comprehension, at least in some cases. Amanda Harris (2001) questions the comprehensibility of shamanic words of *manang* healers of the Iban people of Borneo. Given the *manang*'s muffled performance style and specialized vocabulary, it is difficult to believe that clients or audiences can actually follow their oratories, despite their professed efficacy. While the *manang* busily performs his songs to summon spirits, discover the cause of ailments, and effect cures, the community is involved in other activities essential to the healing, but distracting from the point of view of song comprehension. In Harris's view, the verbal performances of the *manang* make up only one component of the overall healing ritual; perhaps it is the simple fact that the songs occur – as opposed to their explicit content – that lends them their efficacy within Iban experience of healing (see Chapter 8).

MYTHIC ACCOUNTS

The origins of the shamanic calling are often the focus of sacred narratives shared by both shamans and their communities. Through recitation of these myths, the community is reminded of the central importance of shamanic practices for their relations with the supernatural as well as for their day-to-day welfare.

Often, shamanic traditions relate an era of primordial unity, in which pathways between the various realms of the cosmos were open and obvious. Karl W. Luckert (1984: 12) defines this situation in Native American mythologies as a "prehuman flux," and notes its importance both in the sacred narratives of hunter-gatherer cultures and, to a lesser extent, in those of sedentary agrarian cultures. In myths of this kind, communication and movement across cosmic boundaries as well as between people and other beings occurs with ease. Bering Sea Inuit myths of the 1870s, for instance, collected by Edward W. Nelson, often feature characters which shift form and location without difficulty. According to the Bering Sea narrators, however, the situation had gradually changed, so that spirits were now more tightly bound to particular shapes, locales, and identities, and communication between these had thus grown rare (Fitzhugh and Kaplan 1983: 6). Only shamans still possessed the capacity to travel and transform as of old, making them unique and ensuring their centrality in the religious rituals of the broader community.

Tkacz, Zhambalov, and Phipps (2002: 15) record a Buryat myth regarding the advent of shamanic powers among people during such a time of primordial unity. At first, an eagle descended from heaven to offer the human community supernatural assistance, but they did not fully understand or value what he was offering them. Although they could communicate with the eagle, they did not regard him as a credible leader among them. So the eagle returned to the sky and requested that shamanic skills be given directly to a human being instead. The eagle then transferred his powers to a sleeping woman, who thus gained supernatural sight. Not only did the woman thus gain powers previously unknown to humanity, she soon gave birth to a son who became the first shaman. Mircea Eliade (1964: 69–70) notes similar Buryat myths and links them to Sakha (Yakut), Khanty (Ostyak), Teleut, and Orochon myths that portray the eagle as a supreme being and/or the originator of shamanic knowledge. In such narratives, the cosmic importance of shamanic practices is emphasized, adding further notoriety to the tradition within the wider community and enhancing the view of shamans themselves.

The end of this primordial unity is described in a myth that Thai notes concerning the Hmong New Year. The myth links the rupture of primordial unity with a compensatory rise of the shamanic profession in the person of Siv Yis, the first shaman. According to Thai, New Year commemorates the end of the great battle of Siv Yis against the spirits responsible for disease and death, led by a triumvirate known as Dab Tsog. In the beginning, human beings had no disease or death to contend with and thus were blessed with unending life. But this perfect existence bored some people so that they complained to each other about living for so long. A fly overheard their conversation and flew to the heavens, where it reported this view to Ntxwg (Ntxwj) Nyoog. Ntxwg Nyoog was affronted at human ingratitude and declared that if people were not happy about living for so long they might as well die. So he sent to earth the Dab Tsog with an army of assistant *dab* (spirits of disease) to bring about an end to human immortality. When the god of heaven, Saub, found out about Ntxwg Nyoog's act, he in turn sent Siv Yis to earth as the first shaman to fight against the *dab* and help people triumph over disease. At this time, the *dab* were all visible to humanity, making the war possible. The battle raged for centuries, but at last Siv Yis and the human beings won the day. Then the humans, in vengeance for the war, began to wage a policy of destruction against the *dab*, seeking to put them all to death once and for all. When the *dab* saw what was happening, they appealed to Saub, who decided to save them. So he summoned the human beings to him and blew powder in their eyes, asking if they could still see the *dab*. The human beings replied that they could still make them out. So Saub again blew dust in their eyes and asked a second time. Again he received the confirmation that the people could still see the *dab*. For a third time, Saub blew powder in the humans' eyes and asked if they could see the spirits. At this point, the people could no longer see any spirits at all, and when questioned, they asked Saub what he was talking about. So Saub knew his protection of the *dab* would be successful. Then Saub called the dog to him. Now the dog was a tremendously wise being, because he had been a general in a former life. As a human being, however, he had committed adultery with the king's wife and, as punishment for that earthly wrongdoing, was fated to be reincarnated as a dog, to help the human community for ever more as a faithful servant. Saub blew dust in the dog's eyes and asked if he could still see the *dab*. Understanding what Saub intended to do, the dog wisely lied, and said, "No, I can't see them at all anymore." Saub believed him. As a result, dogs can still perceive the spirits, and Thai noted that when dogs bark or howl at night, Hmong people traditionally interpret the behavior as an indication that the dog is seeing spirits no longer visible to humankind. Such narratives pull the shaman and the act of healing disease into a great mythic chronicle, where the modern shaman becomes heir to a prominence and heroism that stretches back to the very first shaman and the end of primordial unity.

In folk songs collected from Karelian epic singers in the early nineteenth century, Elias Lönnrot found numerous accounts of a mythic primordial shaman named Väinämöinen. Lönnrot incorporated these into his Finnish national epic *Kalevala*, making Väinämöinen a cultural hero for modern Finland. In Poem 16 of *The Kalevala* (Lönnrot 1963: 96–102), for instance, Väinämöinen undertakes a journey to the land of the dead (Tuonela, Manala) to obtain magic words for completing a boat. He is met there by the daughter of the dead, who questions him about his manner of dying. Väinämöinen tries to lie, but the guardian catches him in his prevarications, since his body does not show signs of the fates he claims: he is neither bloody from wounds, wet from drowning, nor burned from fire. The guardian then tries to compel him to drink something and attempts to put him to sleep by magic. Väinämöinen escapes, however, by transforming into a snake and slithering back across the river. In a version of the song collected by A. A. Borenius from Jyrki Malinen in 1871, Väinämöinen's escape and return is described thus:

> Then the old Väinämöini
> Felt his doom coming
> His day of distress dawning:
> Changed himself to a brown worm
> Slithered into a lizard
> Swam across Tuoni's river.
> Then he went to his people
> Himself put this into words:
> "Do not, young men,
> go to Mana unless you're killed
> to Tuonela unless dead."   (Kuusi *et al.* 1977: 193–4)

The audience is thus reminded not only of the wonder of Väinämöinen's deeds, but also of the impossibility of ordinary people repeating such acts. The land of the dead, Manala or Tuonela, is accessible only to shamans but is known to the living through the eyewitness reports such persons have brought back over the ages. Epic songs of this type were common evening entertainment in northern Finland and Karelia during the nineteenth century, despite the fact that active shamanism was in strong decline in the culture at that time and Christianity had long since displaced the pre-Christian religion. The narrative songs preserved communal understandings of spirit travel and quests even while firsthand acquaintance with *tietäjä* shamans was disappearing (Pentikäinen 1989; Haavio [1952] 1991; Siikala 2002). The Finnish materials illustrate the ways in which shamanic verbal traditions could long outlast the active practice of shamanism in a given culture area.

LEGENDARY ACCOUNTS

While shamanic knowledge becomes understood through myth, the careers of past living shamans could become remembered in legendry. Sometimes retold generations after the life of the shaman, and sometimes easily merging into the mythic, such narratives constitute a powerful Native discourse concerning the characteristics, efficacy, and potential dangers of shamanic practices.

In his *Eskimo Folk-Tales* (1921) Knud Rasmussen includes a number of accounts of legendary shamanic spirit journeys. Typical is that of a great shaman named Kúnigseq (1921: 38–9). Kúnigseq sets out with his helping spirit to visit the land of the dead. After crossing a treacherously slippery reef and descending a great slope covered with heather, Kúnigseq and his guide arrive at their destination:

Suddenly he heard one crying "Here comes Kúnigseq."
By the side of a little river he saw some children looking for greyfish. And before he reached the houses of men, he met his mother, who had gone out to gather berries. When he came up to her, she tried again and again to kiss him, but his helping spirit thrust her aside.
"He is only here on a visit," said the spirit.
Then she offered him some berries, and these he was about to put in his mouth, when the spirit said:
"If you eat them, you will never return." (1921: 38)

Kúnigseq is able to meet his dead brother as well, and finds the land very appealing, although lacking in any supply of cold drinking water. He returns to the land of the living, but dies soon thereafter, to be reunited with his happy kin, including a recently deceased son.

Such tales seem to have accomplished several tasks at once. First, they established the shaman in question as an expert spirit traveler, one with personal experience of an otherworld of intense interest to community members and clients. In the narrative, we see Kúnigseq as a noted arrival in the land, and we witness the powerful and effective guarding he receives from his protective helping spirit. Second, the tale creates a standard against which to evaluate the reports and experiences of living shamans. Often, living shamans are seen as feeble reflections of earlier, more powerful practitioners, whose marvelous exploits nevertheless helped reinforce communal views of the potential efficacy of shamanic activities. Finally, such accounts convey knowledge of the otherworld to an audience. Most community members would probably be unlikely to need the advice regarding the necessary avoidance of food while in the land of the dead: a widespread motif in traditions about the underworld in many cultures. Nonetheless, the details of the appearance of the land of the dead, and the contentment of the dead who reside there, could prove valuable cosmological information for the community, the members of which would all have relatives in that realm and would expect to reach it themselves someday. Overall, then, the tale of Kúnigseq's journey can be seen as a powerful articulation of the shaman as hero within Inuit culture.

Because shamans often vied with each other for clients and reputations, stories about shamanic duels abound in various traditions around the world. A striking example was recorded from the Sámi informant Per Bær in 1924. According to Bær, a female *noaide* used her magic to murder a former suitor toward whom she felt animosity (Qvigstad 1927: II, no. 142, 1: pp. 488–91). Another *noaide*, a friend of the murdered man, confronted her obliquely, saying "Have you been cracking any reindeer's legbones lately?" The woman replied: "Yes, and I will be cracking another's legbones today as well." With these cryptic challenges, they began to use their magic against each other. The man sent his spirit out of his body and into the sea, where he took the form of a fish. The woman pursued him, seeking to catch him with a line. The man raised a storm that prevented her, however. Then he fled to a river, where he again hid as a fish. The woman took up fishing by a hole in the ice. The man awoke the spirits of dead people who had drowned and they in turn prevented the woman from continuing. They then flew to a churchyard, where the man was at last successful in defeating and killing his opponent. He jested, "It wasn't that easy for you to break another reindeer's legbone." Stories of this kind are widespread in shamanic traditions and often involve elaborate chains of transformations. On a narrative level, they reproduce the kinds of unseen transformations that shamans might describe after a long trance or séance, and they illustrate the mutability of form which the shaman may enjoy upon leaving the physical body.

Kira Van Deusen (1999: 128–9) records another tale of a shamanic duel from a contemporary Yupik teacher in 1990s Chukotka, Siberia. In the story, a young man goes to visit a home inhabited by a girl and her grandmother. After eating dinner, the three go to sleep, but the old woman prepares to kill the man during the night. The man realizes her intent, however, and changes places with the daughter, so that when the old woman throws her knife to kill him, she cuts off the daughter's head rather than the man's. In anger, the woman throws her knife again at the man, but it misses him. He returns the knife by throwing it back at the woman, cutting off her right hand. The story continues:

"All the same you will not live," she said.
She took the knife in her left hand, but he was agile and again he got out of the way.
"I'll show you how to throw," he said.
He took the knife in his left hand and threw it and cut off her left hand. Now she had no hands left.
"All the same you will not live," she said. She took the knife in her teeth, and how she threw it! The fellow just managed to get out of the way.
"I'll show you how to throw!"
Even though he had hands he took the knife in his teeth and threw it, cutting off the old woman's head! (1999: 128–9)

The supernatural nature of this encounter is underscored by the fact that the tent immediately begins to shrink after the old woman's beheading, so that the man manages to escape only just in time. It becomes evident that the women had been spirits and that the man had probably been helped by his own supernatural powers in defeating them. The story represents a striking example of the ways in which shamanic narratives may survive in cultures well after the conscious abandonment of shamanic rituals.

Sámi legends also preserved memories of irascible or dangerous shamans of the past. In the 1920s, Isak Persen Saba recounted tales of a past *noaide* for the folklorist Just Qvigstad (1927). Although Saba was born in 1875, he knew various stories about Káren-Ovllá, a *noaide* who had died in 1849 (Qvigstad 1927: III, no. 149, 1: pp. 420–7). In Saba's accounts, Káren-Ovllá received his helping spirits from his father while still in the cradle. He grew up to be a powerful and much feared *noaide*, whose temper wreaked havoc on his family. One altercation led to the supernatural murder of his son, while another resulted in his wife becoming blind. Later in life, Káren-Ovllá became progressively less able to control his helping spirits. Confronted by an associate about his aggressive acts, Káren-Ovllá said: "I no longer have great control over my *noaide* spirits: they do what they will. I do not have to do anything but think and it happens" (ibid.: 423). When he unintentionally laughed at one of his helping spirits after it fell into the cooking fire, the spirit retaliated by killing Káren-Ovllá's best driving reindeer. Another time, the shaman's daughter found him turned upside down in a grove, again the victim of his spirits' ire. In the end, Káren-Ovllá chose to bequeath his spirits to distant shamans in Russia rather than allow them to fall into the service of his similarly cantankerous local kinsmen, who were their next logical recipients. In Saba's community, such tales recounted the memorable adventures of past *noaide* figures, while also helping explain the fact that their skills were no longer common.

In the introduction to an anthology of Hopi traditional narratives, Ekkehart Malotki (Malotki and Gary 2001: xv) identifies some fourteen motifs in Hopi narratives that he regards as "typical of shamanism." These include drumming, magical flight, travel between different cosmic realms, accounts of healing, and descriptions of a psychopomp role. Malotki links these narratives to a variety of healer known as *povosqa* ("seer"), who used quartz crystals as a diagnostic tool and practiced various forms of healing and divination in the Hopi community as late as the 1920s (2001: xxvii). The narratives would thus represent cultural memories of a shamanic profession parallel to those described above for Sámi and Finnish traditions. As in the Nordic examples, Hopi shamanism had survived a long period of cultural and religious marginalization before finally disappearing altogether as an active practice, and remained strongly remembered in oral narratives of the community.

Tales in various shamanic traditions may also relate the reasons for past practitioners' failures, as, for instance, when a shaman fails to return from a trance state and instead falls into protracted coma. One such tale was collected by the Finnish folklorist Samuli Paulaharju and refers to a Sámi *noaide* by the name of Akmeeli:

Akmeeli was so noble a sorcerer that he could sing himself into a wolf, could lie the whole winter like a bear under a firtree, could fly in the form of a bird, and again swim as a fish. The man sang and beat his sorcerer's drum; then suddenly he tumbled into a corner of the cottage, going lifeless. He was not then to be touched, not on pain of death … And once again Akmeeli sang and beat his drum and told his wife to wake him at such and such a time with such and such words, and he dropped into the corner of the cottage. But when the time came, the wife did not remember the words, nor did Akmeeli have the strength to rise from his trance. [He] just lay in the corner as one dead, and finally the corpse began to stink, the flesh rose and left the hands and cheeks. Finally he had to be taken and buried beyond Sompio River in the shore slope of the Hieta-brook. After thirty years had passed the words rose into the wife's memory, and immediately she hobbled to Akmeeli's grave and cried, "From the bend of the pike's bowels, from the third curve, Akmeeli Antereeus, *paijele jo pajas!*" Then the likeness of the old sorcerer rose from the soil, moved his jaws and muttered something. But soon the jaws dropped, the flesh and bones fell, the sorcerer crashed down and in dust disappeared into the grave. (quoted in Haavio 1991: 125)

The tale reminds an audience of the constant risk the shaman faced: in wandering as a spirit, the shaman could easily become lost and end life in a coma or early death.

PERSONAL EXPERIENCE NARRATIVES

Legends of the sort described above could easily become resources for individuals in their interpretations of their own supernatural experiences, as Dorothy Eggan (1955) suggests in her study of a Hopi informant. The man in question had agreed to record all his dreams, and had amassed some three hundred accounts over the course of sixteen years (1955: 110). Many of these featured a *dumalaitaka*, i.e., a spirit helper, who once took him to the land of the dead, showed him treasures and wisdom, and could change form in various ways. The dreamer reported meeting with a number of powerful deities from Hopi mythology, including Palulukon – a powerful water serpent – and Tuwapongwuhti, the Mother of All Wild Game. His narrated experiences show strong resemblance to the kinds of vision quest narratives recorded elsewhere in North America, as noted in Chapter 5, despite the fact that neither he nor any of his associates were active shamans.

Such personal experience narratives may describe not only communications with spirits but also supernatural events related to the development of a shaman's career or arsenal of tools. The Buryat shaman Bayir Rinchinov reported the supernatural discovery of his shamanic mirrors (*toli*) through the assistance of both dream visions and his teacher:

When I was just starting, I would dream about a *toli*. Babey [a term for father or a male elder] would come to me in my dream. In one hand he held a large *toli*, and in the other he held a small one. He would laugh and disappear. I kept on having this dream till it was too much for me to bear. I went to my teacher. It was a cold morning. A little snow had just fallen. He looked at the vodka bottle I brought and said, "Near the sacred place in the Shandan Valley two *tolis* have fallen. Let's go and find them." I gathered a few of my friends ... and we drove to this area. We got out of the car and my teacher said, "Stop, don't move." It had just snowed and there were no footprints in the snow. He made an offering of wheat grains to the spirits and said, "Outline this area with a silver knife." So I outlined a square three steps by three with a silver knife. "Sit around this," he said and we did so. "Look for it," he said and went back to the car. We started looking, digging. Choboloy dug up the *toli* from under the snow. He found the large *toli*. Then we looked in the area for another half day, but couldn't find anything. My teacher then drank some *arkhe*, or home-brew, and said, "Bayir, give me three coins." He took them and did something with them as he prayed. Then he said, "It is seventy-seven steps from here." He told me to mark off seventy-seven steps in the southwestern direction. I started counting off the steps: "One two, three ..." Just over a small hill was my seventy-seventh step. I stopped and yelled, "Here is the seventy-seventh step." My teacher said, "Step aside." He took the three coins and tossed them straight up. The coins fell in three different directions. He asked me where did the center coin fall and said, "Go and look for it." I went straight to the spot and found a *toli* under the snow. To this day these are the two *toli* on my altar. (Tkacz, Zhambalov, and Phipps 2002: 34–5)

Rinchinov's narrative can be seen as an account of supernatural intervention in the provision of a key element of the shaman's equipment. At the same time, the account can be taken as an illustration of the legendary powers of the young shaman's teacher, a man who had survived Soviet suppression through living in a very remote part of Siberia. In either case, tales of this kind portray shamans as recipients of highly unique supernatural assistance, enhancing their reputations among audience members and underscoring the cosmic endorsement of shamanic practices as a favored means of communication between the various spirit realms.

Reflecting the accumulated knowledge and wisdom of past generations, carefully handed down through processes of initiation and apprenticeship, and at the same time reflecting integrally the unique insights of the living practitioner, shamanic verbal art is both weighty and yet fragile. Often equated with the very essence of shamanic power itself, verbal art has the capacity to defy space and time in a manner as mysterious and inspiring as spiritual flight itself.

PART V

Shamanic politics in a changing world

CHAPTER 12

Shamanism under attack

Describing the activities of US Navy Commander Henry Glass among Alaskan Tlingit people in the 1890s, Sergei Kan (1991: 370) quotes the testimony of a Russian priest who knew Glass well:

[H]unting shamans was his favorite pastime and sport. A captured shaman was usually invited aboard his boat and received with honor. Glass would talk to him in a friendly manner, inquiring about his life, the number of his *yéik* [spirits], the extent of their strength and power, etc. Then he would announce that he was also a shaman who owned *yéik* and suggested that they compete against each other. Upon his order, a charged electric battery was brought out. The shaman was asked to hold the wires in his hands, while the two poles were being connected. The shaman's body would begin to twist. His own people, witnessing his strange and funny poses and hearing his screams and moans, became frightened. The shaman himself learned a practical lesson about the power of his white colleague. But the captain did not stop at that. Shamans always left his boat with their heads shaved and covered with oil paint, and having promised not to practice shamanism anymore.

For myriad populations in various eras and cultural contexts, shamanic traditions have proven cogent, convincing, and quite resilient models for how the world works and how its forces can be controlled. In confronting the most vexing issues of human existence – sickness, misfortune, inter-personal conflict, death, loss – shamanic worldviews offer not only plausible explanations for the occurrence of unwanted events, but also pragmatic means of attempting to reverse or mitigate their effects. The shaman provides the community with essential spiritual services, both through specific ritual procedures performed as needed, and – at a deeper level – through upholding a coherent understanding of the cosmos which clarifies the significance and predictability of life's events. Shamans and shamanic traditions help make sense of the world for their communities, for persons in the throes of disease or misfortune, and for shamans themselves.

Yet in the cultural encounters that have taken place since Western scholars first began to describe shamanic traditions, these religious specialists, rituals, and ways of understanding the world have often faced virulent, even ruthless, aggression. Shamans have been tortured or discredited, religious practices banned, worldviews condemned. It is no exaggeration to state that for the past several centuries, shamanism has faced a formidable and sustained attack.

From a twenty-first-century, culturally relativistic perspective, it may seem difficult to fathom the virulence with which shamanic traditions were stigmatized and suppressed in the past. Clearly, for a figure like Commander Glass in the account cited above, the Tlingit *ixt* represented an enemy who needed to be defeated, for the shaman's own good, for the good of his community, and for the greater good of American society. Glass regarded his actions not as a sadistic hobby, but as part of his duty as a representative of the United States and as a Christian. It might also seem surprising that shamanic traditions continue to face analogous pressures today: if outright torture and humiliation are less common in the religious confrontations of the current era, subtle strategies for marginalizing and discrediting shamanic worldviews or their practitioners often continue, even in societies that profess a deep commitment to religious pluralism. This chapter explores some of the motivations behind attempts to displace shamanic traditions over time and the regimens of suppression or persecution that have developed in various contexts. We examine the shaman as a perceived enemy of progress within a given religion, or as an enemy of new religious notions being imported through missionization. We also look at the ways in which scholars and government officials have perceived shamans as enemies of reason or as sources of unwelcome resistance to colonial power or processes of acculturation. We discuss attacks on shamanism as a product of both intercultural and interfaith confrontations and as a preface to our exploration of shamanic revitalization movements in the chapter that follows. In a very concrete sense, this chapter, along with the two which follow, address those aspects of "religion" that Timothy Fitzgerald (2000) labels "politics."

THE MARGINALIZATION OF SHAMANS WITHIN EVOLVING RELIGIONS

It is wholly inaccurate to claim that shamans enjoy universal and unequivocal esteem within their own communities, even where their traditions remain undisputed as the backbone of local approaches to disease or other human problems. As we have seen in other chapters, shamans are often viewed with suspicion, as possible sources of misfortune rather than assistance, or even as murderers, charlatans, or cheats. Such variability in estimation is expectable in a highly decentralized religious tradition, where individual shamans compete with each other and with other familial or communal entities for authority. As we shall see, this perennial lack of unified support may grow more pronounced as a community develops its religious traditions in more firmly institutionalized, doctrinal directions.

Åke Hultkrantz (1989) explores some of the ways in which shamanism may have operated earlier in religious traditions that gradually evolved toward more complex systems. In these, Hultkrantz argues, shamanism can sometimes be recognized as an underlying stratum: marginalized, but not necessarily completely erased, by later refinements and modifications. Like many scholars of shamanism, Hultkrantz connects shamanic traditions particularly with small-scale hunter-gatherer societies, in which social stratification is kept at a minimum and strong ideals of collective welfare and cooperation prevail. For example, a shaman like Thai operates first within his own clan, maintaining relations with ancestors and interested spirits and negotiating with the spirit world for the good of other clan members. As Thai's effectiveness became manifest through his healing rituals, however, clients from a broader swath of the community began to consult him. Today, Thai notes, he has been invited to virtually every major center of Hmong population in the United States and is recognized as an important healer nationally. Yet his source of authority and network of contacts remain very much those of a traditional hunter-gatherer shaman: rooted in an egalitarian ideal of Hmong society in which individuals help other individuals within a communal setting and in which the shaman's authority arises from a demonstrated ability to heal, contact the spirit world, and negotiate with its unseen denizens. As Barbara Tedlock (2004) has shown, shamanism can also thrive in small-scale subsistence agricultural settings, where the practitioners are often female.

Hultkrantz notes, however, that societies change as they acquire more elaborate, large-scale agriculture or other means of livelihood (1989). Social stratification and division of labor grow as elements of social structure, and the egalitarian ideals of the small-scale society are replaced with notions of class, specialization, and destiny. As societies change, so too religions undergo transformation, reflecting the altered circumstances and norms of their ambient societies.

Harvey Whitehouse (2004) explores the dynamic between what he terms the "doctrinal" and the "imagistic" modes of religion. In Whitehouse's view, the shamanic specialist occupies the imagistic pole in a continuum of religious experiences (2004: 63–77). This pole is characterized by powerful, spontaneous religious experiences which are remembered episodically and interpreted personally. When these are central to a community's religion, they help shape religious institutions which remain highly localized and lack strong hierarchies. In such a framework, figures like the shaman can function as local notables within the ritual activities of an extended family or community. At the opposite pole lies the "doctrinal" mode, in which religious experiences are dominated by routinized rituals and doctrines, stored and recalled in the mind as complex semantic wholes. A profession-alized class of religious specialists base their claims to authority on knowl-edge of this doctrine, and help maintain institutions which examine individuals' beliefs for adherence to an orthodox norm. As a society devel-ops toward greater social complexity and hierarchy, it will gravitate toward the doctrinal mode. The imagistic mode, however, does not necessarily disappear, but may come to alternate with the doctrinal either through instances of visionary dissidence or through a historical oscillation between the two modes over time in a manner similar to that described by A. Thomas Kirsch in his classic of Southeast Asian religions (Kirsch 1973).

Sometimes, in the development toward doctrinal religious expressions, societies have retained shamanic traditions despite their (formerly) sponta-neous and localized nature. Such seems to be the case in the thirteenth-century Mongolian khanate of the Golden Horde, discussed in Chapter 2 (Dawson 1955: 12), as well as, to some extent, in the Manchu Qing dynasty of China during the seventeenth through early twentieth centuries (Vitebsky 1995: 42). Caroline Humphrey (1994) has argued that the textual sources left to us regarding the rise of the empire of Chinggis (Genghis) Khan – written largely by cultural outsiders – provide evidence for a frequent use of divinatory trance. The leader Temüjin acquired his name Chinggis from a sage Kokochu, whom the Persian historian Rashid-al-Din quotes as having declared: "God talks to me and I visit the sky" (Humphrey 1994: 202). Chinggis in turn conferred an honorific title on his diviner, renaming him Teb Tenggri ("heavenly one") and relying on his divination faithfully until the latter began to plot intrigues against the khan. Chinggis is also described as being able to enter divinatory trance himself: falling into an altered state in which he uttered detailed accounts of things that were to come. Writes one Islamic historian:

Every now and then he used to fall into a trance, and in that state of insensibility all sorts of things used to proceed from his tongue … Whenever this inspiration came over him, every circumstance – victories, undertakings, the appearance of enemies, the defeat and reduction of countries – anything which he might desire, would all be uttered by his tongue. A person used to take the whole down in writing and enclose it in a bag and place a seal upon it, and when Chinggis Khan came to his senses again, they used to read his utterances over to him one by one, and according to these he would act. (1994: 203)

Humphrey suggests that such divinatory shamanic practices, consisting apparently of trance, facilitated upward spiritual travel and consultation with a heavenly deity, thus underscoring the patriarchal nature of the khanate and figuring as a source of authority and legitimation within the new empire. They were, to use Whitehouse's terminology, still imagistic and occasional. As the conquering generation of Chinggis gave way to an established dynasty, however, its leaders developed a taste for the greater predictability and stasis of the "doctrinal" mode. The descendents of Chinggis shifted allegiances to Buddhism, relying on lamas as a prime medium between the emperor and the heavens, and marginalizing the older shamanic divination of the past (1994: 195, 199, 206). At the same time, however, shamanic practices persisted outside the imperial court: these continued to involve horizontal spiritual travel and negotiation with unseen spirits in a manner consonant with that described in Chapter 4. Because of their spontaneity and unpredictability, these practices – and their practitioners – remained potentially disruptive forces within the empire (1994: 200).

Humphrey's examination of state shamanism within the Manchu Qing dynasty shows a similar trajectory. External spirits of previous Jurchen shamanic traditions – the unpredictable prime movers of an imagistic religiosity – gradually became redefined as Manchu ancestors, a conceptual move that again favored the patriarchal system of the empire and subsumed the spirits into the doctrinal apparatus of genealogy, prescribed ritual, and trained priesthood. Gradually, shamanic practitioners became a hereditary class of government functionaries, largely devoid of a supernatural calling or duties, apart from making sacrifices for the continued prosperity of the state and its leaders (1994: 211). Writes Humphrey: "By the mid-eighteenth century, if we are to believe what the Qianlong emperor Hongli wrote, the court shamans, who could hardly speak Manchu, had lost touch with earlier traditions and confined themselves to a ritualistic repetition of half-understood formulae" (1994: 211–12). At this point, however, Hongli instituted a process of "remembering" – revitalization – that helped reinvigorate and extend the dynasty's shamanic traditions until the beginning of the twentieth century. Hongli's revitalization contained a good deal of Buddhist influence and a concerted effort to standardize and regulate shamanic formulas: a reflection of the essentially doctrinal mode that he and his state had come to expect in religion. Yet it also preserved some elements of shamanic ritual within the Confucian court structure up until the early twentieth century. The process of shamanic revitalization is a topic to which we will return in the following chapter, in which the Manchu case may be compared with other state-supported attempts to valorize yet control past imagistic religious expression.

Karen Smyers (1999: 40) has described a parallel in the shamanic practices of the murky third-century Queen Himiko (Pimiko) of Wa (Japan), who functioned, much like Chinggis Khan, as a vehicle for communications between the spirit world and her earthly kingdom. Japanese historians note a similarly shamanic Empress Jingū of the same era. Such royal shamanic figures may have represented continuities of past supernatural practices among the people who migrated to Japan, but they also evinced a great degree of transformation as well, as did their Manchu and Mongolian counterparts. Their alterations reflected the interests and agendas of a complex, aristocratic, and royal society with a vested interest in dynastic power.

While such continuities demonstrate at least the theoretical capacity of shamanic traditions to survive into the more doctrinally shaped religious idioms that accompany stratified social configurations, Hultkrantz (1989) argues that, in general, the shamans in such situations are gradually replaced by or transformed into priests, with election and indoctrination maintained by established religious institutions. As a result, rituals which formerly were performed as needed within the local community become codified into procedures and facilities presided over or financed by the upper echelons of society. In the more stratified messianic traditions of Southwest Asia, including Zoroastrianism, Judaism, Christianity, and Islam – but also in the agrarian religions of other parts of the world, including Central America – the old central role of the shaman survives in the figure of the prophet, a voice at the margin of society who has recourse to supernatural experience through vision quests or privations, and who shares these experiences occasionally with a larger (potentially hostile) religious establishment. The prophet may strongly resemble the shaman in supernatural experience, but usually undergoes a very different evaluation within the framework of a religious tradition that possesses a defined orthodoxy and hierarchy. In this sense, many Western messianic religions may be said to possess a shamanic stratum or potential, underlying part, if by no means the entirety, of the religion's activities.

In the context of South and East Asia, Hultkrantz argues that old shamanic techniques of trance gradually evolved into the yogic traditions within the more doctrinal religious systems known by scholars as

Hinduism, Buddhism, and Taoism. As we saw in Chapter 7, early Vedic texts describe ecstatic specialists, *muni*, who strongly resemble shamans. Gananath Obeyesekere (2002: 167) suggests that the shaman common to tribal Indian religions gradually helped give rise to the enstatic yogic meditator, the *samana* of Hindu and Buddhist traditions. This homology between the shaman and the yogic specialist in turn gradually led to the spread of more elaborated rituals and paraphernalia from Buddhism into localized shamanisms within the peripheral areas of the Buddhist world: Central Asia and Siberia. Thus, Hultkrantz argues (1989: 47), terms like *shaman* itself can be seen as adoptions of the Indic *samana*. In Central Asia, this Buddhist element would later receive a further stratum of influence from the spread of Islam in the region. Such events mean that the earlier shamanism becomes transformed into the meditative religious traditions of South and East Asia, while in those areas in which it survived relatively intact (e.g., Siberia and Central Asia) it acquired new layers of symbolism and paraphernalia which helped make it resemble the more stratified, doctrinal religions that had developed out of or alongside it.

INCOMING RELIGIONS AND MERGERS OF BELIEFS

Whereas the above discussion has focused on situations in which shamanic traditions gradually became replaced or obscured within evolving religions, the history of shamanism around the world is replete with cases in which preexisting shamanic traditions were suddenly confronted with new religious ideas arriving from the outside. Sometimes new religious traditions spread through missionization and trade contact; sometimes they resulted from economic colonization or conquest. In general, historical accounts of initial contact situations indicate the resilience of shamans and shamanic traditions in the face of new imports, sometimes rejecting the arriving belief system altogether, but frequently choosing instead to selectively incorporate elements into preexisting practices. Gradually, such contact borrowing could result in new fused religious outlooks, a process which scholars of religion term *syncresis*.

Håkon Rydving (1995) surveys the substantive manner in which Sámi *noaide* shamans were able to assimilate and incorporate Christian elements into their practice, thereby neutralizing the potential for loss of authority within their own communities. Much to the consternation of Lutheran authorities, Sámi of the seventeenth and early eighteenth centuries made open reference to both their traditional religion as well as Christianity in their daily lives. Recourse to the *noaide* for help with luck, illness, or divination was common, and *noaide* practitioners were influential and respected members of the community. Sámi drum heads contained images not only of pre-Christian Sámi deities, but also of Christ, the saints, and churches, integrated into a single, meaningful cosmos. Christianized Sámi ministers occasionally abandoned their new religion to become shamans themselves, or to combine shamanism with elements of their Christian training (Rydving 1995: 71). Aside from these, few men came forward to undergo training as ministers. It was not until the authorities criminalized shamanic religious practices in the eighteenth century and threatened any owner of a drum with execution that the old religious traditions became clandestine or abandoned.

The same persistence and resilience of shamanism is evident in Tlingit oral history of the first contacts between *ixt* shamans and Christian missionaries. The first Russian Orthodox priest arrived in Sitka, Alaska, in the 1830s and began to preach to Tlingit in the area. William Nelson, a Tlingit elder, recounted for the ethnographer Sergei Kan (1991) the experiences of an *ixt* from this period whose paraphernalia came to include a crucifix and holy water and whose primary helping spirit resembled an Orthodox priest:

There once lived a man in the Angoon area who was very sick – he had a strong internal bleeding. One night he saw a man coming through the door. He had a long beard and white hair [looked like a Russian priest]. He was coming closer and closer but then disappeared. He went into the shaman's body. It was a power, a healing power spirit. We call it *kugawasu yéik* [good luck spirit]. After that the sick man became a shaman; he would sing shaman's songs at night. He was getting the power. Pretty soon his bleeding stopped – no more blood came out of his stomach.

He felt good and decided to go to the beach to get some fresh water from a stream. When he scooped up some water, on the bottom of his cup he saw a cross. He drank the water with the cross. That night he began making noises like a shaman does when the spirit comes down on him. He was speaking Russian. People knew it was Russian because the Russian boats were already visiting them at that time. He owned a Russian axe and every time he spoke Russian he would pick it up. That is when the Russian spirit came down to him. We call it *Anóoshi yahaayí* [Russian spirit]. He used that axe to chase away the evil spirits that made his patients sick. He told the people that every seventh day this *yéik* would come down on him and that on that day the house had to be cleaned very thoroughly. He was a strong *ixt'* and he had two powers – the healing good luck spirit (*kugawasu yeík*) and the Russian spirit (*Anóoshi yahaayí*). He could tell when somebody was going to be healed or when witches were doing some wicked things. He lived a long time ago but the Russians were already here. He died in a cave near Angoon. (1991: 375–6)

Kan (1991: 379) points to the likelihood that the story reflects a contact era interaction between an *ixt* and the new religion. The man's career as a shaman follows a traditional pattern, with an initiatory illness followed by contact with a tutelary spirit. His healing activities combined traditional Tlingit features with the novelty of the Sabbath cleaning and the paraphernalia and language of Orthodox priests. Other informants spoke of shamans who wore head garments that looked like those of priests or who raised their hands during their ceremonies in imitation of gestures used by Orthodox clergy. Christianity was clearly seen as a source of ritual acts and items of power, which could be assimilated with ease into the shamanic traditions of the community with little initial likelihood of conversion. By the end of the Russian era in Alaska (1867), the new religion counted only some four hundred converts; not even in Sitka had the Orthodox Tlingit become a majority. It would take more explicitly state-sponsored efforts, such as those connected with the American era that followed, to destroy the reputation and power of the *ixt* and make way for large-scale conversion to forms of Christianity.

Among another indigenous community of Northwestern North America, the Dunne-za (Beaver) people of British Columbia, traditional shamanism and Christianity fused into a seamless and effective syncretic tradition, as Robin Ridington (1988) has documented. Elders in the community could sometimes take on the role of *Naachin* ("Dreamers"), serving as communicative links between the spirit world and that of ordinary life. The earliest such visionary, Makenunatane, was revered in Dunne-za oral tradition, but also strongly associated with the Christian divine intermediary Jesus. Both figures were seen as having accomplished similar tasks: opening up a pathway to heaven for human beings by reporting and clarifying the communications that they had received from above (1988: 78). As the *Naachin* Charlie Yahey expressed it in an oratory of 1965:

> When God's son comes down – lots of good people will be saved
> and the bad people will be left behind and they will cry a lot.
> If somebody sings a song – even dancing –
> There may be lots of people but don't be shy.
> Somebody is like that. We'll be happy again.
> If you die you're going to see your way to heaven.
> By himself he will. If he dreams about heaven
> He's going to tell somebody about it.
> He will be happy about it. He's going to try
> to go to heaven if he dreams about it.   (1988: 82–3)

The Christian Second Coming is merged here seamlessly with the Dunne-za imperative to sing or dance, not only to secure a place in the favored afterworld of heaven, but also for happiness and success in one's present existence. As another *Naachin* Amma Skookum stated to Ridington:

> I dream of heaven and somebody told me,
> "You people should play drums and sing
> so you won't have trouble with meat this summer.
> Sing and drum and you will kill lots of moose this summer." (1988: 86)

Shamanic and Christian outlooks merge here tightly, creating a discourse shaped by Christian teachings but also steeped in continuity with the shamanic past.

While this fusion appears to have occurred without substantial resistance from the Catholic missionaries of the area, the arrival of a major highway through the region produced devastating cultural and religious changes of its own, precipitating the breakdown of Dunne-za spirituality through the massive social and economic transformations it caused (1988: 82). Not surprisingly, the highway was regarded by some elders as a source of confusion for the dead of the community as well, particularly in their afterlife journey to the world of the dead, described through the Christian imagery of heaven. According to the *Naachin* Charlie Yahey:

> This highway fooled many people.
> They thought it was the road to heaven.
> They walk and walk and walk and get nowhere.   (1988: 82)

The passage to heaven entails finding one's way there, often through the crucial assistance provided by the *Naachin* and community members who participate in the *Naachin*'s songs and dance. A parallel to Catholic notions of prayer for the dead, the *Naachin*'s singing is seen as both efficacious and compassionate, a key role in the migration of souls from one realm of the cosmos to another.

Somewhat distinct from the situations described above are those cases in which communities have largely given up the core elements of their shamanic traditions while consciously retaining some features of the old belief system in their practice of the new. The line between this sort of retention of old beliefs within an essentially new religion and the incorporation of new beliefs into a preexisting shamanic tradition can seem slight, but the overall effect is often great. The difference often hinges on the role afforded the shamanic practitioner or shamanic practices in the resultant religious configuration. Where shamans or shamanic practices can be recast in a diminished role within the community's spiritual activities, so that they do not directly contravene the new religion's worldview or authority, they have sometimes been able to remain a part of the community's religious life. Where such recasting has been resisted by the authorities of the new religion, the same continuity can seldom be achieved.

Andrzej Rozwadowski (2001: 72) discusses the syncresis which occurred between shamanic practices and Islam in the dervish tradition of Sufism in the southern Central Asian region. Dervishes pursued knowledge of God through trance experiences, induced through hyperactive states entailing music and dance as well as inebriates such as opium, hashish, and wine. Shamans occasionally identified so strongly with the Islamic elements of these new fusions that they entered Sufist monasteries. Thus, shamanic traditions became assimilated in the new religion rather than being targeted for suppression. According to Jean During (2006), this assimilation of earlier shamanic traditions into lived Islam permitted the preservation and even extension of a variety of musical performance of long significance in the region. Later Islamic reforms would push for a removal of such syncretic elements, as occurred in purist movements within Buddhism and Christianity as well.

Anwarul Karim (2003: 74–8) details shamanic syncresis with both Islam and Hindu religions in contemporary Bangladesh. Karim cites two female practitioners, both of whom began their careers as shamanic healers as a result of supernatural dream visions. Both women used healing charms and song in their work, and both combined these with other procedures to treat illnesses, exorcize spirits, or address client misfortune. Yet they did so as part of opposing religious traditions: one, a middle-aged woman named Sakhina Khatun, grounded her practices in her identity as a Muslim; the other, an elderly healer named Fulkumari, saw her actions as part of her Hindu spirituality. Fulkumari had also learned techniques from Muslim practitioners, however, and felt proficient in both healing traditions. In either case, shamanic practices were not viewed as running counter to active participation in one of the dominant religions of the country.

In surveying shamanic traditions in contemporary Southeast Asia, Ruth-Inge Heinze (1988: 50, 146) notes a wide variety of syncretic phenomena. In Thailand, for instance, *ma khi* shamans describe the desire of spirits to possess human mediums as a result of karmic considerations. While waiting for their next rebirth, the spirits can improve their *karma* by rendering services to others. In this conceptual framework, the *ma khi* can view shamanic duties as part of a broader *Brahmin*-influenced Buddhist religiosity. Similarly, Heinze found that Malay *bomoh* shamans viewed themselves as pious Muslims, while the various Chinese shamans she interviewed were able to conceive of their duties as part of Taoism or Buddhism.

This same tendency toward incorporation can be observed in other contact situations as well. Olivier Lardinois S J (2007) examines the choices of indigenous Taiwanese shamans to maintain their shamanic healing traditions despite their conscious conversion to Catholicism. Lardinois interviewed shaman converts from the Tayal, Bunun, Tsou, Paiwan, and Amis ethnic groups. He found that by and large they continued to value and practice shamanic traditions despite their conversion. Most of the ten shamans interviewed had already become established as shamans before their conversion, and only one underwent shamanic initiation after baptism. This latter practitioner continued to practice shamanism only with the express encouragement of her parish priest, a missionary from Colombia. Catholic shamans were consulted by fellow villagers of both non-Christian and Christian backgrounds (including some clergy), particularly for relief from protracted headaches, arthritis, fever, cancer, depression, and anxiety. Shamans also continued traditional practices aimed at helping clients locate missing objects or resolve social and familial tensions. Shamans justified their practices under the Christian rubric of alleviating the suffering of others, and strongly condemned all forms of shamanic aggression, which they linked to the sins of jealousy and vengeance. Prayer, holy water, and the sign of the cross were incorporated into their practices, along with direct invocation of God and Jesus. The prayer book used by Catholic Amis women in attending to the ill and blessing houses and boats features both Christian texts and melodies drawn from shamanic tradition. In contrast to local Presbyterian converts, indigenous Catholics continued to venerate ancestors, and at least one convert to Presbyterianism had subsequently converted to Catholicism in order to alleviate headaches which a local (non-Christian) shaman had attributed to his abandonment of veneration practices. Lardinois stresses the importance of recognizing the positive motivations behind shamanic practices rather than exercising a blanket condemnation in the manner of missionaries of the past.

The Native American Church represents another example of the conscious retention of elements of prior shamanic traditions within an embrace of a new religious ideology. The religion emerged during the latter half of the nineteenth century, apparently in Oklahoma, and spread rapidly among different Native American communities. In 1918, it was officially incorporated as a formal religion within the United States, and eventually also Canada. Adherents of the church combine the shamanic practice of peyote-induced visionary experiences with a monotheistic ideology drawn directly from Christianity. While rejecting many of the polytheistic aspects of traditional Native shamanisms, the religion places central emphasis on elements of shamanic tradition as practiced by many Native American communities of the past, including the use of the sweat lodge and entheogens and imagery of sacred directions. Such inclusions of old elements can prove strongly affirmative for a community undergoing a shift from a deeply meaningful past religion to a new worldview promoted initially by cultural outsiders (Slotkin 1956; La Barre 1964).

COMPETITION FOR ADHERENTS

The persistence of shamans and shamanic traditions within communities experiencing concerted missionization is a sign of the power and resilience of shamanic belief systems in general. The representatives of encroaching religious movements, however, were not always tolerant of such persistence. Incoming religious traditions that enjoy the prestige and approval of colonizing authorities have often proved highly successful in drawing away adherents over time, particularly those individuals or communities with upward economic aspirations. In such contexts, missionaries as well as new converts sometimes cast the retention of shamanic traditions as backward, self-defeating, and confining, while crediting the encroaching movement with a superior worldview and the potential of attaining a standard of living equal to that of the colonizing polity. In such circumstances, the importance of choice becomes emphasized, and the merging described above becomes rejected as wrongheaded or deleterious.

Sherry Ortner (1995) explores the ongoing conflicts between shamans and lamas in 1960s Nepal. Here, in Sherpa communities, the triumph of new, more institutionalized forms of religion, dominated by Buddhist doctrine, was not complete. In village contexts, shamans remained important figures, but were locked in competition with hereditary Buddhist lamas, who often were consulted for assistance with similar personal or health problems. In other areas of Nepal, further, Buddhist monks and monasteries dominated, as we shall see below. Ortner shows how shamans were losing ground to lamas in village settings, in part because of the greater value now placed on doctrinal learning, knowledge which bolstered the lamas' status. Where the shaman placed value particularly on the individual supernatural experience – the *hlabeu* trance (1995: 360) – and the individual shaman's capacity to diagnose and deal with problems arising from the jealous living (*pem*), unhappy dead (*nerpa*), and local spirits (*lu*), the lama found answers in the texts of Buddhist wisdom which he possessed and interpreted, and in the ceremonies which he enacted according to Buddhist regulations. These activities allowed the lama in turn to control demons that were likely to afflict human beings. The struggle between these two groups of specialists was expressed in part through stories, such as this one told from a lamaist point of view:

There was once a competition between a great lama and a shaman. They both flew to the sky, and both came out the same. This went on for a long time. No matter what the lama did, the shaman matched him. They both made rocks soft. They both made footprints in the rock. Then the lama suggested mountain climbing. The shaman started climbing, but the lama went to sleep. The lama's servants kept trying to wake him, but he kept saying, "Don't worry," and kept on sleeping. The lama said, every time they tried to wake him, "Did the sun rise yet?" They admitted that it hadn't. "Well, then, don't bother me," he said. Finally the sun rose to find the shaman singing and dancing just below the summit, thinking he had won, when the lama came running up the sunrays to the top and won the contest. Then the shaman was humiliated, and hid behind his drum. But the lama said, "Don't worry, don't be ashamed," and he gave him some snow from the mountain, which is why that mountain now has a crimp near its summit. Previously shamans had refused to pay obeisance to lamas, but since then they always do. (1995: 357)

Shamanism and Lamaism had come to occupy the same conceptual and economic niche within Sherpa village life, leading to the kinds of competition described above.

As Håkon Rydving (1995) shows, Lutheran approaches to Sámi religiosity in Norway and Sweden shifted markedly during the eighteenth century. Whereas earlier authorities had accepted syncretic merging as expectable and relatively unimportant, the new missionary approach emphasized making a conscious choice between the old religion and the new. The old religion was to be rejected entirely, and state legislation was passed to criminalize key elements of the old belief system, such as possession of shamanic drums. Sámi reacted to this new discourse quite negatively at first: fear of the new religion stemmed in part from concerns of angering ancestors or the spirits. The fears stemmed also from the fact that those communities who had converted most fully often displayed greater instances of poverty, disease, alchoholism – social ills directly attributable to increased contact with the colonial authorities. The Sámi Anders Person Snadda expressed his views to the missionary Högström in 1745:

[A] certain Sámi named Snadda asked me if I would permit him to speak his thoughts frankly according to the beliefs that he had held until now. He said that he had heard it said by old people, how happily and in what prosperity the people lived when they freely made use of [their] sanctuaries, and also how many strange destinies and peculiar events his people had been subjected to, and now a general poverty had increased since so many obstacles had been laid in the way of the use of these customs. He referred to the so-called Nederbyn community that in former times consisted of a hundred rich and wealthy tax-paying Sámi; but since they began to deviate from the customs of their ancestors, they have become scattered, and nowadays there are in the whole of the community, not more than a few, and most of them are beggars. He told about his father, that he used the drum, and was well; he himself had now put it aside, but found himself not understanding anything else, but soon having to [beg] ... He believed that God gives well, yes as soon, his food to the evil and to witches, as to the pious. He was of the opinion that when the wolf comes, he is not likely to have greater consideration for my reindeer than his. He feared that [the village] would soon be waste if people continued to discard the old customs: which probably they had seen beforehand, who had begun to leave in time and had already fled, etc. To all this, the other Sámi added their words, from which I could notice that they were of the same opinion as he. (Rydving 1995: 86; translation slightly modified)

Given these views, Sámi *noaidit* seemed far from experiencing the kinds of social and economic rejection that would eventually emerge once the state imposed harsh punishment for pagan backsliding.

Rebecca Kugel (1994) writes of the antagonistic contact situation experienced by nineteenth-century Ojibwa (Anishinabe) people of the Fond du Lac area of Minnesota. In 1839, the community received a Presbyterian missionary in the figure of the New England preacher Edmund Ely. As Kugel shows, Ely's brand of Christianity found little resonance among local Ojibwa: his emphasis on Anglo-American Protestant values of truth, independence, self-sufficiency, and faith in God alone conflicted radically with the community's traditional values of unity, harmony, generosity, and multiple spirit helpers. Where Ely sought to incorporate the community into an American national Christianity, the community itself interpreted him from within their own religious traditions as apparently an evil shaman, bent on inflicting harm on a person with whom he had come in conflict.

Using Ely's own diary, Kugel is able to chronicle a particular interpersonal relation that eventually led to Ely's failure as a missionary and departure from the area. Ely had distinguished himself by his refusal to share food with his neighbors, an act which he believed would help teach Ojibwa people the value of self-sufficiency, but which instead stigmatized him as unnaturally miserly, particularly among the extended family led by a young Makwawaian. In the conflicts deriving from Ely's stinginess, the preacher struck and badly frightened Makwawaian's nephew, whom he caught pilfering turnips. Makwawaian responded with barely contained anger, nearly assaulting the preacher, a tremendous breach of Ojibwa etiquette. The Ojibwa community, which had come to regard Ely as a powerful healer – and therefore a potentially dangerous shaman – immediately feared for Makwawaian's health. Ely's reputation as a shaman was further bolstered by his apparently mysterious control over his cattle, which seemed far more subdued and tractable than any of the ruminants then familiar to Ojibwa: moose, buffalo, and deer. More than a year after this open altercation, a further event occurred. Ely's cow gave birth to a calf, and when Makwawaian came to Ely's homestead to inspect the new animal, the protective mother charged and severely butted the visitor. Makwawaian believed that Ely had used his powers to compel his helping animal, the cow, to attack and injure Makwawaian. Not only was Makwawaian greatly shaken by the attack, but he also appears to have suffered considerable internal injury, since he soon began to cough up blood and mucous. In Ojibwa views, it was likely that Ely had at last taken his revenge on his rival through supernatural aggression. Four days after the attack, Makwawaian arrived at Ely's home with a shaman of his own, sang a song of spiritual power before Ely, and then did the same in front of the cow, asking the cow to return his strength. As Makwawaian's health returned during the following days, it became clear to the community that his suspicions of the missionary had been correct. Rather than rescuing the Ojibwa from what he regarded as ignorant superstitions, in other words, Ely reinforced their traditional beliefs, as the community interpreted him as the epitome of a shaman with evil intent. Given this reinscription, it was inevitable that Ely's missionary efforts would fail in the region. Kugel writes:

Alongside their ongoing evaluation of cattle, the Ojibwa in the 1830s also commenced an assessment of the missionaries. With protestations that they had "come here to do good and teach [the] children," and in possession of new and seemingly potent medications, the missionaries ought to have been positive forces within Ojibwa communities. Instead, they quarreled with the people, refused to share food, made incomprehensible demands about work and travel, and in numerous other ways seemed bent on community destruction. (1994: 239)

The Ojibwa were not likely to abandon their old ways of understanding and controlling the cosmos simply because a badly behaved foreign missionary told them to do so, especially one whose actions could be interpreted from within the preexisting shamanic tradition. As in other parts of the world, and given the unwillingness of many missionaries like Ely to adapt their messages to the communities whom they approached, shamanic traditions faced little real threat from outside missionaries. The triumph of foreign religious movements over indigenous varieties of shamanism often occurred only once state coercion was added to the situation.

Sometimes the discourse of confrontation and rejection inherent in the Rev. Ely's approach to Ojibwa religiosity becomes expressed by community members themselves. Paul Radin (1926: 169ff.) details the views of Crashing Thunder, a Ho-Chunk (Winnebago) man who abandoned his community's shamanic traditions for an embrace of the peyotism of the Native American Church (see further discussion in Chapter 14). Crashing Thunder became an outspoken critic of the old traditions while extolling the efficacy of the newly arrived peyote spiritualism. Robin Ridington documents similar internal dissention among Dunne-za people in 1960s British Columbia. As Amma Skookum, a *Naachin*, remarked:

> I dream lots of times about different things
> but the people of Halfway [British Columbia] don't believe me.
> When I sing Ruby's song I said people should dance.
> People should sing that song and dance.
> But nobody sings that song.
> Here I'm the only one who sings in Halfway;
> the people just think it's bullshit.
> When Ruby died I dreamed about him.
> He was drunk when he died and he couldn't get to heaven.
> "Help me," he said. And I did. I sang that song.
> That's why he went to heaven.   (Ridington 1988: 88)

Such internal decline in belief in the importance of shamanic rituals, of course, can be seen as the product of outside influences: the encroachment of a competing worldview presented by the surrounding Canadian society, its popular culture, technology, and social norms. Amma Skookum had come to be viewed not as a central pillar of the community's supernatural economy but as an irrelevant holdover from the past.

STATES AND SUPPRESSION

It should be noted that from the perspective of many Christian missionaries during the eighteenth and nineteenth centuries, the persistence of shamans and shamanism represented not simply a defeat of their efforts to spread the religious traditions they believed in, but a triumph of the powers of darkness and evil. Shamans and their tutelary spirits were explicitly demonized, equated with dualistic concepts like the devil and hell. The non-dualistic worldview of shamans – in which spirits as well as shamans themselves were recognized as being capable of doing both good and ill – was lost on missionaries who regarded their opponents as ignorant at best, if not also sorely deluded or even malevolent. Communal values of helpfulness and generosity, as well as the self-sacrificial attitude of many shamans, were ignored as virtues, or interpreted as further deceptions aimed at hoodwinking a gullible and abused populace. Faced with this seemingly demonic adversary, missionary leaders often showed few qualms about enlisting the aid of the state to impose the new faith upon indigenous communities, under the threat of death if necessary. By outlawing shamanic practices, arresting and incarcerating shamans, and discrediting shamanic traditions in every manner possible, the state-aided missionaries of various countries sought to end forcibly the influence of shamans on their subject communities. With time, they proved notably successful in this effort.

As we saw in Chapter 2, Western Europeans had a long history of suppressing religious heterodoxy within their own nations, one which had unfolded in acts of sometimes striking violence for a number of centuries before the advent of the great voyages of discovery at the outset of the colonial enterprise. Witchcraft trials, the suppression of pagans, Jews, and Muslims, and the relentless quest to root out and punish heresy had all proceeded in medieval and post-medieval European societies through an evolving cooperation of church and state. Church authorities called on states to subdue and punish deviations from the religious norm, while states used the imagery of religion to help maintain and even extend their economic and political control over peasant populations, hinterlands, and subject peoples in general. With the publication of Johannes Schefferus's *Lapponia* (1673), and the establishment of colonies in the New World and elsewhere, this machinery of suppression was turned upon indigenous shamans.

As Glavatskaya (2001: 240) has shown, the West European model of suppression of religious heterodoxy inspired the Russian czar to follow suit as well. Anna Reid (2002: 46) quotes the 1710 order of Czar Peter the Great in which he directs Metropolitan Filofey of Tobolsk to compel conversion among the Khanty of his district:

Find their seductive false god-idols, and burn them with fire, and axe them, and destroy their heathen temples, and build chapels instead of those temples, and put up the holy icons, and baptize these Ostyaks [Khanty] … and if some Ostyaks show themselves contrary to our great sovereign's decree, they will be punished by death.

Peter did not intend to suppress shamanism alone through this decree: Filofey was instructed to apply the same methods to Muslims within his see as well (2002: 47). Two centuries later, these policies remained in place in Siberia. Writing at the opening of the twentieth century, M. A. Czaplicka (1914) notes:

On the whole, the shamans are very much attached to their vocation, in spite of the persecutions which they have to suffer from the [Russian] Government. Tiuspiut was many times punished by the Russian officials and his shamanistic dress and drum were burned; but he returned to his duties after each of these incidents. "We have to do it, we cannot leave off shamanizing," he said to Sieroszewski, "and there is no harm in our doing it." (1914: 176)

Continual suppression by state authorities had severely affected the practice of shamanism in the region. At the same time, the dogged persistence of shamanic practitioners had led authorities to mitigate their stances to a degree.

As coercive as Russian efforts at converting Siberian peoples seem to have been, Alaskan Tlingit people recall their efforts in the Sitka area as mild in comparison with the American-led Presbyterian mission of the 1870s, as Sergei Kan (1991) reports. The resilience described above in the initial Tlingit meeting with Christianity was soon reversed as an American era started for Alaska. American missionaries were virulent in their condemnation not only of shamans and witchcraft, but also of a host of traditional Tlingit customs, such as communal living in the winter and matrilineal descent and inheritance (1991: 367). Military force was used to compel children to attend the new missionary schools, where teachers endeavored to stigmatize all aspects of the old way of life, including shamanism. Graduates were encouraged to marry each other, and to settle in new "Boston style" houses that encouraged nuclear family thinking rather than a continuation of the old clan-based mentality of earlier Tlingit. Commander Glass's torture of shamans (described at the outset of this chapter), along with shamans' ineffectiveness in curing new diseases, such as the newly arrived smallpox, undermined the community's confidence in their traditional healers. Writes Kan:

Humiliated and persecuted, unable to combat new diseases or perform their healing séances without the fear of punishment, shamans increasingly lost their hold on the native community, becoming less and less relevant to its social and religious life. Among the manifestations of this process were the refusal of some of the prominent shamans' descendants to accept the call by inheriting their paraphernalia and by insisting that the shamans' corpses be disposed of, not above ground, in accordance with tradition, but by burial, which prevented their guardian spirits from being inherited. (1991: 371–2)

By the turn of the twentieth century, Tlingit shamans had disappeared from the Sitka area, although they remained in more isolated communities into the 1930s. Kan notes that even in the 1950s "there were still some individuals in conservative communities who, while not full-fledged shamans, were reputed to be fortune-tellers and spiritual healers" (1991: 371). State persecution, along with the discrediting that resulted from failures in the face of ravaging epidemics, spelled the end of a tradition that had existed among Tlingit for countless generations. Tlingit elders today, Kan reports, although generally strongly supportive of Christian viewpoints, nonetheless speak with respect of the *ixt* of the past.

In the Buddhist world, state authorities often sided with religious leaders to marginalize and eventually remove shamanic practitioners. In the Sherpa communities of 1960s Nepal, as Sherry Ortner (1995) details, Lamaism, and eventually Buddhist monasticism, were treated as the more prestigious and suitable religious traditions, favored by authorities over an increasingly disparaged shamanism. Typical of the situation of the era is the following story which Ortner collected from local Sherpas:

Once there was a king whose servant was dying. The king called both the lama and the shaman. The shaman, shaking and speaking in his trance, seemed to know everything, but actually he was possessed by a demon [*du*], and the demon knew everything the servant did. [Here the lama-informant added an aside: "Demons inform shamans; that's how they know everything."] Then the king said, "This is much better than the lamas, the lamas only read religious texts." But then Guru Rimpoche [the culture hero] said, "No, lamas are greater, this shaman is possessed by a demon, which is evil." And Guru Rimpoche put his golden thunderbolt [*dorje*, a weapon against demons] up the king's sleeve and said, "Now go back and see if the shaman speaks so well." He told the king to ask the shaman, "What do we do during [a certain ritual] in the temple?" and similar questions, and the shaman wouldn't know, because during such rituals the demon has been thrown a decoy offering [*gyek*] that has carried him far away to his distant land, so he never sees the ritual. Also, he'll be afraid of the *dorje*. [And everything Guru Rimpoche said came to pass.] (1995: 360)

Here the king and the lama guru are eventually united in their condemnation of the shaman, whose powers are ascribed to "demons" rather than "helping spirits," and whose inferiority is demonstrated by his lack of knowledge of Buddhist ceremonies. At the time of Ortner's fieldwork, Lamaism too was experiencing a similar denigration. Buddhist monasteries enjoyed the greatest state support and used their prestige to promote the removal of old elements of shamanic and Hindu religious practice from Nepali religious life, reorienting the communities' religious practices to coincide with festivals celebrated at the monasteries.

In Japan, on the other hand, Buddhism furnished a covert means of preserving shamanism over time. Takefusa Sasamori (1997: 94) recounts Japanese state attempts to suppress various forms of shamanism during the late nineteenth century:

The Japanese government issued a decree prohibiting shamanic rituals in 1873, during the Meiji Restoration. The reason stated for making such a decree was that the *azusa miko* (or "maiden who uses the *azusa* bow") only speaks in a delusive way, swindling ignorant people and offering no real benefit to them.

The logic behind the attempted suppression appears similar to that adopted in imperial Russia: to end a system that seemed to prey on impressionable and ill-informed peasants whose fidelity to old belief systems represented a barrier to progress. The Meiji suppression paralleled and repeated earlier attempts to oust Shugendō practitioners from the ranks of Buddhist clerics during the eighth century, as Karen Smyers (1999: 43) has shown. In the nineteenth-century case, however, rather than abandon their calling, *itako* shamans joined certain Buddhist sects, obtained the official designation of "missionary," and were able to continue their livelihoods as before. Notes Sasamori: "With time, the decree simply lost its relevance, and at present the *itako* can work without any kind of license" (1947: 94). In a similar fashion, Smyers (1999: 39–43) points out, other shamanic healers (*odaisan*, *ogamiyasan*, *gomiso*) became associated with the worship of the god Inari (a widespread Japanese deity often linked to foxes), and continued to function at Shinto and Buddhist Inari shrines. Shrines that granted licenses to shamans, such as the Takayama Inari, profited through the willingness of grateful practitioners to lead pilgrimages back to the shrine, even when the shamans moved to more distant locales (1999: 40). This fortunate turn of events differs from that experienced by shamanic practitioners in many other places, where suppression took harsher and more permanent forms.

Leonid Potapov (1999) recounts the turning tide of fortunes for Central Asian shamans during the early years of the Soviet Union:

The 1920s were a period of renaissance of shamanism in the Altai ... The renaissance ... developed as a result of Bolshevik pressure on the Russian Orthodox church after 1917, the Church having been the primary opponent of shamanism in the Altai region. Spiritual missions and churches were closed by the government, but shamanistic cults were not interfered with. The Communists were fighting all religions, but did not regard shamanism as a religion, considering it instead as a survival of the local clan system. (1999: 24)

In 1929, however, the state attitude changed abruptly, and shamans became the target of harsh suppression. "The shamans disappeared and those who survived and returned from Stalin's labor camps were extremely unwilling to have contact and in general denied their shamanistic past" (1999: 25). Potapov recounts his attempts to collect shamanic lore from a Khakass shaman in 1946. The man had spent ten years in a *gulag*, and was fearful of sharing his knowledge lest he be arrested and imprisoned once again. Vilmos Diószegi (1968), collecting in Siberia in the late 1950s, found shamanic traditions often entirely obliterated, especially in areas which had become more firmly integrated into the Soviet state, which denigrated shamanism as backward and antiquated (Hultkrantz 1989: 44; 1998: 55–6). Occasionally, he came upon aged former shamans who clearly remembered past rituals and roles but who declined to share them with the ethnographer. Recounting his frustrated efforts to persuade a Beltir elder to speak of shamanic traditions, Diószegi writes: "I could say whatever I wanted, Chibadyakov kept smiling without a word. 'These are things of bygone days. Why should we rake them up?'" (1968: 50). In those cases in which Diószegi was particularly successful in his collecting efforts, it was often because he was accompanied to the community by a trusted cultural insider, sometimes a person with a family history of prominent shamans (1968: 44–5). Among Buryat people of the Aga region of Siberia, local shamans were sometimes able to flee to remote villages of eastern Mongolia to elude Soviet imprisonment (Tkacz, Zhambalov, and Phipps 2002: 12). Shamanism and shamanic practitioners lingered as clandestine elements of such remote communities, allowing for their eventual reemergence in the shamanic revitalizations of the post-Soviet era, as detailed in the following chapter.

Although it is possible to regard state acts of shamanic suppression as simple expressions of the piety of rulers and their concern for their seemingly misguided subjects, it is far more likely that these same acts arose as tools for rulers' consolidation of power. As Chapter 2 details, Western "discovery" of shamanism as a religious tradition coincided closely with colonial expansion. Initial contacts with non-Western communities were often seemingly amicable: explorers and merchants set up trading relations based on notions of reciprocity and relative equality between trading partners, acknowledging cultural differences as sources of curiosity and wonder. With time, however, the leaders of colonizing nations, eager for new wealth, elected to employ their technological superiority to suppress and dispossess the populations they had formerly traded with on an equal basis, imposing a system of economic oppression that rendered indigenous communities subjugated populations. Those people who were not killed or banished in this process were often subjected to programs of enslavement, surveillance, and management, aimed at assimilating the remnant indigenous populations into a rapidly expanding colonial system. Since shamans were often among the primary leaders and potential sources of resistance in this situation, it became expedient for colonial authorities to undermine their status and discredit them, or to subject them to outright persecution under the banner of missionary necessity. A set of religious practices which had provided meaning and assistance in people's lives for countless generations were suddenly stigmatized, defined as inimical to the interests of the state and the welfare of its denizens.

REASON, MODERNITY, AND STATE INTERESTS

State authorities often described their policies toward shamans as acts of earnest devotion to a state religion. In contrast, Western intellectuals of the Enlightenment period onward tended to disparage shamanism not as a demonic obsession, but as mere superstition, a barrier to the edification and improvement of an ignorant populace. Shamans were condemned as self-deluded charlatans or profiteering hoodwinkers, bent on maintaining their hold over impressionable communities through a tyranny of fear, innuendo, and distortion. The virulence of these opinions can be sensed in the description of an Evenki (Tungus) séance which the German naturalist Johann Gottlieb Georgi recorded in 1751:

Prior to my departure, I still had an opportunity to watch a Tungus shaman practice his magic. At our request, he visited us the first night, and when we asked him to give us a demonstration of his art, he asked us to wait till the night, which we willingly agreed to do. At 10 p.m. he took us to a distance of one verst, and then bade us sit down. He stripped himself naked, then put on his shaman's coat, which was made of leather and decked out with all kinds of iron instruments ... He kept running to and fro along the fire, and made an infernal racket with the iron bells inside his dress ... At last, he started leaping and shouting, and soon we heard a chorus that was singing along with him. It was his believers, some of whom he had brought with him ... At length, after a lot of hocus-pocus and sweating, he would have had us believe that the devils were there. He asked us what we wanted to know. We put a question to him. He started his conjuring tricks, while two others were assisting him. In the end, we were confirmed in our opinion that it was all humbug, and we wished in our hearts that we could take him and his companions to the Urgurian silver-mine, so that there they might spend the rest of their days in perpetual labor. (quoted in Hoppál 1989: 75–6)

Georgi's remarks about the shaman's "infernal racket," "hocus-pocus," "conjuring tricks," and "humbug," along with his desire to imprison the practitioner in punishment of his healing practices, can hardly be regarded as illustrations of scientific neutrality, despite the writer's avowed identity as a naturalist.

The Enlightenment view of shamanism as an enemy to human progress lived on in the social planning and reforms of developing countries, many of which retained active shamanic traditions in the twentieth century despite the legacy of colonialism and missionization. Boudewijn Walraven (1994: 3–4) notes the importance of the "New Village Movement" as a force for undermining the traditional importance of *mudang* shamanic practices in rural South Korea. President Park Chung-Lee launched the movement as a means of modernizing the countryside. Village festivals as well as seasonal and crisis rituals in which the *mudang* had formerly presided became increasingly stigmatized, as communities were exhorted to embrace modern farming methods, housing, and social infrastructure. Man-young Hahn (1990: 195) cites government records that report the destruction of 135 shrines in 1969, with a further eleven destroyed in 1970 and another eleven in 1972. Practitioners of rituals were subject to arrest and as a consequence, rituals that had formerly been performed for the entire village became covert and recentered on the home. The *mudang*'s *kut* séance became viewed not as a valued supernatural intervention but as an affront to national progress. Laurel Kendall (2001) traces attendant societal attitudes in recalling a night-time *kut* séance of 1977. Kendall writes:

A policeman from the district office appears at the gate and shouts his insistence that they cease their drumming and dancing. He complains that this sort of activity is precisely why the New Village Movement has not advanced in Enduring Pine Village. He denounces the shamans for dancing and shaking their hips to the drum rhythm in front of schoolboys. This greatly amuses the shamans, but the elderly couple who are sponsoring the *kut* are irate at the policeman's intrusion. (2001: 26–7)

Eventually, the participants bribed the policeman to go away. Although later cultural policy in South Korea would come to view shamanism as a cultural treasure, the effects of such stigmatization were considerable, both in terms of limiting the number of persons willing to carry on the tradition and reducing the number of people willing to pay for shamans' services. And when a populace abandons a tradition, they do so not only for their own day and age, but also for generations to follow. Revival, as we will see in the following chapter, is never exactly the same as continuity, either in terms of diversity of traditions maintained, or in terms of community under-standing or support of the traditions.

Carol Laderman (2001) explores the ongoing challenges to Malay sha-manic traditions in late twentieth-century Malaysia. In the view of Prime Minister Mahathir bin Mohammad, many traditional rural practices, such as consultations with *bomoh* shamans and use of séances (*Main Peteri*) were regarded as "impediments to ... progress" (2001: 42) in a Malaysia aimed at becoming known as a thoroughly modern, urbanized Muslim state. In this context, many traditional healers lost economic and social ground in their villages, while only those individuals who could creatively merge the tradi-tion with elements of Islam and modernity were able to prosper. Urbanized Malaysians were no longer familiar with the norms and practices of a *Main Peteri*, and erred in their preparations or behaviors during the séance on the rare occasions in which they elected to arrange one. By failing to offer the

bomoh proper hospitality before the event, skimping on offerings of payment, laughing at seemingly exotic or naive ritual behaviors during the
séance, and failing to carry out the sacrifices demanded by spirits during
their communications, the would-be clients of *bomoh* further undermined
the very traditions they sought to embrace. These missteps not only
reflected their ignorance of the healing system that had formerly flourished
in rural Malaysia but also held the likelihood of dispiriting or even endangering the practicing shamans. Laderman recounts the illness of one shaman
which was attributed to his urbanized clients' failure to behave properly
after a séance (2001: 46).

While such cultural breakdown adversely affected the shamanic traditions
of rural Malaysian villages, some healers in the same country were able to
combine elements of the tradition with Western medicine and urban Islam
for a new, hybridized religious healing procedure. The resulting repackaging
and rethinking of shamanic categories can be viewed as a form of neoshamanism, and will be discussed in greater detail in Chapter 14. In many
more cases, however, elderly *bomoh* are forced to watch their traditional
knowledge lapse, as no suitable apprentices come forward to accept the call
and carry on the tradition.

In the United States, official respect for religious pluralism has not always
impeded state authorities from infringing upon shamanic traditions, particularly when these run counter to secularist uses of particular resources or
activities in public spaces. David O'Brien (2004) chronicles the efforts of a
city government in the state of Florida to ban animal sacrifice central to a
syncretic Cuban religion (Santeria), a law that was upheld throughout the
US court system until being decisively reversed by the Supreme Court.
Opponents of the religion's practices stated: "Santeria is not a religion. It is a
throwback to the dark ages. It is a cannibalistic, Voodoo-like sect which
attracts the worst elements of society, people who mutilate animals in a
crude and most inhumane manner" (2004: 35). Such discourse, laced with
evolutionary terms like "throwback" and "crude," presents shamanic traditions as pieces of the past: murky, primitive acts that do not deserve the
prestigious designation – or the constitutional protections – of true religion.

Lloyd Burton (2002) has examined the ways in which the US Park
Service has at various times undermined Native American sacred views of
the landscape in favor of the interests of rock climbers and other secular
consumers in the context of national parks and publicly owned lands:

If a tribe's sacred sites are mostly on public lands outside their jurisdiction, and the
agency controlling them decides that one of them would be a perfect spot for an

Figure 13. Contemporary Chukchi shamanic dancer. Photo courtesy Gregory Gusse.

observatory (Mt. Graham), a ski lift (the San Francisco Peaks), or a reservoir (Rainbow Bridge), there is little if anything a tribe can do about it. In allowing the U.S. Forest Service to build an access road through an Indian cemetery on public lands in 1988, the Supreme Court ruled that federal land management agencies have the power to physically destroy a site even if it means literally destroying a tribe's religion. Interestingly, the same decision also held that an agency can manage a site specifically for tribal religious preservation if it chooses to do so. (2002: 15)

As a set of remarkably resilient and enduring religious practices and understandings, shamanism has operated successfully in a vast array of cultures over the course of many centuries. Yet its dynamics have always been based on fragile relations: those between a shaman and spirit helpers, as well as those between the shaman and an ambient community. Failure in the maintenance of any of these relations can lead to the decline of the tradition, as a new generation fails to hear or heed the call to a shamanic profession or a community fails to acknowledge or make use of existing shamans' services. In some cases, changes in the community's own economics and religious institutions have led to the marginalization or even abandonment of shamans as leaders and specialists. In other cases, the decline of shamanism has arisen from pressures placed on these relations by outside groups: missionaries wishing to replace the old religion with a new, governments wishing to enforce allegiance to a state religion, or social agendas that stigmatize the shaman as part of a backward and inferior past. The nuanced system of trust and interreliance described in Chapters 4, 5, 6, and 8 cannot operate in a context of lukewarm support or downright skepticism. And thus, as elder shamans go to their graves without the opportunity to pass on their learning, a new generation arises with no new shamans. In the following chapters, we examine attempts to revitalize or even recreate shamanism in contemporary communities and the challenges faced in a context of lapsed shamanic knowledge.

CHAPTER 13

Shamanic revitalizations

> She was ten when the Kiowas came together for the last time as a living
> Sun Dance culture. They could find no buffalo; they had to hang an
> old hide from the sacred tree. Before the dance could begin, a com-
> pany of soldiers rode out from Fort Sill under orders to disperse the
> tribe. Forbidden without cause the essential act of their faith, having
> seen the wild herds slaughtered and left to rot upon the ground, the
> Kiowas backed away from the medicine tree. That was July 20, 1890,
> at the great bend of the Washita. My grandmother was there. Without
> bitterness, and for as long as she lived, she bore a vision of deicide.
>
> N. Scott Momaday, *The Way to Rainy Mountain*

The widespread and often virulent suppression of indigenous religions
during the era of mass colonization created psychological, social, and
spiritual wounds that did not quickly heal. Ancient traditions and revered
religious specialists were swept aside, sometimes at the behest of conquering
authorities, sometimes as a result of internal rejection in a context of foreign
missionization and rapid or gradual cultural change. As a result, communities often found themselves essentially adrift, hoping to replace old verities
that had anchored their societies with the promised benefits of "modernity"
and full political enfranchisement within a new dominant polity (Kendall
2001: 27). As these new goals fail to materialize, however, or fail to bring
about a renewed social cohesion and stability, community members may
feel a sense of betrayal and anger. Such situations may in turn lead to
revitalization of formerly abandoned traditions: the self-conscious revival of
ways or ideas that had been rejected before. This chapter explores this
tendency, surveying specific North American and Siberian shamanic revivals from both the nineteenth and twentieth centuries to discuss the challenges and potential benefits involved in reinstituting a once abandoned
religious tradition. These are juxtaposed in turn to shamanic revitalizations
that occurred with strong state support and control, as in the eighteenth-
century Qing dynasty or twentieth-century South Korea. A survey of these

experiences establishes a base of comparison with the varieties of neo-shamanic innovation discussed in the following chapter. In some instances, as we shall see, shamanic revitalizations and neoshamanic movements overlap, with differentiation between the two a question of identity and motive.

The term *revitalization* is associated with the important synthetic work of Anthony F. C. Wallace (1956). Surveying a vast array of ethnographic studies of phenomena labeled nativistic movements, cargo cults, and messianic movements among cultures in the throes of extended colonization, Wallace theorized that revitalization permits a culture to reestablish a "steady state" after a long period of individual stress and cultural distortion. In this context of cultural crisis, a visionary leader may arise, one who charts a path back to cultural integrity through the selective revival of prior religious traditions. Wallace's wholly functionalist view of revitalization was later challenged by Theodore Schwartz (1976), who theorized that the cognitive dissonance, tensions, and emotionalism of the situation of Wallace's period of "cultural distortion" are potentially sustained rather than reduced by revitalization movements. In Schwartz's view, revitalization of prior religious traditions emerges out of a situation of cultural heterodoxy and participates in an ongoing back and forth between competing outlooks and social strategies. Its appeal in part is bolstered by a sense of crisis, of which it becomes not a solution but a symptom. In her study of Siberian religious activism, Marjorie Mandelstam Balzer (1999: 75) defines revitalization as "a group-level attempt to recapture an idealized past in order to reintegrate it with an uncertain future." Her definition emphasizes the motivations behind such efforts: the idealization of a past system of belief (in comparison with that existing in the present) and the desire to escape anxiety about an uncertain future. In such situations, a community may choose to revive a past religion because it seems to offer greater surety and stability when facing the challenges of the present. In any case, it is clear from these studies that old religious practices do not immediately disappear from the community's supernatural repertoire: sometimes they can re-emerge as the basis for strategies of cultural renewal and reorganization.

The quotation which opens this chapter illustrates powerfully the lingering memories of old traditions that can become the foundations of revitalization efforts. Writing in 1969 in a lyrical autobiographical work *The Way to Rainy Mountain*, N. Scott Momaday could report the firsthand account of religious suppression that his grandmother witnessed in her childhood. The last successful Kiowa Sun Dance, an elaborate, multiday solstice ceremony aimed at ensuring plentitude of buffalo and other wealth in the coming year, occurred in 1887. Nonetheless, members of today's Kiowa

community remember elements of the old tradition, despite its long suppression by US authorities (Mikkanen 1987). The general characteristics of
the festival are recalled, and some elders still remember in detail songs used
within the ritual despite the fact that it has not been performed during their
lifetimes. Some of the dance steps formerly used are preserved, in altered
form, in the Brush Dance, which used to precede the building of the
ceremonial lodge during the Sun Dance but which now exists as a separate
dance on its own. These elements stand as the raw materials for a potential
revival, should the community choose to follow that course in their spiritual
lives. Naturally, other elements of the tradition may have been lost, and
such gaps in information need to be filled through either conscious innovation or visionary revelation. Indeed, as Wallace points out, it is often the
vision or dream of a charismatic leader that allows the community to effect
this reconstitution, bridging the gap between past and present knowledge
through either the leader's direct decisions regarding details of the revitalization or the revelations which the leader acquires through supernatural
experiences. Writes Wallace:

With a few exceptions, every religious revitalization movement with which I am
acquainted has been originally conceived in one or several hallucinatory visions by a
single individual. A supernatural being appears to the prophet-to-be, explains his
own and his society's troubles as being entirely or partly a result of the violation of
certain rules, and promises individual and social revitalization if the injunctions are
followed and the rituals practiced, but personal and social catastrophe if they are
not. (1956: 425)

The charismatic leader then shares the vision with community members,
using the characterization of the community's problems and the solution
offered within the vision as a means of galvanizing and restructuring the
collective.

MANCHU SHAMANIC REVITALIZATION

The Qianlong Emperor Hongli of Manchuria (r. 1735–96) initiated one of
the first recorded instances of shamanic revitalization in his decree of 1778.
As Caroline Humphey (1994) details, the Qing dynasty had its origin
among the Tungusic Jurchen people of northeast China in the late sixteenth
century. The empire's founder, Nurgaci, drew on both Jurchen and
Mongolian populations to challenge the supremacy of the Ming dynasty,
and eventually created an empire that relied on shamanic divination as a
source of state authority. It also embraced the administrative – and, increasingly, the cultural – characteristics of the region's earlier Han rulers,

gradually replacing shamanic spirit entities with a cult of ancestors that carried significance as the source of supernatural assistance. Buddhist and Confucian notions infused the court religion with doctrinal tendencies and stasis. By the late eighteenth century, when the Qianlong emperor promulgated his decree, court shamans knew little Manchu (Jurchen) language and performed shamanic ceremonies in only a perfunctory manner. Apparently fearing a loss of temporal power as a result of this acculturation, and wishing to buttress his authority at a time of marked state expansion, the emperor instigated a thorough reinvigoration of his dynasty's hereditary religion. Believing that the rituals performed in the sinicized court no longer represented the old religion, Hongli sent mandarins to the outlying margins of the empire to observe and record Jurchen and Mongolian shamanic traditions intact (1994: 210–12). And although his efforts to preserve and standardize the prayers and rituals of Manchu shamans could be seen as a sign of a lack of understanding regarding the variability and adaptability of shamanic traditions in practice (1994: 212), Hongli's revitalized shamanism seems to have displayed many of the characteristics typical of prior Jurchen and Mongolian practitioners. Humphrey writes:

Manchu court shamans and their assistants were in charge of an assortment of rituals: invoking the spirits of the imperial clan; giving thanks for blessings received and asking for new ones; ritually washing the Buddha statue; making sacrifices for the prosperity of saddle horses and of horses in general … driving away evil spirits, especially the exorcism of smallpox; praying over offerings … burning incense and paper money for the spirits; parading the statue of Buddha and the tablets of the ancestral spirits; and playing official music … Shamans in the capital also conducted private curing rituals that were analogous with similar activities all over north Asia. (1994: 214)

This state-endorsed return to shamanic traditions – albeit still blended with the more doctrinal tendencies of Buddhist and Confucian practice – allowed the emperor to remind his court of the ethnic distinctiveness of his dynasty and, by extension, of the heavenly mandate by which the Manchu had come to rule all of China. Such assertions were particularly important in a context in which the real cultural distinctions between Manchu rulers and the empire's Han majority were rapidly dwindling. As Humphrey writes: "The history of the Qing court is the precarious balance of the processes by which the dynasty attempted to solve the contradiction between Manchu rural culture, which still was viable on the frontier, and the political institutions and classical traditions of conquered China. In effect, the court preserved an archaic ideology of Manchuness at odds with the sinicized institutions of government" (1994: 216). Hongli's policies illustrate pointedly the anxieties and motivations that often lie at the base of revitalization movements.

MIDÉWIWIN

A very different case of revitalization can be seen in the Midéwiwin Society of Great Lakes Potowatomi, Ho-Chunk, Sioux, and Ojibwa peoples. Norman Bancroft Hunt (2002: 64–71) provides an overview of the institution and its genesis. Hunt notes that seventeenth-century Jesuit missionaries made no reference to the tradition among Great Lakes Native communities, despite their keen interest in the indigenous religions they sought to displace. Historians suggest that the movement began as a secret society in the late seventeenth or early eighteenth century, in a context of declining or disrupted local shamanisms. Members borrowed the Grand Medicine Lodge tradition of the Iroquois and pooled shamanic visions in a new cooperative institution aimed at healing and mutual assistance. The society spread quickly across tribal lines throughout the Great Lakes and New England regions, partly in response to the new tradition's emphasis on a universal message and ideal of unification, embodied in the mythic accounts of its institution. Hunt writes:

A likely explanation for the origin of the Midéwiwin is that it occurred as a reaction against the social, religious, and cultural upheavals of the late seventeenth and eighteenth centuries. At this time, tribes such as the Ojibwa … were embroiled in the territorial disputes of the English and French during the French and Indian Wars, were subject to rapidly changing economies related to the fur trade and the introduction of European trade goods, and were also under intense pressure from missionaries anxious to convert them to Christianity. The shamans were at the center of these changes, not only because their beliefs were in conflict with those of the missionaries but also because they were seen as hostile traditionalists. Indeed, much of the Native resistance to Europeans was led by so-called "prophets," or shamans. A bonding together of the shamans through the Midéwiwin would have strengthened their position as well as acting as a unifying force for traditional beliefs. (2002: 65)

Here, then, in contrast to the Manchu revitalization, which operated at the very pinnacle of Chinese society, the Midéwiwin movement allowed an increasingly disempowered population to recover a basis for communal action and authority. Through the Midéwiwin institution, members were able to frame a non-Christian and collective response to the missionization that was transforming Native communities at the time. Midéwiwin rituals and activities represented a substantive means of reestablishing cultural and religious authority for communities deeply affected by forced acculturation. It remains an important religious institution among many Great Lakes tribes today, reflecting both its appeal and its effectiveness as a culturally recognized alternative to encroaching religious influences.

WOVOCA

One of the most celebrated shamanic revitalizations in American history occurred among the Numu (Yerington Paiute) people of Nevada in the late nineteenth century. There, a Numu man named Wovoca (referred to in government documents as Jack Wilson) emerged as the center of a new movement that spread rapidly to numerous tribes across the American West. According to the detailed history written by Michael Hittman with the support of the Yerington Paiute tribe (1990), Wovoca experienced a powerful vision sometime around 1889 or 1890, possibly while suffering from scarlet fever. In this vision, Wovoca saw a happy afterlife in which Numu and whites were able to live in harmony. He received five songs of power to control the weather, and was promised the co-presidency of the USA with Benjamin Harrison. Upon his revival from this catatonic state, possibly in conjunction with the solar eclipse of January 1, 1889, he began to preach a moral code of upright life and called for the institution of a new sacred dance, a revival of the earlier 1870 Ghost Dance. Adherents of the movement were promised a recovery of their youth in heaven. Wovoca was credited with performing successful rain dances on several occasions and drew interested visitors from throughout the West, including representatives of over thirty different tribes. Native adherents were particularly drawn to elements of Wovoca's teaching that suggested the rebirth of Native control of their lands and a shirt of invincibility that would render white firearms useless against them. Hittman suggests that these "ghost shirts" may represent an adaptation of Mormon undergarments. Wovoca's movement synthesized religious, social, and political messages and encompassed whites as well as Natives, even if in practice it proved of greater importance to Native activists.

SIBERIAN REVITALIZATIONS

In examining movements from nineteenth-century Siberia, Marjorie Mandelstam Balzer (1999) lays stress on their innovative features, as well as their typical fusion of religious, social, and political motives. Revival of shamanic traditions in Siberia was seldom an isolated spiritual event but rather part of a larger sociocultural response to situations under the czarist or Soviet regimes. Illustrative is the case of revitalization among Vakh Khanty in the late nineteenth century. In 1896, a prominent Khanty woman reported having a dream in which a great illness came to plague her people (Balzer 1999: 84). To stave off the effects of this coming affliction, she called for a rejection of tobacco and alcohol, a collecting of goods within kin networks, and ritual sacrifices of horses at multiple sacred sites. The movement employed elements of Orthodox Christianity such as making sacrifices on particular saints' days and at sites of importance to Orthodox missionization. Word of the visions spread rapidly to an area of more than one hundred kilometers. Followers embraced the substitution of expensive horse sacrifices for the more traditional sacrifice of reindeer, an example of the kinds of innovation Balzer describes. Adherents also made offerings of prestige items from the Russian trade, including objects of brass and pewter and lengths of chintz and calico fabric. The nature of these sacrificial items suggests that the movement was viewed as a response to the growing presence and influence of Russians in the region and the economic and cultural effects of this presence. The new practices drew adherents from towns as well as rural districts, and attracted individuals of both pure and mixed ancestry. The sacrifices reinforced the old lineage orientation of Khanty shamanism and addressed not only the prestigious sky god but also lesser gods of smallpox and disease that were associated with epidemics arising from extended contacts with Russians. Balzer suggests that the revitalization as a whole was largely a response to the persistence of smallpox in the region and the broader sociocultural effects of the colonial situation.

Where the Khanty revitalization of the 1890s arose in response to the pressures of Orthodox missionization and increasing Russian trade, Siberian revitalizations of the 1990s unfolded in the spiritual vacuum of the post-Soviet Russian Federation. Communities that had previously consigned their shamanic traditions to the past – often after a period of harsh suppression and concerted denigration – began in the 1990s to explore and reengage shamanic traditions as sources of identity, as well as potential sources of tourist income. Virlana Tkacz, Sayan Zhambalov, and Wanda Phipps (2002: 12) explore the rituals of a new generation of Buryat shamans who reemerged after the fall of the Soviet Union. Young potential shamans of the Aga region traveled to remote villages in eastern Mongolia to seek out and learn from surviving traditional shamans. Write Tkacz, Zhambalov, and Phipps: "And so the ancient traditions, which had been in danger of being lost because of the seventy-year ban, were revived" (2002: 12). Henri Lecomte (2006), in examining shamanic revitalization movements across contemporary Siberia, juxtaposes such reclamation efforts from two other related movements: new adaptations of shamanic musical traditions as an expression of youth and collective identity, and the establishment of professional shamanic therapy centers in urban areas. Where Lecomte views the first movement as true revitalization, he sees the latter two as varieties of neoshamanism. In any case, Lecomte notes (2006: 50), the multiplicity of shamanic adaptations "is proof that this ancient conception of the world has remained deeply anchored in the collective imagination of the peoples of Siberia at the outset of the twenty-first century" (2006: 50; my translation).

Shamanic revitalization in the Tuva Republic may serve as an example of similar movements which occurred to varying degrees within many indigenous communities throughout the former Soviet Union. The Tuvan people of southern Siberia, possibly descendents of the historical Huns, came under first Mongolian and then Manchu control from the thirteenth to twentieth centuries. In the nineteenth century, their lands began to be settled by Russian migrants, and in the twentieth century, the region was pulled into the Russian Empire, eventually to be incorporated into the Soviet Union. The Tuva Republic today is a part of the Russian Federation and comprises both Native Tuvan and ethnic Russian populations. As a state, the republic has three official religions: Tibetan Buddhism, Russian Orthodoxy, and shamanism. The official status for shamanism here – currently unique internationally – reflects the diligent efforts of Tuvan intellectuals during the 1990s.

As described in Chapter 12, the Hungarian ethnographer Vilmos Diószegi was able to travel widely in Tuvan villages during the late 1950s and recorded a wide variety of shamanic traditions that had survived the harshest era of Soviet religious suppression. In Diószegi's view, the traditions he observed were the final glimmerings of a once robust shamanic culture that was now fated to disappear. In the Glasnost era, however, Tuvan intellectuals like Mongush Borakhovich Kenin-Lopsan (1987) began to collect and publish Tuvan shamanic lore that had persisted in rural areas. His study presented both descriptions of rituals and recordings of shamanic songs, and boldly described itself as an account of Tuvan shamanism from the nineteenth through the twentieth century, rejecting Diószegi's pessimism.

Francis Greene, a visitor to Tuva Republic in 1992, reports the practice of shamanic rituals by one of his educated guides:

I am sure that Shamanism is not really dead in Tuva, and suspect that Valya, the ethnologist-musicologist who arranged a Hoomei [throat-singing concert] for me, is well on the way to becoming a Shamanka. I saw her making little offerings of vodka to the four quarters of the compass during a bonfire picnic in the woods during which we discussed animism, ghosts, and the like. She described nights on the steppe, with stars the size of apples which one could reach up and pluck, and how with forty-one pebbles a Shaman can track down a lost or stolen horse. The last Shaman (he was repressed with the other religions' priests) died on his way home from the Gulag, but appeared to his settlement as a grey wolf and is now buried in an open grave in a place known to all. (Greene 1992)

As Greene's account suggests, Tuvan shamanic revitalization proceeded through the combined efforts of educated Tuvan intellectuals, sympathetic outsiders interested in the topic of shamanism, and a nascent tourist trade in the struggling republic. As we shall see in Chapter 14, Mongush Kenin-Lopsan's work to revitalize Tuvan shamanism was closely bound to the development of neoshamanic tourism, particularly in its early stages. A key moment in that process was the scholar's hosting of a 1993 conference on Tuvan shamanism, organized in the capital city of Kyzyl and attended by Michael Harner and other members of the Foundation for Shamanic Studies. Tamia Marg Anderson (1992), an attendee of the conference and one of ten members of the Foundation for Shamanic Studies who journeyed to Tuva for the event, writes:

Professor Kenin-Lopsang had refused the good life of a Soviet scientist, of one who would toe the party line, and instead dedicated his life to keeping alive the stories of his peoples' shamans. Stalinist repression took an enormous toll on shamanism as well as Buddhism, but now, since the collapse of the Soviet Union in 1991, these practices are beginning to flourish once again ... While shamanism has been virtually extinct for centuries in the West, the tie with the ancient spiritual tradition was never completely lost in the nomadic culture of the Tuvans.

Though officially this meeting was to be an academic conference, we came with the additional intention of assisting the Tuvans in their efforts to rehabilitate their shamanism and reintegrate it into their culture and daily life. Shamans from all over Tuva came to Kyzyl to participate in this seminar. Many told their stories, how they found their power and what they do with it, and they listened to each others' stories with rapt attention. This was essentially the first sanctified "coming out" in three generations and it was taking place in the ex-communist headquarters!

We also toured several days through the countryside with an entourage of Tuvan shamans and others interested in shamanism. Our now large group visited yurts and towns, met with local people, and participated in shamanic events. Whenever we formed a circle of drummers the Tuvans joined in without inhibition. People crowded into auditoriums to see what kind of healing the traveling shamans would do. Our Tuvan hosts took us to one of the sacred springs of Tuva overlooking the snowy peaks that form the southern border of Tuva with Mongolia. They continuously honored us with lavish feasts, great hospitality, and of course throat-singing. (Anderson 1992)

By the time Kenin-Lopsan published a selection of his collection of shamanic lore in English (1997), he could report that the reinvigorated shamanism of his homeland now had thirty-seven practicing shamans, dramatically fewer than the 725 attested in the 1931 Tuvan census, but far more than only a decade earlier (Hoppál 1997: 133). Kenin-Lopsan estimated that an additional one to two hundred persons were then in training in various villages around the republic. These modern-day shamans were registered as genuine practitioners through an official center for the study of Tuvan shamanism, which Kenin-Lopsan helped found in 1993. They belonged to a professional organization, Düngür ("Drum"), which was established in 1992 and which planned to conduct examinations of training shamans before conferring upon them official status. The organization had a health center in the capital city of Kyzyl, as Kenin-Lopsan describes in 1995:

On any given day, one to ten shamans can be working at Düngür ... Düngür sends shamans to the outlying villages when needed. When you arrive, you can see people waiting to see one of the shamans. There are small placards on the room doors which relate the name of the shaman, what his specialities are (female organs, gall bladder, heart and circulation, etc.) and what region s/he is from. Waiting can be an all day affair sometimes. The people sit in the hallway, outside and wait. When their turn arrives, they show their receipt and receive treatment ... The building is a meeting place for the shamans and the people. (quoted in Hoppál 1997: 133)

Mihály Hoppál describes this revitalization as follows:

What is happening in the Düngür centre is in fact an entirely new development in the history of shamanism. It is an authentically late twentieth century phenomenon shaped by circumstances differing from the traditional. On the one hand a very conscious organization, formed at the initiative of local intellectuals, is serving a demand on the part of the common people as the large numbers who come day by day show. Tuva shamanism today is a typical example in the post-communist world of the preservation of changed and changing traditions that have their roots in the past but are adapting well to the present conditions. (1997: 134)

Although Hoppál is certainly correct in noting the substantial alterations that obtain in the reinstituted Tuvan shamanism – e.g., its centralization, its focus on certification and official training, and the dominance of an urbanized elite in its functions – the Tuvan case is not unlike other examples of shamanic revitalization described above. A visionary leader – in this case a university-trained ethnographer – has sought to restore a tradition of healing and supernatural intervention that an imposed colonial authority had striven to eradicate. Kenin-Lopsan makes his own view of the movement clear when he writes: "I trust that the ancient sources of our old culture, our spiritual culture, Tuva shamanism will be reborn ... The shamanic belief is the ancient faith we are born with" (Hoppál 1997: 133). Shamanic practices represent for him – and perhaps for many of his associates within the revitalization effort – powerful links to a cultural past nearly severed by two centuries of oppression. His success in reviving Tuvan practices among a local clientele reflects the willingness of Tuvans to explore these elements of their heritage, despite the populace's strong identification with Tibetan Buddhism and a legacy of secularism born of the Soviet experience.

The Tuvan example provides a model for many other such attempts in other parts of Siberia, such as that which Piers Vitebsky (2005: 386–9) describes in a contemporary Evenki community. There, one of the local leaders convinced an aged Evenki shaman to perform on stage for the benefit of a community that had no firsthand experience of its culture's former shamanic traditions. Writes Vitebsky of the leader: "Tolya had waited for years for an opportunity to show the people of his community what they had lost from the heart of their own culture ... his aim was to raise cultural awareness" (2005: 389). While some Western ethnographers (e.g., Johansen 2001) have criticized Siberian revitalizations as touristic fabrications, Anna-Leena Siikala has pointed out the fact that, at least in the Khanty communities in which she works, the staged ceremonies performed in cities have counterparts conducted out of the sight of most tourists and ethnographers. Siikala notes in an interview about her fieldwork:

> It is wonderful to witness that the rituals and their associated sacrifices have lived on in secret for more than a hundred years. What we imagined were only public performances at festivals is in fact a reality, as the shamans hired for these events by the cultural administration return from the city back to their home villages in the countryside and change roles. (Pohjanpalo 2007: 31)

KOREA AND JAPAN

Indigenous communities of North America and Siberia have at times managed to revitalize shamanic traditions as tools of local cultural survival, often mounted in direct response to processes of acculturation and decay attendant in the colonial experience. In South Korea, on the other hand, as Laurel Kendall (2001) details, state authorities and an urbanized elite themselves have succeeded in reasserting shamanism as a potent symbol of national culture. Kendall describes contemporary Korean interest in shamanism as "both a sign and signification of the distinction between 'modern' Korean urbanites and their 'traditional' past. If the countryside was a place of backwardness and superstition, by the very act of imposing distance, it became for the new middle class a homeland of nostalgic longing ... a site of ambiguous imagining and emotional resonance, simultaneously backward and bucolic" (2001: 32). Kendall chronicles the role of one Korean scholar in particular in achieving this shift in orientation toward shamanic traditions:

> The folklorist, historian and nationalist Ch'oe Namsŏn linked contemporary shaman practices to myths of the culture hero Tan'gun, as recorded in (highly ambiguous) ancient texts, and precipitated an intellectual tradition that regards "shamanism" as a unique spiritual force infusing the Korean people ... These writings moved "shamanism" from the jaws of "superstition" to the embrace of "religion" and "culture" within Korean intellectual discourse. Linked to Tan'gun, ancient shamanic practices were infused, retrospectively, with nationalist spirituality, a theme that has been taken up again with the revival of interest in Korean folklore since the 1970s. (2001: 33)

Kendall notes the ways in which these developments have restored livelihoods for shamanic practitioners, while also recasting their arts as cultural "survivals" rather than contemporary acts. The *kut* often becomes, in Kendall's view, a showcase of past Korea, replacing supernatural practice with simple prognostications and presenting a colorful and symbolic experience for viewers. Man-young Hahn (1990: 219–31) similarly notes the sometimes stultifying and artificial effects state codification has had on shamanic traditions as well as other elements of Korean folklore.

Timothy Tangherlini (1998) presents the Korean shamanic revitalization as a more ambivalent and complex phenomenon. Tangherlini notes the importance of formal research in buttressing the revitalization: university-trained folklorists and scholars of Korean literature have played prominent roles in collecting and codifying *kut* rituals, while also underscoring their historical and cultural significance. State authorities have designated particular *kut* as prized intangible cultural heritage and accorded state stipends to shamans designated as living national treasures. State funding has also been devoted to employing shamans to perform at the Korean Folklore Museum, where school groups and foreign tourists can easily view them. Such acts have much to do with political assertions of an independent and viable modern Korea in touch with its traditional past, but they also directly affect the livelihoods and practices of contemporary shamans who can now make a living in a calling which was largely moribund during the 1970s.

Examining the turbulent political situation of South Korea in the years 1987–8, Tangherlini (1998) notes the symbolic uses opposing factions made of shamanic ritual and paraphernalia. During the long period of protests and counterprotests, both the student reform movement and the state made use of *kut* performance and the hourglass *changgu* shamanic drum as devices for legitimizing their stances by connecting them with potent symbols of Korean traditionality. In the media context of the approaching Olympic games, such shows of tradition were particularly effective, since they readily attracted the attention of foreign television journalists flocking to the country to find cultural interest stories (1998: 128). As Tangherlini notes, this legitimizing role also proved ironic, since the Korean shaman, as an empowered woman within a highly patriarchal Confucian society, often figures as a subversive element in traditional village culture (1998: 132). Student activists drew upon these subversive overtones to employ shamanism as a symbol of political change, while state authorities employed shamanic performances as emblems of social stasis and conservativism. In such political situations, revitalized shamanism becomes a tool of broader cultural debate, an evolving device that has grown to encompass national and nationalist agendas.

In the eclectic and shifting religious context of contemporary Japan, shamanic practitioners have also come to thrive, as Karen Smyers (1999) details. Where at mid-century, Carmen Blacker (1975: 162–3) perceived a shamanic tradition apparently in its final gasps, Smyers found a continuing and even expanding role for shamans in the late twentieth century. Drawing on both Shinto and Buddhist traditions, *odaisan* (*ogamiyasan*) shamans associated with Inari worship amalgamate various religious influences into highly personalized spiritual arsenals. As Smyers writes:

> The shamans, in sharp contrast to Shinto and Buddhist priests, derive their authority from direct experience of the *kami* [spirits] and may engage in various austerities to increase their spiritual powers. Their ethos was eclectic. Each had a constellation of deities and practices garnered from a wide range of possibilities – practically the whole spectrum of religion in Japan. In addition to a connection with the Inari *kami*, shamans were associated with other religious centers (Mount Kōya, Mount Ontake, Tenrikyō), Buddhist figures (Kōbo Daishi, Jizō, Kannon), other *kami* (Sarutahiko, Ebisu, Benten), and various other spirits and beings from the otherworld (ancestors, the unhappy dead, the spirits of miscarried or aborted fetuses (*mizuko*), spirit foxes, dragons, snakes). Personal experience and training were more important than institutional or doctrinal consistency in determining the sources of a shaman's powers and her hermeneutical stance. (1999: 45)

Japanese shamans have remained popular sources of healing and spiritual guidance among the general populace, and continue to incorporate new influences or ideas innovatively in their professional activities. Smyers attributes the continued success of Japanese shamans to a widespread resistance within Japanese culture to processes of religious consolidation, as well as the powerful attractiveness of the shaman's personalized approach to clients' needs (1999: 41).

Robin Ridington (Ridington 1997; Ridington and Hastings 1997) has explored in detail revitalization efforts among the Omaha people of Nebraska. Sacred to the tribe's history were certain objects with shamanic significance that emerged during the eighteenth century. One of these was a sacred pole made from a tree that, according to an Omaha visionary, stood on the earth directly beneath the North Star. Along with the pole, the community held sacred a white buffalo hide and a pipe. These objects had first arisen during the tribe's westward migration from the Ohio Valley toward the Great Plains. A perceived need to keep the tribe together in a new environment was met by the visionary experience of a young man. His visions led to the establishment of annual rituals connected with the objects. By greasing the pole with buffalo fat and ochre, Omaha people believed they could restore balance within the tribe and ensure hunting success (Ridington 1997: 162), a ritual act of a kind explored in greater detail in Chapter 10. In 1888, however, in the wake of the destruction of the wild buffalo herds and the widespread conversion of Omaha people to Christianity, the pole's hereditary custodians decided to donate the sacred objects to the Peabody Museum at Harvard University. The decision was facilitated by the anthropologist Alice Fletcher and her Omaha associate Francis La Flesche, in consultation with the pole's last keeper Yellow Smoke. Although the pole was successfully transferred to the museum, the hide and pipe were stolen and sold to art collectors, eventually coming to the National Museum of the American Indian only late in the twentieth century. The time of the pole seemed over: a ritual innovation had apparently served its purpose and was now consigned to memory, although not without a final flourish. The chief who permitted the recitation of the pole's sacred narrative outside of its proper ritual framework – Francis LaFlesche's father Joseph (Iron Eye) – took ill immediately after breaking the tabu and died two weeks later in the very room in which the narration had occurred. As Ridington and Hastings relate, members of the tribe regarded the chief's untimely death as a "demonstration of the sanctity of the faith of their fathers" (1997: 96).

It was a century later when leaders of the Omaha tribe sought the return of the sacred pole, Umon'hon'ti, "The Real Omaha." Seeking to regain connection with their tribe's past, leaders worked to have the pole repatriated to Nebraska in 1989. Such a move, however, was not without risks. As Ridington writes:

Doing nothing would have brought little risk. For a century, most people had been content to leave matters where Fletcher and LaFlesche had settled them with Yellow Smoke. Furthermore, for most of those years, there had been little chance that the museum would have entertained the thought of "deacquisitioning" such an important holding. Renewing contact was a riskier alternative. Since any possible relationship to Umon'hon'ti was different from the strict order of a traditional keeper's discipline, anyone making contact with him risked being accused of impropriety. They risked being blamed for whatever misfortunes should befall the tribe or individuals within it. (1997: 171)

A return that leaders hoped would refocus and rekindle the community's feelings of unity held the potential of dividing the tribe into rival factions instead. As Ridington reports, although tribal members today agree that Umon'hon'ti is an Omaha, and a central figure in their community, they are not certain how to reincorporate this ancient aspect of Omaha spirituality into their current lives. For the time being, the pole, along with the white buffalo hide and pipe (which were similarly returned to the tribe in 1991) reside at the University of Nebraska State Museum in Lincoln, awaiting the construction of a tribal museum or other suitable place on the tribe's reservation. The revitalization hoped for in requesting the return of Umon'hon'ti has perhaps not occurred with the clarity or the immediacy which some of the tribe's leaders had anticipated, but the process of restoring an ancient ritual is no simple matter. Crucially, the difficulties of striking a balance between according authority to the pole and assuming authority for one's own culture lie at the heart of conflicts regarding the repatriation. As Ridington writes: "The only consensus now seems to be that this balance can be realized only through the passage of time" (1997: 173). As the Omaha situation illustrates, large-scale revitalization is not always spontaneous or successful.

A similar experiment took place among the Makaw people of western Washington state in the late 1980s (Sullivan 2002). The Makaw traditionally relied on whaling for sustenance, and specifically retained the right to whale in their nineteenth-century treaty negotiations with the US government. For several generations, however, whaling was prohibited, as the Gray Whales struggled for survival as a species. As the whale population successfully rebounded from threatened extinction, however, Makaw leaders announced their intention to revive the hunt. Their purpose was not to regain a food source for the community, but to reestablish a sacred relation that lay traditionally at the heart of Makaw mythology and ritual. For

Makaw people, the Gray Whale was a key tutelary figure, one whose relations with humanity were cemented in part by the annual hunt.

The notion of reviving the hunt, however, involved enormous logistic and cultural issues, as Robert Sullivan (2002) relates in his overview of the event. Significant among these was the inevitable loss of ritual and cultural knowledge that had resulted from generations of whaling inactivity. Cultural information had to be regained and choices made regarding how to modernize or adapt traditional methods to the circumstances of late twentieth-century society. Significant as well was the fierce resistance the planned whaling met with among ecologically minded activists and members of the general public outside of the tribe. Massive demonstrations against the whaling, and heated public debate in newspapers and on radio and television, affected the event in ways that the planners could not have foreseen. Although the tribe persevered in its plan, the potential for frustration and disillusionment certainly mounted. The public discussion of the rights and limitations of indigenous rituals within modern secular states reflected the unsettled issues that sometimes arise in the revitalization of past religious practices. Revitalization poses social and cultural risks for the community that embraces it, even while it may offer avenues for strengthening a sense of cohesion or wellbeing. These thorny issues seldom have simple answers and reflect ultimately the perplexing effects that colonial situations have wrought within many communities which once relied upon shamanic rituals as keys to cosmic and social integration.

Addressing assembled participants in a contemporary Buryat *shanar* ritual in the year 2000, Bayir Rinchinov expressed his hopes for his people and their religious practices with near missionary fervor: "We all stand together. Buryats not only from Chelutay and the eleven Khori clans, but all Buryats on this earth will all eventually find their way to shamanism" (Tkacz, Zhambalov, and Phipps 2002: 160). Shamanic revitalization must be seen in connection with the kinds of neoshamanic adaptations discussed in the following chapter. Often the difference between the two phenomena is slight, and often the distinctions made contribute to a political stance regarding cultural heritage, self-determination, and community identity. Shamanic traditions become tools for broader cultural revitalization, conceived of as the reclamation of lost cohesion, identity, and wellbeing. In this way, such phenomena belong to the political dimension of religion as described by Timothy Fitzgerald (2000). Their political nature does not lessen their importance as expressions of religious identity, however. Rather they remind us of the long-standing potential of shamanic traditions and shamans to serve as rallying points for communal identity and action, in the past as well as the present.

CHAPTER 14

Neoshamanism

As we have seen in the preceding chapters, for Thai and his Hmong American community, shamanism represents not simply a means of accomplishing particular goals (e.g., curing illness or ensuring success in some endeavor), but also a deeply meaningful way of understanding the cosmos and the place of the individual and community within it. As such, and in a context of profound cultural change brought on by the refugee experience, shamanism also becomes for many Hmong Americans a powerful link to past traditions: a symbol of the community's continuity from ancient times, a proof of its survival in a new country, and a sign of its ability to endure into the future. Although some of Thai's contemporaries reject shamanism as part of a past that needs to be discarded or replaced by a different religion (e.g., Christianity), Thai finds the tradition deeply satisfying and effective as a way of life within his community and cosmos.

On the same campus at which Thai studies, however, and sometimes within the same classroom, one can find other persons with different links to shamanism. Jim, for instance, came upon shamanism as an outgrowth of his interest in *ayahuasca* and various discoveries via the Internet. He eventually traveled to Peru to experience the transformative effects of the entheogen and associated rituals personally. Facing an array of personal problems, he saw the act as an alternative to suicide. He returned to Wisconsin three months later, finished his undergraduate degree in sciences, and now plans to move to California to continue his explorations of shamanism with a friend. Siv associates shamanism with her personal connections to Norwegian and Sámi cultures, and has taken workshops in shamanic techniques both in the United States and Norway. For her, shamanism is part of a pathway to personal enlightenment that fills a void that she had perceived in her upbringing within Christianity. She has obtained advanced training in film making and massage, and identifies strongly with issues related to ecology, human rights, and indigenous peoples. She is particularly drawn to the therapeutic approach to shamanism promoted by Sandra Ingerman. Lon has also taken shamanic workshops and worked with a teacher for some time in Florida. For him, shamanism is a means of accessing a level of cognition or creativity that is at the heart of his work as an artist. Creating canvases full of mantra-like repeated patterns and images of cryptic inserted spirit helpers and symbols, Lon seeks to present visually and artistically the worldview of a shaman within the mainstream Western idiom of canvas painting and mural. All of these individuals show a deep interest in shamanism as a religious tradition or psychic technique, as well as a desire to incorporate it into their personal spirituality in various ways. They are participants in a lively and growing phenomenon termed by scholars of religion and anthropology "contemporary shamanism" or "neoshamanism." Since the former term implies that extant traditional shamanisms like Thai's are somehow not "contemporary," we shall use the term *neoshamanism* here. Extremely variable and evolving in nature, neoshamanism nonetheless tends to display certain recurrent features, as we shall see in this chapter. In certain ways, it can be seen as part of a larger shamanic continuum stretching from the ancient past to the present. In other ways – such as its typical modes of training or its participants' understanding of the cosmos – it departs markedly from the tendencies discussed in the previous chapters. In any case, its existence can be seen as proof not only of the enduring human interest of shamanism as a religious phenomenon, but also of the creative approaches to religiosity that characterize the contemporary world. Not limited to the urbanized West, neoshamanism exists in a variety of different contexts, including postcolonial and postcommunist societies around the world.

SOURCES OF KNOWLEDGE

Neoshamanism as a phenomenon in contemporary religion draws many aspects of both worldview and practice from descriptions in ethnographic literature. Where shamans like Thai situate their religious activities within long-standing, culturally specific traditions that they have assimilated through associated systems of selection and apprenticeship, neoshamanic practitioners often create improvised rituals and procedures of their own, borrowing elements of belief and ritual acts from traditions that are foreign to them, but which they have come to know through the writings of anthropologists or (more recently) through tourism. Workshops offered by other neoshamans or by persons with a claim of access to a specific traditional shamanism also offer a means of becoming acquainted with shamanic practices. Given the comparative, descriptive nature of much ethnographic writing on shamanism, neoshamans often draw on a variety of different shamanic cultures in formulating the elements of their beliefs and practices. Concepts of worldview identified in the scholarly literature through early twentieth-century ethnography among Siberian peoples, for instance, may be combined with practices derived from extant shamanic traditions among indigenous communities in North or South America. This eclecticism is a distinctive feature of neoshamanism that has attracted the comments of scholars working in the fields of comparative religion and anthropology (Atkinson 1992; Hamayon 2001; Johansen 2001; Svanberg 2003) and will be examined in greater detail below. Given their ethnographic sources, as well, neoshamans often show a strong interest in ongoing ethnographic research on shamanic traditions and sometimes a desire to participate in this discourse as well (Wallis 2001, 2003). Hybridizing the perspectives of ethnographer and practitioner, the neoshaman may thus blur the once sacrosanct line between ethnographer and object of study, a move which links neoshamanism to the broader phenomenon of postmodernism (Svanberg 2003).

GUIDING FIGURES AND CONCEPTS

Although the ideas and practices of neoshamanism derive from a variety of different sources, several figures loom large. Mircea Eliade (1964) often serves as a primary source of information on traditional shamanism, and many of Eliade's characterizations recur frequently in neoshamanic understandings, e.g., his emphasis on a tripartite cosmos and the privileging of astral or upper world journeys over lower world explorations. Also important to the movement are the mythological ideas of Joseph Campbell and the ethnographically inspired explorations of Carlos Castaneda and Michael Harner. We examine each of these latter influences below.

In his explorations of world mythology, Joseph Campbell (1904–87) combines Jungian archetypes with folkloristic motif research to reveal commonalities underlying various religious systems around the world. In his *Hero With a Thousand Faces* (1949) and other works, Campbell posits that human cultures passed through a series of mythologies on their path from simple hunter-gatherer societies to complex urban civilizations. The first stage in this progression, "The Way of Animal Powers," was dominated by mythic concepts tied to shamanism. Campbell's surveys promoted the idea among his audiences that human cultures possess certain common features – a collective unconscious – shared by all people to one degree or another. The effect of this perspective was to convince readers of a comparability between Western and non-Western religious phenomena and to view the specific myths of a given culture as part of a larger human heritage. This viewpoint allows for the relativism and selectivity which is prevalent in many forms of New Age thought, including neoshamanism: once particular religious ideas are viewed as part of a single continuum, it becomes easier to borrow and recombine them, or to understand the features of one tradition through reference to apparently analogous features in another. Many of the neoshamans I have interviewed in the United States note Campbell as a major influence in their thinking.

Another influential figure in the development of Western neoshamanism is Carlos Castaneda (c. 1925–95). Born in either Brazil or Peru, Castaneda eventually became a naturalized US citizen and studied anthropology at the University of California at Los Angeles in the 1960s, taking courses from Michael Harner among others. He wrote a series of books focusing on teachings he attributed to a Yaqui Indian named Don Juan Matus. These works attained cult status in the 1970s, and have been translated into some seventeen languages. Reclusive and guarded regarding his own personal history, Castaneda died in 1995, leaving behind a legacy of ideas regarding the cosmos and supernatural experience that lie at the heart of the New Age movement.

From his very first work, *The Teachings of Don Juan* (1968), Castaneda established key elements of later neoshamanistic explorations, as well as the broader New Age ideology. He recast altered states brought on by psycho-tropic substances not as supernatural experiences but as "nonordinary reality" (1968: 7), a relativizing term that represented such perceptions as equally valid as – although markedly distinct from – the ordinary percep-tions of everyday life. He also emphasized the importance of subjectivity in describing his experiences, noting: "I wanted to describe the emotional impact I had experienced as completely as possible" (1968: 10). And he advocated experiential learning over mere description, attributing the con-viction to Don Juan: "He said that learning through conversation was not only a waste, but stupidity, because learning was the most difficult task a man could undertake" (1968: 34).

Castaneda's first book depicts the author as an ethnographer, gradually initiated at his own request into the altered state experiences of peyote (*Lophophora williamsii*), Jimson Weed (*Datura inoxia*), and psylocybe mushrooms (*Psilocybe mexicana*) through the patient but unrelenting teach-ing of Don Juan. Where peyote acts as a source of knowledge, Jimson Weed or psylocybe mushrooms can become "allies": personified entities "capable of carrying a man beyond the boundaries of himself" (1968: 32) in order to "reveal matters that no human being could" (1968: 32) and to confer upon the adept "power" (1968: 33). Through extensive training and willpower, Castaneda's Don Juan states, an adept (termed "sorcerer") may learn to enter "a crack between the two worlds, the world of the diableros and the world of living men" (1968: 137). Upon entering the crack, one can seek a "spirit helper" (1968: 138) with whom to forge a close and transformative relation of the sort typical of traditional shamanism: "After you return, you will not be the same man. You are committed to come back to see your helper often. And you are committed to wander farther and farther from the entrance, until finally one day you will go too far and will not be able to return" (1968: 138). He also describes experiences of soul-loss resulting from the aggression of other sorcerers (1968: 131).

In his later *Journey to Ixtlan* (1972), Castaneda distanced himself from hallucinogens, stating:

My perception of the world through the effects of those psychotropics had been so bizarre and impressive that I was forced to assume that such states were the only avenue to communicating and learning what Don Juan was attempting to teach me. That assumption was erroneous. (1972: 12)

His subsequent books present an increasingly complex cosmology of alternative realities, peopled by an array of different fellow sorcerers with positive or negative motivations, and incorporating concepts drawn from Eastern religions and philosophy.

As positivist critics such as Richard de Mille (1976) began to uncover discrepancies in accounts given in Castaneda's various books, readers who admired Castaneda's teachings reconceptualized them as possible allegories or as narratives of alternative sensibilities that defied the simplistic dichotomy of "fact" and "fiction." This relativizing stance toward the nature of key experiences combined with the features mentioned above to create a distinctive set of attitudes and perceptions that characterize much New Age discourse today.

Where Castaneda's writings remain at times cryptic and aloof, Michael Harner seeks to present shamanism in as open and welcoming a manner as possible. His manual *The Way of the Shaman* ([1980] 1990) became his chief tool for acquainting interested readers with typical features of shamanism and adapting these to contemporary Western lifestyles. Through a series of workshops as well as his Foundation for Shamanic Studies, Harner has sought to share his adaptation of "Core Shamanism" with the world. Translated into numerous languages, with workshops replicated internationally by students and admirers, Harner's *The Way of the Shaman* has become a major interest and practice among neoshamans in North America and Europe.

Harner's enthusiasm is evident in his preface to the 1990 third edition of his manual:

Ten years have passed since the original edition of this book appeared, and they have been remarkable years indeed for the shamanic renaissance. Before then, shamanism was rapidly disappearing from the Planet as missionaries, colonists, governments, and commercial interests overwhelmed tribal peoples and their ancient cultures. During the last decade, however, shamanism has returned to human life with startling strength, even to urban strongholds of Western "civilization," such as New York and Vienna. (1990: xi)

For Harner, shamanism is a "methodology, not a religion" (1990: xii) and as such can be learned and practiced by persons of any religion or background, provided they are open to the kind of experiential learning advocated and exemplified by Castaneda: "[C]hildren of the Age of Science, myself included, prefer to arrive first-hand, experimentally, at their own conclusions as to the nature and limits of reality" (1990: xii). Crucially, if practitioners follow the instructions in his manual, Harner suggests, they will not only gain a sense of shamanism but actually become shamans themselves:

Using the core or fundamental methods of shamanism emphasized in this book and in my shamanic training workshops, these new practitioners are not "playing Indian," but going to the same revelatory spiritual sources that tribal shamans have travelled to from time immemorial. They are not pretending to be shamans; if they get shamanic results for themselves and others in this work, they are indeed the real thing. (1990: xiv)

This invitation proves deeply meaningful to many seekers in the New Age movement, Harner suggests, because of its reverence for nature, acknowledgement of the power of the environment, and substitution of firsthand experience for religious dogma (1990: xiii). Harner's institute offers workshops at a variety of levels as well as a two-year certificate program, and sponsors ethnographic research on extant shamanic traditions. Harner has also been joined in his work by other instructors, including Sandra Ingerman (1991, 1993), who merges shamanic concepts with psychotherapy, particularly as related to past traumas, which become understood as cases of soul-loss or theft.

SHAMANIC TOURISM

A further element of Harner's project is, as noted above, the Foundation for Shamanic Studies, a non-profit organization devoted to documenting, celebrating, and preserving shamanic traditions in indigenous communities around the world (Harner 2008). Harner's foundation has significantly affected communities in which shamanic practitioners have been offered support as "living treasures of shamanism." Describing this aspect of the foundation, Harner writes:

> Our Living Treasures designation provides an annual lifetime stipend to exceptionally distinguished indigenous shamans in less-developed countries where their age-old knowledge of shamanism and shamanic healing is in danger of extinction. Special care is given to providing the economic assistance necessary to allow these Living Treasures to pass on their knowledge to their people. (2008)

Such support can not only make it possible for a practicing shaman to remain active, but it may also send a powerful message to the shaman's community regarding the intrinsic value of the practitioner's art as viewed from an outside perspective. Where formerly shamans faced denigration from elite forces outside their communities, the Living Treasures program of the Foundation for Shamanic Studies seeks to use the prestige of Western institutions to valorize and preserve local shamanic traditions. Researchers connected with the foundation may also study the stipended shamans so as to incorporate elements of their practices into the broader repertoire of Harner's Core Shamanism.

Harner's foundation and other organizations like it within Western neoshamanism have also played pivotal roles in the development of shamanic tourism, in which interested Westerners journey to indigenous communities to witness or even take part in shamanic ceremonies. The growth of such tourism in the former Soviet Union can be illustrated by the history of shamanic revitalization in Tuva Republic, as noted in Chapter 13. The elements of this history related specifically to neoshamanism and tourist activities are summarized below.

Writing in 1991, before the break-up of the Soviet Union, Ralph Leighton, American founder of the organization Friends of Tuva, suggested that tourism might figure as a means of helping develop the Tuva Republic's economy and identity. In his organization's first newsletter, Leighton states:

> One enjoyable way to help Tuva might be to develop tourism. At present one can travel through Tuva on the "Sayan loop" from Abakan with the local (Russian) branch of the Soviet Travel company Intourist, or by going around the world with InnerAsia Expeditions of San Francisco. However, there is as yet no program that has Tuvans as its organizers and guides (and thus the primary economic beneficiaries). Alan [Leighton] and I want to help establish such a program. We realize, however, that Tuva's charm is in large part due to its isolation, so we want to keep any tourism to a low profile. (Leighton 1991)

That same summer, Leighton was able to travel to the Tuva Republic for the first time, where he observed both elements of Tuvan Buddhism and a sacred spring. He also attended a state celebration that included Tuvan throat singing, wrestling, and horse racing.

In the summer of 1993, after the end of the Soviet Union, Leighton notes in his *Newsletter* the organizing of a conference on shamanism in the city of Kyzyl, arranged through the efforts of Michael Harner and his Foundation for Shamanic Studies. Leighton writes (1993):

A conference on shamanism is being held in Kyzyl at the end of June and in early July. Participants from the US include several persons affiliated with the Foundation for Shamanic Studies, founded by Michael Harner ... After the conference an expedition will foray into the countryside of Tuva, in search of shamans and perhaps their trance enhancers ... A report about the expedition is possible in an upcoming edition of the *Friends of Tuva Newsletter*.

Soon after the conference, an article on Tuvan Buddhism by Gary Wintz (1993) detailed the creation of an exhibit on Tuvan shamanism in the Kyzyl museum as a product of the conference. The exhibit had been overseen by the Tuvan scholar Mongush Kenin-Lopsan, who had also hosted the conference. Wintz notes, however, that the same museum also contained a much larger exhibit commemorating the 1992 visit of the Dalai Lama.

From the mid-1990s onward, staged shamanic ritual performances became a standard part of tourist programs in the Tuva Republic, bringing outsiders into contact with some of the outward (partially reconstructed) manifestations of traditional Tuvan shamanism and helping finance and legitimize the revitalization efforts underway among Tuvan intellectuals at the time. Ulla Johansen (2001) points out the ways in which such performances depart from traditional Tuvan practices, describing staged rituals as "the folklorization of shamanism" (2001: 299). Performances now tend to take place in the day rather than the night, so that they can be viewed by outside observers, who pay admission to witness them. They are staged, with particular features at times emphasized and length modulated so as to hold greater viewer appeal. At the same time, as Anna-Leena Siikala has found in her work among contemporary Khanty shamans (Pohjanpalo 2007: 31), such public display events may help sustain less publicly viewed revitalization efforts that seek to reengage the community with a shamanic tradition that had previously remained covert or moribund. For tourist viewers, such rituals offer a materialization of a world glimpsed only abstractly in the ethnographic writings of earlier scholars and can serve as powerful sources of inspiration in their own explorations of shamanic practices.

THE CHARACTERISTICS OF NEOSHAMANISMS

Although neoshamanism varies greatly from practitioner to practitioner, certain common features emerge from any comparison of practices. Below I detail some of these commonalities with reference to the personal experiences of Jim, Siv, and Lon. One of the most striking elements of neoshamanic practice is its emphasis on volition. Where shamans in many traditional contexts speak of their calling as something that came to them from outside themselves, either through heredity, communal selection, or in the aftermath of an initiatory illness, neoshamans often describe their embrace of shamanic activities as a conscious choice. Practitioners mention coming upon a neoshamanic manual such as Michael Harner's *The Way of the Shaman*, or seeing an advertisement for a workshop run by a neo-shamanic instructor. Although some informants, such as Lon, may describe life-long psychic or spiritual tendencies, or a long-standing feeling of attraction to alternative spirituality (Siv), the neoshamans whom I have interviewed describe themselves generally as simply open-minded and curious, having become interested in shamanism fortuitously as a result of reading or travel. As neoshamans, they seldom discuss feelings of compulsion experienced during their initial periods of activity, nor do they describe any fear regarding a possible decision to cease their practices. For Jim, Siv, and Lon, an embrace of shamanic practices is simply part of a wider spiritual journey that may include various other religious traditions over time.

Scholars have described such an emphasis on volition as characteristic of contemporary Western religiosity in general, particularly in the extremely pluralistic context of the United States, where various denominations and religious movements vie to attract new members from among a circulating pool of potential adepts. Spirit quests are characteristic of some forms of traditional shamanism as well, however, particularly those of Native North America, helping create a traditional background through which to view the volitional tendencies of contemporary neoshamanism.

Jim, Siv, and Lon all describe their pathways to neoshamanism in great detail, emphasizing the individual nature of their experience. It is due to this tendency that Joan Townsend (2005) terms neoshamanic phenomena an "individualist religious movement." Certainly, traditional shamanisms feature highly individualized spiritual experiences and knowledge, which practitioners may guard jealously from counterparts or competitors. But, as we saw in the previous chapters, the traditional shaman generally finds a context through roles assumed in relation to both tutelary spirits and a human community made up of teachers, kin, and clients. These roles direct and control the shaman's activities and shift the shaman's focus from self to a broader embrace of community and cosmos. For Jim, Siv, and Lon, however, the primary focus of their activities is personal, and only Siv has attempted a spiritual journey on behalf of someone else. Jim and Lon are not opposed to helping others in their shamanic activities, but do not consider such undertakings a primary feature of their callings.

A third important distinction between traditional shamans and neo-shamans like Jim, Siv, and Lon lies in the area of cosmology. Where Thai and other Hmong shamans may differ regarding the exact topography of the otherworlds they traverse in their spirit journeys, they nonetheless share a single overall understanding of the cosmos and its levels or layers. No such common ground tends to obtain in neoshamanism, where a Western view of the physical universe may coexist in practitioners' minds with an openness to possible other ways of understanding the cosmos. Shamanism may give access to elements of reality which conventional science has so far failed to discover, neoshamans suggest, or it may reflect an unseen cosmos arrayed alongside the visible one identified by astronomers and other scientists. The spirits and concepts described in shamanic traditions may represent in fact more metaphors than realities in the sense intended by Western empiricism. Given the variety of different views of how to interrelate a shamanic cosmos and other worldviews of modern Western life, neoshamans often offer a choice of different explanations to their clients or counterparts, permitting latitude on how to understand the nature of the spiritual experiences at the heart of the practice. Sandra Ingerman, for instance, writes in the introduction to her manual *Soul Retrieval: Mending the Fragmented Self* (1991: 3):

As you read this book and wonder whether or not what I am talking about is "real," I ask you not to enter into a battle between the right brain and the left brain. Simply read the material and experience it. After eleven years of working with the shamanic journey I know nonordinary reality is real. But I don't intend to convince you of that. For me, the big questions are these: Does the information that comes from a shamanic journey work? Does the information make positive changes in a person's life? If so, who cares if we are making it up?

Ingerman's markedly relativist stance may seem quite different from the situation of past shamanisms, where, presumably, faith in the supernatural nature of the shaman's spirit quests was generally accepted. Past ethnographers noted recurrently that shamans reacted with anger and frustration when confronted with doubters, and sometimes described the open lack of faith of ethnographic observers as harmful to the efficacy of their séances. Evidence exists, of course – as discussed in Chapter 8 – that such an

assumption of undisputed faith among past societies may represent scholarly romanticism in itself: the account of the skeptical George Hunt of
Boas's Kwagul ethnography (Boas 1930) or the suspicious audience members described by Edward Schieffelin (1995) attest to the fact that doubts
could arise within traditional shamanisms as well. Whether or not these are
the product of a *decline* of the tradition is a topic which, as stated in
Chapter 8, cannot be realistically addressed on the basis of the evidence
available today. Nevertheless, the conscious and open acceptance of possible
skepticism expressed in Ingerman's formulation appears a new development, and one characteristic of many New Age religious explorations.

James Beckford (2003: 197ff.) suggests that such relativism can be understood within the framework of postmodernity, in which a certain playful-
ness regarding once sacrosanct boundaries such as *true/false, belief/disbelief*
can permit a hybridity of viewpoint that reflects a fundamental shift in the
understandings of religion within contemporary societies. Beckford (2003:
205) also points to Meštrović's (1997) theory of "postemotional society," in
which individuals have purportedly lost the ability to unequivocally put
faith in religious concepts, preferring instead to retain a degree of skepticism
about articles of belief. In such a context, Ingerman's stance can be seen as a
workable strategy to defuse what might otherwise prove a point of insur-
mountable contention between a neoshamanic instructor and her students.
In a "postmodern," "postemotional" context in which all the world is
consciously acknowledged as a stage, the creation of an agreement concerning a willing suspension of disbelief would seem essential as a first step
toward attempting a reactualization of shamanic traditions.

The linkage of this relativizing viewpoint with the emphasis on experiential learning described in the quotations from Castaneda and Harner
above is evident in the writings of another shamanic instructor, Geo Athena
Trevarthen. She notes on her website:

> I certainly have no objection to people not believing me. In fact, as a shamanic
> teacher I encourage all my students not to believe a word I say. What I know is
> ultimately only true for me. I would never want my students to be satisfied with
> blind faith when they can have experience. I want them to try out anything I say for
> themselves, to think about it, journey on it, and see what value it may have for
> them. (Trevarthen 2007)

Here the differences in interpretation expectable in a neoshamanic context
are regarded as positive, the signs of a healthy attitude that is not tied to
"blind faith," possibly a reference to the demands of belief characteristic of
established Christian denominations.

Merete Jakobsen (1999: 162–82) delineates some further frequent points of contrast between neoshamanic practices and their traditional models or antecedents. Neoshamans tend to be their own monitors of progress, not relying on a master for legitimization of progress and status, as in traditional communities. Not only does Harner emphasize the validity of self-evaluation in his manual, but he explicitly stigmatizes critiques of others' skills as a sign of personal weakness: "A true master shaman does not challenge the validity of anybody else's experiences, although less capable and less humble shamans may" (Harner 1990: 45). Neoshamans also tend to emphasize the concepts of fellowship and love (Jakobsen 1999: 169–70), display an equal openness to both male and female practitioners (1999: 179), and describe spiritual journeys and spirits with markedly less emphasis on fear and aggression than is typical of traditional shamanic practitioners (1999: 180–1).

Joan Townsend (2005: 5) draws a distinction between the Core Shamanism of Harner and the religious movements for which she reserves the term *neoshamanism*. According to Townsend, these latter movements substitute a pantheistic worldview for the belief in spirits shared by traditional and Core shamanism. They also tend to reject the coexistence of shamanic practices alongside organized religions such as Christian denominations. Most importantly, Townsend argues, such movements describe the nature of the universe as wholly benign, filled with positive energies or spirits, largely rejecting or marginalizing the existence of ill-willed spirits with which the traditional shaman must sometimes vie. Although these features point to important distinctions between Core Shamanism and the movements that have developed in the wake of Harner's manual, other scholars (e.g., Jakobsen 1999; Svanberg 2003) use the term *neoshamanism* in a broader sense to encompass all modern adaptations, including Harner's Core Shamanism.

ECLECTICISM

Both the comparative nature of neoshamanism's source materials and the framework of workshops, fairs, and specialty stores that cater to New Age interests contribute to the vigorous eclecticism of much neoshamanic phenomena today. Although practitioners sometimes describe themselves as deeply embedded within a single shamanic tradition – perhaps one which lies within their own cultural heritage, as we shall see below – others are equally proud of the range of different traditions and practices with which they are familiar. These practices may not only include specifically shamanic phenomena but also broader lore, such as Western astrology, yoga, crystal therapy, past-life channeling, aura analysis, health food and vitamin nutrition. Jakobsen (1999: 148–9) records the photocopied advertisement of a British practitioner that illustrates this range of influences:

She Wolf Lodge.
    Native American and Celtic Shamanic Teachings.
    Being a teacher native American & Celtic esoteric traditions. I am a seer of Celtic descent. My grandmother was a Scottish Irish seer & Shaman taught me the art of being a seer, healer & psychic in the Celtic traditional way. I can trace my ancestry back to almost the legendary Firb Olgs: the people of the bogs, also known as the people of the Goddess Domnu. I have used my psychic abilities to help many people for many years. I read the native American sacred path cards and I am a colour healer, dream analyst. Earth astrologer & rebirther which I was taught by native American people. I am a member of the Seneca Indian Historical Society, Brant Reservation Irving New York U.S.A. I am able to show you your pathway in life. I can guide you on your way to reach the pathway you wish to walk.

The advertisement shows the varied influences which the practitioner has assimilated into her personal religiosity, as well as the range of different means of positioning herself as a professional within the neoshamanic trade. On the one hand, she cites a Scottish Irish heritage and identity as well as a link to shamanic traditions within that culture through her grandmother. This familial link is deepened diachronically through reference to archaeological data (bog people) and mythology known to us through medieval manuscripts as well as its modern interpretation and revival in Goddess religion. On the other hand, as her name (She Wolf Lodge) connotes, the practitioner shows an awareness of Native American shamanic traditions, and she reports having learned techniques directly from Native Americans. Membership in the Seneca Indian Historical Society further bolsters this connection. Other practices (e.g., psychic ability, card reading, color healing, dream analysis, astrology, rebirthing) point to extensive experience in a variety of New Age movements, some of which evince a strong discourse of science and objectivity rather than a more subjective enunciation of sacrality. Finally, the advertisement offers the practitioner's guidance in helping clients find their pathways through life, a reference to psychological therapy and the ideology of self-realization. These different elements may be seen as alternative means of legitimizing the practitioner's status and activities, especially within her interactions with potential clients. Where a traditional shaman, such as Thai, depends on his community's recognition of shamanism as an important identity and activity, She Wolf Lodge attempts to appeal to potential clients through a variety of different modes of authentication, negotiating her role and status in a complex, multicultural context by embracing a range of different identities at once.

TRADITIONALIST CONFRONTATIONS

While neoshamans occasionally attract the disapproval of academic researchers, they may also come under fire from members of indigenous communities. In a context of long-term forced acculturation, indigenous community members may come to regard neoshamanic activities among members of the dominant polity as a form of co-option or final colonialism. This viewpoint can take on particular ire when neoshamans borrow elements of ritual or understanding directly from a specific community, sometimes violating in the process age-old systems of secrecy or proprietary rights which had limited access to the traditions in the past. Andy Smith (1993: 168), critiquing New Age appropriations of Native American traditions, writes: "The New Age movement is part of a very old story of white racism and genocide against the Indian people."

Referring to non-Native adapters of shamanic traditions as "plastic medicine men/shamans," many Native American activists have drawn attention to such acts of borrowing as conscious acts of theft. Particularly offensive in many activists' views are workshop leaders who claim Native ancestry or identity when, in fact, they have no such connections. Profiting from their workshops and the image of Native authenticity, they both replicate white stereotypes of Native spirituality and profit from marketing it to fellow whites. An online Wall of Shame (2007) identifies such pretenders and calls upon readers to boycott their products and practices. The custodians of the Wall write:

Every one of the women on this Wall of Shame are fully knowledgeable of Native American objections to their "teachings," yet they continue to prostitute Native American spiritual ways for their own selfish gain: either personal or financial. They have shown no regard for the spiritual well being of either the Native American people objecting to them or the Nuagers [New Agers] whose money they take. (Wall of Shame 2007)

Philip Jenkins (2005) notes the underlying racism in many New Age formulations: the portrayal of Native Americans as intrinsically spiritual, or as more pristine than other contemporary communities, or as more authentic in their relations to nature or religion. These are stereotypes which often plague contemporary Native American experiences within majority culture relations, modern counterparts of the markedly pejorative stereotypes of a century ago.

MOTIVATIONS

In examining this range of neoshamanic traditions occurring in the affluent West, scholars have attempted to explain the motivations underlying personal religious searching. In his study of American fire walking, Loring Danforth (1989) draws on the work of Steven Tipton (1982) to offer a theory for the overt relativism of New Age religiosity. Danforth and Tipton maintain that American society has long valued "individualistic utilitarianism," an attitude by which the concept of good is strongly identified with the attainment of material, social, or even emotional gains in one's current life. Rather than looking toward happiness as a potential state of an afterlife existence, or regarding suffering as instrumental or meaningful in one's earthly life, the individual utilitarianist regards one's current situation as wholly constitutive of one's status as fulfilled or successful. Although earlier generations thus equated the attainment of material wealth and social status with happiness, the generation of the late 1960s rejected these values as unsatisfactory and hypocritical. Gradually, however, Tipton suggests, many formerly estranged members of this generation gradually came to identify emotional satisfaction as a primary end in itself, thereby retaining the entrenched utilitarian worldview of American society (and much of the West) while shifting its notion of the mechanism for attaining its goal. Now happiness could be achieved by finding emotional satisfaction: by realizing one's self, nurturing one's Inner Child, gratifying one's deep-seated emotional needs, and exploring one's personal psychological drives. Various New Age activities and rituals offer means of obtaining this self-realization, but they do so in a highly individualistic and relativized manner. Since what is most important is achieving one's own feeling of fulfillment, the methods and concepts that lead to that goal can be tailored precisely to the views and values of the individual. Thus, the precise details of whether one "believes" or not become subordinated to the more central goal of what leads one to a feeling of wellbeing or completeness. Belief becomes an option, rather than a precondition. In the case of neoshamanism, this shift creates a marked contrast between shamans and clients in traditional contexts and their counterparts in contemporary Western societies. It represents a logical and apparently adaptive set of views for societies with a high degree of physical, economic, and social mobility, and a strong emphasis on individual rights and initiative.

Joan Townsend (2005) offers a different explanation for New Age exploration, locating it not within recent trends of Western societies but within a long-standing human tendency toward religious experimentation.

Drawing on the earlier work of Peter Berger (1969) as well as that of Marilyn Ferguson (1989), Townsend describes neoshamans as "cognitive minorities." Dissatisfied with the religious options as well as the moral inconsistencies within their own cultures, such persons throughout history have been drawn to foreign religious phenomena which they may sample and eventually adopt. Townsend distinguishes two predominant orientations among contemporary cognitive minorities: those who join "In Group movements" (such as the Unification Church or Hare Krishna within Western society) and "Individualists." The latter adopt foreign religious traditions in a highly personalized and idiosyncratic manner, but may nonetheless find inspiration and even validation in contact with others. Townsend suggests that "Cognitive minorities need reinforcement and validation from others to develop and maintain their beliefs; otherwise they often abandon them" (2005: 3). This validation may come through media – television, workshops, websites – creating a virtual community facilitated in a manner different from that of a traditional face-to-face community.

Scholars in the 1990s responded to broader public interest in shamanic traditions in a sometimes dismissive, sometimes openly hostile manner. Roberte Hamayon (2001: 5), for instance, labels Michael Harner a "former anthropologist" and asserts that he "indulged the trend" when advocating neoshamanic adaptations. Ethnographers supportive of and interested in cultural phenomena in other respects nonetheless at times betray a surprising lack of tolerance for neoshamanist movements, particularly if the practitioners seek to make an income through their activities. Such characterizations, of course, may at times amount to a kind of anthropological colonialism in themselves: stifling, under the banner of authenticity, the diverse, evolving, and opportunistic tendencies of religious expression, particularly in affluent societies with ample access to ethnographic data and learning.

NEOSHAMANISM BEYOND THE WEST

The above discussion has focused primarily on neoshamanic phenomena as found among relatively well-educated and affluent members of Western societies, particularly in Europe and North America. Neoshamanism also occurs elsewhere, however. Sometimes its existence is tied economically and culturally to the neoshamanism described above, as when interested Westerners pay to witness shamanic rituals in situ or to participate in them through various forms of arranged excursions. In other cases, however, these non-Western or non-elite neoshamanisms represent independent, culturally specific responses to processes of change in the context of post-colonial or post-Soviet societies. In such cases, they may merge with the kinds of revitalization described in the last chapter.

An important merging of shamanic practices with Christianity occurred in the Native American Church of the United States. Here nineteenth-century religious innovators creatively combined elements of traditional Native spirituality (particularly the visionary use of peyote; see Chapter 9) with the tenets of monotheistic Christianity. The resultant fusion spread rapidly among Native American communities and today can be found on many reservations throughout the United States and Canada.

This adaptation of peyote vision practices has been carefully chronicled by a number of scholars, including Weston La Barre (1964) and James S. Slotkin (1956). La Barre published the first edition of his dissertation *The Peyote Cult* already in 1938. Slotkin not only joined the Native American Church but also became one of its officials; both La Barre and Slotkin spoke forcefully against federal laws that sought to limit peyote use within the religion. The earliest ethnographer to write about "Peyotism," J. Mooney, probably assisted the Native community in the work of incorporating the movement as the Native American Church at the outset of the twentieth century (Slotkin 1956: 58).

Slotkin (1956: 22) cites reports written by Mooney in the period 1891–6 that indicate the existence of communal rituals reminiscent of later Native American Church activities among the Kiowa people of Oklahoma. It is unclear to what extent the movement existed among other tribes at the time, or how it had come to be practiced among the Kiowa. Mooney cites a Kiowa myth about a girl who mistakenly thought her brothers were dead and received the gift of peyote from the sun in consolation (Slotkin 1956: 22–3). The resulting syncretic religion allowed members to merge Christian ideas with the notion of shamanic spirit journey, contextualizing the latter in a supportive ritual structure that allowed for participants' ethical, aesthetic, and philosophical predispositions. Christian elements appear drawn from both Catholicism and forms of Protestantism (Slotkin 1956: 45), while Native elements appear as generalizations of widespread tendencies in Plains Indian religions: e.g., the sacrality of directions, the importance of rituals of long duration, specific ritual roles for men vs. women.

In the autobiography of the Ho-Chunk (Winnebago) man Crashing Thunder edited by Paul Radin (1926: 169), the arrival of peyotism in the Northern United States is detailed from a firsthand perspective. After a tumultuous life that included prison, alcohol abuse, and various supernatural experiences, Crashing Thunder joined his parents in consuming peyote while living in Nebraska. While traditionalists within the community warned that those who ate the cactus destroyed their afterlives, others saw it as an agent for social healing among a troubled and frustrated people. Crashing Thunder recounts the words of his father in deciding to join the movement:

My father and I walked by ourselves and he told me about the peyote. "It does not amount to anything, all this that they are doing. Yet those who partake, stop their drinking. Sick people also get well. We were told these things and therefore we joined. What they claimed is true and your mother is practically well now; and so am I. They claim to offer prayers to Earthmaker, to God." (1926: 171)

At the same time that the father viewed the movement as positive, he also strongly condemned its rejection of many elements of traditional shamanism as practiced previously in the region and in the Midéwiwin movement (discussed in Chapter 13):

They throw away all the medicines that they possess and whose virtues they know. They give up all the blessings they received while fasting, give up all the spirits who blessed them. They stop giving feasts and making offerings of tobacco. They are bad people. They burn up their medicine pouches, give up the Medicine Dance and even cut up their otter-skin bags. They say they are praying to Earthmaker, God; that everything they are giving up comes from the bad spirits, that the bad spirits deceived them. They claim that there are no spirits with the power of bestowing blessings and that there is no other spirit except Earthmaker, God." (1926: 171)

Crashing Thunder eventually joined the movement and similarly rejected all traditional Ho-Chunk religiosity as sinful. As he states in his autobiography: "I learned ... that all I had done in the past had been evil ... It is false, this giving of pagan feasts, of holding the old ... things holy, such as the Medicine Dance and all other customs" (Radin 1926: 202). From this perspective, peyotism appears a rejection of traditional shamanism as well as the revitalization movement known as Midéwiwin, even while retaining the use of an entheogen that stood at the center of shamanic traditions among North American peoples for thousands of years. The issues of religious shift illustrated here are explored in depth in Chapter 12.

Such syncretic amalgamations of local shamanic tradition and an introduced formal religion have occurred elsewhere as well. As Shanon (2002: 20–1) details, Amazonian *ayahuasca* traditions became fused with forms of Christianity in various ways in twentieth-century Brazil. The church of Santo Daime dates to the 1930s and was formed when an Afro-Brazilian rubber tapper named Raimundu Irineu Serra learned about *ayahuasca* from indigenous practitioners in the rain forest. After eight days of repeated use of the entheogen, Serra saw a vision of the Queen of the Forest, who ordered him to establish a church centered on *ayahuasca* use (2002: 21). The resulting movement fuses *ayahuasca* vision quests with elements of Catholicism, as the following portion of a Daime hymn illustrates:

> I have climbed, I have climbed, I have climbed
> I have climbed with joy
> When reaching the Heights
> I encountered the Virgin Mary.
>
> I have climbed, I have climbed, I have climbed
> I have climbed with love
> I have encountered the Eternal Father
> And the redeemer, Jesus Christ. (2002: 66)

The image of spiritual travel here, facilitated by an entheogen prepared along lines specified in long-standing shamanic tradition, is fused with sacred visions integral to Christianity. Comparable but distinct observations can be made of União do Vegetal, founded in the 1960s, or the movement known as the Barquinha, a fusion of Afro-Brazilian Umbanda with shamanic *ayahuasca* use. The former approaches *ayahuasca* ("*hoasca*") use as a tool of esoteric knowledge and maintains a highly formal, restrained decorum in its services (Shanon 2002: 24); the latter adopts the metaphor of a *barquinha* ("little boat") as a means of describing spiritual travel facilitated by the entheogen, and combines it with communal singing and dance shaped by Afro-Brazilian musical and spiritual traditions (2002: 25–6). Although they began in remote population areas where indigenous practitioners and cultural outsiders mixed, all three movements have spread markedly, as Shanon points out:

Nowadays, there are *Daime* and União do Vegetal communities in practically all major Brazilian towns, and their members are from all walks of life, with a growing number of professionals and members of the upper middle class. Recently, these groups have also established communities in Europe and the United States. (2002: 20)

The legal battle of one such offshoot – Centro Espirita Beneficente União do Vegetal (UDV) – to continue their use of *ayahuasca* within American society is detailed in Chapter 9.

In order to distinguish Tuvan neoshamanic performances from surviving traditional shamanism, Ulla Johansen (2001) identifies certain key distinctions. Traditional shamans, she suggests, typically have little or no formal education or travel experience outside of their native districts. They are generally unaware of international shamanic movements dominated by figures like Harner and they thus display a local purism in terms of rituals performed and paraphernalia used. Crucially, they do not practice for anyone except members of their own communities. In contrast, Johansen notes, many of the neoshamans she came upon in Tuva had received college educations and studied shamanism as an academic subject in anthropology or culture courses. They were often very familiar with Harner's Core Shamanism and interested in relating Tuva shamanism to counterparts from other parts of the world. In so doing, such Native practitioners emphasized their similarities to neoshamans in the West, while Western neoshamans in turn looked upon them as illustrations of "traditional" shamanism at work.

While pointing out important elements in the revitalization of Tuvan shamanism, Johansen's work also runs the risk of transforming ethnographers into arbiters of authenticity. Insisting that shamans know only their own tradition or limit their education and travel experience so as to maintain innocence of neoshamanic trends can lead to a self-fulfilling pessimism: by this definition, as time goes by and intercultural communication increases, there will be fewer and fewer such "authentic" shamans regardless of whether the community continues to engage in shamanic practices or not. Yet we may note that a willingness to stage public shamanic rituals does not necessarily mean that the performers do not also practice the traditions privately as well, or that they hold no belief in them as efficacious or sacred. As discussed in Chapters 6 and 8, performativity – "showmanship" – has long been a part of shamanic traditions worldwide to one degree or another, apparently even in the most traditional circumstances. And if an unwillingness to make a profit from one's spiritual acts were universally applied as a standard for true religiosity, then the ranks of professional clergy in many formal religious denominations would undoubtedly be smaller. It is important, thus, to note differences that exist between these latest manifestations of shamanic traditions and those that have come before, but to observe these as part of a changing economic and cultural system in which religious transformation is simply one part.

In many cases in the postcommunist or developing world, the line between revitalization and neoshamanism can appear very slight. Where the cases of renewed Tuvan and Korean shamanic traditions discussed in Chapter 13 can be seen as conscious attempts at religious revitalization, the new fusion of shamanic ritual and Muslim faith healing described by Carol Laderman (2001) qualifies as an entirely new creation. Malaysian officials, like counterparts in many Westernizing nations of the twentieth century, came to regard tradition as an impediment to social and economic progress. In an interpretive framework based on the dichotomization of "tradition" and "modernity," shamanic ritual practices became viewed as emblems of a backward rural culture, plagued with superstition and irrational behavior. Their rejection became a symbolic act of support for Malaysia's "future," a revision of worldview which policy-makers and social leaders believed would ease the country's entry into the ranks of the world's industrialized nations. As Stacey Pigg (1996: 165) writes in describing similar attitudes in Nepal, "the idea of the modern generates a sense of difference while at the same time holding out the promise of inclusion in a global cosmopolitan culture." Resulting policies led to a strong urbanization effort in Malaysia and the suppression of religious practices regarded as inimical to a modern, Islamic state. In this context, many traditional Malay healers (*bomoh*) lost their standing and clientele, as their neighbors left village tracts and customs for a new urban experience. At the same time, as Laderman details, urbanized Malays came to romanticize the countryside and its folk practices. As a result, new forms of healing developed, hybridizations of Islamic faith healing and traditional shamanism. In one particular case examined by Laderman, a male sage Yussof teamed up with a highly dramatic female *bomoh* Cik Su to create a combined séance of great appeal to urbanized Malays. Writes Laderman:

Yussof's admonitions concerning piety, prayer, and devotion to Islam protect their healing treatments from criticism directed at more traditional shamans' séances. This innovative combination of antiquity and modernity, magic and religious orthodoxy succeeded in making Cik Su and Yussof wealthy at a time when traditional Malay shamanism, primarily based in agrarian communities … was on the wane. (2001: 61–2)

The pair's séances, although drawing on many traditional notions of spirits and winds, lacked many of the features of traditional Malay shamanism. The healers made no attempts at negotiating with spirits, nor did they recommend specific sacrifices as therapies. Drawing selectively on Malay ideas of health, Yussof repackaged these in a manner consonant with a contemporary urbanized identity. Herbal cures, prayer, meditation, and social harmony combined in therapies that evinced both the air of traditionality and the wisdom of Islam. Many traditional Malay *bomoh* would not have recognized the pair's techniques as valid; on the other hand, their clientele seem to have regarded them as exemplars of ancient Malay custom.

Where many non-Western neoshamanisms deny influence from Western ideas, some movements emphasize the fusion of local traditions and Western-mediated Core Shamanism as a conscious and beneficial union. Such is the case with some of the *ayahuasca*-related tours and workshops characteristic of contemporary shamanic tourism today. As Hamilton Souther, the founder and leader of Blue Morpho tours, writes in his overview website (2003):

Tens of thousands of years ago shamanism entered into the collective unconscious of the human being and formed the structure to understand the life experience of traditional man through present. Today the westerner, distanced from the inner wisdom of this realm of magic is looking to the mystics to open their ancient connection to Spirit and unveil the boundaries between the westerner's reality of separation and fear to a reality of mystical proportions filled with inner connection to spirit in its various forms.

Tourism becomes for Souther a means of recovering lost spirituality, so that it can be restored to those whose cultures have lost connection with shamanic truths over time:

Through the domination of globalization of western belief systems and commercialization of third world countries, traditional, old world, shamanism is now isolated to the world's most remote locations ... It is here, when the sun descends behind the horizon, that the veil of the westerner's reality lifts and the sights and sounds of shamanism begin to take shape. Shamans (Curanderos), men and women trained in the art of Spirit, turn to and into the realm of the mystical to aid and enrich their patients, communities, and personal path of discovery. Shamans learn, heal, grow, and teach through altered states of consciousness where plants and animals have voice and other worlds hold places of wisdom where the learning and training occurs.

As Kira Salak (2006) points out in her chronicle of her own experiences of *ayahuasca* facilitated by Souther's tours, such personal explorations can be deeply meaningful for those involved, and are readily described by participants as religious. Salak's visions during her *ayahuasca* consumption included spiritual travel, demonic exorcism, recovery of missing souls (soul retrieval), incarnations of past lives, and a conversation with God. Although shaped in part by her readings of Core Shamanism and other elements of New Age spirituality, Salak's visions also display a tremendous similarity to the supernatural experiences of "traditional" shamans, as recorded ethnographically in different parts of the world over the last several centuries.

CREATIVE REVIVALS

As we saw in the last chapters, a number of indigenous communities have sought to recover and/or revitalize their cultures' once abandoned shamanic traditions, searching for ways to revivify a set of spiritual procedures and understandings that had been abandoned during fairly recent colonial contact and forced or volitional religious shift. In the late twentieth century, other communities and individuals have sought to accomplish an even more daunting task: the revival or adoption of shamanic traditions in contexts where they have not existed for centuries or longer. Often drawing on ethnographic data concerning extant shamanic traditions from other parts of the world, and adapting concepts to the worldview and values of contemporary Western urbanites, these new religious innovators display the eclecticism typical of neoshamanic movements within a conscious framework of cultural fidelity.

Ailo Gaup (2005) has written about his personal quest to recover Sámi shamanism. Gaup did not grow up in direct contact with shamanic traditions and learned about shamanic techniques in the United States through taking courses with Michael Harner and Sandra Ingerman. Equipped with Harner's Core Shamanism methods and a broad understanding of shamanic traditions in various parts of the world, Gaup returned to Norway and his birth culture to explore the ways and culture of the *noaide* of the past. Although, in Gaup's view (2005: 25), all people have a natural ability to become shamans, he also sensed a native ability in himself that linked him with other Sámi *noaide* shamans of the past (2005: 35). This special linkage was particularly powerful in the area in which Gaup was born:

I was born in Finnmark, on a mountain that is called Røyehodet. Over the years this place and fate tied me to the power of nature and the shaman's tasks. In my eyes, this is a special place, and everything is to be found in eyes that see. The mountain releases ancient power and knowledge. This has become alive within me, like a *saivo* land, a paradise within. This is where I learn ceremonies and meet with ancestors. (2005: 37; my translation)

Gaup associates the spot both with ancestors and with specific spirit helpers, such as a white reindeer and invisible spirit beings. Although Gaup was raised by an adoptive family that did not have Sámi connections, he became interested in his natal culture as a young adult. Visions of a shamanic drum recurred in his dreams, and he returned to the north of Norway on a dual quest both to respond to this shamanic calling and to embrace his lost Sámi identity. For Gaup, the line between shamanism and ethnic identity blurs into a single meaningful and emotive whole.

A parallel experience is chronicled by Gershon Winkler (2003), who has sought to recover linkages between shamanism and his natal Orthodox Judaism. Writes Winkler in the introduction to his manual *Magic of the Ordinary: Recovering the Shamanic in Judaism*:

My ancestors were a tribal people, they lived and practiced a Judaism that in very few ways resembles the more urbanized Judaism of today. Once upon a time my people enjoyed a relationship with the earth that was more about spirituality than about commerce or industry. Our visionaries came not from rabbinical seminaries and academies of higher learning but from solitary walkabouts and vision quests deep in the wilderness and far from the reaches of civilization. They were masters of sorcery and shamanism, dancing comfortably between the realms of spirit and matter, celebrating the magic of the worlds around them and the worlds beyond them. They knew the language of the trees and the grasses, the songs of the frogs and the cicadas, the thoughts of horses and sheep. They followed rivers to discover truths, and climbed mountains to liberate their spirits. They journeyed beyond their bodily limitations and brought people back from the dead, healed the incurable, talking raging rivers into holding back their rapids, turned pints into gallons, brought down the rains in times of drought, walked through fire, even suspended the orbit of the earth around the sun. My ancestors were powerful warriors and shamans who, like the warriors and shamans of other aboriginal peoples, were swept under the rug by so-called civilization as it overtook an entire planet by force, subjugating spirituality and personal aliveness in the guise of "civilizing the primitives" and "saving souls." (2003: xix)

Winkler characterizes the ancient religious traditions of Judaism as nature-centered and embracing of feminine spirituality, and attributes the historical rupture between this recoverable shamanic belief system and modern Judaism to first the persecution and then the insidious intellectual influence of Christianity (2003: 11–13). Asserting no linkage between true Judaism and its purported outgrowth in Christianity, Winkler writes: "There is just no such thing as 'Judeo-Christian.' 'Judeo-Apache' would be a more authentic and legitimate theological alliance than 'Judeo-Christian'" (2003: 12). Drawing on contacts with shamanic revivalists of Native American background in the American Southwest, Winkler uses the traditions observed there to reenvision Jewish ceremonies he had long practiced as an Orthodox Jew: "watching the Indian medicine people perform their ceremonies, I experienced *déjà vu* and became increasingly conscious of the shamanic traditions of my own people" (2003: xx).

A principal aim of Winkler's work is to reinterpret the Jewish scriptures in the light of shamanic traditions which they may reflect. Great biblical prophets like Moses (Mosheh) and Elijah, as well as famed Talmudic rabbis like Chanina ben Dosa, become seen as "sorcerers" – healing, working wonders, divining, and interacting with spirits described as angels or as *sheydim*, half-angel/half-human beings often described in biblical exegesis as demons (2003: 88–92). The mysticism of the *kabbalah* is read as the fruits of vision quests (2003: 71), and figures like the *golem* from Jewish oral tradition are depicted as the products of "illegitimate magic" (2003: 76–84). The monotheistic deity is described as the "Creator Spirit," which manifests itself through a variety of different spirits and forces within a cosmos that encompasses multiple worlds and realities (2003: 93–4). Traditional Jewish rituals become enactments of a consciousness of this spirit-imbued world, recapturing, in Winkler's view, the sense of communication and wonder that had been part of ancient Judaism but which had gradually become lost in later Jewish-and Christian-influenced exegesis and theology. A set of new rituals is proposed to supplement these, however, such as one to create a "Sacred Circle" (2003: 96–8), underscoring the shamanic logic behind the scriptures and uniting elements of Jewish prayer with rituals drawn from Native American and other traditions of interest within New Age mysticism. Winkler's ideas have led to a foundation and a website in Thousand Oaks, California (Winkler 2008).

Geo Athena Cameron Trevarthen attempts to rehabilitate the much-maligned "Western" worldview of European cultures by restoring its non-Christian spirituality:

The Celtic tradition formed the basis for the Western world-view. In the West, we live on the secular surface of the Celtic cosmology. This facet affirms our value as individuals realizing our potential. It celebrates life in the world and success in the field of action. The problem is that the spiritual part of the tradition was lost to most of us, leaving a gutted cosmology. However, we can heal this rift in our lives. Healing means: "to make whole." When we practice the whole Western way, we can be passionately engaged in the world, and just as passionately connected to Spirit. (Trevarthen 2007)

The pathway to this recovery, for Geo Athena Cameron Trevarthen, draws on a variety of New Age spiritual techniques derived from Asian religions as well as neoshamanism: "Through meditation, energy work, chant, prayer and the visionary technique of the *echtra* or spirit journey, we can learn to experience spiritual reality as personally and vividly today as Celtic shaman-priests did millennia ago." Trevarthen describes herself as "an hereditary shaman-priestess." "Hereditary" here means that she was raised in a Neopagan household, as her mother was a follower of the Golden Dawn magickal revival movement that arose in turn-of-the-twentieth-century Britain and North America. This upbringing, Trevarthen notes, allowed her to be more fully open to spiritual enlightenment that others might initially reject or treat with skepticism:

This was one of the greatest advantages of my upbringing within the tradition. I've learned over the years that my spirit journeys and experiences are a lot more vivid and intense than they are for many other people. I attribute this in part to the fact that Spirit was always part of my day to day reality. My mother talking to my dead great-grandfather was no more unusual than her talking to the neighbour. (2007)

This openness has allowed Trevarthen to provide many innovations in her work within the movement known as modern Druidry. Not only does she seek to recover the core aspects of that religious tradition, but she also draws on elements from the spiritual traditions of India and Sumeria and knowledge that she gained through her Master's and Ph.D. studies at the University of Edinburgh, such as facility in Old Irish and an acquaintance with the writings of medieval Irish theologian John Scotus Eriugena. Study of Michael Harner's *The Way of the Shaman* as well as the writings and teaching of Sandra Ingerman have also added important elements to her practice and understanding.

Gaup, Winkler, and Trevarthen illustrate the serious personal commitment modern seekers may evince in their quest to recover lost spiritual traditions. Their efforts are profoundly personal, yet also offered as invitations to people of shared ethnic background with the hopes of reconstituting the kinds of cultural and communal cohesion that Western individualism seems inevitably to undermine.

For many Western intellectuals over the past several centuries – scholars as well as religious leaders – shamanism has represented the epitome of the primitive, the irrational, and the outdated. It was regarded as a set of misguided superstitions, to be jettisoned in favor of a more perfect religiosity or an embrace of modern "realism" and "progress." This discourse, as we saw in Chapter 2, often coincided with a process of cultural destruction and colonization, in which indigenous communities were forced off their lands and away from their livelihoods – as well as their belief systems – by an incoming polity bent on co-opting sources of local wealth and power. In the centuries of vilification and suppression that followed, many shamanic traditions were abandoned. Yet today, neoshamanisms seem to call for a reversal of the trend: the reinvigoration of shamanic worldviews and the reintroduction of them in new contexts, not only within the indigenous communities that had practiced them until relatively recently, but also among groups within the dominant polity long estranged from shamanic traditions. Scholars have described such trends as characteristic of postmodern Western society, or as the product of the intense individualism and self-creation that marks empowered Western culture today. But the effect of such neoshamanisms in formerly shamanic cultures is decidedly more contentious, as participants negotiate the complexities of cultural maintenance, exoticization, and co-option, particularly in relation to emerging economic niches such as education, tourism, and cultural display. Perhaps never before has shamanism held so much appeal for so many people in the world. It remains to be seen, however, what the long-term effects of this widespread interest will be, both for those communities that currently maintain age-old shamanic traditions largely intact, and for those whose relation to shamanism has been mediated through scholarly or marketing channels.

Epilogue

When an interdisciplinary group of faculty members at the University of Wisconsin-Madison met in the late 1990s to formulate a new curriculum in religious studies, the scholars involved decided to require coursework in a variety of different areas. In addition to depth in particular religious traditions, they wished to ensure that students come away with more general understandings, so they identified seven different breadth categories for students to choose from. Alongside Judaism, Christianity, Islam, South Asian traditions, Buddhism, and East Asian traditions was the category "Ancient, Indigenous, and Folk Traditions." I was invited to offer instruction in this latter category, and my course on shamanism resulted. The material presented in the preceding chapters reflects the content and orientations of that course. It is an overview of current understandings of the phenomena captured by the term *shamanism*, supplemented at times with insights from my own fieldwork and students' input.

Much has changed since 1964, when Mircea Eliade's *Shamanism: Archaic Techniques of Ecstasy* first appeared in English. For one thing, ethnographic and theoretical foci have shifted from a search for overarching universals or evolutionary stages of human culture to a preoccupation with the specificities of particular cultural situations as politically and socially constituted. Broad terms like *shamanism* have become highly suspect, despite scholars' continued reliance on them in research and teaching. As Chapters 1 and 2 show, the very concept of "shamanism" can be regarded in some measure as a product of Western imperialism, a device for homogenizing and diminishing the distinctiveness of indigenous religious traditions and of displaying them as somehow a single entity, inferior to the religious traditions of empowered polities. There are few scholars today who would not wince at the confident and superioristic ways in which earlier scholars like Marett (1909) and Otto (1950) described beliefs like "animism" and approached the comparison of indigenous religions with idealized images of Christianity. As cultural relativism developed from theory to practice in twentieth-century scholarship, these earlier formulations came in for substantive critique.

At the same time, and partly as a further product of this same process of cultural relativism, the sharp boundary between those who write about cultures and those whose cultures are written about began to dissolve. The "ethnographer" and the "primitive" no longer inhabit separate worlds, either in reality or in the imagination of scholars' writing. As Chapter 14 demonstrates, shamanic traditions are nearly as likely to be found today among college-educated Westerners or well-connected urbanites in a variety of cultures around the world as among small subsistence communities living in close reliance on the land or natural resources. As Chapter 13 shows, further, indigenous revitalizers are often college trained today, with a firm knowledge of shamanism as it occurs elsewhere in the world and a thorough familiarity with the ideas of Eliade or even Harner. Scholarly pronouncements on particular religions are as likely to be read by adherents of the religion in question as by persons from outside the community. Dichotomies like primitive/civilized, traditional/modern, and authentic/spurious have all become highly problematic and open to considerable scholarly debate as a result of this widened conversation.

Given these developments, one can rightly ask if there is any value, or any validity, in discussing a blanket concept of "shamanism" at all. Yet at the same time, it remains strikingly clear that at least some of the cultural commonalities brought into focus under the term *shamanism* in past research do indeed exist. I believe the chapters presented here – particularly the prime descriptive Chapters 4–6, as well as the supplemental Chapters 9–11 – underscore this reality, and confirm the impression of similarities noted by scholars already centuries ago.

Acknowledgement of commonality does not necessarily mean denigration of difference or value. Personally, I remember the first time a Hmong student took my course on Sámi culture. After the course was over, he told me how exciting it was for him to hear about religious traditions from a culture from the distant north of Europe that so closely paralleled the ones he knew from his own community, rooted in the tropical highlands of Laos. For that student, and for many individuals from other cultures in various parts of the world, the term *shamanism* can connote not colonial domination and disparagement, but rather affirmation. One's local traditions can be seen as part of a wider set of understandings regarding the seen and the unseen, ones that hold great antiquity in human culture and that have exerted a shaping influence on many societies the world over. Such affirmation can prove valuable in the politics that form the third category in

Fitzgerald's (2000) provocative revision of the phenomena formerly described by the term *religion*.

These viewpoints become of great importance when examining the historical processes dicussed in Chapters 12–14. Communities sometimes choose to revitalize or even recreate lapsed shamanic traditions as both an act of resistance against the tragedy of forced "deicide" (N. Scott Momaday's term, 1969: 10), and as a response to feelings of social disintegration or decay. In part, such movements are also a response to the newfound acceptability of shamanism in Western society. Restoring a sense of scholarly respect for shamanic traditions has become embraced as a necessary part of contemporary research, a further demonstration of the blurring of the line between the arenas of action of scholars and the communities which they study.

A further change that has occurred in Western scholarship since the time of Eliade is a reduction of the once rigid boundary between notions of "science" or "fact," on the one hand, and that of "belief," on the other. Scholars today are more comfortable looking at worldviews as well as Western science as heuristic, provisional models of the world. Frequently, scholars are willing to posit that no particular way of looking at the cosmos is inherently more "real" or "correct" than any other, but rather, that human communities constantly seek to explain their world through models based on the evidence available to them and the traditions of interpretation which they have developed. An individual may indeed adopt a particular view as a preferred way of explaining the cosmos, but acknowledge in so doing that the choice is based on belief rather than "fact." In this light, the ease with which past scholars labeled beliefs that differed from their own as "superstitions" or "delusions" seems misguided and counterproductive, and the discourse is opened to the possibility of discussions between people who hold separate, even opposed, beliefs.

While supernatural explanations in particular have thus gained greater legitimacy as epistemological grounds in the study of human cultural phenomena like religion, cognitive science has in its own way blurred the boundary between supernatural experience and the physically measurable neural functioning of the brain and body. As Chapters 7 and 8 show, scholars have endeavored to interrelate brain function and religious or healing experiences in ways that scholars half a century ago could not have imagined. Researchers are increasingly convinced that religious experience is physical – bodily – but this physicality does not lessen its significance as religious. Cognitive research can bolster rather than undermine our recognition of shamanism as an important set of ritual traditions, ones that operate through the body as a tool for supernatural experience.

A final area of change since the middle of the last century lies in the scholarly views of intellectual property. As Chapters 9–11 make clear, shamanic activities often feature elaborate and memorable expressive traditions, be they musical, medicinal, verbal, or material. In many ways, these belong to shamanic practitioners and their communities as valuable commodities, and scholars must treat them with respect, even to the point of giving them back when a community makes such a request. The issues of cultural ownership and repatriation discussed in Chapter 10 could not have surfaced in the era of the mid-twentieth century, when the authority of the man of science and of the museum as a benign repository of human knowledge remained largely unquestioned. The issues of neoshamanic co-option of traditions, discussed in Chapter 14, are a further manifestation of the recognition that shamanic traditions are intellectual property, as is the knowledge of plants and other substances which can lead to heightened supernatural experiences and potent cures (Chapter 9).

With so many profound changes in the way scholars conceptualize their work, the writing of an overview of shamanism can prove daunting. Yet the task also offers new possibilities for creating a framework that is both responsive to cultural specificities and respectful of practitioners' viewpoints and interests. The present study has tried to accomplish these ends. I hope it leads the reader to a deeper appreciation of the profoundly significant and widespread body of soteriological, ritual, and political traditions that make up shamanism, a body of knowledge of great intrinsic value and tremendous import to individuals as well as communities in their experience of the cosmos. I concur wholeheartedly with Eliade (1964: xx) when he states that a knowledge of shamanism is "a necessity for every true humanist," and I hope that this survey will serve as an opening for the reader to explore the intricacies of this rich and varied set of religious traditions.

Bibliography

Ahlbäck, Tore and Jan Bergman (eds.) 1991. *The Saami Shaman Drum*. Stockholm: Almqvist & Wiksell International.

Aldhouse-Green, Miranda and Stephen. 2005. *The Quest for the Shaman*. London: Thames & Hudson.

Anderson, Tamia Marg. 1992. "Shamanism in Tuva." *Friends of Tuva Newsletter* 9 (1992), www.fotuva.org/newsletters/fot9.html, accessed February, 2008.

Arbman, Ernst. 1970. *Ecstasy or Religious Trance in the Experience of Ecstatics and from the Psychological Point of View*. Uppsala: Bokforlaget.

Arnett, Amy M. 1995. "Jimson Weed (Datura stramonium) Poisoning." *Clinical Toxicology Review* December, 18(3); online version at: www.erowid.org/plants/datura/datura_info5.shtml, accessed Nov. 1, 2007.

Athanassakis, Apostolos N. 2001. "Shamanism and Amber in Greece: The Northern Connection." In: *Shamanhood, Symbolism and Epic*. Eds. Juha Pentikäinen, Hanna Saressalo, and Chuner M. Taksami. Budapest: Akadémiai Kiadó. 207–20.

Atkinson, Jane Monnig. 1987. "The Effectiveness of Shamans in an Indonesian Ritual." *American Anthropologist* New Series 89(2): 342–55.

1989. *Art and Politics of Wana Shamanship*. Berkeley, CA: University of California Press.

1992. "Shamanisms Today." *Annual Review of Anthropology* 21: 307–30.

Aubert, Laurent. 2006. "Chamanisme, possession et musique: quelques réflexions préliminaires." *Cahiers de Musiques Traditionnelles* 19: 11–20.

Austin, James H. 2006. *Zen-Brain Reflections: Reviewing Recent Developments in Meditation and States of Consciousness*. Cambridge, MA: Massachusetts Institute of Technology.

Bacigalupo, Ana Mariella. 2004. "The Mapuche Man Who Became a Woman: Selfhood, Gender Transgression, and Competing Cultural Norms." *American Ethnologist* 31(3): 440–57.

Bäckman, Louise and Åke Hultkrantz (eds.) 1977. *Studies in Lapp Shamanism*. Stockholm: Almqvist & Wiksell International.

Bahn, Paul C. 2001. "Save the Last Trance for Me: An Assessment of the Misuse of Shamanism in Rock Art Studies." In: *The Concept of Shamanism: Uses and Abuses*. Eds. Henri-Paul Francfort and Roberte N. Hamayon. Budapest: Akadémiai Kiadó. 51–94.

Balzer, Marjorie Mandelstam (ed.) 1997. *Shamanic Worlds: Rituals and Lore of Siberia and Central Asia.* Armonk, NY and London: New Castle Books.

1999. *The Tenacity of Ethnicity: A Siberian Saga in Global Perspective.* Princeton, NJ: Princeton University Press.

Basilov, Vladimir N. 1997. "Chosen by the Spirits." In: *Shamanic Worlds: Rituals and Lore of Siberia and Central Asia.* Ed. Marjorie Mandelstam Balzer. Armonk and London: New Castle Books. 3–45.

Becker, Judith. 2001. "Anthropological Perspectives on Music and Emotion." In: *Music and Emotion: Theory and Research.* Eds. Patrick N. Juslin and John A. Sloboda. Oxford: Oxford University Press. 135–60.

Beckford, James A. 2003. *Social Theory and Religion.* Cambridge: Cambridge University Press.

Bennett, Bradley C. 1992. "Hallucinogenic Plants of the Shuar and Related Indigenous Groups in Amazonian Ecuador and Peru." *Brittonia* 44: 483–93.

Berger, Peter. 1969. *A Rumour of Angels: Modern Society and the Rediscovery of the Supernatural.* Baltimore, MD: Penguin.

1990. *The Sacred Canopy, Elements of a Sociological Theory of Religion.* New York: Anchor Books.

Blacker, Carmen. 1975. *The Catalpa Bow: A Study of Shamanistic Practices in Japan.* London: George Allen & Unwin.

Boas, Franz. 1930. *Religion of the Kwakiutl Indians. Part II – Translations.* New York: Columbia University Press.

Bogoras, W. 1904–9. *The Chukchee.* Publications of the Jesup North Pacific Expedition vol. VII. Memoirs of the American Museum of Natural History XI. New York: G. E. Stechert.

Booth, Martin. 1998. *Opium: A History.* London: Simon and Schuster.

Brady, James E. and Wendy Ashmore. 1994. "Mountains, Caves, Water: Ideational Landscapes of the Ancient Maya." In: *Archaeologies of Landscape: Contemporary Perspectives.* Eds. Wendy Ashmore and A. Bernard Knapp. Oxford: Blackwell Publishers. 124–48.

Briggs, Charles and Richard Bauman. 1999. "'The Foundation of All Future Researches': Franz Boas, George Hunt, Native American Texts, and the Construction of Modernity." *American Quarterly* 51(3): 479–528.

Burton, Lloyd. 2002. *Worship and Wilderness: Culture, Religion and Law in Public Lands Management.* Madison, WI: University of Wisconsin Press.

Campbell, Joseph. 1949. *Hero With a Thousand Faces.* Princeton: Princeton University Press.

Castaneda, Carlos. 1968. *The Teachings of Don Juan.* Berkeley: University of California Press.

1972. *Journey to Ixtlan.* New York: Simon and Schuster.

Chaumeil, Jean-Pierre. 1982. "Représentation du monde d'un chamane Yagua." *L'Ethnographie* 88(87–8): 49–54.

Chilson, Clark and Peter Knecht (eds.) 2003. *Shamans in Asia.* New York: Routledge Curzon.

Clottes, Jean, and J. David Lewis-Williams. 2001. *Les chamanes de la préhistoire: transe et magie dans les grottes ornées.* Paris: Maison des Roches.

Cocchiara, Giuseppe. 1981. *The History of Folklore in Europe.* John N. McDaniel, trans. Philadelphia: Institute for the Study of Human Issues.

Commission on Classification and Terminology of the International League Against Epilepsy. 1981. "Proposal for Revised Clinical and Electroencephalographic Classification of Epileptic Seizures." *Epilepsia* 22(4): 489–501.

Connor, Linda H. and Geoffrey Samuel. 2001. *Healing Powers and Modernity: Traditional Medicine, Shamanism, and Science in Asian Societies.* Westport, CT: Bergin and Garvey.

Conquergood, Dwight and Paja Thao. 1986. *I Am a Shaman: A Hmong Life Story with Ethnographic Commentary.* Evanston, IL: Northwestern University Press.

Cooper, Robert (ed.) 1998. *The Hmong.* Singapore: Times Editions.

Covell, Alan Carter. 1983. *Ecstasy: Shamanism in Korea.* Elizabeth, NJ: Hollym International.

Cowell, E. B. and W. F. Webster (eds.) 1977. *Rig-Veda Sanhita: A Collection of Ancient Hindu Hymns of the Rig-Veda.* H. H. Wilson, trans. Vol. VI. New Delhi: Cosmo Publications.

Crocker, Jon Christopher. 1985. *Vital Souls: Bororo Cosmology, Natural Symbolism, and Shamanism.* Tucson, AZ: University of Arizona Press.

Czaplicka, M. A. 1914. *Aboriginal Siberia: A Study in Social Anthropology.* Oxford: Clarendon Press.

Danforth, Loring. 1989. *Firewalking and Religious Healing: The Astenaria of Greece and the American Firewalking Movement.* Princeton: Princeton University Press.

d'Anglure, Saladin. 1992. "Rethinking Inuit Shamanism through the Concept of 'Third Gender.'" In: *Northern Religions and Shamanism.* Eds. Mihály Hoppál and Juha Pentikäinen. Budapest: Akadémiai Kiadó. 146–51.

Dawson, Christopher. 1955. *The Mongol Mission: Narratives and Letters of the Franciscan Missionaries in Mongolia and China in the Thirteenth and Fourteenth Centuries.* London and New York: Sheed and Ward.

de Mille, Richard. 1976. *Castaneda's Journey: The Power and the Allegory.* Santa Barbara, CA: Capra Press.

Desjarlais, Robert. 1995. "Presence." In: *The Performance of Healing.* Eds. Carol Laderman and Marina Roseman. New York: Routledge. 143–64.

Devereux, George. 1961. "Shamans as Neurotics." *American Anthropologist* New Series 63(5): 1,088–90.

Devlet, Ekaterina. 2001. "Rock Art and the Material Culture of Siberian and Central Asian Shamanism." In: *The Archaeology of Shamanism.* Ed. Neil Price. London and New York: Routledge. 43–55.

DeVos, George A. (ed.) 1976. *Responses to Change.* New York: Van Nostrand.

Dick, Lyle. 1995. "Pibloktoq (Arctic Hysteria): A Construction of European-Inuit Relations?" *Arctic Anthropology* 32(2): 1–42.

Diószegi, Vilmos. 1968. *Tracing Shamans in Siberia: The Story of an Ethnographical Research Expedition.* Oosterhout, Netherlands: Anthropological Publications.

Dirks, N. B. 1994. *The Hollow Crown*. Ann Arbor, MI: University of Michigan Press.

Dow, James. 1986. "Universal Aspects of Symbolic Healing: A Theoretical Synthesis." *American Anthropologist* New Series 88(1): 56–69.

DuBois, Thomas A. 1999. *Nordic Religions in the Viking Age*. Philadelphia, PA: University of Pennsylvania Press.

2006. *Lyric, Meaning, and Audience in the Oral Tradition of Northern Europe*. South Bend, IN: The University of Notre Dame Press.

DuBois, Thomas D. 2005. *The Sacred Village: Social Change and Religious Life in Rural North China*. Honolulu, HI: University of Hawai'i Press.

During, Jean. 2006. "Du samā' soufi aux pratiques chamaniques: nature et valeur d'une expérience." *Cahiers de musiques traditionnelles* 19: 79–92.

Durkheim, Émile. 1915. *The Elementary Forms of the Religious Life*. New York: The Free Press.

Edda. 1987. *Snorri Sturluson. Edda*. Anthony Faulkes, trans. and ed. London: Everyman.

Eggan, Dorothy. 1955. "The Personal Use of Myth in Dreams." In: *Myth: A Symposium*. Ed. Thomas A. Sebeok. Bloomington, IN: Indiana University Press. 107–21.

Ekstrom, A., M. Kahana, J. Caplan, T. Fields, E. Isham, E. Newman, I. Fried. 2003. "Cellular Networks Underlying Human Spatial Navigation." *Nature* 425: 184–8.

Eliade, Mircea. 1964. *Shamanism: Archaic Techniques of Ecstasy*. Willard R. Trask, trans. Princeton: Princeton University Press.

Elwin, Verrier. 1955. *The Religion of an Indian Tribe*. London and New York: Oxford University Press.

Erowid. 2007. *The Vaults of Erowid*. www.erowid.org/, accessed September 27, 2007.

Evans-Pritchard, E. E. 1940. *The Nuer: A Description of the Modes of Livelihood and Political Institutions of a Nilotic People*. Oxford: Clarendon Press.

Fedorova, Natalia. 2001. "Shamans, Heroes and Ancestors in the Bronze Castings of Western Siberia." In: *The Archaeology of Shamanism*. Ed. Neil Price. London and New York: Routledge. 56–64.

Ferguson, Marilyn. 1989. *The Aquarian Conspiracy: Personal and Social Transformation in the 1980s*. London: Paladin Grafton Books.

Findeisen, Hans. 1934. "Zweitausend Kilometer auf Hundeschlitten durch die Jagdgebiete des Nordens." In: *Menschen in der Welt*. Berlin: Repr. *Arbeiten zur Ethnographie Sibiriens und Volkskunde Zentral-Europas*. Asian Folk and Social Life Monographs 51. Taipei: The Orient Cultural Service. 5–56.

1957. *Schamanentum dargestellt am Beispiel der Besessenheitspriester nordeurasiatischer Völker*. Zurich: Europa Verlag.

Fitzgerald, Timothy. 2000. *The Ideology of Religious Studies*. New York and Oxford: Oxford University Press.

Fitzhugh, William and Susan A. Kaplan (eds.) 1983. *Inua: Spirit World of the Bering Sea Eskimo*. Washington, D.C.: Smithsonian Institution Press.

Flaherty, Gloria. 1992. *Shamanism and the Eighteenth Century.* Princeton: Princeton University Press.

Flattery, D. V. and M. Schwartz. 1989. *Haoma and Harmaline: The Botanical Identity of the Indo-Iranian Sacred Hallucinogen "Soma" and Its Legacy in Religion, Language, and Middle Eastern Folklore.* Near Eastern Studies 21. Berkeley: University of California Press.

Flood, Gavin. 1996. *An Introduction to Hinduism.* Cambridge: Cambridge University Press.

Francfort, Henri-Paul. 2001. "Prehistoric Section: An Introduction." In: *The Concept of Shamanism: Uses and Abuses.* Eds. Henri-Paul Francfort and Roberte N. Hamayon. Budapest: Akadémiai Kiadó. 31–50.

Francfort, Henri-Paul and Roberte N. Hamayon (eds.) 2001. *The Concept of Shamanism: Uses and Abuses.* Budapest: Akadémiai Kiadó.

Frecska, Ede and Zsuzsanna Kulcsar. 1989. "Social Bonding in the Modulation of the Physiology of Ritual Trance." *Ethos* 17(1): 70–87.

Gaup, Ailo. 2005. *Sjamansonen.* Oslo: Tre bjørner forlag.

Geertz, Clifford. [1965] 1979. "Religion as a Cultural System." In: *Anthropological Approaches to the Study of Religion.* Ed. Michael Banton. London: Tavistock Publications. Repr. in *Reader in Comparative Religion: An Anthropological Approach.* Eds. William A. Lessa and Evon Z. Vogt. New York: Harper & Row. 78–92.

Ginzburg, Carlo. [1966] 1983. *The Night Battles: Witchcraft and Agrarian Cults in the Sixteenth and Seventeenth Centuries.* Baltimore: The Johns Hopkins University Press.

Glavatskaya, Elena. 2001. "The Russian State and Shamanhood: The Brief History of Confrontation." In: *Shamanhood, Symbolism and Epic.* Eds. Juha Pentikäinen, Hanna Saressalo, and Chuner M. Taksami. Budapest: Akadémiai Kiadó. 237–48.

Gold, Daniel. 2003. *Aesthetics and Analysis in Writing on Religion: Modern Fascinations.* Berkeley: University of California Press.

Gračeva, Galina N. 1989. "Nganasan and Enets Shamans' Wooden Masks." In: *Shamanism Past and Present.* Eds. Mihály Hoppál and Otto von Sadovszky. Budapest: ISTOR. 145–53.

Greene, Francis. 1992. "Report from Tuva – April 1992." *Friends of Tuva Newsletter* 4 (Summer 1992), www.fotuva.org/newsletters/fot4.html, accessed February, 2008.

Grob, Charles S. 1999. "The Psychology of Ayahuasca." In: *Ayahuasca: Human Consciousness and the Spirits of Nature.* Ed. Ralph Metzner. New York: Thunder's Mouth Press. 214–49.

Grusman, Vladimir, Alexei Konovalov, and Valentina Gorbacheva. 2006. *Between Worlds: Shamanism and the Peoples of Siberia.* Moscow: Khudozhnik i Kniga.

Haavio, Martti. [1952] 1991. *Väinämöinen, Eternal Sage.* FF Communications no. 144. Helsinki: Suomalainen Tiedeakatemia.

Hahn, Man-young. 1990. *Kugak: Studies in Korean Traditional Music.* Inok Paek and Keith Howard, trans. and eds. Seoul: Tamgu Dang.

Hamayon, Roberte N. 1982. "Des chamanes au chamanisme." *L'Ethnographie* 88 (87–8): 13–48.

1993. "Are 'Trance,' 'Ecstasy' and Similar Concepts Appropriate in the Study of Shamanism?" *Shaman* 1(2): 3–25.

2001. "Shamanism: Symbolic System, Human Capability and Western Ideology." In: *The Concept of Shamanism: Uses and Abuses*. Eds. Henri-Paul Francfort and Roberte N. Hamayon. Budapest: Akadémiai Kiadó. 1–30.

Harner, Michael. 1972. *The Jívaro: People of the Sacred Waterfalls*. Berkeley: University of California Press.

(ed.) 1973. *Hallucinogens and Shamanism*. New York: Oxford University Press.

[1980] 1990. *The Way of the Shaman*. San Francisco: HarperSanFrancisco.

2008. "The Foundation for Shamanic Studies." www.shamanism.org, accessed February, 2008.

Harris, Amanda. 2001. "Presence, Efficacy and Politics in Healing among the Iban of Sarawak." In: *Healing Powers and Modernity: Traditional Medicine, Shamanism, and Science in Asian Societies*. Eds. Linda H. Connor and Geoffrey Samuel. Westport, CT: Bergin and Garvey. 130–51.

Harva, Uno. 1927. *Finno-Ugric, Siberian [Mythology]*. Mythology of All Races. Boston, MA: Archaeological Institute of America, Marshall Jones Company.

Harvey, Graham (ed.) 2000. *Indigenous Religions: A Companion*. London and New York: Cassell.

Heinze, Ruth-Inge. 1988. *Trance and Healing in Southeast Asia Today*. Bangkok: White Lotus Co.; Berkeley: Independent Scholars of Asia Inc.

Her, Vincent K. 2005. "Hmong Cosmology: Proposed Model, Preliminary Insights." *Hmong Studies Journal* 6: 1–25.

Hittman, Michael. 1990. *Wovoca and the Ghost Dance*. Yerington, NV: The Yerington Paiute Tribe.

Hollimon, Sandra E. 2001. "The Gendered Peopling of North America: Addressing the Antiquity of Systems of Multiple Genders." In: *The Archaeology of Shamanism*. Ed. Neil Price. London and New York: Routledge. 123–45.

Hoppál, Mihály. 1989. "Changing Image of the Eurasian Shamans." In: *Shamanism Past and Present*. Eds. Mihály Hoppál and Otto von Sadovszky. Budapest: ISTOR. 74–89.

1997. "Tracing Shamanism in Tuva: A History of Studies." In: *Shamanic Songs and Myths of Tuva*. Mongush B. Kenin-Lopsan. Budapest: ISTOR. 123–40.

Hoppál, Mihály and Juha Pentikäinen (eds.) 1992. *Northern Religions and Shamanism*. Budapest: Akadémiai Kiadó.

Hoppál, Mihály and Otto von Sadovszky (eds.) 1989. *Shamanism Past and Present*. Budapest: ISTOR.

Huhm, Halla Pai. 1980. *Kut: Korean Shamanist Rituals*. Seoul and Elizabeth, NJ: Hollym International.

Hultkrantz, Åke. 1953. *Concepts of the Soul among North American Indians: A Study in Religious Ethnology*. Stockholm: Ethnographical Museum of Sweden.

1979. *The Religions of the American Indians*. Berkeley: University of California Press.

1989. "The Place of Shamanism in the History of Religions." In: *Shamanism Past and Present*. Eds. Mihály Hoppál and Otto von Sadovszky. Budapest: ISTOR. 43–52.

1991. "The Drum in Shamanism: Some Reflections." In: *The Saami Shaman Drum*. Eds. Tore Ahlbäck and Jan Bergman. Stockholm: Almqvist & Wiksell International. 9–27.

1998. "On the History of Research in Shamanism." In: *Shamans*. Eds. Juha Pentikäinen, Toimi Jaatinen, Ildikó Lehtinen, and Marjo-Riitta Saloniemi. Tampere Museums' Publications 45. Tampere: Tampere Museums. 50–8.

2001. "Shamanism: Some Recent Findings from a Comparative Perspective." In: *Shamanhood, Symbolism and Epic*. Eds. Juha Pentikäinen, Hanna Saressalo, and Chuner M. Taksami. Budapest: Akadémiai Kiadó. 1–10.

Humphrey, Caroline. 1994. "Shamanic Practices and the State in Northern Asia: Views from the Center and Periphery." In: *Shamanism, History, & the State*. Eds. Nicholas Thomas and Caroline Humphrey. Ann Arbor: University of Michigan Press. 191–228.

Humphrey, Caroline and Urgunge Onon (eds.) 1996. *Shamans and Elders: Experience, Knowledge, and Power among the Daur Mongols*. Oxford: Clarendon Press.

Hunt, Norman Bancroft. 2002. *Shamanism in North America*. Toronto: Key Porter Books.

Hutton, Ronald. 2001. *Shamans: Siberian Spirituality and the Western Imagination*. London and New York: Hambledon and London.

Iliff, Barbara. 1994. "Spirits Like the Sound of the Rattle and Drum: George Thornton Emmons' Collection of Tlingit Shamans' Kits." Seattle: Unpub. Ph.D. dissertation, University of Washington.

1997. "Tlingit Shamans' Art." *Northwest Folklore* 12(1): 35–63.

Ingerman, Sandra. 1991. *Soul Retrieval: Mending the Fragmented Self*. San Francisco: HarperSanFrancisco.

1993. *Welcome Home: Life After Healing: Following Your Soul's Journey Home*. San Francisco: HarperSanFrancisco.

Jacobs, Sue Ellen, William Thomas, and Susan Lang (eds.) 1997. *Two-Spirit People: Native American Gender Identity, Sexuality, and Spirituality*. Urbana, IL: University of Illinois Press.

Jakobsen, Merete Demant. 1999. *Shamanism: Traditional and Contemporary Approaches to the Mastery of Spirits and Healing*. New York and Oxford: Berghahn Books.

Jankovics, M. 1984. "Cosmic Models and Siberian Shaman Drums." In: *Shamanism in Eurasia I*. Ed. Mihály Hoppál. Göttingen: Herodot. 150–65.

Jenkins, Philip. 2005. *Dream Catchers: How Mainstream America Discovered Native Spirituality*. New York: Oxford University Press.

Jensen, Tim and Mikael Rothstein (eds.) 2000. *Secular Theories on Religion: Current Perspectives*. Copenhagen: Museum Tusculanum Press.

Jochelson, Waldemar. 1908. *The Koryak*. Publications of the Jesup North Pacific Expedition vol. 6. New York: G. E. Stechert.

Johansen, Ulla. 2001. "Shamanism and Neoshamanism: What is the Difference?" In: *The Concept of Shamanism: Uses and Abuses*. Eds. Henri-Paul Francfort and Roberte N. Hamayon. Budapest: Akadémiai Kiadó. 297–303.

Jolly, Karen, Catharina Raudvere, and Edward Peters. 2002. *Witchcraft and Magic in Europe: The Middle Ages*. Eds. Bengt Ankarloo and Stuart Clark. Philadelphia: University of Pennsylvania Press.

Jourdain, Robert. 1997. *Music, the Brain, and Ecstasy*. New York: Avon Books.

Kan, Sergei. 1991. "Shamanism and Christianity: Modern-Day Tlingit Elders Look at the Past." *Ethnohistory* 38(4): 363–87.

Karim, Anwarul. 2003. "Shamanism in Bangladesh." In: *Shamans in Asia*. Eds. Clark Chilson and Peter Knecht. London and New York: Routledge Curzon. 51–85.

Kehoe, Alice. 2000. *Shamans and Religion: An Anthropological Exploration in Critical Thinking*. Prospect Heights, IL: Waveland Press.

Kendall, Laurel. 1995. "Initiating Performance: The Story of Chini, a Korean Shaman." In: *The Performance of Healing*. Eds. Carol Laderman and Marina Roseman. New York: Routledge. 17–58.

    2001. "The Cultural Politics of 'Superstition' in the Korean Shaman World: Modernity Constructs Its Other." In: *Healing Powers and Modernity: Traditional Medicine, Shamanism, and Science in Asian Societies*. Eds. Linda H. Connor and Geoffrey Samuel. Westport, CT: Bergin and Garvey. 25–41.

Kenin-Lopsan, Mongush B. 1987. *Obriadobaia praktika i fol'klor tuvinskogo shamanstva, kon'ets XIX – nachalo XX s*. Novosibirsk: Izdaltel'stvo <<Nauka>> Sibirskoe otdelenie.

    1997. *Shamanic Songs and Myths of Tuva*. Selected and edited by Mihály Hoppál with the assistance of Christiana Buckbee. Budapest: ISTOR.

Kensinger, Kenneth M. 1973. "*Banisteriopsis* Usage Among the Peruvian Cashinahua." In: *Hallucinogens and Shamanism*. Ed. Michael Harner. New York: Oxford University Press. 9–14.

Kippenberg, Hans G. 2002. *Discovering Religious History in the Modern Age*. Princeton: Princeton University Press.

Kirsch, A. Thomas. 1973. *Feasting and Social Oscillation: A Working Paper on Religion and Society in Upland Southeast Asia*. Cornell University Southeast Asia Data Paper no. 92. Ithaca, NY: Cornell University Southeast Asia Program.

Kors, Alan C. and Edward Peters (eds.) 1986. *Witchcraft in Europe 1100–1700: A Documentary History*. Philadelphia: University of Pennsylvania Press.

Kugel, Rebecca. 1994. "Of Missionaries and Their Cattle: Ojibwa Perceptions of a Missionary as Evil Shaman." *Ethnohistory* 41(2): 227–44.

Kuusi, Matti, Keith Bosley and Michael Branch. 1977. *Finnish Folk Poetry: Epic*. Helsinki: Finnish Literature Society.

Kvideland, Reimund and Henning K. Sehmsdorf (eds.) 1988. *Scandinavian Folk Belief and Legend*. Minneapolis, MN: University of Minnesota Press.

La Barre, Weston. 1964. *The Peyote Cult*. New York: Schocken Books.

    1989. *The Peyote Cult*. Norman, OK: University of Oklahoma Press.

Laderman, Carol. 1995. "The Poetics of Healing in Malay Shamanistic Performances." In: *The Performance of Healing*. Eds. Carol Laderman and Marina Roseman. New York: Routledge. 115–42.

    2001. "Tradition and Change in Malay Healing." In: *Healing Powers and Modernity: Traditional Medicine, Shamanism, and Science in Asian Societies*. Eds. Linda H. Connor and Geoffrey Samuel. Westport, CT: Bergin and Garvey. 42–63.

Laderman, Carol and Marina Roseman (eds.) 1995. *The Performance of Healing*. New York: Routledge.

La Hontan, Louis Armand, baron de. [1703] 1905. *New Voyages to North-America: Giving a Full Account of the Customs, Commerce, Religion and Strange Opinions of that Country. With Political Remarks upon the Courts of Portugal and Denmark and the Present State of the Commerce of these Countries*. Reuben Gold Thwaites, trans. 2 vols. Repr. Chicago: A. C. McClurg & Co.

Landy, D. 1985. "Pibloktoq (Hysteria) and Inuit Nutrition: Possible Implication of Hypervitaminosis A." *Social Science Medicine* 12(2): 173–85.

Lang, Sabine. 1998. *Men as Women, Women as Men: Changing Gender in Native American Cultures*. Austin, TX: University of Texas Press.

Lardinois, Olivier SJ. 2007. "Theological and Pastoral Reflections on the Practice of Shamanism Still Found in the Catholic Indigenous Communities of Taiwan." *eRenlai Magazine*. Online journal article, www.erenlai.com/index. php?aid=763&Jan=3, accessed July 14, 2007.

Lecomte, Henri. 2006. "Approches authochtones du chamanisme sibérien au début de XXe siècle." *Cahiers de musiques traditionnelles* 19: 37–52.

Lee, Yong-Shik. 2004. *Shaman Ritual Music in Korea*. Korean Studies Dissertation Series no. 5. Edison, NJ and Seoul: Jimoondang International.

Leete, Art. 1999. "Ways of Describing Nenets and Khanty 'Character' in Nineteenth Century Russian Ethnographic Literature." *Folklore* 12. Online journal article, www.folklore.ee/folklore/vol12/charactr.htm, accessed January 1, 2007.

Leighton, Ralph. 1991. "What Ever Happened to Tannu Tuva?" *Friends of Tuva Newsletter* 1 (May 1991), www.fotuva.org/newsletters/fot1.html, accessed February, 2008.

    1993. "Shamanic Conference in Kyzyl." *Friends of Tuva Newsletter* 7 (Summer 1993), www.fotuva.org/newsletters/fot7.html, accessed February, 2008.

Lévi-Strauss, Claude. 1963. *Structural Anthropology*. New York: Anchor Books.

Levitin, Daniel J. 2006. *This Is Your Brain on Music: The Science of a Human Obsession*. New York: Plume (Penguin Group).

Lewis, I. M. 1971. *Ecstatic Religion: An Anthropological Study of Spirit Possession and Shamanism*. Harmondsworth: Penguin Books.

Lewis-Williams, J. David. 2001. "Southern African Shamanistic Rock Art in its Social and Cognitive Contexts." In: *The Archaeology of Shamanism*. Ed. Neil Price. New York and London: Routledge. 17–42.

    2002. *A Cosmos in Stone: Interpreting Religion and Society through Rock Art*. Walnut Creek, Lanham, New York, Oxford: AltaMira Press.

Li, Lisha. 1992. "The Symbolization Process of the Shamanic Drums Used by the Manchus and Other Peoples in North Asia." *Yearbook for Traditional Music* 24: 52–80.

Lincoff, Gary. 2005. "Is the Fly-Agaric (*Amanita muscaria*) an Effective Medicinal Mushroom?" Paper delivered at the Third International Medicinal Mushroom Conference, held at Port Townsend, Washington, October 2005 (www.nemf.org/files/various/muscaria/fly_agaric_text.html, accessed November 1, 2007.

Lindsay, A. D. (trans.) 1977. *Plato. The Republic.* New York: Everyman's Library.

Lommel, Andreas. 1967. *Shamanism: The Beginnings of Art.* New York: McGraw-Hill.

Lönnrot, Elias. [1849] 1963. *The Kalevala or Poems of the Kaleva District.* Francis Peabody Magoun, trans. Cambridge, MA: Harvard University Press.

Lowie, R. H. 1934. *An Introduction to Cultural Anthropology.* London: George G. Harrap.

Luckert, Karl W. 1984. "Coyote in Navajo and Hopi Tales." In: *Navajo Coyote Tales: The Curly Tó Aheedlíinii Version.* Ed. Father Berard Haile, OFM. Lincoln, NE and London: University of Nebraska Press. 3–19.

Maenchen-Helfen, J. Otto. 1973. *The World of the Huns: Studies in their History and Culture.* Berkeley: University of California Press.

Malotki, Ekkehart and Ken Gary. 2001. *Hopi Stories of Witchcraft, Shamanism, and Magic.* Lincoln: University of Nebraska Press.

Manker, Ernst. 1938. *Die lappische Zaubertrommel: Eine ethnologische Monographie I.* Acta Lapponica I. Stockholm: Thule.

     1950. *Die lappische Zaubertrommel: Eine ethnologische Monographie II.* Acta Lapponica IV. Stockholm: Gebers.

Marett, Robert Ranulph. 1909. *The Threshold of Religion.* London: Methuen & Co.

Maskarinec, Gregory C. 1995. *The Rulings of the Night: An Ethnography of Nepalese Shaman Oral Texts.* Madison: University of Wisconsin Press.

McKinney, Lawrence O. 1994. *Neurotheology: Virtual Religion in the 21st Century.* Cambridge, MA: American Institute for Mindfulness.

Mebius, Hans. 2003. *Bissie: Studier i samisk religionshistoria.* Östersund: Förlaget för Jemtlandica.

Meštrović, Stjepan. 1997. *Postemotional Society.* London: Sage.

Metzner, Ralph (ed.) 1999. *Ayahuasca: Human Consciousness and the Spirits of Nature.* New York: Thunder's Mouth Press.

Meuli, Karl. 1935. "Scythica." *Hermes* 70: 121–76.

Mikkanen, Arvo Quoetone. 1987. "The Kiowa Sun Dance," http://rebelcherokee. labdiva.com/Kiowasundance.html, accessed January 24, 2007.

Miller, Thomas R. 1999. "Mannequins and Spirits: Representation and Resistance of Siberian Shamans." *Anthropology of Consciousness* 10(4): 69–80.

Mills, Antonia and Richard Slobodin. 1994. *Amerindian Rebirth: Reincarnation Belief among North American Indians and Inuit.* Toronto: University of Toronto Press.

Momaday, N. Scott. 1969. *The Way to Rainy Mountain.* Albuquerque, NM: University of New Mexico Press.

Mottin, Jean. 1983. "A Hmong Shaman's Séance." *Asian Folklore Studies* 43(1): 99–108.

Naoko, Takiguchi. 2003. "Miyako Theology: Shamans' Interpretations of Traditional Beliefs." In: *Shamans in Asia*. Eds. Clark Chilson and Peter Knecht. New York: Routledge Curzon. 120–52.

Newberg, Andrew, Eugene D'Aquili, and Vince Rause. 2001. *Why God Won't Go Away: Brain Science and the Biology of Belief.* New York: Ballantine.

Nicoletti, Martino. 2004. *Shamanic Solitudes: Ecstasy, Madness and Spirit Possession in the Nepal Himalayas.* Kathmandu: Vajra Publications.

Nioradze, Georg. 1925. *Der Schamanismus bei den sibirischen Völkern.* Stuttgart: Strecker und Schröder.

Noll, Richard. 1983. "Shamanism and Schizophrenia: A State-Specific Approach to the 'Schizophrenia Metaphor' of Shamanic States." *American Ethnologist* 10 (3): 443–69.

——— 1985. "Mental Imagery Cultivation as a Cultural Phenomenon: The Role of Visions in Shamanism." *Current Anthropology* 26(4): 443–61.

Obeyesekere, Gananath. 2002. *Imagining Karma: Ethical Transformation in Amerindian, Buddhist, and Greek Rebirth.* Berkeley: University of California Press.

O'Brien, David. 2004. *Animal Sacrifice and Religious Freedom: Church of the Lukumi Babalu Aye v. City of Hialeah.* Lawrence: University Press of Kansas.

Ohlmarks, Åke. 1939. *Studien zum Problem des Schamanismus.* Lund: C. W. K. Gleerup.

O'Keefe, J. and J. Dostrovsky. 1971. "The Hippocampus as a Spatial Map: Preliminary Evidence from Unit Activity in the Freely-moving Rat." *Brain Research* 34: 171–5.

O'Keefe, J. and Lynn Nadel. 1978. *The Hippocampus as a Cognitive Map.* New York: Oxford University Press.

O'Neil, Maryadele *et al.* 2006. *The Merck Index: An Encyclopedia of Chemicals, Drugs, and Biologicals.* 14th edition. Rathway, NJ: Merck and Co.

Ortner, Sherry B. 1995. "The Case of the Disappearing Shamans, or No Individualism, No Relationism." *Ethos* 23(3): 355–90.

Ott, Jonathan. 1993. *Pharmacotheon: Entheogenic Drugs, their Plant Sources and History.* Kennewick, WA: Natural Products Co.

Otto, Rudolf. 1950. *The Idea of the Holy: An Inquiry into the Non-Rational Factor in the Idea of the Divine and Its Relation to the Rational.* New York: Oxford University Press.

Paulson, Ivar. 1964. "Zur Phänomenologie des Schamanismus." *Zeitschrift Religions- und Geistesgeschichte* 16: 121–41.

Pearson, James L. 2002. *Shamanism and the Ancient Mind: A Cognitive Approach to Archaeology.* Walnut Creek, CA: AltaMira Press.

Pentikäinen, Juha. 1989. *Kalevala Mythology.* Ritva Poom, trans. Bloomington: Indiana University Press.

——— 1995. *Saamelaiset – Pohjoisen kansan mytologia.* Helsinki: Suomalaisen Kirjallisuuden Seura.

Pentikäinen, Juha, Toimi Jaatinen, Ildikó Lehtinen, and Marjo-Riitta Saloniemi (eds.) 1998. *Shamans*. Tampere Museums' Publications 45. Tampere: Tampere Museums.

Pentikäinen, Juha, Hanna Saressalo, and Chuner M. Taksami (eds.) 2001. *Shamanhood, Symbolism and Epic*. Budapest: Akadémiai Kiadó.

Persinger, Michael B. 1987. *Neuropsychology Bases of God Beliefs*. New York: Praeger Publishers.

Peters, Edward. 1978. *The Magician, the Witch and the Law*. Philadelphia: University of Pennsylvania Press.

Peters, Larry G. 2004. *Trance, Initiation & Psychotherapy in Nepalese Shamanism: Essays on Tamang and Tibetan Shamanism*. Delhi: Nirala Publications.

Pigg, Stacey. 1996. "The Credible and the Credulous: The Question of 'Villagers' Beliefs' in Nepal." *Cultural Anthropology* 11(2): 160–201.

Pohjanpalo, Virve. 2007. "Ancient Rituals and Closed Cities." *Universitas Helsingiensis* 4/2007: 30–2.

Potapov, Leonid P. 1999. "Shaman's Drum: A Unique Monument of Spiritual Culture of the Altai Turk Peoples." *Anthropology of Consciousness* 10(4): 24–35.

Price, Neil (ed.) 2001. *The Archaeology of Shamanism*. London and New York: Routledge.

2002. *The Viking Way: Religion and War in Late Iron Age Scandinavia*. Uppsala: Uppsala University Press.

Prince, Raymond and Françoise Tcheng-Laroche. 1987. "Culture-Bound Syndromes and International Disease Classifications." *Culture, Medicine and Psychiatry* 11 (1): 3–52.

Purev, Otgony, and Gurbadaryrn Purvee. 2004. *Mongolian Shamanism*. 3rd edition. Ulaanbator: Admon Publishing.

Qvigstad, Just (ed.) 1927. *Lappiske eventyr og sagn*. 4 vols. Oslo: H. Aschehoug & Co.

Radin, Paul (ed.) 1926. *Crashing Thunder: The Autobiography of an American Indian*. New York and London: D. Appleton and Company.

Ramachandran, V. S. and Sandra Blakeslee. 1998. *Phantoms in the Brain*. New York: Quill.

Rasmussen, Knud. 1921. *Eskimo Folk-Tales*. London: Gyldenhal.

Rätsch, Christian. 2005. *The Encyclopedia of Psychoactive Plants: Ethnopharmacology and Its Applications*. Rochester, VT: Park Street Books.

Reid, Anna. 2002. *The Shaman's Coat: A Native History of Siberia*. New York: Walker & Company.

Riboli, Diana. 2000. *Tunsuriban: Shamanism in the Chepang of Southern and Central Nepal*. Kathmandu: Mandala Book Point.

Ridington, Robin. 1988. *Trail to Heaven: Knowledge and Narrative in a Northern Native Community*. Iowa City, IA: University of Iowa Press.

1997. "All the Old Spirits Have Come Back to Greet Him: Realizing the Sacred Pole of the Omaha Tribe." In: *Present is Past: Some Uses of Tradition in Native Societies*. Ed. Marie Mauzé. Lanham, MD: University Press of America. 159–74.

Ridington, Robin and Dennis Hastings (In'aska). 1997. *Blessing for a Long Time: The Sacred Pole of the Omaha Tribe.* Lincoln: University of Nebraska Press.

Roscoe, Will. 1998. *Changing Ones: Third and Fourth Gender in Native America.* New York: St. Martin's Press.

Roseman, Marina. 1991. *Healing Sounds from the Malaysian Rainforest: Temiar Music and Medicine.* Los Angeles: University of California Press.

1995. *Dream Songs and Healing Sounds: In the Rainforests of Malaysia.* Washington, D.C.: Smithsonian/Folkways Recordings. SF CD 40417. CD plus descriptive notes.

2001. "Engaging the Spirits of Modernity: The Temiars." In: *Healing Powers and Modernity: Traditional Medicine, Shamanism, and Science in Asian Societies.* Eds. Linda H. Connor and Geoffrey Samuel. Westport, CT: Bergin and Garvey. 109–29.

Rouget, Gilbert. 1980. *La musique et la transe: esquisse d'une théorie générale des relations de la musique et de la possession.* Paris: Éditions Gallimard.

Rozwadowski, Andrzej. 2001. "Sun Gods or Shamans? Interpreting the Solar-Headed Petroglyphs of Western Siberia." In: *The Archaeology of Shamanism.* Ed. Neil Price. London and New York: Routledge. 65–86.

Rydving, Håkon. 1995. *The End of Drum-Time: Religious Change among the Lule Saami, 1670s–1740s.* Acta Universitatis Upsaliensis. Historia Religionum 12. Uppsala: Almqvist & Wiksell International.

Sagard, Gabriel. [1632] 1939. *The Long Journey to the Country of the Hurons.* Ed. George M. Wrong. Toronto: The Champlain Society.

Salak, Kira. 2006. "Hell and Back." *National Geographic Adventure* (March 2006): 54–8, 88–92.

Sasamori, Takefusa. 1997. "Therapeutic Rituals Performed by *Itako* (Japanese Blind Female Shamans)." *The World of Music* 39(2): 85–96.

Schaefer, Stacy B. 1996. "The Crossing of the Souls: Peyote, Perception, and Meaning among the Huichol Indians." In: *People of the Peyote: Huichol Indian History, Religion, and Survival.* Eds. Stacy B. Schaefer and Peter T. Furst. Albuquerque: University of New Mexico Press. 136–68.

Scheff, T. J. 1979. *Catharsis in Healing, Ritual, and Drama.* Berkeley: University of California Press.

Schefferus, Johannes. [Johan Scheffer] 1673. *Lapponia, id est regionis Lapponum et gentis nova et verissima descriptio, in qua multa de origine, superstitione, sacris magicis, victu, cultu, negotiis Lapponum, item animalium, metallorumque indole, quae in terris eorum proveniunt, hactenus incognita produntur, & eiconibus adjectis cum cura illustrantur.* Francofurti: Typis J. Andreae, ex officina C. Wolffii.

Schieffelin, Edward. 1995. "On Failure and Performance: Throwing the Medium Out of the Séance." In: *The Performance of Healing.* Eds. Carol Laderman and Marina Roseman. New York: Routledge. 59–89.

Schultes, Richard Evans, Albert Hofmann, and Christian Rätsch. 2001. *Plants of the Gods: Their Sacred, Healing and Hallucinogenic Powers.* Rochester, VT: Healing Arts Press.

Schwartz, Theodore. 1976. "The Cargo Cult: A Melanesian Type-Response to Change." In: *Responses to Change*. Ed. George A. DeVos. New York: Van Nostrand. 157–206.

Sethna, Tehmurasp Rustamjee. 1977. *Yasna, Excluding the Gathas, Visparad, Blessings, Afringans, Afrins*. Karachi: Ma'aref Printers.

Shanon, Benny. 2002. *The Antipodes of the Mind: Charting the Phenomenology of the Ayahuasca Experience*. Oxford: Oxford University Press.

Shirokogoroff, S. M. 1935. *The Psychomental Complex of the Tungus*. London: Kegan Paul, Trench, Trubner and Co.

Shternberg, Lev. 1925. "Divine Election in Primitive Religion." Congrès International des Américanistes, compte-rendu de la XXIe session, pt. 2. Göteborg. 472–512.

————— 1999. *The Social Organization of the Gilyak*. Anthropological Papers of the American Museum of Natural History no. 82. New York: American Museum of Natural History, distributed Seattle: University of Washington Press.

Siikala, Anna-Leena. 1978. *The Rite Technique of the Siberian Shaman*. Helsinki: Suomalainen Tiedeakatemia.

————— 2002. *Mythic Images and Shamanism: A Perspective on Kalevala Poetry*. Helsinki: Suomalainen Tiedeakatemia.

Simons, Ronald C. and Charles C. Hughes. 1985. *The Culture-Bound Syndrome: Folk Illnesses of Psychiatric and Anthropological Interest*. Boston: G. Reidel.

Singer, Philip. 1990. "'Psychic Surgery': Close Observation of a Popular Healing Practice." *Medical Anthropology Quarterly* 4(4): 443–51.

Slotkin, James S. 1956. *The Peyote Religion: A Study in Indian–White Relations*. Glencoe, IL: The Free Press.

Smart, Ninian. 1973. *The Science of Religion and the Sociology of Knowledge*. Princeton: Princeton University Press.

Smith, Andy. 1993. "For All Those Who Were Indian in a Former Life." In: *Ecofeminism and the Sacred*. Ed. C. Adams. New York: Continuum. 168–71.

Smyers, Karen A. 1999. *The Fox and the Jewel: Shared and Private Meanings in Contemporary Japanese Inari Worship*. Honolulu: University of Hawai'i Press.

Sommarström, Bo. 1991. "The Saami Shaman's Drum and the Star Horizons." In: *The Saami Shaman Drum*. Eds. Tore Ahlbäck and Jan Bergman. Stockholm: Almqvist & Wiksell International. 136–68.

Souther, Hamilton. 2003. "Tourism: Bridging the Gap Between the Mystical and the Western Worlds." *Blue Morpho Center for Shamanic Studies and Workshops*, www.bluemorphotours.com/testimonial.asp, accessed December 16, 2007.

Steinberg, Michael K., Joseph J. Hobbs, and Kent Mathewson (eds.) 2004. *Dangerous Harvest: Drug Plants and the Transformation of Indigenous Landscapes*. Oxford: Oxford University Press.

Strömbäck, Dag. 1935. *Sejd: Textstudier i nordisk religionshistoria*. Stockholm: Hugo Gebers Förlag.

Sullivan, Robert. 2002. *A Whale Hunt: How a Native American Village Did What No One Thought It Could*. New York: Scribner.

Svanberg, Jan. 2003. *Schamantropologi i gränslandet mellan forskning och praktik. En studie av förhållandet mellan schamanism-forskning och neoschamanism.* Turku: Åbo Akademis förlag.

Tangherlini, Timothy. 1998. "Shamans, Students, and the State." In: *Nationalism and the Construction of Korean Identity.* Eds. Hyung Il Pai and Timothy R. Tangherlini. Korea Research Monograph 26. Berkeley: Institute of East Asian Studies. 126–47.

Tapp, Nicholas. 1989. "Hmong Religion." *Asian Folklore Studies* 48(1): 59–94.

Tedlock, Barbara. 2001. "Divination as a Way of Knowing: Embodiment, Visualisation, Narrative, and Interpretation." *Folklore* 112: 189–97.

  2004. *The Woman in the Shaman's Body: Reclaiming the Feminine in Religion and Medicine.* New York: Bantam Books.

Terry, Patricia (ed. and trans.) 1990. *Poems of the Elder Edda.* Revised edition. Philadelphia: University of Pennsylvania Press.

Thomas, Nicholas and Caroline Humphey (eds.) 1994. *Shamanism, History, & the State.* Ann Arbor: University of Michigan Press.

Tipton, Steven M. 1982. *Getting Saved from the Sixties: Moral Meaning in Conversion and Cultural Change.* Berkeley: University of California Press.

Tkacz, Virlana, Sayan Zhambalov, and Wanda Phipps. 2002. *Shanar: Dedication Ritual of a Buryat Shaman in Siberia as conducted by Bayir Rinchinov.* New York: Parabola Books.

Toelken, Barre. 2003. *The Anguish of Snails: Native American Folklore in the West.* Logan, UT: Utah State University Press.

Townsend, Joan B. 2005. "Individualist Religious Movements: Core and Neo-Shamanism." *Anthropology of Consciousness* 15(1): 1–9.

Tremlin, Todd. 2006. *Minds and Gods: The Cognitive Foundations of Religion.* New York: Oxford University Press.

Trevarthen, Geo Athena. 2007. *Celtic Shamanism.* www.celticshamanism.com, accessed December 16, 2007.

Turi, Johan. [1910] 1935. *Turi's Book of Lappland.* Emilie Demant Hatt, ed. E. G. Nash, trans. New York: Harper and Brothers.

Turi, Johan and Per Turi. 1918–19. "Noaide Tales." In: *Lappish Texts.* Copenhagen: Høst & Son. 133–49.

Tylor, Edward Burnett. 1871. *Primitive Culture.* New York: Holt.

Van Deusen, Kira. 1999. *Raven and the Rock: Storytelling in Chukotka.* Seattle and London: University of Washington Press; Edmonton: Canadian Circumpolar Institute Press.

  2004. *Singing Story, Healing Drum: Shamans and Storytellers of Turkic Siberia.* Montreal and Kingston: McGill-Queen's University Press.

Vitebsky, Piers. 1995. *The Shaman.* Boston: Little, Brown and Company.

  2000. "Shamanism." In: *Indigenous Religions: A Companion.* Ed. Graham Harvey. London and New York: Cassell. 55–68.

  2005. *The Reindeer People: Living with Animals and Spirits in Siberia.* Boston: Houghton Mifflin Company.

Von Gernet, Alexander. 2000. "North American Indigenous Nicotiana Use and Tobacco Shamanism: The Early Documentary Record, 1520–1660." In: *Tobacco Use by Native Americans: Sacred Smoke and Silent Killer.* Ed. Joseph C. Winter. Norman: University of Oklahoma Press. 59–80.

Wafer, Lionel. [1699] 1934. *A New Voyage and Description of the Isthmus of America.* Ed. L. E. Elliott Joyce. Oxford: The Hakluyt Society.

Wall of Shame. 2007. http://shameons.bravepages.com/, accessed December 16, 2007.

Wallace, Anthony F. C. 1956. "Revitalization Movements." *American Anthropologist* 58: 264–81. Repr. *Reader in Comparative Religion.* 4th Edition. Eds. William A. Lessa and Evon Z. Vogt. New York: Harper & Row. 421–9.

Wallis, Robert J. 2001. "Waking Ancestor Spirits: Neo-Shamanic Engagements with Archaeology." In: *The Archaeology of Shamanism.* Ed. Neil Price. London and New York: Routledge. 213–30.

    2003. *Shamans/Neo-Shamans: Ecstasy, Alternative Archaeologies and Contemporary Pagans.* London: Routledge.

Walraven, Boudewijn. 1994. *Songs of the Shaman: The Ritual Chants of the Korean Mudang.* London and New York: Kegan Paul International.

Walsh, Roger. 1997. "The Psychological Health of Shamans: A Reevaluation." *Journal of the American Academy of Religion* 65(1): 101–24.

Wasson, Gordon R. 1963. *Soma, the Divine Mushroom of Immortality.* Ethnomycological Studies 1. New York: Harcourt, Brace and World.

Waterfield, Robin (trans.) 1998. *Herodotus. The Histories.* Oxford: Oxford University Press.

Weiss, Gerald. 1973. "Shamanism and Priesthood in Light of the Campa *Ayahuasca* Ceremony." In: *Hallucinogens and Shamanism.* Ed. Michael Harner. New York: Oxford University Press. 40–8.

Westman, Anna and John E. Utsi. 1999. *Drum-Time: The Drums and Religion of the Sámi.* Luleå: Luleå Alltryck.

Westmeyer, Joseph. 2004. "Opium and the People of Laos." In: *Dangerous Harvest: Drug Plants and the Transformation of Indigenous Landscapes.* Eds. Michael K. Steinberg, Joseph J. Hobbs, and Kent Mathewson. Oxford: Oxford University Press. 115–32.

Whitehead, Neil. 2002. *Dark Shamans: Kanaimà and the Poetics of Violent Death.* Durham and London: Duke University Press.

Whitehead, Neil and Robin Wright (eds.) 2004. *In Darkness and Secrecy: The Anthropology of Assault Sorcery and Witchcraft in Amazonia.* Durham, NC and London: Duke University Press.

Whitehouse, Harvey. 2004. *Modes of Religiosity: A Cognitive Theory of Religious Transmission.* Lanham, MD: AltaMira Press.

Williams, Maria P. 1995. "The Wolf and the Man/Bear: Public and Personal Symbols in a Tlingit Drum." *Pacific Review of Ethnomusicology* 7: 79–92.

Winkelman, Michael. 1986. "Trance States: A Theoretical Model and Cross-Cultural Analysis." *Ethos* 14(2): 174–203.

1992. *Shamans, Priests and Witches: A Cross-Cultural Study of Magico-Religious Practitioners.* Arizona State University Anthropological Research Papers no. 44. Tempe, AZ: Arizona State University.

2000. *Shamanism: The Neural Ecology of Consciousness and Healing.* Westport, CT: Bergin and Garvey.

Winkelman, Michael and Philip M. Peek. 2004. *Divination and Healing: Potent Vision.* Tucson: University of Arizona Press.

Winkler, Gershon. 2003. *Magic of the Ordinary: Recovering the Shamanic in Judaism.* Berkeley: North Atlantic Books.

2008. Walking Stick Foundation, www.walkingstick.org/, accessed February, 2008.

Wintz, Gary. 1993. "Buddhism in Tuva." *Friends of Tuva Newsletter* 8 (Fall 1993), www.fotuva.org/newsletters/fot8.html, accessed February, 2008.

Wolf, Margery. 1990. "The Woman Who Didn't Become a Shaman." *American Ethnologist* 17(3): 419–30.

Wright, Peggy A. 1991. "Rhythmic Drumming in Contemporary Shamanism and Its Relationship to Auditory Driving and Risk of Seizure Precipitation in Epileptics." *Anthropology of Consciousness* 2(3–4): 7–14.

Index

abstinence, sexual 61, 64
Afghanistan, cultures of 27
Africa, cultures of: Nuer culture 9; San culture 31–2
afterlife. *See* dead
age, as factor in shamanic calling 66–8; adolescence 59, 64, 67
aggression, shamanic 13, 84, 94–9, 103, 112, 141, 144, 149, 161, 213–15, 232, 235–6, 268, 287
alcohol 112, 140, 170–1, 172, 175, 196, 207, 216, 231, 234, 237, 254, 256, 280
altered state of consciousness. *See* trance states
Amanita muscaria (Fly Agaric) 23, 27–8, 162–4
animals, as element of shamanic traditions 16, 28, 30, 43, 72, 95, 111, 140, 180, 190, 191, 195, 199, 245, 285; transformation into 13, 28, 34, 165, 182, 186, 188, 210, 211, 213, 215; particular species: bear 33, bird 46, 49, 62, 149, 177, 182, 192, cattle 73, 235, dog 73, 97, 101, 210–11, feline 28, fish 99, 112, 213, fox 241, 260, frog/toad 64, 287, goat 16, horse 31, 45, 73, 194, 195, 196, 251, 254, insect/scorpion 49, 99, lizard 49, otter 182, pig 46, ruminants (buffalo, deer, eland, elk, reindeer) 32, 60, 73, 111, 176, 177, 192, 235, snake 49, 99, 167–8, 177, 186, 187, 211, 260, walrus/seal 58, 96, whale 13, 262, wolf 60–1, 72
animism 46, 291
archetypes, Jungian 266–7
Armand, Louis, baron de la Hontan 21
Asian cultural area 184, 186, 224, 226–7, 231, 241. *See also* specific countries
assistants, of shaman 86, 88–9, 111, 112, 155–6
Avvakum, Russian Orthodox priest 19
awe 7, 8, 9, 11
Ayahuasca 165, 167, 169, 171, 173, 175, 264, 281–2, 285; component plants: *Banisteriopsis spp.* 167, 169, *Brugmansia spp.* 165, *Diploterys cabrerana* 167, 168, *Psychotria viridia* 167, 168

Bacchic revels 28, 30
Bangladesh, cultures of 231

birch (*Betula ermanii*) 164, 189
black shaman 84, 85
bones, in shamanic visions 64, 65, 66
Borneo, cultures of 137, 208
brain 55, 110, 113–15, 116, 117–20, 121–4, 146, 159–60, 161, 163, 168, 169, 171, 273; brain chemicals: Dopamine 160, 169, Monoamine oxidase 169, opioids 146, 160, 169, serotonin 169; memory: 66, 113, 121–4, 293
Brazil, cultures of 62, 94, 168, 173, 190, 267, 281
Buddhism 7, 85, 130–1, 157, 196, 206, 225, 227, 231, 233–4, 240–1, 251, 256, 260, 271; Lamaism 233, 240, 255, 258

call, refusal of 58, 61, 62, 63, 78
Campbell, Joseph 266–7
Canada, cultures of 18, 49, 70, 119, 158, 186, 187, 229, 232, 237, 280
cannabis 29, 164
cannibalism 95, 99, 245
Castaneda, Carlos 162, 266, 267–8, 269, 274
Catherine the Great, empress of Russia 22
Celtic culture 276, 288
Ch'oe Namsŏn 259
charisma, charismatic leader 250, 257
Chile, cultures of 80
China, cultures and scholarship of 14, 26, 30, 69, 130, 140, 177, 206, 224, 225–6, 231; Han culture 27, 250, Jurchen culture 225, 250–2, Manchu culture 91–2, 157–8, 177, 180, 224, 225–6, 250–2, 255, Ming dynasty 250, Qing dynasty 224, 225–6, 248, 250–2, Xiong-nu culture 26, 30, Yuan dynasty 14
Chinggis (Genghis) Khan 14, 130, 224–5, 226
Christianity 4–5, 6, 7, 8, 9, 12, 14, 15–18, 19, 23, 25, 31, 48, 49, 51, 85, 99, 112, 116, 167, 173, 208, 213, 222, 226, 227–30, 231, 232, 234–6, 237, 239, 261, 264, 274, 275, 280–2, 287, 288, 291; varieties of: Anglicanism 18, Barquinha 282, Catholicism 14, 18, 230, 232, 252, 280, 282, Church of Santo Daime 173, 281–2, Hmong Missionary Alliance

volition, as element in shamanic calling 24, 57–61, 62, 272–3

Wafer, Lionel 20
white shaman 84, 85
witchcraft 15–18, 19, 20; trials 16, 17, 18, 238
Witsen, Nicolas 20

workshops, within neoshamanism 265, 268, 272, 277, 279, 286
Wovoca 253

Yoga 130–1, 226, 227, 276

Zoroastrianism 26, 27–8, 226

CPSIA information can be obtained
at www.ICGtesting.com
Printed in the USA
LVHW021221220123
737704LV00004B/548